Spotting and Discovering Terms through Natural Language Processing

Spotting and Discovering Terms through Natural Language Processing

Christian Jacquemin

The MIT Press
Cambridge, Massachusetts
London, England

This book was set in Times Roman by Windfall Software using ZzTEX.

Printed and bound in the United States of America.

Library of Congress Cataloging-in-Publication Data

Jacquemin, Christian.
  Spotting and discovering terms through natural language processing/Christian Jacquemin.
p. cm.
  Includes bibliographical references and index.
  ISBN 0-262-10085-1
  1. Terms and phrases–Data processing. 2. Language and languages–Variation–Data processing. I. Title.

P305.18.D38J33   2001
418–dc21   00-135245

Contents

Acknowledgments

The work presented in this book was started about ten years ago when I worked on the transformation of compound nouns under Maurice Gross at the Laboratoire d'Automatique Documentaire et de Linguistique of the University of Paris 7. Although the content of my work was not what Maurice had been expecting, I am greatly indebted to him for pointing me at very interesting research issues.

It was during this early research for my dissertation that I met Benoît Habert, another student in Gross's laboratory. I could not have desired a better guide to the marvels of language processing. Our association has been rich and intensive. We have further joined the same laboratory (LIMSI-CNRS) and still share many projects and discuss our ideas.

Since then my work has gradually shifted from compounding to terminology. Somewhere along the line, when I ran against a problem downloading corpora and term lists from the Web which was in those years not an easy task, I started an especially productive collaboration with Jean Royauté on using term variant recognition in information access and representation. We spent hours scanning piles of correct-or-spurious-variants in order to uncover the hidden nuggets of term variations that affirmed our intuitions.

When Béatrice Daille joined my laboratory in Nantes, we already knew each other, but I could not have imagined that her contributions would be so stimulating. Béatrice has the remarkable ability to apply rigorous formal reasoning to linguistic analyses. She can immediately focus on the essential issue of a problem, and she always proposes innovative solutions.

I must further mention the important influence of Evelyne Tzoukermann during the semester I spent working at Bell Labs. I remember it as a sunny afternoon. She offered me very friendly and cooperative scientific challenges that opened new fields of investigation. We proved to complement each other well, and I benefited much from her expertise in morphology. Judith Klavans joined our group and immediately brought compelling new issues. We had terrific discussions and great fun.

It is last, with pleasure, that I acknowledge Joseph Mariani and Gérard Sabah. My having been accepted at their LIMSI laboratory has resulted in many other collaborations. I am greatly indebted to all the people there whose cooperative spirit has make this book possible.

In addition to the people mentioned above, I wish to thank Marc El-Beze, Jacques-Henri Jayez, Bernard Lang, Bernard Levrat, and Christiane Marchello-Nizia for participating on the committee of my "Habilitation Thesis"; Fernande Dupuis and Philippe Barbaud for their friendly discussions on compounding; Yannick Toussaint for managing the ILIAD project; Nabil Hathout, Fiammetta Namer, and Georgette Dal for their help with computational morphology; Marie-Claude L'Homme and Didier Bourigault for the adventure into computational terminology; Cécile Fabre for the analysis of nomino-verbal variants; Kyo Kageura, Yoshikane Fuyuki, Jorge Vivaldi, and Antje Schmitt Wigger for their expansions of *FASTR* to unexplored languages; Brigitte Grau, Gabriel Illouz, Olivier Ferret, Martine

Hurault-Plantet, and Nicolas Masson for the question-answering track; Michèle Jardino, Yannick de Kercadio, and Patrick Paroubek for the SDR track; Marie-Paule Péry-Woodley and Jacques Virbel for the Cognitique project; and Emmanuel Morin for interesting discussions during his dissertation work.

Finally, I am very grateful to Lin Chase who accepted the hard task of reviewing the first version of the manuscript. She gave me excellent editorial advice. In addition she helped me reformulate some passages, clarify the overall organization, and correct mistakes. I am especially indebted to her critical eye. Any remaining errors are mine. Thank you so much, Lin.

To any person whom I do not cite and whose cooperation played a significant role in the development of this book, I apologize.

1 Introduction

Peut-être serait-il utile aujourd'hui d'instituer une langue écrite qui, réservée uniquement pour les sciences, n'exprimant que ces combinaisons d'idées simples qui se retrouvent exactement les mêmes dans tous les esprits, n'étant employée que pour des raisonnements d'une rigueur logique, pour des opérations de l'entendement précises et calculées, fût entendue par les hommes de tous les pays, et se traduisît dans tous leurs idiomes, sans pouvoir s'altérer comme eux en passant dans l'usage commun.

Alors, par une révolution singulière, ce même genre d'écriture, dont la conservation n'eût servi qu'à prolonger l'ignorance, deviendrait, entre les mains de la philosophie, un instrument utile à la prompte propagation des lumières, au perfectionnement de la méthode des sciences.[1]

Esquisse d'un tableau historique des progrès de l'esprit humain *(Sketch of the Progress of the Human Mind)*, Condorcet, 1793. ©1988, *Éditions Flammarion, Paris.*

1.1 Motivation

Because of the recent dramatic increase in the number of electronic documents, the retrieval of information from texts is a crucial issue for the future, whether these texts be abstracts, full texts, or simply titles. In accessing documents through keywords or bags of words—as in an Internet search—a user may fail to express the formulation that matches the relevant documents. For example, when searching for *loan offers*, it is necessary to consider that *offer our commercial customers credit commercial loans*, *offer a complete range of home investment and business loans*, *offering a special jumbo mortgage loan*, etc., are all valid instances of a query. Conversely, it would be misleading to believe that any co-occurrence of the words *loan/loans* and *offer/offers/offering* in a 15-word window is an expression of *loan offers*. For instance, *loan continues to offer* from the sentence *interlibrary loan continues to offer a full range of services to our graduate students . . . ,* or *loan center offers* from *education loan center a offers tutorials and references about financing through grants scholarships . . .* are not valid occurrences for the *loan offers* querying.

Failure to consider the complete range of variants will result in misses during the process of information access. Considering variants that are too broadly defined will result in a huge mass of documents, many of which will be inappropriate. This work proposes methods that balance these two effects in reaching the goal of qualitative and accurate information retrieval.

1.2 Term Spotting through Term Normalization

This book describes *FASTR*, a natural language processor for the normalization of term occurrences.[2] Term normalization is a compromise between rigid and constrained querying through controlled keywords and excessively loose querying through bags of words (as commonly proposed by Web search engines). It consists in linking occurrences of correct term variants with the corresponding normalized term. Proper term normalization is expected to relate *offer a complete range of home investment and business loans* with *loan offer*, but not to relate *loan continues to offer* with *loan offer*.

The input to *FASTR* is a set of documents and a set of terms resulting from human or automatic acquisition. The output is a set of linguistic links between text sequences and an initial list of terms.

FASTR is a unique combination of several natural language processing techniques. It serves both as an efficient parser, capable of processing large amounts of terminological and textual data, and as an accurate term spotter, capable of distinguishing subtle linguistic differences between correct and spurious term occurrences. *FASTR* was constructed based on a detailed observation of numerous types of term variations in French and English documents from various specialized domains. Its design combines shallow parsing, exploitation of large terminological and lexical data, and novel transformational unification-based techniques. Optimization techniques ensure that the parser can handle efficiently large amounts of texts quickly, making the approach usable in real applications.

The design of *FASTR* and the exceptional accuracy of the resulting term spotting demonstrate that no in-depth understanding of target documents is necessary for a correct identification of terms and variants. The basic component of the parser is a metagrammar, which is a set of metarules describing acceptable linguistic transformations of terms. The tuning of such a metagrammar is based on corpus investigation and is not prohibitively time-consuming.

1.3   Is In-depth Understanding a Viable Alternative?

Apart from very specific domains of knowledge—such as a specialized medical field—automatic text understanding encounters two major difficulties:

• Texts are heterogeneous and may pursue various expository strategies. Unlike normalized documents such as medical reports, most documents adopt their own progression and make use of a variety of rhetorical processes and means of expression.

• The knowledge involved in documents is vast and organized into complex ontologies and relations. Although defining the ontology of some restricted domain may be possible, there is no reason to believe that a huge multi-domain knowledge base will soon be available.[3]

Is it a reasonable belief that understanding the content of raw documents is a viable alternative to automatic indexing? Is it really necessary to understand in-depth the content of a document in order to assess its relevance to a query of information? Is it realistic to aim at elaborating the ever-moving target of a universal multipurpose knowledge base?

The automatic indexing tool *FASTR* supports the argument that access to full text documents does not require a complete understanding of their content. A network of superficial clues—such as those perceived by an inattentive reader skimming through a text—are sufficient for deciding whether a document fits search criteria. Because of their conceptual values, occurrences of terms in texts give clues to the information content of documents.

Since large amounts of textual and terminological data must be processed, I prefer a partial analysis of multi-domain documents to an in-depth understanding restricted to a specific domain. Because of their local nature (they do not span entire sentences) and because of their high information content, terms are privileged keys for information description. Therefore, term extraction is an unavoidable preliminary phase to correct document indexing.[4]

To sum up, text-skimming through *term identification* is an essential component of automated information retrieval. To this end, this book provides a full discussion of the design of a shallow parser and evaluates its use for both precise and broad-coverage extraction of controlled terms from large corpora.

1.4   Term Variation: A Central Issue

Terms are vehicles of scientific and technical information. The "life" of terms is closely connected to the evolution of the domain to which they belong. A look at the scientific literature of an emerging technology—such as aircraft in the second half of the nineteenth century, easily illustrates the various means of term creation, the integration of terms in "general" language and their eventual extinction (Guilbert 1965). Term *fluidity* is another important aspect of the evolution of terms. Denotations, spellings, syntactic properties, and usages of terms are continually evolving. The unsettled characteristics of terms are not only diachronic in their nature. Scientists working in a large domain, such as the Human Genome Project, may underestimate the fluidity of the terminology that they are using, which can be a detriment to scientific communication (Frenkel 1991). The useful life of terms is further characterized by their mobility. The *migrations* of terms, from donor to borrower disciplines or to general language, and the terminological differentiation of scientific domains, have been the subject of discriminative statistical studies (Losee 1995; Losee and Haas 1995).

In creating an automatic information-processing system that deals with scientific or technical texts, close attention must be given to term variability. Ignoring term variability may lead to the conception of inefficient indexing engines that are unable to relate conceptually close but linguistically different occurrences.[5]

The cornerstone of the automatic recognition of controlled terms is therefore the representation and processing of *morphological, syntactic, and semantic variations* described by the following definition:

Definition 1.1 (Morphological, syntactic, or semantic variation) A morphological, syntactic, or semantic variation is a transformation of a controlled multi-word term that satisfies the following four conditions:

1. The "content" words of the controlled term are preserved by the transformation or transformed into morphologically or semantically related words. For example, *recognized neural cells* is a correct variant of *Cell recognition* because *cell* is preserved and because *recognition* is transformed into *recognize*, a morphologically related word. Only some "empty" words, such as prepositions or determiners, can be deleted or replaced by the transformation. For example, in French, *réserve en eau* (literally *reserve in water*) is a variant of *Réserve d'eau* (literally *reserve of water*).[6]

2. Full words may be morphologically or semantically related:

a. Variations that involve neither relationships of derivational morphology nor semantic relationships are called *syntactic variations*. Thus *comprehension of language* is a syntactic variation of *Language comprehension*.

b. Variations that involve a morphological relation of derivational morphology are *morphological variations*. For instance, *determine the structures* is a morphological variation of *Structure determination* because *determine* and *determination* are morphologically related.

c. Variations that involve a semantic relationship are called *semantic variations*. Thus *speech comprehension* is a semantic variant of *Language comprehension* because *speech* and *language* are semantically related.

3. The order of the words composing the controlled term can be modified by the transformation and new words can be inserted into the variant, but the dependency relations existing in the original term must be preserved by the transformation. For example, *fluctuations in mean arterial blood pressure* is a variant of *Pressure fluctuation,* and the dependence of *pressure* on *fluctuation* in the controlled term is still present in the variant.

4. The variant should not contain the original term (or one of its inflections). For example, *mean arterial pressures* is not a variant of *Arterial pressure* because the word string of the controlled term is not modified by the variation.

This is the definition that will be used throughout this book in building *FASTR*, the computational tool intended for the extraction of term variations and for evaluating the results of the extractions. The four conditions described above are the result of experimental observations of various scientific corpora. There will be provided in this book numerous examples that will help the reader to relate these conditions to the observed linguistic phenomena. Indeed, the definition above is the result of many lengthy manual and automatic investigations of term variants in retrieving text occurrences that are morphologically, syntactically, or semantically related to controlled terms. Apart from the notions of morphological, syntactic, and semantic variations, the main element of definition 1.1 is dependence, which is a syntactic invariant characterizing the various phrases that denote the same concept.

Contrary to the *ISO* guidelines (see Sager 1990, pp. 88–89), terms are not "ideal and unambiguous identifiers whose textual utterances are systematically identical to their baseform." Terms, when they are used for scientific and technical communications, are treated as linguistic objects with peculiar characteristics but with a rich variety of possible linguistic transformations. Among the peculiarities of terms, Guilbert (1973) has pointed out the following striking differences between terms and "ordinary" lexical units of general language:

• Terms have a monosemous denotative function whose meaning is only weakly influenced by the context of utterance.

• The "life" of terms (creation, semantic shifts, migrations, death) depends strongly on the evolution of their technical or scientific domain.

• Terms are constructed according to characteristic morphological, syntactic, and semantic patterns and are easily influenced by foreign imports.

Despite the constant and characteristic features that give an illusion of fixedness, terms are genuine complex lexical entries—possibly polysemous, possibly structurally ambiguous—that can be modified by morphological, semantic, and syntactic transformations and integrated into the construction of novel lexical entries. In brief, the full complexity of terms in language reflects the complexity of human cognition and its many means of communication.

For a proper identification of terms and their ongoing evolutions in different corpora, it is essential to consider the variety of terms, to accept their linguistic and communicative dimensions and to reject misleading beliefs that terms are fixed labels, the same as with identifiers in computer programs. Extant corpora attest to the continual renewal of terms through numerous transformations. Linguistic analyses presented in this book show that scientific and technical terms are genuine linguistic expressions whose linguistic motivation is more closely related to *conventional expressions* (Langacker 1987, sec. 1.2.3) than to the codes of a fixed nomenclature.

Recognition of variants is a means of overcoming incompleteness in term banks. Controlled term lists are created by human experts working with a variety of textual sources with different linguistic dimensions. These data are thus necessarily flawed by the subjectivity of the experts and their various levels of competency, as well as by the variety and heterogeneity of their sources. The reduction of terminology to finite lists always results in oversimplification and incompleteness.

For this reason *FASTR* is designed to represent and extract term variants. A term is represented by a local syntactic structure and a set of feature structures—mainly morphological ones—linked to the nodes of the structure. In addition to the grammar of terms, a metagrammar is used to transform the term rules into term variant rules, which are used to extract *term variations* from scientific corpora. In Jacquemin (1999), I show that term variants represent approximately a third of the term occurrences in an English scientific corpus (9% are syntactic variants, 6.5% are morphosyntactic variants, and 22% are semantic variants).[7] Indeed, variation is a crucial characteristic of terms. Any approach to term extraction has to deal with this complexity; overly simplified tools are not likely to produce good results. *FASTR* succeeds in providing an accurate and efficient technique for the extraction of term variants without suffering the inefficiency of in-depth parsers.

1.5   Overview of the Study

The first third of the book reviews the state-of-the-art in automatic term extraction and automatic indexing. Various tools are described and their relative merits are compared. The rest of the book presents the formalism and the computational devices of *FASTR*, the natural language processor for term spotting and thesaurus enrichment.[8]

Chapter 2 gives a detailed account of some concurrent approaches to automatic term extraction and automatic indexing. In these two domains mostly statistical filters and finite-state automata are applied to tagged corpora. Some solutions combine both approaches by ranking the output of a finite-state filter through statistical measures. Automatic term extraction is designed to build terminological databases with conceptual information and semantic links, while automatic indexing is used to prepare subsequent information access by linking documents with descriptors that are expected to represent the content of the documents. These two domains are covered in this book because *FASTR* is simultaneously a tool for terminological enrichment—a subtheme of term extraction—and a tool for multi-word term recognition—a subtheme of automatic indexing.

Chapter 3 describes the grammar of *FASTR*, a unification-based formalism inspired largely by *PATR-II* and *Lexicalized Tree Adjoining Grammar* (*LTAG*). The decision to use a unification grammar was motivated by the flexibility of feature-based structures that permit various types of data to be represented within the same formalism. The decision to add a lexicalized grammar was motivated by the fact that multi-word terms are syntactic trees that include more than one lexical item.

Chapter 4 complements the discussion of *FASTR*'s grammar with a discussion of the metaformalism used for describing term variations. Metarules are formally expressed in a way that resembles the formalism of the grammar. In the course of parsing, metarules transform term rules into variant rules and retrieve variant occurrences from documents.

Term variant generation is performed dynamically and is accompanied of several optimization procedures that ensure high parsing speed despite the use of a unification-based (meta)grammar.

Chapter 5 presents the design and the fine-tuning of a metagrammar for term variations in the English language. First, syntactic transformations are created according to the standard syntactic structures of noun phrases and their combinations in the construction of term variants. Four families of term variations are described: coordinations, permutations, modifications/substitutions, and elisions. Then these paradigmatic variations are complemented with additional constraints through experimental tuning on a training corpus and a training term list. The resulting metarules are used for evaluating the quality of the extraction on a test corpus according to standards imported from information retrieval.

Chapter 6 describes how the parser *FASTR* is applied to the acquisition of terminological, conceptual, and linguistic data. The data acquisition results in an enrichment of terms through candidate terms, and the acquisition of conceptual links can be exploited in automatic thesaurus construction. In using this mode of acquisition, the parser can participate in the maintenance of its own knowledge source. Through term acquisition the terms recycled into the parser for term variant extraction are continuously enriched through data mining: relevant knowledge is learned from the corpora being processed.

Chapter 7 shows that *FASTR* can be extended to recognize full-fledged morphosyntactic variations. The parser is equipped with a finite-state machine for a surface analysis of variant phrase structures. It is also enhanced with an extended lexicalization mechanism that links a term with morphological families instead of single lexical items.

Chapter 8 concludes the book with a discussion of semantic variation. The formalism of *FASTR* metarules is extended in order to allow semantic links to be embedded in the expression of variations. The resulting tool is a novel and powerful architecture that efficiently combines local morphosemantico-syntactic transformations and shallow syntactic parsing. This chapter also presents some important applications of *FASTR* to multilinguality, cross-lingual information retrieval, and cascaded information retrieval combining Web search and variant recognition.

Two corpora and two associated lists of controlled terms are used for the English language throughout this study: a training corpus [Medic] and a training term list [Pascal] in the medical domain, and a test corpus [Metal] and a test term list [Pascal-Metal] in metallurgy. These data are presented in full in appendix C. Both corpora are raw and untagged; they are composed of scientific abstracts from journal articles. These data were provided by the documentation center INIST/CNRS, and the author would like to thank Jean Royauté and Xavier Polanco of the PRI department at INIST/CNRS for their continual support of this work. The fine-tuning and the evaluation results of applying metarules are reported in section 5.5 for syntactic variations, in section 7.2 for morphosyntactic variations, and in section 8.1 for semantic variations.

2 Studies in Term Extraction

Terms are extracted from textual corpora for two main applications: *knowledge acquisition* and *automatic indexing*. These two activities have motivated the development of techniques for automatic term extraction with both good coverage and good precision. The techniques are slightly different depending on their exact application, but they share many features. This chapter gives an overview of the different studies in automatic term extraction, in the field of corpus-based terminology and knowledge extraction, and in the field of information retrieval.

Depending on whether we work with single-word terms or multi-word terms, the central issues in the design of a term extraction system are very different:

- Single-word terms are generally polysemous and call for word-sense disambiguation and context analysis.
- Multi-word terms are far less polysemous than single-word terms, but since they have a phrase structure, they are prone to variations. Their identification calls for morphosyntactic analyzers or n-ary statistical measures.

Word-sense disambiguation, on the one hand, and phrase parsing and n-gram statistics, on the other hand, are very different, so they can be studied independently. The chapter focuses on the techniques for multi-word term identification and on the associated techniques for phrase extraction, whether they be statistical or NLP techniques. Particular attention is paid to the description and the computational processing of term variations.

This chapter is organized into four sections. A general introduction is provided in section 2.1. Sections 2.2 and 2.3 are dedicated to term acquisition and automatic indexing. The concluding section 2.4 sketches out the lines of research that have led to the conception of *FASTR*, the tool for term spotting presented in the next chapters.

2.1 Basic Concepts and Techniques

This section provides details about concepts and techniques that will be used throughout this book. First, the basic concepts are covered in section 2.1.1: What is a term? How is a term bank or a thesaurus organized? What kind of information is provided? The examples come from the *AGROVOC* and *UMLS* bases which are available for the agricultural and the medical domains, respectively. Section 2.1.2 then briefly outlines the two possible uses of term extraction: term acquisition for knowledge acquisition and thesaurus construction, and automatic indexing for information access. Section 2.1.3 provides details about the different levels of linguistic analysis used for capturing the characteristics of terms. Section 2.1.4 presents some computational techniques used for extracting terms from corpora: finite-state techniques, grammar-based parsers, and statistical filters. The last section, section 2.1.5, covers the basic measures of quality used in information retrieval and shows how they can be extended to term recognition and automatic indexing.

The reader who is familiar with these basic concepts can safely skip to the next section.

2.1.1 Terminology

According to Sager (1990, p. 3), *terminology* has three contemporary meanings:

1. A set of practices and methods used for the collection, the description, and the presentation of terms.

2. A theory for explaining the relationships between concepts (abstract meanings) and terms.

3. A vocabulary of a special subject field (e.g., the terminology of aeronautics).

In retrieving terms for corpora, the first and third meanings of terminology are the most relevant: specialized lexical data and their management. Since this work focuses on the application of natural language processing techniques to the extraction of terms, it must cope with the linguistic dimension of terms. The two sides of the coin of linguistics for terminology are, on the one hand, the representation of terms in terminological data-bases with respect to normalization constraints and, on the other hand, the capture of terms in written corpora where several types of neologisms or variant forms are encountered.

Terms in Dictionaries

Terms are linguistic representation of concepts. Otman (1995, p. 27) distinguishes two types of terms:

1. Technical terms, which denote instruments, artifacts, observations, experiments, measures.

2. Scientific terms, which denote theoretical concepts in scientific domains.

Both types of terms are predominantly represented by nouns or noun phrases in dictionaries even though they may sometimes be more appropriately expressed as verb or adjective phrases in technical and scientific corpora.

The data used for representing terms in a term bank belong to the following five broad categories (Sager 1990 p. 172):

• Management data (numeric keys, record number, terminologist's name, date of coding, etc.).

• Conceptual data (subject, scope, definition, related concepts and type of relation, etc.).

• Linguistic data (lexical entries, synonymous entries, equivalents in other languages, variants, etc.).

• Pragmatic data (usage restrictions, contextual data, etc.).

• Bibliographical data.

Let us illustrate briefly some of these data from two different thesauri, *UMLS* (UMLS 1995) and *AGROVOC* (AGROVOC 1995).

AGROVOC *Thesaurus*

The entry for *immunisation* (immunization) in the French version of (AGROVOC 1995) is shown in table 2.1. It contains, first, the descriptor (the preferred linguistic expression of this concept) and a short note for clarifying its meaning. The next three fields, labeled *ep*, provide linguistic variants with synonymous meanings. Then the conceptual hierarchy above and under the current concept is traversed and the corresponding descriptors. Four more generic concepts, labeled **TG1** to **TG4**, are reported. There is only one more specific concept; it is reported by the next field **TS1**. The fields labeled **ta** (associated terms) provide the opportunity to express additional conceptual relations that are not hierarchical (as opposed to the generic and specific relations above). The last two fields are equivalents in two foreign languages.

Table 2.1
Entry of the French term *Immunisation* in AGROVOC

Code	Text	Gloss
	IMMUNISATION	[descriptor]
	(immunisation spécifique d'antigène)	[note of usage]
ep	*immunisation active*	[nondescriptor (synonym)]
ep	*immunisation croisée*	—
ep	*sensibilisation immune*	—
TG1	*immunostimulation*	[generic term (level +1)]
TG2	*immunothérapie*	[— (level +2)]
TG3	*thérapeutique*	[— (level +3)]
TG4	*contrôle de la maladie*	[— (level +4)]
TS1	*vaccination*	[specific term (level -1)]
ta	*antigène*	[associated term]
ta	*réponse immunitaire*	—
ta	*résistance aux maladies*	—
ta	*résistance induite*	—
En	*immunization*	[English equivalent]
Es	*immunización*	[Spanish equivalent]

UMLS *Metathesaurus*

The *Unified Medical Language System* (*UMLS*) database is an ambitious project with the purpose of unifying medical terminological data from different sources. The *Metathesaurus* is the central vocabulary component of the *UMLS*, which combines the scopes of its source vocabularies. The organization of the *UMLS* is more atomized than that of *AGROVOC*, and several files must be scanned in order to collect the complete data about a concept. This presentation considers on only some of the main aspects of the *UMLS*. More information is available at the Web site given in the bibliographical reference (UMLS 1995).

The Metathesaurus of the *UMLS* is organized by concept or meaning. A concept is represented by one or more synonymous terms. Each term is the group of all strings that are lexical variants of each other. One of the terms representing a concept is chosen to be the preferred name of this concept. For instance, *Atrial fibrillation* and *Atrial fibrillations* are two strings linked to the same term $T_1 =$ ATRIAL FIBRILLATION. Similarly *Auricular fibrillation* and *Auricular fibrillations* are linked to another term $T_2 =$ AURICULAR FIBRILLATION. Both terms T_1 and T_2 denote the same concept; therefore they are said to be synonymous. T_1 is the preferred name.

The Metathesaurus of the *UMLS* also contains several types of relationships among concepts, such as generic/specific relations for *Atrial fibrillation is_a Arrhythmia*, or *Paroxysmal atrial fibrillation narrower_than Atrial fibrillation*. The other features in the Metathesaurus are attributes of a concept, attributes of a term, or attributes of a string. For example, the semantic type *pathologic function* and the definition "*Disorder of cardiac rhythm characterized by rapid, irregular atrial impulses and ineffective atrial contractions*" are attributes of the concept with the preferred name *Atrial fibrillation*.

In addition to the Metathesaurus, the *UMLS* has three other knowledge sources: a semantic network, a lexicon, and a map of information sources. The semantic network contains a categorization of the concepts in the Metathesaurus and a set of relationships between these concepts. Figure 2.1 illustrates a portion of the *UMLS* semantic network. The lexicon provides lexical information for the purpose of facilitating natural language processing (NLP) with the UMLS data. These data are in a format that is compatible with the NLP system provided with the *UMLS*. The NLP system is a lexical variant generation package which consists of several modules generating graphical or morphological variants of the words in the lexical base.

Terms in Texts

The choice between the two possible motivations for exploiting corpus-based terminology depends on whether terms are the means or the purpose of the investigation. Automatic indexing is an activity that exploits terms as a means for assigning descriptors to documents in order to facilitate information access later on. Conversely, corpus-based terminography

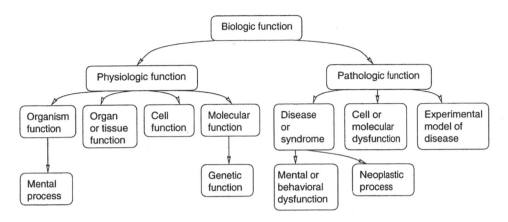

Figure 2.1
Hierarchy of *biological functions* in the UMLS.

and acquisition of terminological knowledge are activities for which the ultimate purpose is the construction of terminological database. Before presenting these two activities in the following section, I will review some of the differences among terms in a text and terms as they appear in terminological databases.

Terms in corpora are used for communication purposes and should satisfy three criteria: *economy*, *precision*, and *appropriateness* (Sager 1990, p. 106). Economy influences the introduction of new terms: there is a tendency to reuse existing lexical material through juxtaposition and overcomposition. For instance, *Capillary blood flow* is a ternary term built from the binary term *Blood flow* through overcomposition with *Capillary flow*. Economy also shows its face in the use of concepts denoted by complex terms through shorter expressions. These shorter expressions include acronyms (*CAPD = Continuous ambulatory peritoneal dialysis*), suppressions of linguistic information that can be pragmatically rebuilt (*Sunflower oil = sunflower seed oil*) or that can be contextually complemented (*Colorectal carcinoma = hereditary nonpolyposis colorectal carcinoma* in the appropriate context).

On the contrary, the need for precision may yield opposite linguistic observations. In a context in which a term can be ambiguous, it receives additional modifiers which disambiguate its meaning. Thus a *mandibular salivary gland* is more precise than a *mandibular gland* through the addition of the modifier *salivary*.

Finally, appropriateness results in a compromise between precision and economy, according to the current context, the focus of the passage, the knowledge of the domain, the level of technicality of the document, etc.

All these factors work together to modify the linguistic expression of a concept and produce several types of variants that differ from the normalized expressions found in thesauri or dictionaries. The purpose of a robust term spotter is to accept all the different types of variants that can be encountered in corpora, and only these.

2.1.2 Automatic Term Acquisition and Indexing

Automatic Term Acquisition

It is now widely accepted that corpora are a reliable source for the constitution of terminologies (Sager 1990, p. 130). The systematic investigation of corpora for corpus-based term acquisition is the focus of the studies presented in section 2.2.

The recent developments in corpus-based term acquisition are due to several converging factors: the widespread availability of part-of-speech taggers such as Brill's tagger (Brill 1992), the increasing volume of electronic corpora, the conception of robust and efficient shallow parsers such as *Cass* (Abney 1990), the combination of statistical and linguistic processors into hybrid systems (Klavans and Resnik 1996), and other recent developments in large-scale natural language processing.

Automatic Indexing

Corpus-based terminology is not the only domain concerned with the automatic extraction of terms from corpora. The purpose of automatic indexing is to assign to documents terms capable of representing the content of these documents (Salton and McGill 1983, sec. 3.3.A). Basic automatic indexing techniques consist of the following steps:

1. Text simplification:

a. Removal of high-frequency words, generally in reference to a *stop list*.

b. Conflation of morphologically related words through *stemming*.

2. Selection of the best indexes, generally based on frequency criteria such as the *discrimination value*.

3. Addition of a weight to terms in order to reflect term importance for the retrieval of information.

The terms traditionally used in automatic indexing are single words. However, *phrase indexing* is a complementary technique that improves precision by exploiting multi-word terms that are more specific than single-word terms (Salton and McGill 1983, sec. 3.5.D). In section 2.3 several techniques for phrase indexing are presented, all of which are essentially statistical techniques based on co-occurrences and NLP techniques. Phrase indexing is one of the capabilities accomplished by *FASTR* through multi-word term spotting.

Table 2.2
Subdomains of term extraction

	Indexing	Corpus-based terminology
With initial data	Controlled indexing	Thesaurus enrichment
Without initial data	Free indexing	Term acquisition

Exploitation of Prior Knowledge

Both term acquisition and automatic indexing divide into two distinct subfields depending on whether or not initial terminological knowledge is available (see table 2.2). Manual indexing is generally performed with reference to a controlled vocabulary; this is called *controlled indexing*. The indexes assigned to documents must belong to the controlled vocabulary, even though they might not occur in the documents which they are assigned to. Conversely, indexing without reference to any initial specific terminological vocabulary is called *free indexing*.

The same criterion can be used to identify two classes of studies on corpus-based terminology. If the acquisition complements prior terminological knowledge, it is called *thesaurus enrichment*; otherwise, it is called *term acquisition*. The difference between these two domains does not only lie in the final goal (adding terms to a base or creating it from scratch) but also in the possible exploitation of prior terminology during thesaurus enrichment (discovering terms from terms **and** corpora).

The work presented in the next chapters of this book falls into the first line of table 2.2. My approach to the recognition and acquisition of terms is intentionally based on prior terminological knowledge. Indexing with *FASTR* is controlled indexing because the goal is to recognize occurrences or variants of terms from authority lists. Similarly corpus-based terminology with *FASTR* is focused on thesaurus enrichment. My purpose is to discover terms that are not yet in a thesaurus and to provide links between acquired terms and initial controlled vocabulary.

2.1.3 Linguistic Levels

This section illustrates some techniques in computational linguistics that are frequently exploited in automatic term spotting. Of course any natural language processing module can be of some use in term extraction. I nevertheless focus on the most commonly used techniques, namely those that pertain to the "lowest" linguistic levels: morphology and syntax. For these two levels, a set of classical methods is proposed that will be used in the remainder of this book for presenting other studies and for detailing my own work.

Morphology

The scope of morphology is the study of words and their structure (Matthews 1974, chs. 1–3). The first step of morphological analysis is to segment sentences into separate word forms; the second stage is the analysis of words into morphemes. If a word is not further analyzable it is termed a *root*. For instance, *deny* is a root.

Roots or associations of roots with affixes construct bases. Affixes are named prefixes if they are located before the base, infixes if they are inserted into the base, and suffixes if they follow the base. Affixes can be of two kinds: derivational or inflectional. Derivational affixes produce new words from a base. For instance, the derivational suffix *-able* produces *deniable* from *to deny*. The process is obviously recursive since *-y* builds *deniably* from *deniable*. On the contrary, inflectional suffixes do not yield new lexemes, they only produce new word forms. For instance, the inflectional suffixes that can be associated with *to deny* produce the different inflections of this verb: *denies*, *denied*, and *denying*.

A final family of word constructions is composed of compounds: lexemes formed through the combination of two or more lexemes. Most compounds encountered in terminology are endocentric compounds; they are composed of a head word with the same category as the compound and a modifier attached to the head noun. Thus a *sea-bird* is a nominal compound with *bird* as nominal head word. Syntactic endocentricity is generally accompanied by semantic endocentricity. Here a *sea-bird* is a kind of *bird*.

Affixing (whether inflectional or derivational) and compounding combine frequently in the construction of terminological units. For example, *Autoregressive model* is a term in which the first word is a compound *auto + regress* with a derivational suffix *-ive*.

I now turn to the two main ways in which morphological analysis is exploited in automatic term extraction through stemming and dictionary-based analysis.

Stemming

Stemming covers a set of dictionary-free techniques that are used for transforming words into stems. A stem is a string that is common to a set of morphologically related words. For the sake of computational simplicity, the stem of a word can be different from its root. For example, the Porter stemmer associates *deny* with the stem *deni* even though the linguistic root is *deny*. Stemmers simultaneously and indiscriminantly account for inflectional and derivational morphology.

The purpose of stemming is to conflate all the different linguistic forms of a concept in order to facilitate information access. Therefore stemming is different from morphological analysis. Two words with the same linguistic root can have different stems because their meanings are not (synchronically) related or because the stemming algorithm does not cope with these endings. For example, the Porter stemmer associates *coronation* with the stem *coron* and *coronarian* with *coronarian* although both words are derived from the same Latin stem *corona* (crown). Daille and Jacquemin (1998) compare the conflation made by a stemmer (Porter stemmer) and the conflation made by a lexicographic database with information on the structure of words (CELEX database). They show that the conflation of words with identical linguistic stems (from CELEX) yields better results than stemming (through Porter) for a term variant conflation task. They also report that neither technique obtains perfect results. The stemmer incorrectly relates words with different linguistic roots such as *training* and *train* (with the meaning of *railway*). Conversely, the lexical database assimilates words that have little semantic proximity but that—generally diachronically— share a common stem. Thus *form* and *formalism* or *classic* and *classification* belong to the same derivational family, but exploiting this fact in information retrieval applications hurts more than it can help.

Stemming algorithms perform basically two operations: *suffix stripping* and *recoding*. The suffix stripper removes from each word a word ending that is expected to be the longest suffix. Actually this suffix can correspond to a concatenation of several linguistic suffixes. For instance, when *-arization* is removed by the Lovins stemmer from *summarization*, three linguistic suffixes are simultaneously pulled out: *-ar*, *-ize*, and *-ation*. Then stems produced by the suffix stripper are normalized by a recoding function in order to account for possible graphic variations such as *adher-e/adhes-ion*.

I will now sketch two significant algorithms used for stemming English words: the *Lovins stemmer* (Lovins 1968) and the *Porter stemmer* (Porter 1980). Stemming of morphologically richer languages such as French raises particular issues such as the combination of rules with exception lists (Dal, Hathout, and Namer 1999).

Lovins Stemmer The stemmer possesses a list of removable word endings sorted by decreasing length and associated with conditions. These conditions are restrictions on the minimal length of the remaining stem or on the letters immediately preceding the suffix. The Lovins stemmer is a two-phase process (see figure 2.2). The first phase is the removal of the suffix with the longest match, subject to verification of the associated conditions. For instance, *absorption* is transformed into *absorpt-* by removing *-ion* and checking that the remaining stem is longer than three letters and that its final letter is not *l-* or *n-*.

The second phase of the stemming algorithm is composed of two steps during which transformational rules are used for recoding stem terminations. First, the double final consonants are undoubled under certain conditions. Then, the first recoding rule matching the ending of the remaining stem is applied. In the case of *absorpt-*, a recoding rule *rpt-* → *rb-* produces the final stem *absorb-*. The application of this rule results in the conflation of a verb such as *to absorb* with the other words in the same derivational family, such as *absorption*.

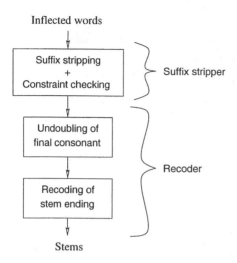

Figure 2.2
Simplified flowchart of the Lovins stemmer.

Table 2.3
Some sample rules of Porter's algorithm

Step	Condition	Input/output	Sample input/output
1	—	$-ies \rightarrow -i$	$ponies \rightarrow poni$
1	*v*	$-y \rightarrow -i$	$pony \rightarrow poni$
2	$m > 0$	$-ational \rightarrow -ate$	$relational \rightarrow relate$
3	$m > 0$	$-icate \rightarrow -ic$	$triplicate \rightarrow triplic$
4	$m > 1$	$-ate \rightarrow \emptyset$	$activate \rightarrow activ$
5	$m > 1$	$-e \rightarrow \emptyset$	$probate \rightarrow probat$

Porter Stemmer In contrast with the case of Lovins stemmer, the two basic stemming transformations—suffix stripping and recoding—are performed simultaneously by the Porter stemmer. The algorithm is composed of five sets of transformational rules which are applied in a stepwise fashion. Step 1 deals with plurals, gerunds, and past participles. Steps 2 to 5 deal with derivational suffixes, removing the outermost ones first. Table 2.3 illustrates some sample rules of each of the processing steps. Condition *v* means that the stem must contain a vowel. A condition $m > \alpha$ states that the measure of the stem must be greater than α. Roughly speaking, the measure of a string is a count of its consonant/vowel groups.

Table 2.4
Three examples of stemming by Porter's algorithm

Word	Step 1	Step 2	Step 3	Step 4	Step 5	Final stem
rational	—	—	—	—	—	*rational*
relational	—	*relate*	—	—	*relat*	*relat*
derivational	—	*derivate*	—	*deriv*	—	*deriv*

Each rule is typically composed of a condition, an input suffix and an output suffix. Thus we have the following step 2 rule:

$$(m > 0) \; -ational \rightarrow -ate$$

indicates that the suffix *-ational* is transformed into the suffix *-ate*, provided that the measure *m* of the stem is strictly positive. The constraint on the measure is intended to avoid the transformation of words such as *rational* into *rate*. On the contrary, longer stems such as *relational* and *derivational* are respectively transformed into *relate* and *derivate*.

At the fourth step another rule transforms the words ending with *-ate*, but it only affects stems of measure strictly greater than 1:

$$(m > 1) \; -ate \rightarrow \emptyset$$

The stem *relate* is not modified by this rule because the length of its stem *rel-* is 1. Conversely, the stem *derivate* is transformed into *deriv* because the length of its stem *deriv-* is 2. A final rule, at step 5, removes final *-e*, thus transforming *relate* into *relat-*.

To sum up, the three words *rational*, *relational*, and *derivational* are transformed by the Porter stemmer according to table 2.4.

Dictionary-Based Morphology
I now turn to the description of morphological analyzers that rely on dictionaries or lexical databases instead of rules.

The complexity of systems in computational morphology depends crucially on the complexity of the language under study. The *two-level approach* (Koskenniemi 1983) is a major reference for an efficient morphological analysis of linguistically complex languages, but its presentation would require more space than it is reasonable to allow for this topic within a study on terminology. The reader interested in a more detailed overview of several techniques in computational morphology can refer to Sproat (1992).

In order to present some principles of computational morphology, I will focus on two techniques simpler than the two-level model: a word- or paradigm-based approach (Byrd et al. 1986; Byrd and Tzoukermann 1988) and a concatenative approach (Tzoukermann and Liberman 1990).

Word-Based Approach   The principle of the word-based approach, as described by Aronoff (1976), is that words can be derived from other words through transformation rules. The implementation of this theory for the English language is described in Byrd et al. (1986). In this system, words are stored together with associated idiosyncratic information used for constructing new words. After analysis the system produces, for each word, the list of the words derived from it, together with their inflections. For instance, the following words are built from the word *beauty*:

Word	Analysis
beautified	`<<<*>N +ify>V +ed>A`
beautification	`<<<*>N +ify>V +ion>N`
beautifier	`<<<*>N +ify>V #er>N`
beautiful	`<<*>N #ful>A`
etc.	
unbeautified	`<un# <<<*>N +ify>V +ed>A>A`
unbeautified	`<un# <<<*>N +ify>V -ed1>V>V`
unbeautiful	`<un# <<*>N #ful>A>A`
etc.	

As mentioned by Sproat (1992, p. 199), the word-based approach is interesting because it relies on genuine words instead of abstract root. This means that it is well-adapted to the use of on-line dictionaries in computational morphology. The approach was also applied successfully to French, a language with a more complex morphology than English (Byrd and Tzoukermann 1988). For instance, the following rule

```
-pn: aux21* (noun + masc +sing -plur) (noun +plur -sing)
```

transforms the plural noun *chevaux* (horses) into its singular form *cheval*. This yields the following analysis of *chevaux*:

chevaux `cheval(noun plur masc)   <<*>N -pn>N`

Concatenative Approach   The concatenative approach is based on an *arc-list*, a list of all the base forms and associated inflectional suffixes. For instance, the Spanish verb *forzar* (to force) is described through four stems *forz-*, *forc-*, *fuerc-*, and *fuerz-* and their concatenations with the appropriate inflectional suffixes.

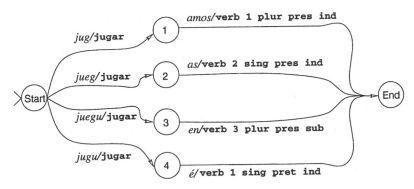

Figure 2.3
A portion of the arc-list describing the inflections of the verb *jugar* (to play).

The system is equipped with an arc-list compiler that takes as input a list of lexical items from a machine-readable dictionary and produces as output the corresponding lists of stems and suffixes. Computationally speaking, the arc-list is a transducer. Figure 2.3 shows a subpart of the arc-list describing the verb *jugar* (to play). Each arc has a double label: the leftmost label is an input label, and the rightmost one is the corresponding output label. The arc-list of figure 2.3 recognizes *jugamos* (we play) and outputs

```
jugar verb 1 plur pres ind
```

by traversing the arc-list from Start to End through state 1.

The system of Tzoukermann and Liberman (1990) is implemented as a set of finite-state transducers and is very efficient. It is used in Jacquemin, Klavans, and Tzoukermann (1997) for the inflectional analysis of French corpora, as a preprocessing stage before term variant identification.

My presentation of terminological morphology has been simplified because I have mainly focused on the word level. However, terms are noun phrases that obey specific inflectional and graphical rules that should be modeled somehow. For example, in French, Noun-Noun terms agree in number only if the second noun is an epithet or a coordinate of the first noun (Grevisse 1988; Noailly 1990). Thus the plural of *Avocat-conseil* (consultant lawyer) is *avocats-conseils*. Conversely, if the second noun is a complement of the first one, it does not vary in number. The plural of *Timbre poste* (postage stamp) is *timbres poste* because this compound can be paraphrased as *timbre pour la poste* (lit. stamp for postage).

In addition to inflectional variations, compounds can also exhibit graphical variations. In French and in English, the components of a compound term can be hyphenated, such as *Aminoacyl-lysine dipeptidase*, separated by a blank, such as *Micro focus tube*, agglutinated, such as *Microfocus X-ray tube*, or uppercased, such as *Achievement Risk Scale Mehrabian* (Sager 1990, sec. 3.2.1).

The rich combinations of inflectional and graphical variations of compounds and complex terms call for specific linguistic descriptions with information on agreement, invariable words, and possibility of hyphens (e.g., Mathieu-Colas 1990 and 1994). Specific tools should also be designed for the morphosyntactic analysis of complex lexical entries (e.g., Maurel 1991 and Silberztein 1993).

Syntax

In this section I focus on the description of the syntax of multi-word terms and their variants. A parallel is made with the syntax of idioms and compounds both of which are also multi-lexical entries.

Characterization of Idioms

Barkema (1994) and Nunberg, Sag, and Wasow (1994) propose criteria that characterize idioms and compounds and differentiate them from regular noun phrases. In both studies none of the criteria are mandatory, and each can be only partially satisfied.

Three criteria are proposed by Barkema (1994):

• *Compositionality*. The extent to which the meaning of a linguistic expression is inferred from both its lexical content and its syntactic structure.

• *Collocability*. The extent to which it is possible to substitute lexical items with other words in the same paradigm such as antonyms or synonyms.

• *Flexibility*. The extent to which standard morphological and syntactic rules can or cannot be used to build a variant of the original expression.

Six criteria are used for characterizing idioms in Nunberg, Sag, and Wasow (1994):

• *Conventionality* and *inflexibility*. The converses of compositionality and flexibility as proposed by Barkema (1994).

• *Figuration*. The extent to which figures of speech are involved in the construction of an expression, such as a metaphor or a hyperbole.

• *Proverbiality*, *informativity*, and *affect*. Three characteristics of the language registers in which idioms are more typically used.

Syntax is mostly concerned with flexibility, the criterion which evaluates the extent to which idioms appear only in a limited number of syntactic constructions and associated morphological transformations. Wasow, Sag, and Nunberg (1984) and Nunberg, Sag, and Wasow (1994) advocate that the semantic properties of idioms are directly relevant in predicting their syntactic versatility. Reciprocally, so that a part of an idiom can be modified by a syntactic transformation such as an adjectival modification, it is necessary that this part of the idiom has a meaning which is an autonomous contribution to the meaning of the entire idiom.

Description of Syntactic Flexibility

Two studies focus on the characterization of the flexibility of idioms and, interestingly, tackle this problem by two opposite and contradictory means. Barkema (1994) proposes a corpus-based approach which contrasts the use of an idiom with the use of a standard noun phrase of the same structure. Gross (1988) proposes an introspective characterization of syntactic flexibility which relies on acceptability values given by a linguist for each possible transformation of each idiom. İ describe in turn these two approaches before providing a list of syntactic modifications encountered in the literature.

Barkema(1994) compares the limited flexibility of idioms with the full flexibility of free constructions. This method is used to build a *flexibility profile* of idioms by determining the list and the number of forms each idiom can take. The patterns considered by Barkema are only syntactic variants: external or internal modifiers and coordinations. The full flexibility of a syntactic pattern is determined by counting the number of occurrences of this pattern and its variants in the reference corpus. (The corpus is analyzed with the large-scale grammar of Aarts and Meijs 1991 and Oostdijk 1991.)

Then, for each idiom I and each variation pattern V_i, the expected frequency of the variant if it were a free construction is given by $e(V_i(I))$:

$$e(V_i(I)) = \frac{I + \Sigma_k V_k(I)}{P_I(f) + \Sigma_k V_k(f)} \times V_i(f)$$

where I is the number of idioms I, $V_k(I)$ the number of variants V_k of I, $P_I(f)$ the number of patterns of I found in free constructions, and $V_k(f)$ the number of variant patterns V_k found in free constructions.

Then the flexibility profile is determined as the difference between the observed frequencies of variation and the expected frequencies calculated by the above formula $e(V_i(I)) - V_i(I)$. It is used to determine the systematic absence of certain variations, the systematic reduction or increase of frequencies of certain patterns, as shown in table 2.5 taken from (Barkema 1994).

Gross (1988) defines a set of generic transformations that can modify a nominal compound with a Noun-Adjective structure. These variations are expected to be accepted by any free construction and selectively rejected or accepted by compounds. The variations studied by Gross (1988) are as follows:

Table 2.5
An excerpt of the flexibility profile of *Cold War*

	Form	Example	Difference
1	Base form	*Cold War*	+49.88%
2	Adjectival premodifier	*melting Cold War*	-0.17%
3	Postnominal clause (tensed)	*the Cold War that existed . . .*	-4.52%
4	Postnominal prepositional phrase	*Cold War against . . .*	+13.92%
5	Postnominal clause (past-participle)	*Cold War thought up by . . .*	-0.78%

1. *Predicativity.* The acceptability of an attributive construction. In French, *une chambre est froide* (a room is cold) is not an acceptable variant of the term *Chambre froide* (a cold room).

2. *Nominalization.* The acceptability of a nominalization of the adjective. In French, *la blancheur de l'examen* (lit. the blankness of the test) cannot be used to refer to the quality of *Examen blanc* (a practice test, lit. a blank test).

3. *Selection restriction on the adjective.* The acceptability of other adjectives. In French, *une omelette norvégienne* (lit. a Norwegian omelet) is a type of icecream, whereas *une omelette écossaise* (a Scottish omelet) has no idiomatic meaning.

4. Five other criteria for determining the idiomaticity of a compound which consist of *number variation* (whether a compound can be singular and plural), *adverb adjunction* (the acceptability of an adverbial modification of the adjective), *adjectival adjunction* (the acceptability of an additional adjectival modifier), *adjective removal* (the optionality of the adjective), and the *selection restriction on the head noun* (the acceptability of other head nouns).

For each compound and each variation, a judgment of acceptability is formulated by a linguist and reported in a table. For example, table 2.6 illustrates the acceptabilities of the first three types of variation mentioned above for some compounds. These variation patterns tend to define classes of similar linguistic behaviors among idioms.

This technique stems from the notion of lexicon-grammar developed at the *Laboratoire d'Automatique Documentaire et de Linguistique* of the University Paris 7 (Gross 1986b). This framework intends to provide a lexicalized description of grammar in which syntactic constructions are related to the lexical elements involved in these structures. Information is encoded in boolean tables such as table 2.6 which associates each entry with a list of acceptable structures.

The high number of terms and corresponding variants makes such a method labor intensive. Furthermore it is not certain whether a linguist, even a specialist in a particular domain, is likely to provide a reliable judgment of the acceptability of a given variation on a given

Table 2.6
Examples of acceptabilities for Noun-Adjective compounds.

Compound	Predicativity	Nominalization	Selection restriction on adjective
Accent grave (grave accent)	−	−	+
Cinéma muet (silent films)	+	−	−
Fait historique (historic event)	+	+	−
Nuit blanche (a sleepless night)	+	−	+

term. Instead, a systematic corpus-based evaluation of the flexibility profile, as proposed by Barkema (1994), seems more appropriate for the description of a compound or a term and its possible associated variants.

Some Different Types of Variations

I now turn to a presentation of the main families of term variations. Since terminology is mainly concerned with the expression of concepts, term variations are studied and classified according to their ability to preserve the conceptual content of linguistic occurrences.

The variations considered by Barkema (1994) are syntactic variants that do not involve morphological transformations. For the idiom *Cold War*, the variations can be classified in two categories: on the one hand, external modifications such as *the melting Cold War* and, on the other hand, internal modifications. Internal modifications divide further into coordinations such as *a period of cold and hot civil war* and modifications/substitutions such as *a kind of cold civil war*.

In Gross (1988) the range of variations is wider since it covers the whole range of possible types of variations: syntactic, morphosyntactic, and semantic variations. The following syntactic variations are described: the transformation of an epithet structure into an attributive one such as *le climat est froid* (the weather is cold), a variant of *Climat froid* (cold weather), the adverbial modification such as *un ami très intime* (a very close friend), a variant of *Ami intime* (a close friend), and the adjunction of another adjective which covers coordinations and modifications/substitutions as described in the previous paragraph.

Nominalization and symmetric adjectivization are the only morphosyntactic variations proposed by Gross (1988). They concern only the symmetric transformation of an adjective into a noun such as *la blancheur du teint* (lit. the whiteness of the color), a nominal variant of *Teint blanc* (white color). Finally, semantic variations are handled by Gross as a negative criterion. The extend to which a synonym word cannot replace a content word is expected to denote the lack of flexibility of a term. Thus *Mercredi Gras* (lit. Shrove Wednesday) is not a correct variant of *Mardi Gras* (lit. Shrove Tuesday). This property is also mentioned by Barkema (1994) as collocability but is not exploited for measuring flexibility.

In Dunham, Pacak, and Pratt (1978) different types of variations are exploited for the purpose of relating linguistic occurrences in pathology diagnostics with terms in a medical nomenclature. No rigorous classification is proposed, but various illustrative examples are given. These authors address all the types of syntactic variations:

• Coordinations, such as *gastric, pyloric, celiac, right colic, and axiliary lymph nodes*, a variant of *Gastric lymph nodes*.

• Modifications/substitutions such as *acute transmural posteroapical left ventricular myocardial infarction*, a variant of *Acute infarction*.

• Permutations and elisions.

The authors also propose morphosyntactic variations such as nominalizations and adjectivizations (e.g., *Abdominal wall/Abdomen wall*) and semantic variations that rely on links in the SNOP indexing language (e.g., *Subdural hemorrhage/Subdural space*).

    This section has provided an inventory of the main types of variations. They will be studied in more detail in the following chapters.

2.1.4   Computational Techniques

This section presents three techniques that are frequently used in natural language processing methods for term extraction: finite-state machines (automata and transducers), context-free grammars, and association measures. For a more detailed presentation of the applications of finite-state techniques to natural language processing, the reader can consult Roche and Schabes (1997b). In Bunt and Tomita (1996) several parsing techniques based on context-free grammars are presented. Charniak (1993) gives an overview of various statistical techniques exploited in natural language processing.

Finite-State Machines

Before turning to the definition of finite-state machines, I introduce regular expressions that define the class of languages recognized by finite-state automata.

Regular Expressions

A regular expression defines a type of language, that is a set of strings built from an alphabet. The power of such a description is that it allows for a finite description of potentially infinite sets.

    Let us consider the alphabet $\Sigma = \{N, A, P\}$. Then $ANPN$ is a string composed out of symbols of the alphabet Σ, and $\mathcal{L} = \{\epsilon, NN, ANPN\}$ is a language over the alphabet Σ, where ϵ denotes the empty string.

    Each regular expression over the alphabet Σ defines a language over this alphabet as follows (Aho and Ullman 1992):

1. Atoms:

a. If x is a symbol in Σ, x defines the language $\{x\}$.

b. ϵ defines the language $\{\epsilon\}$, a set with only one element, the empty string.

c. $\emptyset$ defines the language with no string, the empty set.

2. Operations (R and S are two regular expressions):

a. Union. $R \mid S$ is a regular expression denoting the union of the languages represented by R and S.

b. Concatenation. $R\, S$ is a regular expression denoting the concatenation of each string in R with each string in S.

c. Kleene star. $R^\star$ is a regular expression composed of the empty string, the strings in R, the concatenation of each string in R with each string in R, etc.: $R^\star = \epsilon \mid R \mid R\, R \mid R\, R\, R \mid \ldots$.

3. Extended operations (representational facilities, R is a regular expression):

a. Optional expression. $R^?$ denotes R as an optional element: $R^? = \epsilon \mid R$.

b. Nonempty closure. R^+ is equivalent to one or more occurrences of R: $R^+ = R\, R^\star$.

Let us illustrate the exploitation of a regular expression in the description of term patterns through an example. Section 2.2.5 presents the software *TERMS* (Justeson and Katz 1995) for term extraction. It relies on the filtering of part-of-speech patterns through the following regular expression:

$$((A \mid N)^+ \mid (A \mid N)^\star\, (N\, P)\, (A \mid N)^\star)\, N \tag{2.1}$$

The alphabet is composed of part-of-speech categories: A for adjective, N for noun, etc. The formula describes well-formed noun phrases in English. From the preceding definitions, I provide some strings of the language denoted by this expression:

$$(A \mid N)^+ = \{A, N, A\, A, A\, N, N\, A, N\, N, \ldots\}$$
$$(A \mid N)^\star\, (N\, P)\, (A \mid N)^\star = \{N\, P, A\, N\, P, N\, N\, P, N\, P\, A, N\, P\, N, \ldots\}$$

and finally

$$((A \mid N)^+ \mid (A \mid N)^\star\, (N\, P)\, (A \mid N)^\star)\, N$$
$$= \{A\, N, N\, N, A\, A\, N, A\, N\, N, N\, A\, N, N\, N\, N, N\, P\, N, \ldots\}$$

For every regular expression there is a unique minimum deterministic finite-state automaton that defines this set. Conversely, for every deterministic finite-state automaton, there is a regular set denoting its language (Aho and Ullman 1972, sec. 2.3). I illustrate the first property by building the minimum finite-state automaton corresponding to the regular expression (2.1).

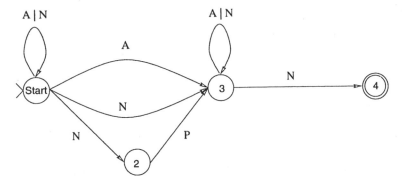

Figure 2.4
The automaton representing the language defined by the regular expression (2.1).

Finite-State Automata

A nondeterministic finite-state automaton is defined by a graph composed of nodes (the states of the automaton), and oriented edges labeled by the symbols of an alphabet (the transitions of the automaton). Two special types of nodes are distinguished from regular states: the start node (the initial state of the automaton) and the set of final nodes marked by double circles (the final states of the automaton).

An input string is accepted by a finite state automaton if and only if there is a path from the initial state Start to a final state corresponding to this string. The language defined by a finite state automaton is the set of strings accepted by this automaton. For instance, the language accepted by the automaton in figure 2.4 is the language defined by the regular expression (2.1). The succession of states and edges leading to accept the string A N P N is

$$\text{Start} \overset{A}{\vdash} \text{Start} \overset{N}{\vdash} 2 \overset{P}{\vdash} 3 \overset{N}{\vdash} 4$$

This automaton is nondeterministic because there are states with more than one transition for a given label. For instance, from the initial node Start and for the label N, there are three possible transitions to the nodes Start, 2 or 3. A deterministic finite-state automaton is an automaton which has no epsilon-transitions (transitions labeled with an ϵ which do not read a symbol of the input string) and such that there is at most one transition for a given node and a given label. The advantage of deterministic automata is their run-time efficiency, since the time for processing an input string is proportional to its length.

The languages defined by nondeterministic automata and deterministic automata are identical. From any nondeterministic automaton $\mathcal{A}$, a deterministic automaton $\mathcal{A}_d$ can be constructed which recognizes the same language (Hopcroft and Ullman 1979, sec. 2.3).

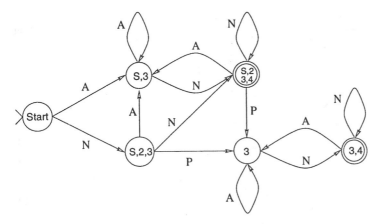

Figure 2.5
The deterministic automaton equivalent to the non-deterministic automaton of figure 2.4.

The deterministic finite-state automaton that defines the same language as the automaton of figure 2.4 is illustrated by figure 2.5.

For constructing a deterministic automaton from a nondeterministic one, new nodes are created that correspond to sets of states of the initial automaton. Then the edges correspond to the union of the edges of the initial automaton between the elementary states. In figure 2.4, since both states Start and 3 are reached from the initial state through symbol A, a new state Start,3 is created, together with an edge labeled A linking the initial state to this state.

Although deterministic automata have a minimal time complexity, their number of states (their space) may not be minimal. A deterministic automaton can be reduced to an equivalent automaton that has a minimal number of states (Hopcroft 1971). The minimization of an automaton is made by merging redundant states (and by removing inaccessible states). Two states are *equivalent* if and only if they yield the same result whatever the input string. The minimization algorithm iteratively marks pairs of inequivalent states. The remaining nonmarked pairs of states are equivalent states that can be merged (Hopcroft and Ullman 1979, sec. 3.4).

First, final states are marked as nonequivalent to each of the nonfinal states. Then, recursively, each pair of states s and s' such that there are transitions labeled with the same symbol x to two nonequivalent states are marked as nonequivalent. For instance, in the automaton of figure 2.5, states Start and 3 are nonequivalent because there are transitions labeled N from these two states to two nonequivalent states (Start,2,3 and 3,4). Since each pair of states in the automaton of figure 2.5 is nonequivalent, this automaton is also minimal.

Finite-state techniques are used in several tools for term extraction presented in section 2.2. They are also part of the algorithm used for morphosyntactic variant extraction, which is presented in chapter 7. Mostly they are used in several domains of natural language processing such as morphology (see section 2.1.3), part-of-speech tagging (Roche and Schabes 1997a), syntax (Voutilainen 1997; Senellart 1998), and semantics in information extraction (MUC-6 1995; Hobbs et al. 1997).

Context-Free Grammars

Context-free grammars represent languages that are more complex than the regular expressions seen in the preceding section. In particular, they can be used to represent arbitrarily distant dependencies and deep recursive structures.

A *context-free grammar* is a finite set of variables, called *nonterminals*, each of which represents a language (Hopcroft and Ullman 1979, ch. 4). The origin of context-free grammars is found in Chomsky (1956), who proposes several types of grammars for the description of natural language.

Context-Free Rules

A context-free grammar is described by rules with a unique nonterminal as the left component and with a right-hand component composed of a concatenation of nonterminals and strings of the language.

Let us consider the set of nonterminals $V = \{\langle NP \rangle, \langle Adj \rangle, \langle Noun \rangle, \langle PreMod \rangle\}$ for the description of noun phrases in English. I can write a grammar of noun phrases such as

$$\langle NP \rangle \rightarrow \langle PreMod \rangle \langle Noun \rangle \tag{2.2}$$

$$\langle PreMod \rangle \rightarrow \langle PreMod \rangle \; and \; \langle PreMod \rangle \tag{2.3}$$

$$\langle PreMod \rangle \rightarrow \langle PreMod \rangle \langle PreMod \rangle \tag{2.4}$$

$$\langle PreMod \rangle \rightarrow \langle Adj \rangle \mid \langle Noun \rangle \tag{2.5}$$

$$\langle Adj \rangle \rightarrow normal \tag{2.6}$$

$$\langle Noun \rangle \rightarrow blood \mid bone \mid cell \mid marrow \tag{2.7}$$

The meaning of the first rule is that the string of a noun phrase (category $\langle NP \rangle$) can be formed by concatenating the string of a premodifier (category $\langle PreMod \rangle$) and the string of a noun (category $\langle Noun \rangle$). The preceding grammar also includes terminal rules that do not contain nonterminals on the right side. The last rules stands, in fact, for four terminal rules. One of them is $\langle Noun \rangle \rightarrow blood$. It means that the syntactic category $\langle Noun \rangle$ denotes a language containing the string *blood*.

Derivation

The language generated by a grammar is obtained by calculating the derivations of a special nonterminal, called the start symbol. Here the start symbol is ⟨NP⟩. A derivation is the substitution of a nonterminal X by one of the strings α such that there exists a rule $X \rightarrow \alpha$. The language generated by a grammar is the set of strings of terminals that can be obtained from the start symbol through one or more derivations.

For example, *blood and bone marrow cell* is a string generated by the preceding grammar. There is only one rule ⟨NP⟩ $\rightarrow \alpha$ that applies for the first derivation:

⟨NP⟩ $\overset{2.2}{\Longrightarrow}$ ⟨PreMod⟩ ⟨Noun⟩

Then, by applying other rules from the grammar, the expected string is finally obtained:

⟨PreMod⟩ ⟨Noun⟩ $\overset{2.3}{\Longrightarrow}$ ⟨PreMod⟩ *and* ⟨PreMod⟩ ⟨Noun⟩

$\overset{2.5}{\Longrightarrow}$ ⟨Noun⟩ *and* ⟨PreMod⟩ ⟨Noun⟩

$\overset{2.7}{\Longrightarrow}$ *blood and* ⟨PreMod⟩ ⟨Noun⟩

$\overset{2.4}{\Longrightarrow}$ *blood and* ⟨PreMod⟩ ⟨PreMod⟩ ⟨Noun⟩

$\overset{2.5}{\Longrightarrow}$ *blood and* ⟨Noun⟩ ⟨PreMod⟩ ⟨Noun⟩

$\overset{2.7}{\Longrightarrow}$ *blood and bone* ⟨PreMod⟩ ⟨Noun⟩

$\overset{2.5}{\Longrightarrow}$ *blood and bone* ⟨Noun⟩ ⟨Noun⟩

$\overset{2.7}{\Longrightarrow}$ *blood and bone marrow* ⟨Noun⟩

$\overset{2.7}{\Longrightarrow}$ *blood and bone marrow cell*

This derivation can be displayed as a tree, called a *derivation tree*. The interior vertices are labeled with nonterminals and the frontier vertices with terminals. Figure 2.6 displays the derivation tree (α) corresponding to the preceding derivation. Each interior node and its daughter nodes is associated with one rule in the grammar and one derivation in the preceding sequence of derivations. The derivation is called a leftmost derivation because, at each step, a derivation is applied to the leftmost nonterminal.

The string *blood and bone marrow cell* has another parse tree (β) in the same grammar, which is given in figure 2.7. A grammar such that some string has more than one parse tree is said to be *ambiguous*. The parse tree corresponding to the correct linguistic structure is (α) because *blood marrow* is not a correct substructure of *blood and bone marrow* while *blood* and *bone marrow* are correct substructures.[9]

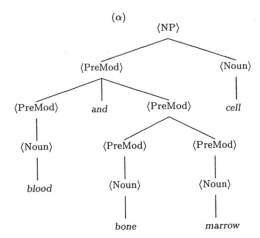

Figure 2.6
Derivation tree (α) of *blood and bone marrow cell*.

Efficient techniques for parsing context-free languages, such as predictive tabular parsers, are presented in Aho, Sethi, and Ullman (1986, ch. 4).

Word Associations

Multi-word terms are a sort of collocations. They are sets of words that tend to co-occur repetitively with a specific meaning that is not just the composition of the components. In this section on word associations, I present some classical measures for the automatic extraction of collocates. One of them, *Mutual Information*, was designed in the domain of information theory. The Mutual Information of two outcomes w_1 and w_2 is the amount of information that one event gives about the other (Charniak 1993, sec. 9.2). Another measure, the *t*-score, is used to differentiate collocates, not to establish them (Church et al. 1991). I present three other measures that come from information retrieval and evaluate the similarity between vectors. In the case of a pair of words, the measures are based on vectors which capture the joint and marginal probabilities of the component words (Smadja, McKeown, and Hatzivassiloglou 1996).

Statistical techniques for term extraction rely on the observation of word occurrences and exploit little or no information about their linguistic properties. The simplest measure for observing two words w_1 and w_2 that are likely to build a term is the frequency of isolated occurrence and the frequency of co-occurrence. The four frequencies characterizing a pair of words in a text are represented in the following contingency table (Daille 1994, chap 4.3.2):

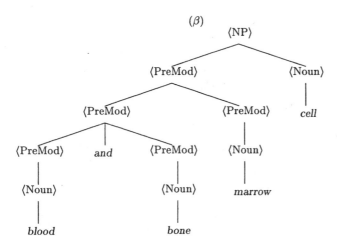

Figure 2.7
Derivation tree (β) of *blood and bone marrow cell*.

	w_2	$w' \neq w_2$
w_1	$a = f(w_1, w_2)$	$b = \sum_{w' \neq w_2} f(w_1, w')$
$w \neq w_1$	$c = \sum_{w \neq w_1} f(w, w_2)$	$d = \sum_{w \neq w_1, w' \neq w_2} f(w, w')$

The measures of co-occurrence $f(w, w')$ vary according to the size of the window in which they are observed. If, for example, the size of the window is 2, the words are contiguous.

In computational linguistics, *Mutual Information* is a widely used information-theoretic measure (Fano 1961, ch. 2):

$$MI(X, Y) = \log_2 \frac{P(w_1, w_2)}{P(w_1)\ P(w_2)} = \log_2 \frac{a}{(a+b)(a+c)} \tag{2.8}$$

X and Y are random variables that correspond to samples taken in which $x = w_1$ and $y = w_2$, respectively. Mutual Information represents the log-likelihood ratio of the joint probability of seeing w_1 and w_2 in the same window over the probability that such an event would have if the two variables were independent. Mutual Information provides a measure of departure from independence. Given X, Mutual Information indicates how much more predictable is Y.

If both words w_1 and w_2 are lexicosemantically associated, w_2 tends to occur more frequently after w_1 than it would just by chance and their Mutual Information is positive (Smadja, McKeown, and Hatzivassiloglou 1996).[10] Mutual Information is null if the words occur independently and negative if w_2 occurs less frequently after w_1 than if they were independent.

Church and Hanks (1990) exploit Mutual Information for measuring the lexical associations of pairs of words for lexicographical acquisition. By merging pairs of words for which the loss of Average Mutual Information is least, Brown et al. (1992) build clusters of words that tend to share the same contexts in a corpus and therefore have related meanings.

Mutual Information is an absolute measure. It is not the most appropriate measure to establish differences among nearly synonymous words w_1 and w_2 that share many identical collocates. Church et al. (1991) propose to use the *t-score* to establish which words w are more likely to appear after w_1 than w_2:

$$t(X, Y) = \frac{P(w \mid w_1) - P(w \mid w_2)}{\sqrt{\sigma^2(P(w \mid w_1)) + \sigma^2(P(w \mid w_2))}} \tag{2.9}$$

Each value $P(w \mid w_i)$ is the conditional probability that the word w_i is followed by the word w in the corpus. The t-score indicates the difference between the two conditional probabilities $P(w \mid w_1)$ and $P(w \mid w_2)$ in standard deviations.

In the domain of document processing and information retrieval, there is a constant need for classifying vectors, either terms represented as vectors of documents or documents represented as vectors of terms. Documents are represented as vectors of terms and similar documents are grouped to facilitate the access to large document databases, and thesauri are built automatically by grouping terms described as vectors of documents to improve term-based querying. The following measures are used to compute term or document similarities in information retrieval (Salton and McGill 1983, sec. 3.3.A):

Dice (1945) coefficient,

$$\text{Dice}(x, y) = \frac{2 \sum_i (x_i \cdot y_i)}{\sum_i x_i + \sum_i y_i} \tag{2.10}$$

Jaccard coefficient or Tanimoto (1958) measure,

$$\text{Jaccard}(x, y) = \frac{\sum_i (x_i \cdot y_i)}{\sum_i x_i + \sum_i y_i - \sum_i (x_i \cdot y_i)} \tag{2.11}$$

Cosine (Salton and Lesk 1968)

$$\text{Cosine}(x, y) = \frac{\sum_i (x_i \cdot y_i)}{\sqrt{\sum_i x_i^2 \cdot \sum_i y_i^2}} \tag{2.12}$$

The two vectors (x_i) and (y_i) represent the weights of terms (t_i) assigned to documents x and y (Salton and McGill 1983, sec. 6.2).

In the case of term extraction, the vectors are given by the contingency table. For example,

$$\text{Dice}(X, Y) = \frac{2P(w_1, w_2)}{P(w_1, w \neq w_2) \, P(w \neq w_1, w_2)} = \frac{2a}{b + c} \tag{2.13}$$

Daille (1994, ch. 4) cites several other measures used for testing the independence, evaluating the correlation, or the similarity of statistical variables. In the same study a systematic observation of the quality of term extraction through the exploitation of these measures is also provided. Daille shows that frequency, despite its simplicity, is a good criterion for term selection. The frequency measure nevertheless has two drawbacks: rare terms are ignored, and repeated sequences without terminological status are incorrectly selected.

From an analysis of terms collected by different measures, Daille (1996) concludes that the *log-likelihood ratio* (Dunning 1993) is a measure that can distinguish rare events and rank high good candidates. The log-likelihood ratio of two words is

$$\lambda(X, Y) = a \log(a) + b \log(b) + c \log(c) + d \log(d) \tag{2.14}$$
$$- (a + b) \log(a + b) - (a + c) \log(a + c) - (b + d) \log(b + d)$$
$$- (c + d) \log(c + d) + (a + b + c + d) \log(a + b + c + d)$$

2.1.5 Evaluation of Term Extraction

The measures of the quality of controlled indexing are taken by analogy from the evaluation in information retrieval. In information retrieval, the goal is to retrieve all the documents relevant to a query and only these documents; in controlled indexing, the purpose is to extract all the occurrences of terms and variants and only them. Obviously the actually extracted occurrences $\mathcal{I}_\mathcal{E}$ only partially overlap with the relevant ones $\mathcal{I}_\mathcal{R}$, resulting in a certain *noise* (incorrect retrieved occurrences) and a certain *silence* (correct unretrieved occurrences) (see figure 2.8).

The basic measures of quality in information retrieval are *precision* and *recall* (Salton 1989, p. 248):

$$P = \frac{|\mathcal{I}_\mathcal{E} \cap \mathcal{I}_\mathcal{R}|}{|\mathcal{I}_\mathcal{E}|}, \qquad R = \frac{|\mathcal{I}_\mathcal{E} \cap \mathcal{I}_\mathcal{R}|}{|\mathcal{I}_\mathcal{R}|} \tag{2.15}$$

Precision is the proportion of retrieved documents that are relevant, and recall is the proportion of relevant documents retrieved. Precision is high (close to 1.0) when noise is low and recall is high (close to 1.0) when silence is low. These two measures do not give a complete picture of the quality of extraction because the system described in figure 2.8

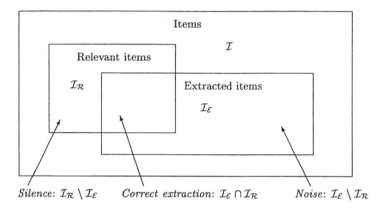

Figure 2.8
Evaluation in an information retrieval system.

has three degrees of freedom. The measure generally used for completing the preceding description is *fallout* (Van Rijsbergen 1975, p. 100). I prefer its complement, which I call *precision of fallout* because its value is high when the quality of the extraction is high (as with precision and recall):

$$\Pi = \frac{|(\mathcal{I} \setminus \mathcal{I}_\mathcal{R}) \setminus \mathcal{I}_\mathcal{E}|}{|\mathcal{I} \setminus \mathcal{I}_\mathcal{R}|} \tag{2.16}$$

Precision of fallout is the proportion of nonrelevant documents which are not retrieved.

Ruge (1991) legitimizes the parallel between evaluation methods used in information retrieval and automatic indexing and suggests a semimanual method for extracting a set of reference terms to measure recall. First, an approximate and overpermissive automatic technique extracts a set of candidate terms that is expected to include all the correct terms and some additional spurious occurrences. Second, a human postfiltering retains only correct indexes among the approximate set extracted at the first step, thus constituting a correct and exhaustive reference set. I will use a similar technique in the evaluation of my tools for term recognition in sections 5.5 and 7.3.

2.2 Term Acquisition

In this section I present some significant studies in corpus-based term acquisition. The input to the programs developer for these experiments is a corpus (either raw or tagged). The output is a list of candidate terms, possibly enhanced with conceptual links. Each system is presented in two steps: first a general outline of the method, and then a more detailed description. This section ends with an overall comparison of the algorithms for term acquisition. The reader who is interested in another analysis of the state-of-the-art in term acquisition may consult Habert and Jacquemin (1993, in French) or Cabré Castellví, Estopà Bagot, and Vivaldi Palatresi (2000 forthcoming, in English).

This overview of term extraction systems deliberately ignores tools for term management in which term extraction is only a small subcomponent of the system. I have intentionally not included systems, such as *Quirk* (Ahmad 1993), which do not focus on the term extraction task per se and, instead, provide complex environments for creating, examining, extracting, and organizing terminological data. In such systems, more efforts are devoted to the integration and the interfacing of the term extractor than to its core development.

2.2.1 *ACABIT*: A Hybrid Model for Term Acquisition

Synthetic Presentation

ACABIT is a program for term acquisition that processes tagged texts through a hybrid analyzer composed of a shallow linguistic parser and a statistical filter (Daille 1994, 1996). The parser is a finite-state machine that relies on part-of-speech categories and morphological features. The linguistic descriptions used in *ACABIT* for noun phrase extraction are positive patterns that capture the inner structure of terminological noun phrases (compare with *LEXTER*, presented in section 2.2.3, which uses similar finite-state techniques but uses negative patterns for noun phrases).

In *ACABIT* the maximal substrings of each sentence that are accepted by the automaton are sorted in relation to statistical measures such as Φ^2, log-likelihood ratio, or frequency. Only the top-ranked substrings are proposed as candidate terms.

In addition to a tool, Daille's study provides a detailed experimental analysis of the syntactic structures of terms and their variations in order to motivate the linguistic filters of *ACABIT*. This study also evaluates several statistical measures with respect to their ability to separate terms from nonterminological sequences.

Implementation

ACABIT arose from a systematic study of the different possibilities of term structures in French (Daille 1994; Daille et al. 1996). Making the assumption that most n-ary terms result from the nested combination of binary terms, the description of term structures focuses mainly on binary terms (terms with two content words). The three main structures considered are N A such as *Station terrienne* (earth station), N P D? N such as *Liaison par satellite* (satellite link), and N N such as *Diode tunnel* (tunnel diode).

Variants are generated from these basic structures through syntactic transformations:

- Combinations of terms through *coordination*. *Assemblage de paquets + Désassemblage de paquets → assemblage/désassemblage de paquets* (packet assembly/disassembly),

- Combinations of terms through *overcomposition*. *Réseau à satellites + Réseau de transit → réseau de transit à satellites* (satellite transit network),

- Syntactic modifications of terms through the addition of an *adjectival modifier*. *Liaison par satellites → liaisons multiples par satellites* (multiple satellite links).

Linguistic Filtering and Conflation

The preceding linguistic analysis of terms and variants is used for constructing a set of transducers. The role of these transducers is (1) filtering—only acceptable term or variant patterns are selected—and (2) conflation—each variant is reduced to its base form(s), one or two binary terms. The patterns of term and variant structures are transformed into regular expressions that define the acceptable patterns for the transducers. The input to these transducers is a tagged corpus with part-of-speech categories and the output is a set of binary candidate terms. If the input pattern is a term pattern, it is reported as output. If the input pattern is a variant pattern, the output is the base form(s) of this variation—the binary term(s) from which the variant is calculated. For example, the text occurrence of the overcomposition *réseau de transit à satellites* (satellite transit network) is transformed into the binary candidates *réseau de transit* (transit network) and *réseau à satellites* (satellite network).

The text to be used for term acquisition is first processed by the finite state machines; they extract all the substrings with acceptable part-of-speech patterns and produce the corresponding candidate base forms. For instance, the base form *Ester acide* (acid ester) corresponds to the following five occurrences in an agricultural corpus: *ester méthylique d'acide* (acid methyl ester), *ester d'acide* (acid ester), *ester de l'acide* (ester of the acid), *ester éthylique d'acide* (ethyl ester of acid), and *ester de sucre et d'acide* (ester of sugar and acid). Thus the linguistic filtering of *ACABIT* prepares the next step of the process, statistical filtering, by reducing all the acceptable segments to pairs of words.[11]

Statistical Filtering

For scoring the output of the first step, a set of statistical measures of association and diversity is proposed in the final output of *ACABIT*. The *measures of association* indicate whether both words in a term tend to co-occur independently one from another or whether they tend to co-occur more frequently than they would just by chance. According to Daille's experimental results, the *log-likelihood ratio* (Dunning 1993) is the most appropriate measure for filtering out relevant candidates (see formula 2.14 above). She also observes that the core frequency is a good indicator of terminologization, even though it is generally taken for granted in the literature that frequency is not a relevant criterion for selecting terms. A similar conclusion about the appropriateness of frequency is reached in Kageura (1999) for the task of extracting valid morphological units from Japanese Kanji sequences.

The *measures of diversity* indicate how frequently the head or argument words of a term combine with other words in the same configuration. Head words with a high diversity denote central concepts in a domain (generic key concepts from which are derived several more specific ones). For instance, in the domain of telecommunications, *network*, *antenna*, and *satellite* are head nouns with a high diversity. Conversely, arguments with a high diversity are of little terminological interests since they correspond to nonspecific modifiers. They generally denote occasional properties instead of intrinsic features. In the same domain, *necessary*, *important*, and *following* are highly combining modifiers that obviously rarely produce a new concept when associated with a head word.

A final measure is calculated by *ACABIT*, a *measure of distance*, that evaluates whether the occurrences of a base term tend to vary from its base form. Terms with several variants legitimate, a posteriori, the conflation of variants performed by *ACABIT*. Not considering such variants would lead the method to miss the terms which accept many variations.

Comments

ACABIT takes advantage of the combination of a linguistic filter and a statistical score. The relative simplicity of the linguistic filter is compensated for by the posterior statistical filter, which rejects nonterminological occurrences. The simplicity of the linguistic knowledge embodied in *ACABIT* makes this tool easily adaptable to different domains and languages. (Currently there are versions of *ACABIT* for French, English, and Malagasy.)

Another specific feature of *ACABIT* is that it accounts for term variation during acquisition. Thus all variants of binary terms detected by the pattern matchers are reduced to corresponding base forms. Ultimately the acquisition process yields only one canonical candidate term for all the variants associated with this term. The advantage of the technique is twofold. First, terms with or without variations are scored as equals during acquisition. This characteristic is necessary since observation of diversity shows that terms are equally as likely to accept variations as not. Second, the final set of candidate terms proposed as output is smaller than it would be without concern for variation. This makes the human filtering and organizing of candidate terms that follows much less tedious.

The open issue in *ACABIT*, as in any statistical approach, is the tuning of the parameters for statistical filtering so as to assign high scores only to correct candidates. Contrary to the linguistic filters which are used for eliminating the spurious occurrences and retaining the correct ones, statistical criteria are only used for sorting candidates and for ranking those proposed to the human expert.

2.2.2 *ANA*: A Statistical Termer

Synthetic Presentation

ANA is a tool for term acquisition that relies on text simplification, approximate equalities between words and phrases, and observation of recurring patterns (Enguehard 1992; Enguehard and Pantera 1995). The approach is incremental in the sense that it is bootstrapped by a set of seed terms and enriched step by step with new terms discovered in the vicinity of previously acquired terms.

The software requires three initial sets of data:

1. A set of *stop words* resulting from frequency filtering.

2. A set of *seed terms* that are built manually and contain some of the major concepts in the domain of the corpus.

3. A set of *scheme words*, mainly prepositions and determiners, used for building complex terms from single-word terms.

Stop words are removed from the texts with the goal of text simplification. Then, three types of recurring patterns are observed in order to acquire new terms: co-occurrences of two terms, and two cases of co-occurrences of a term and an unknown content word: those separated by a scheme word and those not.

Ultimately a network of the acquired terms is built. It mirrors the links of acquisition between single-word terms and complex terms.

Implementation

The purpose of *ANA* is to provide a set of techniques for term acquisition that rely only on graphical properties of texts and that make no use of any linguistic data. The cognitive metaphor of the software is the learning of its mother tongue by a child. Since a child acquires the vocabulary, the syntax, and the semantics of a language without being taught explicitly what they really are, it should be conceivable to acquire the vocabulary of a specialized domain through the mere a investigation of a corpus without referring to any explicit linguistic knowledge.

Acquisition with *ANA* is based on the detection of recurrent co-occurrences in which at least one of the content words is already considered as a term. It relies on Choueka's (1988) assumption that collocations (recurring associations of words) denote meaningful concepts in a domain. Thus the terminological vocabulary of *ANA* is progressively enhanced by adding complex terms composed of pairs of single-word terms, and single-word terms repeatedly observed in the vicinity of a term.

The acquisition process consists of two phases:

1. A *familiarization module* that collects the three aforementioned initial sets of words that will be used during the second step.

2. A *discovery module* which incrementally acquires candidate terms and builds the corresponding semantic network.

Familiarization Module

Before processing texts with *ANA*, the textual data are first simplified. This preliminary cleanup is necessary because the tool does not use any NLP technique and therefore cannot examine the dependency between a pair of words whatever their actual syntactic context. Text cleanup in *ANA* is inspired from the text simplification methods used in information retrieval as a preprocessing to automatic indexing (Salton and McGill 1983, sec. 3.3.A). However, instead of removing indistinctly all the frequent words, only those which are not involved in the construction of complex terms are removed.

In addition to these deletable stop words, two other sets of initial data are built: a set of seed terms and a set of so-called scheme words (mainly determiners and prepositions).

Stop Words   The frequency cutoff under which frequent words are excluded is calculated in order to remove a given ratio of the surface of the Zipf curve of a corpus (the curve relating the frequency of words and their rank order; Van Rijsbergen 1975, p. 14). The cutoff value depends on the type of the corpus: more low frequency words must be removed from multi-domain corpora than from single-domain corpora. This difference is due to the lower ratio of stop words in multi-domain corpora than in single-domain corpora: the number of low-frequency domain-specific content words increases as the diversity of the corpus increases. In English the stop-list thus extracted contains from 60 to 100 items such as *a*, *any*, *for*, *in*, etc.

Seed Terms   The set of seed terms is used for bootstrapping the acquisition of terms. Since the final result of the acquisition is relatively independent from the initial set of seed terms, they can be approximately and inaccurately collected without damaging the subsequent acquisition process. Enguehard (1992) suggested collecting seed terms through manual and statistical observation. Seed terms can be manually collected by selecting terms which represent the major concepts of a domain. They can be statistically gathered by selecting frequent words that do not belong to the stop-list and that frequently follow stop words. From a corpus on nuclear power plants, the following seed terms are acquired: *automate* (automaton), *centrale* (power plant), *chaudière* (boiler), *circuit* (circuit), etc.

Scheme Words   Seed terms are used twice by the software, in the discovery stage for acquiring new terms and, here, in the familiarization module, for automatically constructing the set of scheme words. Scheme words are detected through their role in the construction of complex terms from single-word seed terms. Scheme words W are collected from repeated $T \; W \; T'$ patterns in which T and T' are two seed terms. The extraction of frequent phrases composed of a word between two seed terms yields a set of approximately ten scheme words: *de* (of), *de_la* (of the), *en* (in), *à* (at), etc.

Term Discovery

The process for discovering term is based on the detection of recurring binary associations of content words (possibly separated by a scheme word) such that at least one of the content words is a term. Any seed term or any word acquired during one of the preceding steps of the acquisition process is called a term. The three schemes of term discovery are expressions, candidates, and expansions.

Expressions   Two repeatedly associated single-word terms yield a new term:

$$T + T' \rightarrow T'' = [T \; T']$$

For instance, *cœur du réacteur* (reactor core) is an expression acquired through the association of the terms *cœur* (core) and *réacteur* (reactor).

Candidates   A single word repeatedly collocated with single-word terms and separated by a scheme word is candidate term:

$$\{T\} + Scheme\_Word + W \rightarrow T' = [W]$$

and

$$W + Scheme\_Word + \{T\} \rightarrow T'' = [W]$$

For instance, the repetition of *T du barillet* (*T* of the barrel), in which *T* is a term such as *cuve* (tank), produces the candidate *barillet* (barrel).

Expansions   A single word and a single-word term, repeatedly associated, are proposed as a two-word term:

$$T + W \rightarrow T' = [T \; W] \text{ and } W + T \rightarrow T'' = [W \; T]$$

For instance, *structure interne* (internal structure) is the frequent association of the term *structure* (structure) and the single word *interne* (internal) which produces the new binary term *structure interne*.

   Before calculating the frequencies of the bigrams used for term acquisition, the bigrams are conflated through an approximate equality between single words which is based on a *string-edit distance* (Wagner and Fisher 1974; Hall and Dowling 1980).

Figure 2.9
The three modes of construction of a semantic network from the acquisition of terms by *ANA* (terms from the preceding steps are underlined).

Contrary to the familiarization phase which is a one-step process, the discovery phase is incremental. The initial set of terms is the set of seed terms. At each step, the set of terms is enriched with the unary or binary terms produced by one of the three modes of discovery. Each acquisition adds a node to a conceptual graph (called a semantic network) and possible conceptual links. Figure 2.9 illustrates the three types of completion of the semantic network corresponding to the three schemes of term discovery given above.

From a 120,000-word French text, 100 stop words are acquired, 6 scheme words, and 125 seed terms. Then the incremental discovery process produces more than 3,000 terms.

Comments
The key idea of *ANA* is that terms can be extracted from corpora without calling for complex NLP modules or hand-crafted linguistic data. This approach is similar to the techniques for automatic thesaurus construction, encountered in information retrieval, which rely on the observation of recurring associations (Crouch 1990). *ANA* also shares common features with approximate string matching techniques that are commonly used for spelling checkers or access to large databases (Wagner and Fisher 1974; Hall and Dowling 1980). In the same fashion, Paice and Aragon-Ramirez (1985) propose to conflate complex terms and text occurrences through a two-level matching: approximate equality between words, and similarity between sequences of words in the documents and complex terms. When compared with these similar studies, *ANA* is richer because it combines techniques from different origins: frequency cutoff for term detection, observation of repeated bigrams for phrase acquisition, and approximate equality for the conflation of morphologically similar occurrences.

Such techniques are usually accompanied by an evaluation via an information access experiment. Here the terms are acquired with the purpose of constructing a knowledge base; thus automatic evaluation is not straightforward. An evaluation with human experts shows that the precision ranges from 59.5 to 75.6%.

The radical choice to avoid any form of linguistic processing has the immediate advantage to provide a tool that can be applied to any language. So far *ANA* has been applied to French, English, and Malagasy. Nevertheless, it remains to be shown that the modes of compositions of single words, proposed by *ANA* for building terms are universal. Morphological analysis may turn out to be mandatory for agglutinative languages, for instance.

The second major feature of *ANA* is its "natural" incremental process for the discovery of new terms. This process is robust and does not depend crucially on the initial set of terms.

2.2.3 *LEXTER*: A Tool for Term and Conceptual Knowledge Acquisition

Synthetic Presentation

LEXTER (Bourigault 1993, 1994, 1996) is a natural language processing tool for term acquisition from French corpora. The software extracts maximal noun phrases through finite state machines. The grammar contains patterns describing the frontiers of noun phrases in order to extract their maximal-length expansion.[12] These maximal chunks are then split into subphrases according to the following principle: if several decompositions compete, the decomposition corresponding to subgroups appearing elsewhere in the corpus in an unambiguous situation is preferred. The selected subphrases are proposed by *LEXTER* as *candidate terms*—that is to say, linguistic units that are most appropriate for inclusion in a thesaurus, in relation to other terms through conceptual links.

Several studies have focused on the exploitation of the data produced by *LEXTER*; they propose interesting follow-ups for structuring and conceptually enriching the automatically acquired network of candidate terms. First, in Bourigault (1995), a structuring module and a corresponding browsing tool are proposed for building and observing a terminological network built on terms sharing common constituents. The second extension exploits the bracketing of noun phrases in sentences generated by *LEXTER* on medium-size corpora (Assadi and Bourigault 1996, Habert, Naulleau, and Nazarenko 1996, Assadi 1997). The elementary dependencies between words within noun phrases are used for calculating distributional regularities and building up clusters of words.

Implementation

Extraction of Maximal Noun Phrases

The input to *LEXTER* is a tagged corpus in which each word is accompanied by a part-of-speech category and a set of morphological features such as gender and number for nouns, adjectives, and past participles. The linguistic knowledge embodied in *LEXTER* for locating maximal noun phrases is a form of negative knowledge. Instead of describing the structure of well-formed noun phrases, the grammar is composed of a set of *splitting rules* indicating the most likely frontiers of noun phrases.

The splitting rules are used by the software for breaking the sentence into text chunks corresponding to maximal-length noun phrases. Some patterns are obvious: strong punctuations, conjugated verbs, subordinating conjunctions, pronouns, etc. Other patterns span larger windows in order to exploit the context for a more accurate splitting. Thus an epithet past participle followed by a preposition is eliminated and the sentence is split. For instance, *les clapets* <u>situés</u> <u>sur</u> *les tubes d'alimentation* (the valves <u>located</u> <u>on</u> the feeder pipes) is split into *les clapets* (the valves) and *les tubes d'alimentation* (the feeder pipes). The corresponding rule is

Splitting rule: $V_{past\_participle} + P \rightarrow$ *split & eliminate*   (2.17)

This linguistic rule is however not systematically relevant. The splitting is legitimate only if the phrase introduced by the preposition is a complement of the past participle. The following exception must be described: if the preposition P is *de* (of), the preposition phrase is possibly attached to the head word of the noun phrase instead of the past participle. For example, in *registre motorisé <u>de</u> réglage* (powered regulation register, lit. <u>register</u> powered <u>of</u> regulation), *de réglage* (of regulation) depends from the head noun *registre* (register), not from *motorisé* (powered). These exceptions are described by the following rule which overrides Splitting rule (2.17) if the preposition is *de*:

Exception rule: $V_{past\_participle} + de \rightarrow \emptyset$ (2.18)

This rule states that nothing should be done in the case of the preposition *de*. It postpones the decision to a second step of the process during which the corpus is used as a source of subcategorization knowledge for making the correct disambiguation.

During the second stage, a learning procedure detects unambiguous occurrences in which a past participle accepts a *de* (of) preposition phrase as a complement. This clue is provided by passive constructions *être* $+ V_{past\_participle} + de$ (to be $+ V_{past\_participle} +$ of) such as *chaque pompe <u>est</u> <u>équipée</u> d'une ligne* (each pump <u>is</u> <u>equipped</u> <u>with</u> a pipe).

The learning procedure scans the corpus in order to detect such constructions and collects the corresponding verbs in an exception list $\mathcal{E}$. A new rule is applied that overrides Exception rule (2.18):

Splitting rule: $V_{past\_participle} + de$ & $V \in \mathcal{E} \rightarrow$ *split & eliminate*   (2.19)

The verb *équiper* (to equip) is likely to belong to $\mathcal{E}$, whereas the verb *motoriser* (to motor) is not. Consequently the preceding term *registre motorisé de réglage* remains correctly unsplit by Exception rule (2.18), whereas *pompe <u>équipée</u> d'une ligne* (pump <u>equipped</u> <u>with</u> a pipe) is correctly split by Splitting rule (2.19). This learning procedure is called *endogenous learning*.

The output of the splitting module is a set of non-overlapping maximal-length noun phrases; the remaining chunks of the text are ignored.

Decomposition of Maximal Noun Phrases

The second module for term acquisition in *LEXTER* is a local parser that decomposes the maximal noun phrases produced by the preceding module into binary subgroups. These binary phrases, together with the maximal noun phrases, make up the candidate terms. Each binary candidate is composed of a head and an expansion.

Some of the maximal noun phrases are not ambiguous; they are parsed by nonambiguous transducers that take as input the pattern of the maximal noun phrase and produce subparts of this pattern as candidate terms. The following *decomposition rule* extracts a unique subgroup from $N\,P\,A\,N$ phrases:

Decomposition rule: $N_1\,P\,A\,N_2\ \rightarrow\ A\,N_2$ (2.20)

For ambiguous noun phrases, the disambiguation technique is a corpus-based technique similar to the endogenous learning of splitting rules. An ambiguous parsing rule first generates all the competing subgroups associated with the current maximal noun phrase. Then a disambiguation module scans the corpus, searching for nonambiguous situations elsewhere in the corpus in which one of the competing subgroups occurs. Finally, a set of *disambiguation rules* is used to choose some of the unambiguously detected subgroups and discard the remaining ones.

For instance, *rejet d'air froid* (cool air exhaust) is an ambiguous $N_1\,P\,N_2\,A$ noun phrase from which the following three possible subphrases are generated: $N_1\,P\,N_2$, $N_2\,A$, and $N_1\,A$ (here *rejet d'air* [air exhaust], *air froid* [cool air], and *rejet froid* [cool exhaust]):

Decomposition rule: $N_1\,P\,N_2\,A\ \rightarrow\ N_1\,P\,N_2\ \&\ N_2\,A\ \&\ N_1\,A$ (2.21)

Disambiguation is performed through sets of mutually exclusive rules that are triggered by the nonambiguous subphrases discovered during the endogenous corpus-based investigation. For instance, the Disambiguation rules associated with the preceding Decomposition rule (2.21) are[13]

Disambiguation rules:

if $N_2\,A$ is confirmed by corpus investigation, produce $N_2\,A$ (2.22a)

if one of $N_1\,P\,N_2$ or $N_1\,A$ is encountered in the corpus, produce $N_1\,P\,N_2$ (2.22b)

if none of $N_1\,P\,N_2$, $N_2\,A$, or $N_1\,A$ is found, produce $N_2\,A$ (2.22c)

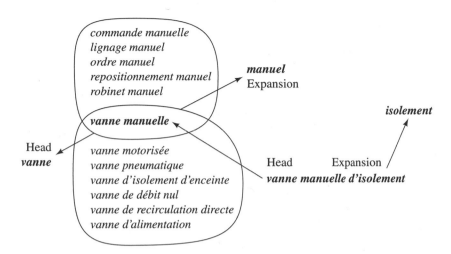

Figure 2.10
A network of connected words built from the output of *LEXTER*.

For example, if among the three competing subgroups, only *air froid* (N_2 A) is encountered in a nonambiguous situation in the current corpus, the Disambiguation rule (2.22a) yields the candidate *air froid*.

An experiment on a 200,000-word corpus produces 12,000 candidates. Recall and precision are not evaluated. Recall is expected to be maximal since most of the noun phrases are extracted. Precision is difficult to evaluate, as it depends on the judgment of experts.

Structuring Module

The structuring module exploits the lexical regularities in the candidates produced by the decomposition phase and organizes them into a network structure. This module connects terms sharing the same head noun or terms sharing the same expansion (an adjectival modifier or a prepositional phrase). For instance, *vanne manuelle* (manual valve) is connected by a *head link* to *vanne* (valve), to which *vanne motorisée* (powered valve), and *vanne de débit nul* (null outflow valve) are also linked. Similarly *vanne manuelle* is connected by an *expansion link* to *manuel* (manual). Figure 2.10 shows a sample network built from the terms extracted by *LEXTER* from a power-plant maintenance manual. The highly productive head nouns, such as *vanne* (valve), should be considered first by a knowledge engineer because they correspond to generic concepts with several hyponyms.

Application of **LEXTER** *to Knowledge Acquisition*
I now turn to the application of the analysis of noun phrase subcategorizations extracted by
LEXTER to the construction of word classes (see also the passage on Context Analysis in
section 6.1.1).

LEXTER is a partial parser specialized in the extraction of noun phrases that are likely
to be terms. These partial structures can be used for semantic classification through the
observation of distributional similarities. As shown by figure 2.10, in the semantic network
built from *LEXTER* output, terms with the same head or with the same expansion are grouped
into classes that can serve as a basis for the distributional analysis of a given head noun or
a given modifier.

A first approach to such a second-order classification is performed by grouping adjectives
with similar distributions, as in Assadi and Bourigault (1996). For example, the adjectives
aérien (air) and *souterrain* (underground) are grouped because they both share the same
head nouns *conducteur* (conductor), *liaison* (link), *ligne* (wire), *ligne électrique* (electric
wire), *poste* (extension), *réseau* (network), and *technique* (technique).

The software *ZELLIG* offers a second exploitation of distributional regularities from
the output of *LEXTER* (Habert, Naulleau, and Nazarenko 1996). The study is based on
the Harrisian approach to semantics in relation with regularities of selectional restriction.
The first step of the algorithm is a reduction of the complex nominal phrases provided by
LEXTER into elementary trees exhibiting core head/argument dependencies. Thus *sténose
serrée du tronc commun gauche* (tight stenosis of left common mainstem) yields four
elementary dependencies: *sténose serrée* (tight stenosis), *sténose du tronc* (stenosis of
mainstem), *tronc commun* (common mainstem), and *tronc gauche* (left mainstem). The
second step of the algorithm is a classification that connects words sharing similar contexts.
For instance, *sténose* (stenosis) and *calcification* (calcification) share the same modifiers
aortique (aortic), *coronarien* (coronarian), and *proximal* (proximal). A graph of words with
common contexts is built and subgraphs of words with reciprocal contextual similarities are
highlighted. Figure 2.11 illustrates a part of the graph extracted from a corpus on coronary
medicine.

A third approach to the clustering of terms produced by *LEXTER* is proposed by *LEXI-
CLASS* (Assadi 1997). Instead of decomposing noun phrases into elementary dependencies,
the head and expansion dependencies of candidate terms are directly used. The tool is designed for use by knowledge engineers for the construction of ontologies.

Comments
LEXTER is a purely symbolic processing tool for terminological acquisition, since it makes
use of no statistical information. Term detection is made through linguistic rules based on
part-of-speech patterns and lexical data. Filtering and disambiguation are based on a corpus

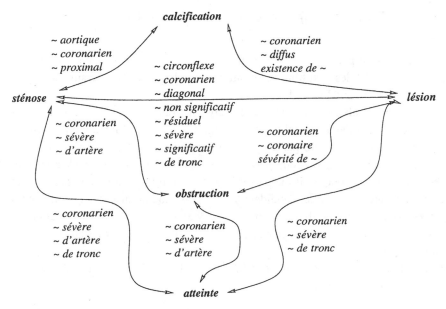

Figure 2.11
A graph of connected words extracted by *ZELLIG* from the output of *LEXTER*.

investigation for which the only criterion is the presence or the absence of a structure. No counts are made; no frequency thresholds are used.

The positive aspect of this approach is that candidates that occur only once in the corpus (hapax legomena) can be extracted by the software. Consequently the output contains occurrences with uncertain terminological knowledge that must be validated through human postfiltering. But the rate of misses is very low.

The drawback of such a labor-intensive method is that the resulting software is language-dependent. Its adaptation to another language requires an as big effort as for any other grammar-based approach to term extraction such as *NPtool* (Voutilainen 1993; see section 2.3.7) or *Termino* (David and Plante 1990a; see section 2.2.4).

In contrast with other tools for term acquisition, *LEXTER* offers an integrated environment for the structuring, browsing, and analysis of candidate terms. This novel feature is due partly to the industrial environment in which *LEXTER* was developed and partly to the choice of avoiding statistical filtering. The philosophy of *LEXTER* is to produce as many candidates as possible so as to avoid misses and provide an environment that helps the knowledge engineer cope with large amounts of data.

2.2.4 *TERMINO*: A Parser for Term and Compound Extraction

Synthetic Presentation

TERMINO is a software package for term extraction and management composed of the following sequential modules: text filtering, grammar-based noun phrase parsing, and term bank construction (David and Plante 1990a, b).

The morphological analyzer and lemmatizer rely on grammatical rules instead of a dictionary in order to handle technical texts and large vocabularies. Since the purpose of *TERMINO* is to extract terms, the parser does not attempt to provide a full analysis of sentences, and, instead, focuses on noun phrases. In order to elicit only noun phrases with a terminological value, the output of the parser is processed by a specific component that is expected to generate only correct candidate terms. This module discards certain words and certain syntactic structures that are unlikely to yield terms. The software contains a final component for the interactive management of term bases with visualization and classification facilities.

In Lauriston (1994), an evaluation of *TERMINO* is made which gives a good insight to the outcome of the term extractor.

Implementation

TERMINO is a parser dedicated to the extraction of terms seen as a subset of the noun phrases in a document. Contrary to *ACABIT* (section 2.2.1) and *LEXTER* (section 2.2.3), *TERMINO* does not expect a preliminary unambiguous tagging of the input textual data. *TERMINO* possesses its own morphological analyzer and tolerates possible part-of-speech ambiguities. The sequence of operations that achieves the extraction of terms from raw corpora is as follows:

1. **Preprocessing**. Text filtering and removal of format characters.

2. **Parsing and term extraction.** Morphological analysis, noun phrase parsing, and term generation.

3. **Interactive term bank construction and management**. An additional tool provides a user-friendly interface to the construction of terminological banks from terms extracted by the preceding steps.

Preliminary Text Filtering

The first module of *TERMINO* filters out spurious characters that are not likely to participate to the construction of words, acronyms, or punctuations. The same module tokenizes the text (identifies the individual word tokens) and sets the sentence boundaries. Because of the approach taken by this module and the following one for morphological analysis, no

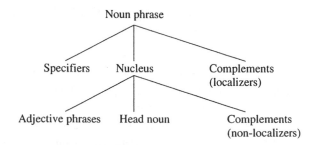

Figure 2.12
The noun phrase grammar of *TERMINO*.

preprocessing of the input text is expected by the termer that can therefore cope with raw corpora.

Morphological Analysis and Lemmatizing

The first step of the proper linguistic processing by *TERMINO* is a morphological analysis of the word tokens. The analysis is performed without dictionary lookup; it relies on the graphical form of words (their prefixes and suffixes) and some exception lists. Each inflected word processed by this module receives a syntactic category associated with morphological features such as tense, gender, and number. In addition the lemma of the word is calculated: the infinitive of verbs, the singular of nouns, and the masculine singular of adjectives. Even an unknown inflected verb—such as *parsions* ([we] parsed)—will be assigned a correct lemma *parser* (to parse) and a correct morphological analysis.

Since the morphological analysis is a noncontextual process, ambiguous words are not disambiguated. One of the functions of the following step—the noun phrase parser—is to disambiguate the morphological analysis of words by choosing, in context, the most relevant among several competing analyses.

Syntactic Parsing

The parser does not intend to provide a full syntactic analysis of the input sentences because noun phrases are the focus of the analysis. The parser is a partial parser, specialized in noun phrase extraction and based on a two-tier grammar of noun phrases inspired from X-bar theory. This grammar for noun phrases in French is shown in figure 2.12.

The upper level of the noun phrase structure corresponds to the compositional part of the noun phrase, while the lower part is a nondecomposable opaque nucleus. The complements in the nucleus differ from the complements in the compositional part in that they cannot participate to the contextual anchoring of the referent of the noun phrase. For instance, the utterance *un traitement de textes très performant* (a very efficient word processor) is analyzed as a nucleus *traitement de texte* (word processor) nested in a noun phrase structure where it receives the localizer modifier *très performant* (very efficient).

Term Recognizer

Candidate structures are generated in four steps from the dependencies between head words and complements found in the noun phrases produced by the syntactic parser. Exhaustive candidate generation is made possible thanks to the tree manipulation facilities offered by the parser (steps 1 to 3). Only some of the possible structures are ultimately kept as valid candidate terms by the fourth step of term recognition (comparator and evaluator of synapsies).

The candidate terms—called here *synapsies* after Benveniste (1966)—are constructed according to the following steps:

1. **Synapsy builder**. First the head word of a noun phrase is chosen as the head of a synapsy. Then each of the complements of this head noun receives a syntactic role in order to generate the possible valid nested structures of each noun phrase. For instance, the utterance *Le système de gestion de bases de données qui est installé* . . . (The database management system that is installed . . .) yields the following candidate synapsies: *système de gestion de bases de données* (database management system), *gestion de bases de données* (database management), and *base de données* (database) (this example and most of the following ones are from a description of *TERMINO* in Bourigault 1994, pp. 73–74).

2. **Expansion categorizer**. For each possible substructure, the complements, also called *expansions*, can be placed in one of two categories:

a. The first category ascertains whether or not the complement is ambiguously attached to the head noun. For instance, in the noun phrase *traitements de textes gratuits* (free word processors), *textes* (word) is unambiguously attached to *traitements* (processors) whereas *gratuits* (free) is ambiguously attached to *textes* or *traitements*.

b. The other category ascertains whether or not a complement is part of the nucleus of the noun phrase. For instance, in *traitement de texte* (word processor), the complement *texte* (word) is unambiguously placed at the nucleus level. On the contrary, in *logiciel intégré* (integrated software), *intégré* (integrated) is ambiguously located at either the nucleus or the noun phrase level because of its epithet role.

3. **Synapsy generator**. All the combinations of head nouns, with each of their expansions, are generated as candidate terms. The expansions are accompanied by the categorizations made in the preceding step.

4. **Comparator and evaluator of synapsies**. This module's purpose is to select the most likely terms. Therefore it evaluates and compares the candidate associations of head words

and complements furnished by the synapsy generator. Among the criteria used for preferring some constructions over others are:

a. The category and the syntactic role of some of the individual words composing the structure (prepositions, complements, head words). For instance, the structure *présence du bruit* (presence of noise), from the utterance *La présence du bruit nuit à* . . . (the presence of noise harms . . .), is not generated because the head word *présence* (presence) belongs to a stop-list of nouns that are not likely to build a term.

b. The comparison of the ambiguous constructions with other nested nonambiguous structures. The utterance *définition de mur du son* (definition of sound barrier) is produced by the synapsy builder and categorized as an ambiguous structure by the expansion categorizer. The complement *son* (sound) is labeled as ambiguously attached to *définition* (definition) or *mur* (barrier). If the synapsy *mur du son* (sound barrier) is unambiguously generated elsewhere in the corpus, the pending attachment of *son* is resolved by linking it to *mur* in *définition de mur du son*. This technique bears some similarities with the endogenous learning of *LEXTER* presented in section 2.2.3.

Term Bank Construction and Management

TERMINO is a tool for corpus-based terminology. Its ultimate goal is the construction of term banks from the candidates collected from corpora by the term recognizer. In order to facilitate the construction and the updating of a term base, *TERMINO* offers an interactive environment for the creation and management of term descriptions. Creation is facilitated by the possibility of scanning the lemmatized words and the candidate terms sorted by head words or expansions. In addition all the occurrences of the current terms in the corpus are displayed with their different contexts. Management of a terminological database is facilitated by an environment that supports browsing, sorting, and updating of term descriptions.

Evaluation

A very illuminating evaluation of the capacities and limits of *TERMINO* is provided by Lauriston (1994). In this study the output of the program on an 8,500-word corpus about radio telecommunication engineering is systematically compared with a set of 592 complex terms identified by manual scanning.

Two different criteria are used for measuring the quality of term extraction produced by *TERMINO*. The first criterion assesses that a term is recognized by *TERMINO* if it is a subconstituent of a candidate term. The second criterion is more selective: it requires that the manually extracted term exactly matches the candidate provided by the software, without any extraneous word.

Under the less restrictive criterion, recall is 74% and precision 72%, whereas the more rigorous standard yields a recall of 51% and a precision of 48%.

The *misses* of *TERMINO*, reported in Lauriston (1994), are due to the lack of consideration for term variants such as the coordinations *programmation locale ou subrégionale* (local or subregional programming), and a nondetection of occurrences comprising an acronym or a capitalized word such as *émetteur AM* (AM transmitter). The *false positives* of *TERMINO* are mostly spurious syntactic constructions or correct noun phrases without terminological value. The incorrect syntactic structures are due to parsing errors such as the nondetection of frozen phrases. For instance, *fins de planification* (ends of planning) is not a correct term occurrence in the utterance *à des fins de planification* (for the purpose of planning, lit. to the end of planning) because *à des fins de* (for the purpose of) is a prepositional locution. Correct structures that are not good candidates generally include a modifier that does not build a hyponym of the concept denoted by the head word such as *renseignements suppémentaires* (additional details). The errors are thus distributed: 47% incorrect syntactic structures and 53% nonterm correct structures.

Comments

TERMINO, despite being geared toward a knowledge acquisition task, is deeply grounded in the tradition of generative linguistics and phrase structure parsing. From the former, it takes a hierarchical representation of noun phrases customized to focus on the description of terminological noun phrases. From the latter, it takes a stratified organization into modules that perform, in turn, morphological analysis, phrase parsing, and filtering of terminological phrases. (The last module is a kind of weak semantic filtering based on lexical and surface clues.)

Some of the shortcomings of the approach arise from the omission of several critical NLP components. For instance, coined phrases and their syntactic and typographic variations are not recognized. These problems are not as simple as it may seem at a first glance. They often correspond to ambiguous situations in which the correct decisions are not systematically the most obvious ones. For instance, coined phrases, such as idioms, cannot be systematically recognized. Thus *relatif à* (relative to) is an idiom that is not present in the utterance *elle a calculé une fréquence relative à l'aide d'un quotient* (she has calculated a relative frequency with the help of a quotient). A blind recognition of the idiom *relatif à* in this utterance would prevent the syntactic parser from extracting the terminological noun phrase *fréquence relative* (relative frequency).

Other shortcomings arise from the radical generative approach employed; they could be remedied through a cooperation with procedures of disambiguation and statistical filtering. One of the simplest modifications would be to add an unambiguous part-of-speech tagger as a preprocessor of the corpora.

However, the generative radicalism of *TERMINO* offers a very precise view of all the benefits that can be expected from syntactic analysis for term extraction. For a good payoff, phrase-parsing techniques must be based on a solid linguistic modeling and associated extraction procedures that mirror as accurately as possible the constraints highlighted by the linguistic model.

2.2.5 *TERMS*: A Pattern Matcher for Term Detection

Synthetic Presentation

TERMS is a tool for the acquisition of multi-word terms from raw corpora (Justeson and Katz 1995). It relies on two assumptions based on the linguistic analysis of technical texts and terminological dictionaries:

1. Terms are repeated in a technical document more frequently than nonterminological noun phrases.

2. Terms have a structure different from the structure of nonterminological noun phrases. Terms generally do not accept inserted modifiers and determiners. On the contrary, regular noun phrases are compositional and flexible constructions which accept a wider range of syntactic modifications.

In accordance with the first hypothesis, the approach uses a statistical filter that rejects strings that appear only once in a document. The second observation is used to build a finite-state automaton that selects terms with a compound structure possibly followed by a simple prepositional phrase. Contrary to concurrent tools that exploit filters based on part-of-speech patterns, the input to *TERMS* is an untagged corpus. This avoids inaccuracies due to tagging errors. Input texts are morphologically analyzed with the help of an important lexical base of inflected words. In case of ambiguity, the part-of-speech category is chosen according to an order of preference.

In Justeson and Katz (1995) the terminological extraction is tested for its recall and its precision against manual term extractions performed by experts or by the authors of the documents. The evaluation is performed on three scientific articles for which recall is 71% and precision ranges from 67 to 96%.

Implementation

As mentioned above, the background information that is reflected in the design of *TERMS* comes from both a dictionary and a corpus study. Through the systematic analysis of the terms in technical dictionaries (fiber optics, medicine, physics, mathematics, and psychology), the authors show that noun phrases constitute from 92.5 to 99% of the multi-word terms. Furthermore 97% of these noun phrases are built only from nouns and adjectives (including verbal gerunds and verbal participles), and 99% consist of nouns, adjectives, and the preposition *of*. This analysis is used for building a filter based on a syntactic description of terms. The filter is embodied in the following regular expression based on part-of-speech categories:[14]

$$E = ((A \mid N)^+ \mid (A \mid N)^\star (N \, P) (A \mid N)^\star) \, N \qquad\qquad (2.23)$$

The regular expression E corresponds to two types of terms, either compounds (C), or compounds followed by a postmodifying prepositional phrase (NP):

$$\begin{cases} E = C \mid NP \\ C = ((A \mid N)^+ \, N) \quad NP = ((A \mid N)^* \, N) \, P \, ((A \mid N)^* \, N) \end{cases} \qquad (2.24)$$

For instance, *linear coefficient*, *word sense*, or *cumulative distribution functions* are accepted by the compound filter C, and *degrees of freedom* is a term that corresponds to the noun phrase filter NP.

The preceding linguistic filtering is followed by a statistical filtering rejecting strings which occur only once in the text.

Implementation of Part-of-Speech Filtering

The most straightforward approach to part-of-speech filtering is part-of-speech tagging followed by pattern selection. This approach was not adopted in the implementation of *TERMS*. The authors argue that tagging errors inevitably lead to recognition errors and, thereby, to a loss of coverage. Instead of requiring a tagged corpus, *TERMS* exploits a lexical database of morphologically analyzed inflected words that associates each input word with its morphological analyses (lemmas and syntactic categories).

Inflected words with ambiguous syntactic categories are disambiguated according to a preference scheme: the word is identified preferably as a noun and, then, as an adjective or a preposition. Words which are not associated with at least one of these categories cannot be part of a candidate string. The preference algorithm is biased toward a noun phrase-friendly disambiguation which systematically—and noncontextually—prefers the acceptable categories. For instance, an ambiguous verb-adjective (e.g., *fixed*) is systematically identified as an adjective, even in occurrences (e.g., *fixed malfunctioning drives*) in which it is in fact a verb.

This algorithm ensures a maximal syntactic coverage: whenever a possible combination of the syntactic categories allows recognition of a valid phrase, the corresponding string is chosen as a valid candidate provided that it occurs more than once in the document. Misses are only due to incorrect exclusions of terminological strings that are not repeated in the document.

The crude preference algorithm is tempered by using a stop-list of words which are only rarely used in admissible part-of-speech patterns. This list contains, for example, *or* categorized as a conjunction and not a noun and *can* tagged preferably as a modal verb. The authors suggest that this stop-list can be modified according to the domain of application (e.g., in heraldry, *or* could be tagged as a noun).

Evaluation

In Justeson and Katz (1995) *TERMS* is evaluated on term extraction from three scientific articles in pattern classification, lexical semantics, and liquid chromatography. The program is parametrized with a minimal frequency of repetition of 2. Additionally prepositions are not allowed in part-of-speech patterns (i.e., only pattern C of formula 2.24 is used for filtering acceptable strings). The reference lists against which the output of *TERMS* is compared are manually established and were provided by the authors or the editors of the articles.

Coverage   *TERMS* identifies 71% of the terms in the reference list for the pattern classification paper. Since most misses are due to the statistical filtering stage, the coverage of the termer is higher for topical terms than for the complete terminological vocabulary. Therefore *TERMS* identifies 146/149 (98%) of the terms that are assessed to be topical or methodological foci by the author of the pattern classification paper. The valid terms that the termer fails to extract are mainly background terms that tend to occur sporadically in the document.

Precision   Precision is evaluated separately on types (several occurrences count for one type) and instances (possibly repeated occurrences of terms). For types, the precision ranges from 67 to 92% and, for instances, the precision ranges from 77 to 96%. The exclusion of noun phrases with a preposition (expression NP in formula 2.24) is an appropriate choice for a strategy in which precision is preferred over coverage. Adding terms containing a prepositional phrase would only slightly enhance the coverage and would severely damage the precision. For instance, for the pattern classification article, this change would yield 58 additional candidates, only 6 of which would be valid terms.

The loss of precision is mainly due to the repeated noun phrases without terminological content such as *different senses* or *desired product*. Therefore the value of the precision declines as the length of the paper increases. This effect could be corrected by adjusting the frequency threshold with the length of the document. The second source of error is the noun-phrase bias of the part-of-speech preference algorithm, which yields candidate strings that are not noun phrases. For instance, *positing separate* is not an adjective-noun structure but a verb-adjective one.

Comments

TERMS is an efficient algorithm for the discovery of candidate terms in raw corpora. *TERMS* exploits only three economical procedures: (1) a simple part-of-speech disambiguation based on a preference selection, (2) a surface pattern filtering, and (3) a frequency cutoff. The algorithm certainly takes advantage of the specific configurations of right-headed compounds in English—so-called Germanic compounding—as opposed to the structure of compositional left-headed noun phrases with prepositional modifiers. The less clear-cut structural segregation between terminological and nonterminological noun phrases in French (and, in general, in any Romance language) calls for more sophisticated procedures such as the ones implemented in *LEXTER* (section 2.2.3) or in *TERMINO* (section 2.2.4).

Apart from the linguistic issue, other issues remain unresolved in this approach:

• It is reasonably argued by the authors that taggers are prone to errors, but they do not provide a systematic comparison between the errors in term extraction due to their preference algorithm and errors that would result from the exploitation of a classical tagger. Thus their choice of technique for part-of-speech disambiguation remains undefended.

• It is correctly noted that the coverage of technical corpora by specialized dictionaries is poor (see also Haas 1992), but no details are given on the coverage of single words by the lexical database. Here 100,000 entries is not a very large vocabulary for processing documents from different technical domains. The authors never tell how or if *TERMS* handles unknown words.

• It is observed that the grammar of *TERMS* satisfactorily covers the terms observed in several specialized dictionaries. However, dictionaries only describe the normalized form of terms and do not account for all the possible variants that are likely to be encountered in corpus occurrences, including nonnominal utterances (mainly verb phrases). The retrieval of these nonstandard forms is not considered in this study.

Despite these questions the performance of the termer are surprisingly good and compare very favorably with a manually extracted terminology.

2.2.6 *Xtract*: A Hybrid Tool for Collocation Extraction

Synthetic Presentation

Xtract is a package of software tools intended for the extraction of collocations from corpora (Smadja 1993b, b). *Collocations* are recurrent combinations of words that co-occur more frequently than it would be expected just by chance and that correspond to arbitrary word usages. Collocations differ from one language to another, are weakly compositional, and are difficult to guess for a nonnative speaker. They are also typically insufficiently described in dictionaries (an exception is the *BBI* dictionary of Benson, Benson, and Ilson 1986).

Strictly speaking, *Xtract* is not a termer, although some of the collocations extracted by the software are compound nouns and terms. I present this tool in my review of term extractors for the following reasons:

• *Xtract* is a seminal work that has inspired several following studies on term extraction such as Daille (1996), Frantzi and Ananiadou (1996b), Ikehara, Shirai, and Uchino (1996), and Shimohata, Sugio, and Nagata (1997) among others,

• *Xtract* shares many common features with other approaches to term extraction that are not directly inspired by Smadja's work (statistical scoring, syntactic filtering, incremental structure building, etc.).

• Terms are part of the lexicon. *Xtract* is a prototypical example of the application of NLP to the extraction of lexicographic data, improving upon the influential work of Church and Hanks (1990).

The corpus-based extraction of collocations by *Xtract* begins with the measure of the frequencies of pairwise word associations with respect to their relative positions within a ± 5 word window. In order to eliminate general contextual similarities, only pairs repeatedly encountered in similar relative positions are retained. Two independent components are used for processing the binary collocations produced at the first stage: a component that extends binary collocations to n-ary ones, and a component that associates binary collocations with a syntactic label.

The evaluation of the output of *Xtract* by a lexicographer reports a precision of 80% and a recall of 94% on a set of 4,000 collocations extracted from a stock market corpus (Smadja 1993a).

Implementation
The techniques exploited by *Xtract* for the extraction of collocations rely on the two following assumptions:

• The words involved in a collocation appear together significantly more often than expected by chance (a similar assumption motivates the use of Mutual Information in Church and Hanks 1990).

• The words appear in a restricted range of relative positions corresponding to particular syntactic constraints.

The software is organized into three modules represented in figure 2.13. The first stage yields binary collocations through statistical filtering. The second stage proposes two parallel and independent postprocessors. One reiterates the first step (in a simpler way) for extending binary collocations to n-ary ones. The other exploits the parsing of the binary collocates by *Cass* (Abney 1990) for labeling them with syntactic roles.

First Stage: Extraction of Binary Collocations
The input to the first stage of *Xtract* is a tagged corpus. First, concordances are built (aligned single words and their environment) so as to collect frequency data about the relative

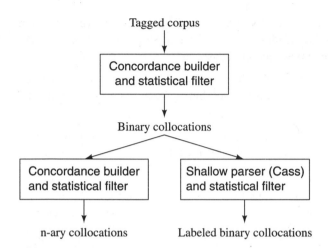

Figure 2.13
Flow-chart of *Xtract*.

positions of pairs of words. For instance, the histogram of figure 2.14 indicates that *net* thus occurs with *cost* as follows: five times *net* immediately precedes *cost* (*net cost*), three times *net* is the second word after *cost* (*cost* X *net*), and *net* occurs once 3 words and once 4 words after *cost* (*cost* X X *net* and *cost* X X X *net*).

These combined position/frequency data are statistically filtered in order to reject the spurious collocations and to select the relevant positions of collocations. There are three means of selection:

1. The elimination of the collocates that are not frequent enough (a very selective criterion that rules out up to 95% of the collocates). Through this filtering, collocates such as {*takeover*, *dormant*}, {*takeover*, *dilute*}, or {*takeover*, *ex.*} are excluded.

2. The rejection of the collocates with a flat histogram in order to select pairs of words that are repeatedly used within specific syntactic constructs. This criterion accepts {*takeover*, *possible*} and rejects {*takeover*, *federal*}.[15]

3. The selection of the interesting relative positions of two collocates which correspond to peaks in the histogram. This criterion selects two positions for the pair {*takeover*, *expensive*}: *takeover* X *expensive* and *takeover* X X *expensive*. The former one corresponds, for instance, to the occurrence *making a hostile takeover prohibitively expensive by enabling* . . . . These positional patterns are used in the second stage of the process for the enrichment of binary collocations.

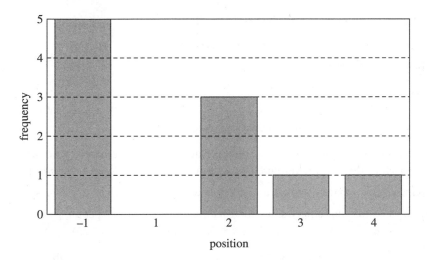

Figure 2.14
An example of histogram used for collocation extraction by *Xtract*: the adjective collocate *net* of the noun *cost*.

The output of the first stage is processed independently by two modules. I detail them in turn.

Expansion of Collocations

The module for the expansion of binary collocations into *n*-ary ones is a simplified reiteration of the first module in which the concordances of single words are replaced with concordances of collocations. The ultimate filtering of *n*-ary collocations relies on the frequency of the observed collocates and avoids the repeated output of nested collocations. First, if several collocates are nested into another one, only the largest one is retained. Since *the Dow Jones industrial average* is selected as a five-word collocation (built from the binary collocation {*industrial*, *average*}), subcollocates such as *Dow Jones industrial* are discarded.

Second, if several collocations overlap partially and only differ in words with the same category and the same position, paradigmatic collocations are produced. Thus the collocation {*index*, *composite*} entails the discovery of the following concordances:

The NYSE's composite index of all its listed common stocks fell 1.76 to 164.13.

The NYSE's composite index of all its listed common stocks fell 0.98 to 164.91.

The NYSE's composite index of all its listed common stocks rose 0.50 to 166.54, etc.

Only the following subsuming pattern is produced as output:

The NYSE's composite index of all its listed common stocks
$\langle VERB \rangle \ \langle NUMBER \rangle \ to \ \langle NUMBER \rangle$
(2.25)

Labeling of Collocations

The collocations produced by the first stage correspond to a large variety of collocations. Three main families of collocations are identified in Smadja (1993a):

1. *Predicative relations* consisting of two words repeatedly used together in a similar syntactic relation such as the support verb/predicative noun association {*make*, *decision*}.

2. *Rigid noun phrases* consisting of uninterrupted sequences of words such as *stock market*.

3. *Phrasal templates* containing empty slots filled with by words with a specific part-of-speech category, such as $\langle NUMBER \rangle$ and $\langle VERB \rangle$ in the above pattern (2.25).

Terms belong to the first two categories. I would advocate that they are somewhere in between because (1) terms are not completely rigid noun phrases since they accept variants, and (2) terms are not genuine syntactic structures since they are not as compositional as phrase constructions.

Xtract compares favorably with the work on collocation of Choueka (1988) because it produces grammatical associations of words instead of core repeated sequences. The output of *Xtract* contains genuine syntactic collocates that would not be retrieved by Choueka's techniques because they are not totally rigid.

In order to enhance the lexicographic values of predicative collocates, this stage associates each of them with a syntactic label. The collocates are parsed by *Cass* (Abney 1990), a robust parser. According to the analysis each collocation is either rejected or enriched with a label denoting the nature of the syntactic relation holding between the two collocates.

If no label is produced by the parser, the relation remains undetermined. Otherwise, the most frequent label is associated with the collocation. For instance, since the collocation {*rose*, *price*} receives the label subject-verb seven times and the label verb-object only once, it is ultimately labeled as a subject-verb relation.

Comments

Xtract is a hybrid lexicographic tool that combines statistical filters and NLP modules (a tagger and a parser). Contrary to *ACABIT* (section 2.2.1), the linguistic filtering follows the statistical filtering instead of preceding it.

Apart from the combination of heterogenous techniques, *Xtract* improves on previous work for collocative computational lexicography through closer attention to nonrigid syntactic constructions, arbitrary long phrases, and syntactic roles. This work has paved the way to the combination of different techniques (statistical filters, syntactic parser, concordance tools) in order to produce multidimensional linguistic knowledge (multi-lexical entries enriched with syntactic features).

The application of these techniques to terminography requires further improvements because of the specific features of terms. First, the collocates must be filtered out in order to discard phrases without terminological value such as {*study*, *said*}. Second, the collocates produced by the system must be conflated in order to group various linguistic forms corresponding to the same concept such as {*price*, *rise$_V$*}, {*price*, *rose$_V$*}, {*price*, *rise$_N$*}, {*price*, *go up*}, or {*price*, *shoot up*}.

2.2.7 Synthesis of Term Acquisition

The tools for corpus-based term acquisition presented in this section share a common purpose—they identify as many correct terms as possible in a text—but exploit therefore a large variety of techniques.

Table 2.7 sums up the various characteristics of these tools. The first three lines indicate whether words are preprocessed by a tagger, morphologically analyzed (without part-of-speech disambiguation), or simplified by a stemming or a truncation procedure. Lines 4 and 5 indicate the type of natural language processing technique used for selecting terminological phrases: either finite-state technique or grammar-based techniques are employed. Line 6 indicates whether a statistical criterion is used for rejecting incorrect occurrences and/or selecting correct terms. Finally, the last two lines of the table provide additional

Table 2.7
Comparative features of the different termers.

		ACABIT	ANA	LEXTER	TERMINO	TERMS	XTract
1	Tagging	×		×			×
2	Morphological analysis				×	×	
3	Stemming		×				
4	Syntactic patterns	×		×		×	×
5	Grammar			×			
6	Statistical filtering	×	×			×	×
7	Text simplification		×				
8	Incrementality		×				
9	Language	Fr/En/Mal	∀	Fr	Fr	En	En

details: whether or not the tool exploits a text simplification technique, and whether it is incremental or not.

This table shows that the tool *ANA* is relatively atypical. The reason is that *ANA* exploits several techniques that are more common in the field of information retrieval than in corpus-based terminology. Conversely, in *ANA*, linguistically motivated techniques are deliberately ignored. This tool excepted, the other tools tend to share similar techniques (mainly morphological analysis and part-of-speech filtering, syntactic filtering through grammars or regular expressions, and possible statistical filtering). For these "similar" tools, the differences lie mainly in the linguistic grounding of the procedures and in their modes of cooperative organization.

2.2.8 Term Extraction for Bilingual Term Alignment

Rey (1995), a dictionary-maker interested in terminography, suggests that manual term discovery should be performed on multilingual data for a language-independent learning of concepts. Multilingual automatic term acquisition is only possible when parallel—or, at least, comparable—corpora are available. On domains for which such data exist, some works focus on the exploitation of multilingual texts in the process of term acquisition.

The termers presented in table 2.7 are dedicated to monolingual term acquisition. However, terminology management is also a central issue for the development of translation aid tools such as bilingual thesauri and multilingual lexical databases. For the purpose of improving the construction of such data, programs are developed for the (semi-)automatic acquisition of bilingual terminological data. Most applications operate on aligned corpora and perform the acquisition of aligned terms in two steps: monolingual acquisition and bilingual alignment. I focus here on the acquisition phase of four tools for term alignment (Van der Eijk 1993), (Dagan and Church 1994), (Hull 1998), and (Gaussier 1998).[16]

The termers used by Van der Eijk (1993), Dagan and Church (1994), and Gaussier (1998) are simple pattern matchers described through regular expressions of syntactic categories. They capture term occurrences from tagged corpora in English. For the former study, they consist of sequences of adjectives followed by a noun, and for the second study, they are restricted to sequences of nouns. Gaussier (1998) does not report the exact patterns used for term acquisition.

In Hull (1998), the patterns exploited for term acquisition from a tagged corpus through regular expressions are described into more detail for the French and the English languages:

English:

$$(A \mid N)^+ \tag{2.26}$$

$$V^+ \tag{2.27}$$

French:

$$(N^+ A^\star) ((de \mid à) (le \mid la \mid les \mid l')^\star ((N^+ A^\star) \mid A \mid V))^+ \qquad (2.28)$$

$$V^+ \qquad (2.29)$$

The first rule for English (2.26) was originally designed as a sequence of adjectives followed by a head noun. The revised rule proposed here handles Noun/Adjective tagging errors and is reported to introduce very little noise. The author admits that, among the sequences extracted by his termer, a significant portion does not correspond to valid terminology units. However, this imprecision is not problematic in a bilingual alignment task, since a term in one language can be correctly aligned with a nonterm in another one.

The overall impression gained from studies on term alignment is that term extraction is not a central issue. The bulk of the work is the alignment of bilingual units, whether terms, single words, or phrases. The extraction of terms can be slightly noisy or inaccurate without degrading significantly the outcome of the alignment algorithm.

2.2.9 Retrieving Extended Collocations

When exploiting statistical procedures for retrieving collocations from texts, such as *Xtract* (section 2.2.6) the yield contains strings that are included inside each other or that should be joined together to build larger collocations. The former problem is referred to as *nested collocations* and the latter *interrupted collocations*. These problems are not ignored in Smadja's study; they are implicitly addressed by the procedure for expanding binary collocations into *n*-ary ones during the second stage of the process. Here I present four subsequent studies on the extraction of collocations that focus more specifically on the issues of merging or joining collocations: Chen and Chen (1994), Frantzi and Ananiadou (1996a, 1996b), Ikehara, Shirai, and Uchino (1996), and Shimohata, Sugio, and Nagata (1997).

Connection of Nominal Collocations

Chen and Chen (1994) present a method for the extraction of maximal nominal collocations in a two-step fashion. First, a probabilistic chunker breaks sentences into probabilistically optimal constituents. These chunks are then grouped into larger noun phrases through a finite state machine. The chunker uses a bi-gram language model and calculates the sequences with the maximal probability. This calculation is made through dynamic programming and the scores of the probabilities are collected from a training corpus (in this case the SUSANNE corpus, Sampson 1995). The syntactic head of the chunks is calculated using a priority on syntactic tags. Only chunks corresponding to noun phrases are kept for the final part of the algorithm. At this ultimate stage the nominal chunks are connected into larger

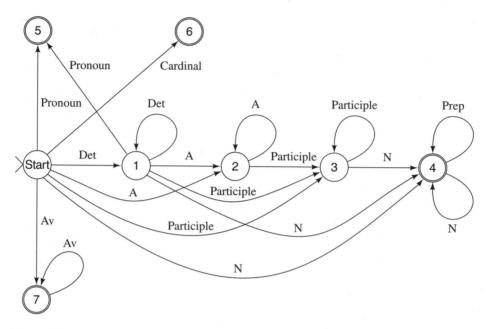

Figure 2.15
Finite-state machine for grouping nominal chunks into noun phrases in English (Chen and Chen, 1994).

noun phrases by using the finite-state automaton shown in figure 2.15, which describes an extended noun phrase grammar.

Extraction of Nested Collocations

Instead of expanding core collocations into larger ones, Frantzi and Ananiadou (1996b) directly collect n-ary collocations filtered by a measure of frequency. They then eliminate some collocations that are substrings of other candidate collocations. The rule for selecting the largest collocations relies on a relevance measure that estimates the likelihood of the string to be a good candidate. The relevance measure is calculated according to the following three criteria:

1. If a collocation c has the same frequency as a longer collocation c' that contains c, c is not a candidate.

2. If c is not a subcollocation, c becomes more relevant the longer and the more frequent it is.

3. Subcollocations that are a substring of one or more collocations and that are not in situation 1 are assigned a relevance that is proportional to the relative number of collocations they appear in.

Table 2.8
Relevance scores of *Wall Street* and its supercollocations.

Score	Frequency	Candidate collocation
114	19	*Staff Reporter of the Wall Street Journal*
37.34	26	*Wall Street Journal*
36	22	*The Wall Street Journal*
33	38	*Wall Street*
31.34	23	*The Wall Street*
6	3	*Wall Street analysts*
4	20	*of The Wall Street Journal*
0	19	*Reporter of the Wall Street*
0	19	*Reporter of the Wall Street Journal*
0	19	*Staff Reporter of the Wall Street*
0	20	*of the Wall Street*

Table 2.8 illustrates the scores of all the collocations containing the string *Wall Street* out of a 40,000-word corpus from the *Wall Street Journal* newswire.

Extraction of Interrupted Collocations

Nested collocations are not the only issue in the possible interactions between collocations that must be taken into account for reducing the volume of acquisition. The other interesting problem, addressed by Ikehara, Shirai, and Uchino (1996), is the possibility of building larger collocations from collocations which are separated by a certain number of words. These authors use the algorithm for counting *n*-gram statistics of Nagao and Mori (1994) to collect the primary collocations. They then combine uninterrupted or interrupted collocations.[17] For the process of extracting interrupted collocations, the order of appearance of the candidate collocations is noted along with their number of occurrences. The pairs of collocations that co-occur more than twice—without intervening punctuation marks—are joined into a unique interrupted collocation. The algorithm is applied to a Japanese corpus of Nikkei Industrial News of 9 millions characters and outputs interrupted collocations such as *price ~ sell time*, *Iran ~ Japan Oil Industry*, *did ~ but said that*, etc. (These examples are English translations of actual Japanese collocates.)

Shimohata, Sugio, and Nagata (1997) also combine repeatedly co-occurring collocations. Contrary to Ikehara, Shirai, and Uchino (1996), each pair of overlapping collocations is not considered independently but rather is merged into a single larger collocation that subsumes both initial ones. Nonoverlapping collocations that co-occur more than twice are also agglutinated into a single collocation with possible intervening words. Since this process is iteratively repeated, arbitrary numbers of collocations can be thus merged. The interesting fact is that such collocations cover several actual occurrences with flexible

Table 2.9
Four utterances of the interrupted collocation *Refer to ∼ the ∼ manual ∼ for specific instructions*

<u>Refer to</u> <u>the</u> appropriate <u>manual for specific instructions</u> on . . .
<u>Refer to</u> <u>the</u> <u>manual for specific instructions</u>.
<u>Refer to</u> <u>the</u> installation <u>manual for specific instructions</u> for . . .
<u>Refer to</u> <u>the</u> <u>manual for specific instructions</u> on . . .

intervening words. Table 2.9 lists the different utterances with their unique corresponding interrupted collocations. The collocated words are underlined.

2.2.10   Term Acquisition in Asian Languages

This section presents two tools intended for term extraction from Japanese and Chinese texts. *JBrat*—a term extractor from Japanese texts—is inspired by *TERMS* and relies on pattern matching. *CXtract*—a term extractor from Chinese corpora—is statistically driven and focuses on the notion of collocation. It is inspired by Smadja (1993a) work on *Xtract*.

When compared with Indo-European languages, natural language processing for Asian languages raises specific issues that may render the task of term acquisition more difficult. The most striking difference is that the extraction of terms from Chinese or Japanese corpora must cope with the lack of delimiters between words (Fung 1997, sec. 1.1.3.). Thus, for most natural language processing tools in these languages, the first task is to insert word boundaries. This operation is called *tokenizing* and consists of finding groups of characters that belong together for building words. This issue and other specific linguistic features, such as the possibility of mixing words in different character sets for a single language (Japanese has three), call for specific tools that are not just a slight modification of softwares developed for other languages. This is the reason why I have dedicated this section to term acquisition in the case of Asian languages.

JBrat Term Extraction from Japanese

For the purpose of term extraction, Japanese offers two facilities that are not available in Chinese. First, Japanese is a language with more inflectional information than Chinese. In term extraction, this information can be exploited for the selection of correct terminological sequences. When compared with other Asian languages, the other advantage of working on Japanese is that tokenizers, part-of-speech taggers, and disambiguators were previously developed for this language, and make the extraction of terms from Japanese corpora easier than starting from scratch.

JBrat (Fung 1997, sec. 3.2.) is a tool for the acquisition of terms from Japanese corpora based on regular expressions. The approach is similar to *TERMS* (see section 2.2.5), but does not use a frequency threshold, with the argument that correct terms may have single occurrences in a corpus.[18]

The syntactic and morphological rules of Japanese technical terms are learned from Japanese examples collected from a parallel English/Japanese corpus. The examples are obtained through automatic term extraction from the English corpus and a manual alignment of English terms with Japanese ones. The exact algorithm is composed of two stages: a training stage in which the patterns for Japanese are learned and an extraction stage in which the patterns are exploited for acquiring terms from the Japanese data. Training is divided as follows:

1. Tagging of a bilingual corpus.

2. Automatic acquisition of terms from the English corpus.

3. Manual alignment of English terms with Japanese ones.

4. Sorting by decreasing frequency of the part-of-speech tag sequences corresponding to Japanese terms.

5. Creation of the regular expressions covering the most frequent tag sequences.

Then, during the acquisition stage, the regular expressions are used for retrieving terms from a tokenized and tagged Japanese corpus through pattern matching.

Since words in Japanese are built from combinations of single ideograms, unknown words are tagged as sequences of ideograms, any subsequence of which is likely to be a word. In *JBrat* the solution for dealing with the problem of the unknown word is to include sequences of tags corresponding to possible unknown words in the regular expressions for term extraction. This facility significantly increases the number of acquired terms without degrading precision.

CXtract Term Extraction from Chinese

The lack of morphological information and the difficulty of distinguishing morphemes, words, and compounds in Chinese makes term extraction in this language more difficult than in Japanese. In this section I report on *CXtract*, a termer for Chinese that operates on corpora without word boundaries. *CXtract* is directly inspired by *Xtract*, a termer developed for the English language and presented in section 2.2.6.

The issue of tokenizing in Chinese is addressed in *CXtract* by looking for repeated adjacent character groups. Multi-word terms are then acquired by detecting multi-word collocations through a modified version of the *Xtract* software (Fung 1997, sec. 3.1). The steps of the algorithm for term extraction are as follows:

1. A list of relevant bigrams is extracted from an unsegmented corpus. The window of observation is ten characters. The criteria for filtering the bigrams are taken from *Xtract*:

bigrams are retained only if they occur significantly more than by chance and if they appear in fixed positions.

2. In addition to both preceding criteria, it is also required that the two components of the bigram occur contiguously somewhere in the corpus.

3. Each bigram is possibly extended to n-grams by observing characters that occur recurringly in its vicinity.

The output of the preceding stages has a high recall at the expense of a low precision because it contains some ill-formed candidate terms. The candidate terms produced by the preceding algorithm are postprocessed by a linguistic filter to reject incorrect candidates using a set of basic morphological features. First, the candidate terms are segmented using a machine readable dictionary. The remaining characters are treated as affixes of the component words. These affixes and their positions are then compared with a predefined set of incorrect affixes containing case, numeral, number, and aspect markers. If a candidate term matches such a filtering pattern, it is rejected.

With the presentation of these termers for Asian languages, I have reached the conclusion of this overview on tools for term extraction from corpora. Termers are not the only applications to focus on the discovery of term occurrences in texts. Since terms represent text chunks with high information content, they are also extracted by indexers for building up condensed representations of documents for the purpose of information access. For this reason I now turn to the presentation of some phrase indexers which, to varying degrees of explicitness, address the issue of term extraction.

2.3 Parsers for Phrase Indexing

The basic purpose of automatic indexing is to assign content descriptors to documents that should fulfill the three following purposes (Keen 1977; cited by Salton and McGill 1983, sec. 3.1):

1. Locate items within a document that deal with particular topics.

2. Build hypertext links that connect documents with similar content.

3. Assist information retrieval by predicting the relevance of individual documents with respect to a query.

Automatic indexers are generally part of larger applications for information access, as opposed to term extractors (section 2.2), which are normally autonomous.

Even though the primary purpose of an automatic indexer is not term extraction, automatically extracted indexes frequently correspond to terms actually present in the indexed documents. The close correspondence between terms and indexes has led to a confusion of language: in the field of information retrieval, indexes are named *terms* although they may not be genuine terms.[19]

In Salton and McGill (1983, sec. 3.5.D) a distinction is made about the vocabulary used for indexing purposes whether it consists of single-word terms or multi-word terms (combinations of single-word terms). Since this book is devoted to multi-word term recognition, I focus here on *phrase indexing*, the indexing through multi-word units. The motivation of phrase indexing is to improve the *specificity* of the indexing vocabulary by avoiding polysemous single words.

The construction of phrase descriptors involves two processes: *phrase identification* and *phrase normalization* (Fagan 1987, sec. 1.4). The identification of phrases in documents can take into consideration a variety of characteristics of words such as individual word frequencies, frequencies of co-occurrences, frequencies of co-occurrences with restriction about the context of co-occurrence, or syntactic structures of the text that is being indexed. Phrase normalization is used for grouping phrase indexes with different forms and similar meanings. The purpose of phrase normalization for phrase indexing is exactly the same as the purpose of term variant conflation for term spotting.

In the remainder of this section, I present several approaches to phrase indexing. Since I am interested in NLP methods, only syntactic approaches to phrase indexing are covered. Some statistically driven term grouping techniques are presented in section 6.1, which is an introduction to automatic thesaurus acquisition. The reader who is interested in a wider presentation of NLP techniques for information retrieval can consult (Lewis, Croft, and Bhandaru 1989). In addition to syntactic approaches, these authors present semantic techniques and knowledge representation methods for information access. Mauldin (1991, chs. 2 and 3) also describes some knowledge-rich representations for information retrieval including semantic and case frame methods.

I now describe in turn eleven studies in syntax-based natural language processing for phrase indexing. I conclude this section with a synthesis that sums up the main features of these tools.

2.3.1 *CLARIT* NLP-Based Indexer

Synthetic Presentation

CLARIT is an environment for automatic indexing that exploits large scale natural language processing resources for identifying noun phrases (NPs) in free text (Evans et al. 1991). The linguistic indexes are augmented with statistical scores. If a controlled vocabulary is available, the indexes are paired with the controlled terms through an approximate window-based matching procedure tolerating partial overlaps. The matching process yields a match score and list of matched controlled terms.

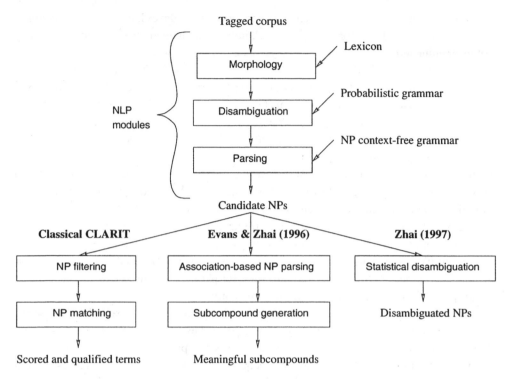

Figure 2.16
Flow-chart of *CLARIT*.

Interestingly the extraction of noun phrases made by *CLARIT* is improved and enhanced by following studies on noun phrase parsing and disambiguation. Evans and Zhai (1996) propose two techniques for the enhancement of the output of *CLARIT*: a filter for complex lexical atoms and a bottom-up association-based parser that groups words on the basis of an association score. Zhai (1997) also improves upon the parsing of *CLARIT* by providing an additional probabilistic model for the structural disambiguation of noun phrases.

CLARIT System

The *CLARIT* system exploits three large-scale shallow NLP procedures for automatic index-ing which are pipelined as described by figure 2.16. The first procedure is a morphological analysis through dictionary lookup. The dictionary contains 100,000 lemmas and 1,000,000 corresponding inflected forms. The morphological analyzer associates each known word with a list of lemma/category pairs. Unrecognized lexical items are labeled as candidate proper names.

The second step of natural language analysis is part-of-speech disambiguation, which ranks the part-of-speech categories of ambiguous words by decreasing order of probability.

The third and most original step is a noun phrase context-free parser. The parser focuses on the most relevant characteristics of the noun phrases for the purpose of information access, namely distinguishing the head word and its dependencies. At this stage the parser intentionally ignores the structural disambiguation of noun phrases. For example, the noun phrase *the redesigned R3000 chips from DEC* is analyzed as $[the]_{Det}$ $[redesigned$ $R3000]_{PreMod}$ $[chips]_{Head}$ $[from\ DEC]_{PostMod}$, where PreMod and PostMod are the pre- and postmodifiers of the head noun *chips*.

The output of the last NLP module—the parser—is passed to a filtering and a matching module. This model's design reflects a compromise between controlled and free indexing:

• The filtering module gathers unigram statistics of noun phrases and calculates relevance scores.

• The matching module compares the noun phrases with terms from a controlled vocabulary.

The combination of these two modules produces free indexes enriched with scores and conceptual information in relation with a controlled vocabulary.

The filtering module calculates a matching score together with a classification of the candidate NPs depending on the type of approximate matching with controlled terms. The primary statistics recorded for each word in each candidate NP by the filtering module are frequency counts (the number of times a word is encountered in the document), document count (the number of documents in which the word in encountered), and two domain-specific measures, the frequency of the word in a reference domain corpus and the frequency of the word in a general English corpus. Three measures are calculated from these statistical data: frequency (an overall frequency estimate), distribution (a domain-specific frequency), and rarity (a frequency in general English).

The matching module is also an original device that is intended to provide a rich framework for the comparison of free indexes (candidate NPs) with a controlled vocabulary (terms from a thesaurus). The degree of matching between a term and a noun phrase is calculated by determining the number of substring matches. For example, the candidate noun phrase A B C D is decomposed into ten substrings A, B, C, D, A B, B C, C D, A B C, B C D, and A B C D. In the matching process all the substrings are compared with the set of substrings derived from the terms in the controlled vocabulary. Every exact match is recorded and used for calculating a fuzzy match score giving the proportion of each candidate NP that matches controlled terms. In addition to this score, the matching module also provides a rough characterization of the conceptual link that holds between a candidate and the controlled terms:

1. An *exact match* corresponds to the equality of the candidate NP with a controlled term.

2. A *general match* occurs when a candidate NP is a substring of a controlled term.

3. A *specified match* occurs when a substring of a candidate NP is equal to a controlled term.

4. *Compositional* and *scored matches* are the matches that do not belong to any of the three preceding classes and that nevertheless receive high scores.

Structural Disambiguation

The output of the NLP module, corresponding to the three topmost components in figure 2.16, is a set of candidate NPs represented by flat dependency structures composed of a head word and pre- and/or postmodifiers. Since it is desirable to disambiguate these unstructured phrases for a proper exploitation in information retrieval, two posterior studies have addressed this issue.

The study of Evans and Zhai (1996) enhances the output of *CLARIT* with meaningful subcompounds. The two stages of the process are, first, an iterative discovery of lexical atoms and, second, an exploitation of these atoms in a bottom-up association-based parsing. Lexical atoms are word pairs w_1 w_2 that co-occur frequently and such that neither w w_1 w_2, nor w_1 w_2 w, is frequent. Thus *operating system*, *data structure*, and *decision table* are compounds extracted by this technique from the CACM corpus.

These atoms are used together with an association score for a structural disambiguation of candidate NPs in a second stage of the process. For example, *general purpose high-performance computer* is disambiguated as [[*general purpose*] [[*high-performance*] *computer*]] through this endogenous disambiguation technique.

Zhai(1997) also provides a method for improving the output of *CLARIT*. The "hidden" structure of a candidate NP is calculated through an iterative algorithm that maximizes the probabilities of intra-NP head/modifier associations. From each disambiguated NP, three sets of indexing units are generated: single words, head/modifier relations, and full NPs. For instance, from the noun phrase *heavy construction industry group*, disambiguated as [[[*heavy construction*] *industry*] *group*], the following items are generated:

Single words:

heavy, construction, industry, group

Head/modifier relations:

heavy construction, construction industry, industry group

Full NP:

heavy construction industry group

Comments

Contrary to other natural language approaches to automatic indexing, the output of *CLARIT* and the output of the *TTP* parser presented in section 2.3.11 are structurally ambiguous. The reason for this ambiguity is that unambiguous parsing is a knowledge intensive task that requires rich subcategorization and selectional information. Even though some studies, such as Pohlmann and Kraaij (1997), present a phrase indexer exploiting semantic information for breaking compounds into subcompounds, such semanticosyntactic data are nevertheless not easily available for large-scale and multi-domain applications. They can be replaced by corpus-based knowledge acquisition techniques that avoid the use of linguistically rich data. In the studies that have followed Evans et al. (1991) presented in the paragraph above, the disambiguation is performed after parsing through such statistically driven corpus-based learning procedures.

Thus *CLARIT* and its complementary studies offer a rich and scalable architecture for automatic indexing, with a concern for the all the intermediate levels between free and automatic indexing. The natural language processor is efficient enough to process large sets of data and rich enough to extract correct syntactic structures. A limit of *CLARIT* is due to its focus on noun phrase extraction, although some other phrase structures can convey conceptual information. As is pointed out in studies on term variations, such as Sparck Jones and Tait (1984a, b) presented below in section 2.3.9, verb phrases are conceptually equivalent to noun phrases and are equally good descriptors.

To sum up, *CLARIT* is a complete NLP front-end to information retrieval, not just a tool for automatic indexing. The fine-grained description of the various matching possibilities between candidate NPs and controlled terms is a unique contribution to bridge the gap between the output of a parser and the input of a retrieval engine.

2.3.2 *Constituent Object Parser*

Synthetic Presentation

The *Constituent Object Parser* (*COP*) is a generative parser for information retrieval that relies on large grammatical and lexical data (Metzler and Haas 1989; Metzler et al. 1989; Metzler et al. 1990). Contrary to other concurrent approaches, such as *COPSY* (section 2.3.3) or the Fagan phrase parser (section 2.3.4), the purpose of the *COP* is not to produce phrase descriptors. The output of the *COP* is a set of syntactic structures, the parse trees of the sentences in the documents and the query. Afterward the information retrieval module exploits parse trees directly instead of using phrase descriptors.

The parser is supposed to treat different types of syntactic structures, including verb, noun, and adjective phrases, and different type of discursive variations such as anaphora, ellipsis, and coordination. Conjunctions are particularly well described in the *COP*. They are represented by two grammars, an *equal-grammar* for isomorphic conjunctions, and an *unequal-grammar* for conjunctions with ellipsis in which some structures are complemented with constituents from coordinated structures.

The *COP* is a prototype that has been tested on a small corpus of abstracts of Cognitive Science from 1984 to 1987. The retrieval procedure consists of two steps. First, documents are prefiltered through keywords contained in the query. Then, the parses of the queries and the prefiltered documents are exploited for selecting relevant documents through a specific matching procedure based on dependency relations.

Syntactic Description through Binary Trees

In this presentation, I first introduce the *COP* formalism for representing syntactic dependencies through binary trees and the exploitation of these data for document retrieval. Then the treatment of ambiguous constructions and the treatment of conjunctions by the *COP* are detailed, since they both constitute original features of the parser.

Principles of Description

The *COP* and the information retrieval matching procedure it employs are based on the assumption that the essential information conveyed by natural language entities can be captured by binary trees expressing *dependency* relations. Figure 2.17 shows several noun phrases represented by binary structures in which the head word is marked by a star. Each internal node in a binary tree indicates which branch contains the dominant concept at that point and which is serving as a modifier. Each frontier node is labeled by a lexical word. A similar binary decomposition of compounds is proposed by Selkirk (1982) and illustrated through examples such as [[*bathroom* [*towel-rack*]] *designer*].

The *dominance* relationship is assumed to be transitive. A constituent dominant over a concept is also dominant over the dominant subconstituent of that constituent. In the utterance *small liberal arts college for scared junior* (tree ζ in figure 2.17), *small liberal arts college* dominates *for scared junior* and its dominant subconstituent *junior*. Transitivity of dominance makes it possible to rate the likehood of a dominance between two nonadjacent words in two different phrases. (Here *small liberal arts college* and *junior* are involved in a dominance relation and are not adjacent.)

Because of the computational complexity of the parser, the system operates in two steps: first, documents are filtered through conventional boolean keyword techniques and then filtered documents and queries are parsed by a genuine NLP-based information retrieval system. Step 1 involves the formulation of a boolean query containing the keywords that are likely to be present in the document. This is typically a disjunction of single-word terms. The documents corresponding to this first query are retrieved. They constitute a filtered subset over which the parser and the corresponding retrieval procedure of step 2 operate. At

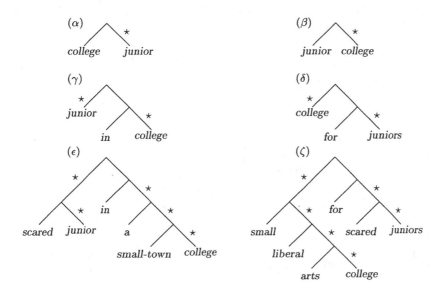

Figure 2.17
Binary parse trees produced by the *COP*.

step 2, a natural language query is formulated, and it replaces the boolean query of step 1. The documents filtered at step 1 and the natural language query are parsed by the *COP*. The parse trees are converted into pairwise dependency relationships; each document is then ranked according to the number of dependencies shared by the query and the document.

Ambiguous Structures

A conservative approach is adopted for parsing ambiguous structures with the *COP*. The parser avoids producing multiple analyses for ambiguous sentences by forcing the attachment of modifiers to the constituent immediately to the left. Subsequent processing during the matching process produces all the possible interpretations from this canonical structure by considering the transitivity of dominance.

Prepositional phrases and adverbs are treated in a similar manner, except that adverbs are attached to existing constituents rather than causing the construction of new constituents. The basic purpose of the strategy of disambiguation is to build structures that represent all the possible interpretations, and to eliminate as many inappropriate relations between terms as possible. For example, the tree *α* of figure 2.18 is preferred to the tree *β* because the modifier *under 35 years old* is attached to *delegates*, the head of the closest constituent on its left, instead of *candidate*.

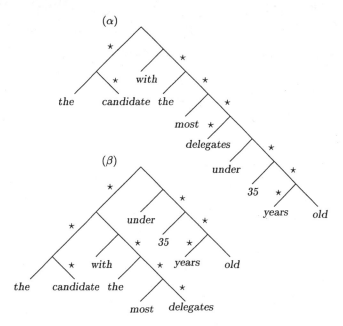

Figure 2.18
Parsing ambiguous phrases with the *COP*: (α) is preferred to (β).

Conjunctions

The grammar for *conjunctions* is divided into two conjunction grammars: the *equal-grammar* and the *unequal-grammar*. Both grammars describe conjoined constituents based on the grammar of regular unconjoined constituents.

The equal-grammar describes the conjunction of syntactically similar constituents, such that each of the constituents would be well-formed if appearing alone.

Conversely, the unequal grammar rules describe context-sensitive conjunctions in which some of the constituents can only be conjoined if they can be complemented with subconstituents of other particular syntactic structures. For instance, the conjunction *he is a cop and good at it* is valid because *good at it* is the attribute of the verb *to be*, a subconstituent of the conjoined clause *he is a cop*. During the processing of the second constituent of this coordination, a function looks for a nonadjacent constituent (*to be*) that can be used to built a verb phrase with *good at it*.

Comments

The *COP* is a very appealing model for the representation of complex phrase structures in a fashion that facilitates subsequent information retrieval. The decomposition of phrase structures into binary dependencies makes sense in an application in which fine-grained structural disambiguation is not necessary. Furthermore the technique of syntactic analysis is complemented with a tree-matching algorithm that exploits elementary dependencies for pairing texts and queries, thus remedying the possible insufficiencies of the syntactic analysis.

The major problem with the *COP* is that no large-scale evaluation is proposed in the literature. It is therefore difficult to evaluate the applicability of this parser to real-word experiments. Would it really cope with multi-domain textual data? Is the retrieval procedure really accurate in terms of precision and recall?

The contribution of this study is thus to offer a theoretical framework for the exploitation of phrase structure grammars in information retrieval. The *COP* is a kind of maximally rich approach to the automatic construction of phrase indexes and to the analysis of natural language queries. Additionally the study avoids the use of explicit indexes by letting the matching process rely on full-fledged syntactic structures. This study is a kind of syntactic counterpart to the semantically rich approach to information retrieval of Mauldin (1991).

2.3.3 *COPSY* Automatic Indexer

Synthetic Presentation

COPSY is an automatic indexer based on natural language processing techniques through the extraction of dependency relations encountered in noun phrases (Schwarz 1988, 1989, 1990). First, a list of regular suffixes and a restricted dictionary composed of negative and positive examples are used for calculating word lemmas and word categories. Then the bulk of the work in *COPSY* is done by a noun phrase parser and a normalization process that converts phrase structure into dependency trees.

The resulting dependency trees permit the partial or total match between queries and documents for information access.

Stemming, Parsing, and Normalization with *COPSY*

The morphological data in *COPSY* consist of a list of regular suffixes together with part-of-speech categories and a list of exceptions. Suffixes are organized into a prefix tree with an output for efficiency considerations (the system corresponds to an actual large scale implementation). In actual fact this tree could be easily translated into a finite state transducer that removes inflectional suffixes and replaces them with normalized endings.

The stemmer operates in two steps. First, the stem is calculated through the prefix tree. For instance, the stem of words ending with *-oes* is obtained by replacing the suffix *-oes* with *-o*: *heroes* is transformed into *hero*. Then, an exception list composed of negative and positive examples is consulted. The positive list contains examples of words ending with *-s* in which the final *s* must not be deleted, such as *afterwards*. The negative list contains

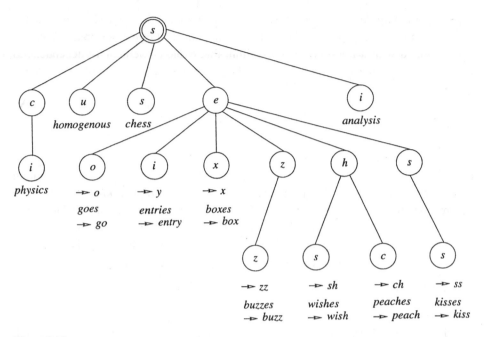

Figure 2.19
The prefix tree for stemming words ending with *s*.

irregular cases ending with -*s* and the corresponding stem, such as *shoes* associated with the singular word *shoe*, and not with *sho*. Figure 2.19 illustrates the prefix binary tree for stemming words ending with -*s*.

Stemmed and categorized words are used as input to the NP parser which operates in two steps. First, noun phrases are isolated, based on noun phrase delimiters such as verbs or punctuations. Then, the dependency structure of these noun phrases is calculated by applying syntactic rules that make the head/modifier relations in these noun phrases explicit. For exemplification purpose the syntactic structure of the noun phrase *scientific analysis of amino acids in cheese* is reported in figure 2.20. The dependencies are materialized by arrows between modifier nodes and head nodes (mother nodes).

The dependency between words in a noun phrase is based on configurational properties enriched with word categories. For instance, the dependency between two nouns depends on whether or not a preposition intervene between these nouns. Through this rule the dependency in *milk storage* is identical to the dependency in *storage of milk*. In addition to nominal subphrases, such as the ones highlighted in figure 2.20, adjectival subphrases are considered. For example, the phrase *a piston movable in a cylinder* is associated with

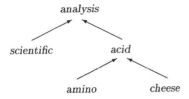

Figure 2.20
Parse of the noun phrase *scientific analysis of amino acids in cheese* by *COPSY*.

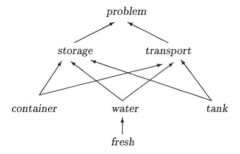

Figure 2.21
Parse of the coordinated noun phrase *problems of fresh water storage and transport in containers or tanks* by *COPSY*.

the dependencies *cylinder → movable → piston*. The analysis of coordinated structures by *COPSY* may yield multiple dependencies such as the ones found in the graph illustrated by figure 2.21.

These syntactic structures made of dependency relations are used for information retrieval through total or partial match between the dependency trees of the noun phrases in a query and the noun phrases in documents. The speed of the retrieval is improved through a presearch of documents: only documents that contain at least one of the words of the query are preselected. This prefiltering is similar to the prefiltering through boolean query in the *Constituent Object Parser* presented in section 2.3.2. It is a kind of precoordination and corresponds to a disjunction on the words of the query. Symmetrically the partial match with dependency relations corresponds to a postcoordination, that is to say, the exploitation of phrase indexes built from single-word terms.

Comments
COPSY is part of a larger and ambitious industrial project, called *TINA*, for text analysis, automatic indexing, and information retrieval. The industrial environment in which *COPSY*

was developed has forced its designer to devise an efficient tool that can process quickly large volumes of data with a reasonable rate of success. The parsing speed, given in Schwarz (1990), is 19 kb/s.

Since the morphological analysis relies on a stemming procedure and exception lists instead of an exhaustive vocabulary, the parser can cope with raw corpora whatever their domain of origin. The quality of the parser is a function of the empirical tuning of the rules against texts from commercial databases. On the whole, about 15,000 sentences were tested against 200 rule hypotheses so as to arrive at a final set of 45 rules.

The major flaw of *COPSY* is that the simplistic model of noun phrases cannot differentiate several types of semantic variants and can ultimately lead to errors in information access. This problem is due to the reductive approach to the representation of phrases by dependencies between words. For instance, *transport in containers*, *transport of containers*, and *transport from containers* are represented by the same dependency relation *container* → *transport*, although they denote different concepts. The misleading similarity between these three description will eventually result in the retrieval of documents about the *transport of containers* when querying for *transport in containers*.

2.3.4 Fagan Phrase Indexer

Synthetic Presentation

The purpose of Fagan's thesis (Fagan 1987) is to compare the effectiveness of single term indexing, and syntactic and nonsyntactic phrase indexing through retrieval experiments. The results show that phrase indexing has little effect on retrieval effectiveness. Several factors might explain this counterintuitive result: for example, the low number of phrase descriptors in documents when compared with single terms, and the exploitation of average performances, which tend to hide significant variations in the performance of individual queries.

In this section I only present the syntactic phrase indexing technique because Fagan's statistical phrase indexing method is a generalization of the method proposed by Salton, Yang, and Yu (1975) without additional NLP.

Fagan Syntactic Phrase Indexer

Fagan's phrase indexing method relies on the output of a general purpose syntactic parser (*PLNLP*; Heidorn 1975), enriched with lexical information provided by a dictionary. In addition closed exception lists are used for rejecting incorrect phrase descriptors. The major contribution of Fagan's indexer is to show how the output of a "classic" syntactic analyzer can be manipulated so as to produce binary phrase indexes from phrase structures.

Basically each parse tree from *PLNLP* is composed of a head word and a list of premodifiers and/or postmodifiers. The descriptors are produced from phrase structures through

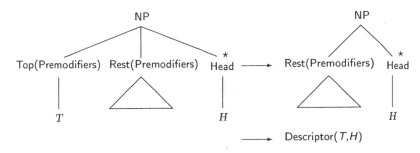

Figure 2.22
Encoding rule from Fagan's thesis.

encoding rules. Each encoding rule is composed of a left-hand side that specifies the object that the rule can be applied to. The right-hand side indicates (1) a transformed phrase structure that can be iteratively produced by the encoding rule and (2) a phrase descriptor. The encoding rule given in figure 2.22 applies to a noun phrase that contains one head word and at least one premodifier. The output of the rule is as follows:

- A copy of the noun phrase in which the leftmost premodifier is removed.
- A descriptor composed of the leftmost premodifier and the head noun.

Table 2.10 illustrates the double application of the rule from figure 2.22 to the noun phrase *automatic text analysis* with two premodifiers and one head noun. The descriptor *automatic analysis* is produced at the first stage, and the remaining noun phrase is *text analysis*. At the second stage, the rule from figure 2.22 applies to the remaining noun phrase *text analysis*; it produces the descriptor *text analysis* and the noun phrase *analysis* which cannot be further transformed by this rule.

A large variety of grammatical constructions are treated by the encoding rules to produce descriptors. Let us illustrate some of the major types of structures dealt with in Fagan's work:

General Noun Phrases The descriptors with determiners as premodifiers are not produced as output. In

the efficiency of these four sorting algorithms

    → *algorithm efficiency*

    → *sorting algorithm*

descriptors, such as *the efficiency*, *four algorithms*, *these algorithms*, are rejected by consulting a stop list of premodifiers made of the determiners *the*, *four*, *these*, etc.

Table 2.10
Production of phrase descriptors from the parse tree of *automatic text analysis*

Parse tree	Phrase descriptor

Original noun phrase

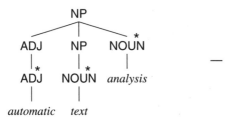

—

First application of rule from figure 2.22

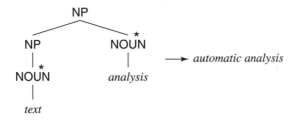

Second application of rule from figure 2.22

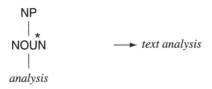

Conjoined Noun Phrases The premodifiers and postmodifiers are distributed on the head words, and all the possible combinations of head/modifier associations are produced. In

the philosophy, design, and implementation of an experimental interface

- → *interface philosophy*
- → *interface design*
- → *interface implementation*
- → *experimental interface*

each of the conjoined head words, *philosophy*, *design*, and *implementation*, is associated with the common modifier *interface*.

Adjective Phrases In addition to noun/modifier associations, adjectival phrases—composed of an adverbial modifier and an adjective—can also be produced. In

a system for encoding, automatically matching, and automatically drawing chemical structures

- → *automatically matching*
- → *automatically drawing*
- → *structure encoding*
- → *structure matching*
- → *structure drawing*
- → *chemical structure*

the first two descriptors are adjectival phrases, and the four remaining ones are nominal phrases. A stop-list of nonrelevant adverbs (*absolute*, *abundant*, *also*, etc) is used for rejecting incorrect adjectival descriptors.

Verb Phrases Verb phrases are also produced as descriptors but thematic roles are not distinguished. In

the machine coding these chemical structures

- → *machine coding*
- → *structure coding*
- → *chemical structure*

the first two descriptors are verb phrases. In the former, *machine* is the subject, and in the latter, *structure* is the object of the verb *to code*.

The quality of phrase descriptors is further improved by removing semantically empty heads in order to avoid the production of descriptors of doubtful quality. In the following example, the semantically empty head noun is removed (*procedure*) and the nearest premodifier is raised to the position of head (*clustering*):

an automated document clustering procedure

$\Rightarrow$ *an automated document clustering*

$\rightarrow$ *automated clustering*

$\rightarrow$ *document clustering*

Three nonappropriate descriptors—*automated procedure, document procedure,* and *clustering procedure*—are not generated thanks to the deletion of *procedure*. The stop-list of semantically empty heads comprises nouns that refer to very general concepts such as *ability*, *activity*, *amount*, and *analysis*.

Comments

The phrase indexing technique proposed by Fagan suffers from the well-known problems raised by generative phrase parsing and by parsing without structural disambiguation. Some of the problems of generative phrase parsing are due to a lack of consideration for some idiomatic and noncompositional constructions. For example, the recognition of *as a function of* as an unbreakable prepositional phrase would avoid the generation of the incorrect descriptor *base function* in the following example:

as a function of the data base $\rightarrow$ *⋆base function*

$\rightarrow$ *data base*

The nondetection of specific discourse structures, such as defining contexts, also leads to the generation of spurious descriptors. For instance, the nonrecognition of the discourse marker *in such areas as* cause the production of three incorrect descriptors with *area* as head noun, in the following example:

applications of automation in such areas as circulation, cataloging, and acquisitions

$\rightarrow$ *⋆circulation area*

$\rightarrow$ *⋆cataloging area*

$\rightarrow$ *⋆acquisition area*

$\rightarrow$ *automation application*

The lack of structural disambiguation is surely the most serious problem raised by the approach proposed by Fagan. Since overindexing that may decrease precision is preferred to underindexing that may reduce recall, all the phrase descriptors are used in case of ambiguous constructions. In the following sentence, *interface* is incorrectly analyzed as an object of *browsing* and yields the incorrect descriptor *interface browsing* instead of *browsing interface*:

they design software for browsing interfaces   → *★interface browsing*

→ *browsing software*

Obviously some of the shortcomings of Fagan's approach—due to the *PLNLP* parser—could be remedied by exploiting some of the recent advances in massive NLP. Structural disambiguation techniques would help selecting the correct dependency relations. Recognition of specific constructions, such as compounds, idiomatic expressions, or defining contexts, would prevent the parser from processing them as generic phrase structures. Partial parsing techniques would help to focus on the most conceptually significant chunks in a sentence.

Despite these problems Fagan's work has paved the way for the exploitation of broad coverage parsers in information retrieval. The decomposition of phrase structures into elementary dependencies and the exploitation of the resulting binary descriptors, advocated in the seminal work of Fagan, has become well-established tradition in the application of NLP to information retrieval.

2.3.5 *FASIT* Syntactic Indexer

Synthetic Presentation

FASIT proposes a large-scale natural language processing module for the automatic indexing of documents that is inspired by the traditional practices of automatic indexing through the use of text simplification techniques (Dillon and Gray 1983). The processing divides into a tagging module through suffix-based morphology and disambiguation rules, and an index extraction modules through pattern matching. Indexes are then grouped into classes through the traditional techniques of stemming and word reordering. The output is evaluated through information retrieval experiments and compared with thesaurus indexing and with single-word indexing using *s*-plural removal.

Index Extraction

The extraction of indexes from documents by *FASIT* exploits a technique that is very similar to the tools for term acquisition proposed in section 2.2.

First, the text is morphologically analyzed through a set of suffix-based rules and an exception list. The complete tag-set consists of a list of 71 part-of-speech categories and possible additional features such as number or tense. Since some word endings may refer to more than one category, more than one tag may be assigned during the morphological analysis.

In order to avoid spurious tagging ambiguities, the exception dictionary contains five types of words: (1) a closed class of frequently occurring words, among which are *to be* or *to have*, conjunctions, etc., (2) words with apparently regular endings that do not conform to the rules, such as *bring* which is not a gerund, (3) nouns or adjectives without informational content, such as *certain* or *basis*, (4) some frequently occurring proper nouns, and (5) a list of domain-dependent words.

Any word not found in the dictionary is tagged through its suffix or is given a default tag (Adjective | Noun | Verb). The ambiguity of tagging that would be a problem in providing a full parse of the sentence is well tolerated by *FASIT* because the patterns for term extraction contain these possible ambiguous tags.

The second stage of the indexing process is a disambiguation of multiply tagged words through contextual rules. At the third stage, the tagged text is matched against a dictionary of part-of-speech patterns to extract indexes. Index selection employs 161 patterns built on tags or combinations of tags in case of ambiguity. The length of the patterns is from 1 to 4 words, and the longest match is selected. The most frequently used patterns and corresponding examples are shown in table 2.11.

Adjective-noun ambiguities are easily accommodated through the use of ambiguous (Adjective | Noun) tags in index selection. As indicated by table 2.11, adjective-noun ambiguities are found in many frequently occurring index patterns (patterns 5, 8, 9, 14, and 15). They result in a very few inappropriate terms. (A similar technique used by Hull 1998 is presented in section 2.2.8.) On the contrary, noun-verb ambiguities, although less frequent, generate more spurious indexes. Many plural nouns, such as *adults* or *books*, are falsely tagged as ambiguous noun-verb tokens. Problems also arise from inflected verbs through the confusion between past-participle and preterite. For instance, *developed group*—a verb/object association—is incorrectly considered as a possible past-participle/noun combination.

Index Grouping

The second operation for automatic indexing is concept grouping which conflates the selected indexes to a canonical form in order to group synonymous indexes. The three steps of index grouping are (1) function word delection (prepositions, conjunctions, and general nouns), (2) stemming, and (3) word reordering. For example, the index *library catalogs* is transformed into *catalog librar* through concept grouping.

This technique is traditionnally used in information retrieval (e.g., Salton, Yang, and Yu 1975); it has the advantage of grouping occurrences such as *library catalogs*, *library cataloging*, and *catalogs of library*. Internal sorting nevertheless produces some classical errors such as the conflation of *school library* and *library school*.

Table 2.11
Most frequently used patterns for index extraction by *FASIT*

	Pattern	Frequency	Example
1	Noun	2,316	*administration*
2	Noun-plural	1,370	*administrators*
3	ProperNoun	619	*Davidson*
4	(Noun-plural | Verb-singular)	457	*budgets*
5	(Adjective | Noun)	378	*adolescent*
6	Noun Noun	346	*art history*
7	ProperNoun ProperNoun	299	*Albrecht Dürer*
8	(Adjective | Noun) Noun	245	*academic library*
9	(Adjective | Noun) Noun-plural	216	*academic libraries*
10	Adjective Noun	212	*administrative decision*
11	Adjective Noun-plural	188	*bibliograhic annotations*
12	Noun Noun-plural	159	*book publishers*
13	Noun Preposition Noun	131	*automation of circulation*
14	(Adjective | Noun) (Noun | Verb)	104	*audio-visual center*
15	(Adjective | Noun) (Noun-plural | Verb-singular)	100	*boolean queries*
16	Others	4,000	
	Total	8,864	

In addition concepts are grouped on the basis of their component words. For instance, the phrase index *continuing education courses* is attached to three groups which are characterized by the single-word indexes *continuing*, *education*, and *courses*. As in *LEXTER* (section 2.2.3), each group represented by the single word w contains any index that has w as one of its component.

Comments

The NLP techniques used by *FASIT* are morphological analysis, disambiguation of part-of-speech tagging, and pattern matching for index extraction. Later studies have addressed these issues in a general framework and have proposed techniques that are now considered standard and are widely used. As described in the *morphology* entry of section 2.1.3, good morphological analyzers now exist for large vocabularies. Unambiguous part-of-speech tagging is now possible with a good accuracy due to work by Church (1988) and Brill (1992). Also, as indicated in section 2.2, improved pattern-matching techniques for term extraction are now to be found in the literature.

FASIT's schemes date from 1983. Their merit was in bringing shallow NLP techniques together at a time when it was not possible to download the softwares from the Internet, and to propose a coherent and unified framework for integrating these pieces of software in a single application. This approach exploited reasonably simple linguistic tools with little manual work. It was possible to apply *FASIT* to large-scale corpora at a time when NLP for information retrieval was a rather speculative matter.

The flaws of *FASIT* fell into two classes. Some were due to the state of the art at the time of the study. They concerned the inaccuracies of part-of-speech tagging and morphological analysis. Other flaws were due to the rough conflation of index synonyms through three nonlinguistic approaches to index normalization: stop-word removal, stemming, and word sorting. In this book I show that it is possible to overcome the inherent limitations of these three simplification methods by conceiving NLP techniques for handling term normalization.

There are some subsequent studies that provide strong arguments against the use of nonlinguistic techniques in information access. Krovetz (1993) argues against stemming in stressing the importance of morphology in information retrieval and its impact on performance. Riloff (1995) shows how stop-word removal incorrectly conflates terms that could be used to create more effective indexing terms. Last, Jacquemin (1996b) provides arguments against word reordering in showing the low rate of genuine variants among permuted co-occurrences.

2.3.6 *IRENA* Phrase Indexer

Synthetic Presentation
IRENA is a recent NLP-based system for automatic indexing (Arampatzis, Koster, and Tsoris 1997; Arampatzis et al. 1998). This system recognizes the three main families of variations: syntactic, morphological, and lexicosemantic variations.

IRENA is composed of four NLP components: a syntactic normalizer in charge of giving a canonical order to a head and its constituents, a morphological normalizer for lemmatizing, an unnesting module for transforming phrases into binary terms, and a lexicosemantic normalizer that normalizes semantic variants. The system is evaluated in the framework of a single-domain information retrieval system in which the ranking of the documents depends both on the type of semantic variants and on the distances between the query terms and the corpus variants. The results show that the combination of phrase indexing and term normalization increases both recall and precision when compared with single-word indexing.

NLP Components
The *IRENA* system combines recent advances in NLP that replace classical indexing procedures using a combination of phrase recognition and term normalization. The pipeline architecture of *IRENA*, shown in figure 2.23, is very similar to earlier classical NLP systems

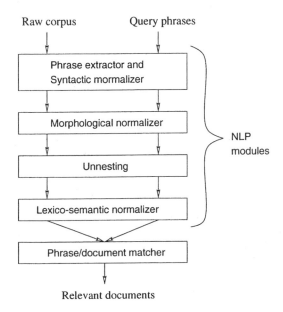

Figure 2.23
Flow-chart of *IRENA*.

for information extraction or information retrieval such as Debili's parser (Debili 1982), presented in section 2.3.10, or *FASTUS* (Hobbs et al. 1997).

The first level is a *phrase extractor and normalizer*, which is composed of a tagger, a shallow parser of noun phrases and verb phrases, and a syntactic normalizer. Through syntactic normalization, each phrase is represented as a head and a set of modifiers. (The modifier part can be empty in case of a bare head.) For instance, *air pollution* and *pollution of the air* are mapped onto the same phrase frame [*air, pollution*].

Both noun and verb phrases are proposed by the extractor and processed by the normalization module. The normalization of verb phrases is more complicated than noun phrases. In addition to word reordering, verb phrases are brought to active forms, time and modality are eliminated, and attributive verb phrases (Noun *is* Adjective) are ultimately transformed into noun phrases (Adjective Noun).

The *morphological normalizer* is a lemmatizer that replaces each inflected word by its lemma (the infinitive of a verb, the singular of a noun, the base form of a comparative adjective, e.g., *easier*). Only inflectional morphology is taken into consideration through a revised Porter stemmer that checks words against an exception dictionary before using regular stemming. Adjectival participles and gerunds are not stemmed because they cannot be inflected.

The following *unnesting* step is a process for decomposing complex phrases into binary dependencies. This technique is used in other tools presented here, such as *CLARIT* (section 2.3.1), the *Constituent Object Parser* (section 2.3.2), and *COPSY* (section 2.3.3). The purpose of unnesting is to facilitate the structural matching of phrases by breaking up complicated phrase frames. For instance, the phrase *man visited conference on software engineering* is transformed into three binary dependencies: [*conference, visit*], [*engineering, conference*], and [*software, engineering*].

The last NLP module is a *lexicosemantic normalizer* dedicated to the normalization of semantic variants. The description of the types of semantic variants taken into consideration by *IRENA* depends on the publication. In Arampatzis, Koster, and Tsoris (1997), a manual expansion of synonyms from WordNet is used in order to avoid the problem of polysemy and its negative effect on information retrieval. In Arampatzis et al. (1998), three interesting possibilities of lexicosemantic normalization are proposed: a semantic clustering of single words which is a sort of semantic analogue to stemming, a semantic expansion in which terms are linked with semantically related terms, and a semantic similarity at the level of document retrieval. The last possibility has some resemblance to the notion of *semantic variation* which I will describe in section 8.1. Two head/argument dependencies are considered as semantically similar if and only if heads and arguments are identical, synonymous, or hypernyms. Only few details of these techniques are given by the authors in these two publications.

Information Retrieval through Phrase Indexes
The retrieval of documents with the *IRENA* system is based on phrase indexes or variants found in the query and the documents. The documents are ranked according to a measure of confidence that depends on the types of variants and on the distances between the components of each variant. The co-occurrence categories, in descending order of importance, are identity, morphological variation, and semantic variation.

The usefulness of phrase indexes and their variants for information retrieval was evaluated in a small experiment involving one million words collected from 633 documents on music. The results showed that phrase indexes lead to very high precision and low recall. When the queries were expanded to include lexical and morphological variants, recall increased up to 60% and precision droppped slightly from 70 to 57%. In this case, an important characteristic was that the corpus contained a large number of proper names which facilitated the retrieval of relevant documents through phrase indexes.

Comments
The *IRENA* system provides several interesting and realistic applications of NLP in information retrieval. The results on a limited experiment demonstrate the advantages of phrase indexing combined with flexible term variant recognition techniques.

The impact of phrase indexing and semantic expansion on information retrieval is further a subject of debate. In the study of Fagan (1987), presented in section 2.3.4, it is shown that phrase indexing does not outperform classical single-word indexing. Similarly in Gonzalo, Peñas, and Verdejo (1999), it is shown that retrieval efficiency decreases when phrases are used as indexing terms unless the query is precise. The same conclusion was reached by Mitra et al. (1997) who also compared the relative merits of single-word indexing, statistical phrase indexing, and syntactic phrase indexing. Mitra et al. used statistical phrases based on co-occurrences and syntactic phrases extracted through tag patterns and decomposed into binary terms. These authors found that syntactic and statistical phrases performed equally well in association with single-word terms. The phrases did not significantly affect high precision retrieval, but they were useful in determining the relative ranks of low-ranked documents.

Unfortunately, all these conclusions are not being considered seriously in the evaluation of the *IRENA* system. The high quality of retrieval with *IRENA* phrase indexing in the music corpus may be only due to the important number of proper names.

The requirement of semantic disambiguation is a crucial factor for the success of semantic expansion, but it is not certain whether users are really willing to cope with this task. Semantic expansion through WordNet on disambiguated words is generally reported to improve recall by Voorhees (1998) and Gonzalo et al. (1998). However, the most promising approach to semantic normalization, which relies on semantic relations of phrase components, is not investigated and implemented in the experimental framework used to evaluate *IRENA*.

In sum, *IRENA* proposes several promising approaches to NLP for information retrieval. The small scale of the applications (compared with those of TREC) and the lack of implementation and evaluation of its innovative aspects are not sufficient to provide conclusions on the validity of the phrase indexing techniques. *IRENA*, however, does present several convincing methods for using phrase indexes in order to improve recall without significant loss of precision. The *IRENA* system certainly deserves further experimental evaluation.

2.3.7 Noun Phrase Parser *NPtool*

Synthetic Presentation

NPtool (Voutilainen 1993) is a finite state parser for noun phrase extraction. The grammatical framework is the *Constraint Grammar* (Karlsson et al. 1995), a system in which syntactic structures are partially specified through dependency relations. The noun phrases are extracted through a double grammatical description composed of hostile and friendly rules. The possibly ambiguous sequences satisfying both grammars are ultimately produced as output of the system.

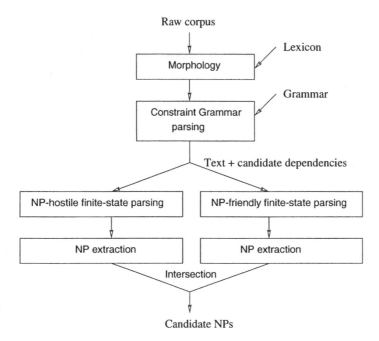

Figure 2.24
Flowchart of *NPtool*.

The focus of *NPtool* is not a term extraction per se, the techiques implemented in this parser are very similar to other tools for term acquisition such as *LEXTER*, presented in section 2.2.3. A more systematic comparison of these parsers and their interest with respect to the design of *FASTR* are detailed in section 5.4.

A Specialized Parser
The architecture of *NPtool* is built upon the *Constraint Grammar* and is complemented with two additional specialized modules for noun phrase filtering. The overall organization of *NPtool* is shown in figure 2.24.

In the *Constraint Grammar* framework, parsing is performed by its two main modules: a context-insensitive dictionary lookup during the morphological analysis and the elimination of unacceptable or contextually impossible alternatives during the parsing stage. The morphological analyzer uses a two-level approach and associates each inflected word with a set of morphological features and corresponding syntactic roles. The morphological analysis is followed by morphological and syntactic disambiguations that exploit syntactic constraints for discarding word analysis that violate these constraints.

For example, the sequence *cylinder head* in *The inlet and exhaust manifolds are mounted on opposite sides of the cylinder head . . .* receives the following analysis after dictionary lookup and disambiguation:

```
"cylinder"
     "cylinder"  N   (@>N  @NH)
"head"
     "head"      V   (@V)
     "head"      N   (@NH)
```

The analysis of *cylinder* indicates that it is a noun, that its lemma is *cylinder*, and that it has two possible syntactic roles: either pre-nominal modifier (@>N) or head noun (@NH). *Head* is also ambiguously analyzed: it is either a head verb (@V) or a head noun (@NH).

All the readings of a sentence are generated from the output of the parsing stage, depending on the remaining ambiguities. In the preceding sequence, two analyses are reported. One corresponds to *head* as a verb, and the other to *head* as a head noun. These analyses are then passed to two NP parsers. The NP-friendly parser retains the analysis with the highest number of words as part of a maximally long NP analysis, and an NP-hostile parser retains the analysis with the lowest number of words as part of a maximally short NP analysis. The NP-hostile parser would prefer the analysis `cylinder/@NH head/@V` and the NP-friendly parser selects the analysis `cylinder/@>N head/@NH`. The candidate NPs that are agreed upon by both parsers are likely to be correct unambiguous noun phrases.

The output of each of the NP-hostile and NP-friendly parsers is processed by an NP extractor that selects the parts of the output strings corresponding to correct NP syntactic patterns. The extractor is a finite state machine represented by the following regular expression based on the syntactic tags of *Constraint Grammar*:

$$((\text{M} > \text{N}^+ (\text{CC M} > \text{N}^+)^\star)^\star)^\star \ \text{HEAD} \ (\text{N} < (\text{D/M} > \text{N}^+ (\text{CC D/M} > \text{N}^+)^\star)^\star \ \text{HEAD})^\star)$$

where M>N stands for premodifiers, CC for coordinating conjunctions, HEAD for head nouns, D/M>N for determiners, and N< for prepositions starting postmodifying prepositional phrases. The expression above is composed of a central head noun and possible pre- and postmodifiers, coordinated or not.

Comments

NP parsing of *NPtool* takes advantage of the rich linguistic knowledge embodied in the lexicon and in the grammar of the *Constraint Grammar*. The dependency-based model is well suited for representing the output of a parser that is used as a front end to information retrieval, as in other existing approaches to syntactic phrase indexing. The *Constraint*

Grammar is also adopted in Sheridan and Smeaton's phrase matcher, which is presented in section 2.3.8.

The alternative approaches to NP recognition are based on lexical patterns. For instance, Senellart (1998) has built fine-grained subcategorization frames for each semantic class of lexical items. Each distributional class must be tuned manually, so this nonsyntactic technique is better adapted to information extraction than automatic indexing and information retrieval. However, to be realistic, such a knowledge-intensive lexical description cannot be utilized in large-scale multi-domain information retrieval experiments.

In *NPtool*, two complementary modules are used for the selection of NPs. The positive module forces the acceptance of noun phrases, and the negative one reduces as much as possible the coverage of NPs within a sentence. This approach has appeal in that it exploits the advantage of negative description. However, the actual mechanisms of NP selection are obscured by the lack of an explicit NP grammar.

2.3.8 Sheridan and Smeaton Phrase Matcher

Synthetic Presentation

Elaborate correspondences between parse trees were used by Smeaton and Sheridan (1991) and Sheridan and Smeaton (1992) in an application of NLP to information retrieval that avoids the use of indexes. The natural language component in these studies was a morphosyntactic analyzer that generated shallow syntactic dependencies from which ambiguous parse trees were built. Then a matching procedure produced a score, indicating the degree of correspondence between phrases. The overall phrase-matching technique was designed as a part of a larger system for information retrieval, but it was only evaluated for its scores on tree matching compared with scores produced by human judges.

The natural language parser used in this study was composed of two modules developed for English at the University of Helsinki: the two-level morphological analyzer of Koskenniemi (1983) and the parser based on Karlsson's *Constraint Grammar* framework (Karlsson 1990; Karlsson et al. 1995). The generator of the structured representation of texts, called *tree structured analysis*, was developed specifically for this project. It transforms the output of the morphological and syntactic stages into partially ambiguous binary trees. Then a tree-matching algorithm is used for pairing texts and queries. It is based on a tree traversal algorithm which is enhanced with flexible matching procedures.

When processing a user query and a set of documents, the complete system produces a set of parse trees for both the query and the documents. The matching algorithm yields a set of ranked analyses according to the similarities between the parse trees in the document and in the user queries.

Table 2.12
Analysis of *remove the fuel pump and filter*

Word	remove	the	fuel	pump	and	filter	
Lemma	remove	the	fuel	pump	and	filter	filter
Morphological	V	DET	N	N	CC	N	V
features	IMP	ART	NOM	NOM		NOM	IMP
	VFIN	SG/PL	SG	SG		SG	FGIN
Syntactic tag	@@MAINV	@@DN>	@@NN>	@@OBJ	@@CC	@@OBJ	@@MAINV

Tree Representation

The morphosyntactic analyzer is a three-stage procedure. First, the text is tokenized and each word receives one or more morphological analyses consisting of a lemma and a set of morphological features. In the next stage, any ambiguous words such as *fuel* and *filter*, which are either noun or verb, are analyzed using local disambiguation rules, Through local rules many of the irrelevant word analyses are discarded. For example, the word *fuel* is disambiguated as a noun in the sentence *remove the fuel pump sediment bowl and filter from the top of the pump unit*. No such disambiguation rule applies to the noun *filter*.

In the third and final stage, the natural language processor applies a set of mapping rules that assigns syntactic function labels that indicate the syntactic dependencies between head words and arguments. An example of the syntactic labels and morphological analyses associated with the words in the utterance *remove the fuel pump and filter* is provided in table 2.12.

Note that the syntactic tags in the last line of the table show *remove* to be the main verb, *pump* the object of this main verb, *filter* ambiguously an object or another main verb, and *the* and *fuel* premodifiers of a noun. These tags retain some ambiguities about the exact scope of the dependencies. Thus the tag @@NN> assigned to *fuel* refers to a noun modifying some other noun to the right. It does not specify whether the modified noun is a single noun, a compound, or a conjoined construct. Here the function of the word *fuel* is ambiguous between being a modifier of *pump* or a modifier of *pump and filter*. The meanings of both interpretations are different, the former can be paraphrased as *the fuel pump and the filter*, and the second one as *the fuel pump and the fuel filter*.

The output of the morphosyntactic analysis is transformed into a tree-structured representation that encodes the dependency relationships between words. The representation consists of binary trees in which most words are leaf nodes. Only prepositions and coordinations are stored at the ancestor nodes that govern prepositional phrases or conjunct constructions. At some parent nodes, the head/modifier relationship is emphasized by a star (⋆). Figure 2.25 illustrates such a tree-structured representation.

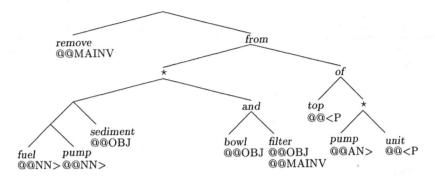

Figure 2.25
Tree representing *remove the fuel pump sediment bowl and filter from the top of the pump unit*.

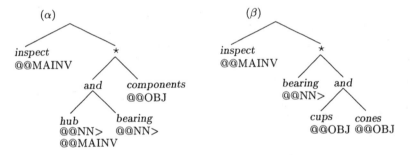

Figure 2.26
Two ambiguous trees representing *inspect hub and bearing components* and *inspect bearing cups and cones*.

The cases of ambiguity are not retained in the tree-structured representation because there is only one tree structure built for every utterance. The tree representation favors one representation over the others. For example, the representation α of *inspect hub and bearing components*, shown in figure 2.26, favors the interpretation paraphrased as *inspect the hub components and the bearing components* over the interpretation *inspect the hub and the bearing components*. The second interpretation is implicitly encoded in the second syntactic tag of the word *hub*.

In the case of the sequence *inspect bearing cups and cones*, represented by tree β in figure 2.26, the interpretation carried by the tree is *inspect bearing cups and bearing cones*. Contrary to tree α, no ambiguous tag retains the interpretation paraphrasable as *inspect the bearing cups and the cones*. This interpretation can be recovered thanks to the tree-matching procedure at the retrieval stage. It is retrieved by skipping the "residual" part *bearing cups* between the words *inspect* and *cones*.

Tree Matching

Since there is a certain loss of information in the process of normalization of syntactic trees into binary indexes, no index are produced in the Sheridan and Smeaton phrase matcher. Instead, a tree matching algorithm is developed to make judgments about the similarity of phrases at retrieval time.

The tree matcher is based on a reverse post-order tree traversal algorithm with possible approximate matches between leaf nodes or between syntactic nodes. At the lowest level the match occurs between two child nodes of a simple binary tree. The syntactic relationship between these nodes is then matched by comparing the parent nodes of the two nodes in the query and in the document. Finally, the residual structure lying between the two matched nodes is used to validate the match.[20] For example, in the matching of the query phrase *classification systems* and the textual utterance *the development of a classification schema using library system theory*, the possible identification of a head modifier relation between *system* and *classification* is invalidated by the presence of the verb *using* in the residual structure.

The second stage of the tree-matching procedure is the calculation of the scores to indicate the degree of match between two tree-structured representation. The recursive computation of the score relies on maximal scoring of exact matches and various inferior scores for approximate matches. The effectiveness of the tree matching procedure is evaluated through a comparison with human judgment. The test set consists of 32 queries and 288 artificially generated phrases that are close in some sense with the original queries. A *Spearman Correlation Coefficient* is calculated in order to evaluate the degree of overlap between the mean human ranking and the ranking provided by the algorithm. The average correlation value is high, but not as high as the authors had been expecting. Remaining errors are due partly to some differences between the task of a human judge and the task of the program, and partly to some insufficiencies of the program such as the inability to handle some types of variants.

Comments

The approach proposed in this study is original in the sense that it exploits the output of a syntactic analysis as it is, without attempting to derive indexing units.[21] The gamble is interesting because it avoids the loss of information that inevitably results from the simplification techniques used for transforming parse trees into binary or unary indexes. This radical approach is made legitimate through the provision of a flexible technique for matching parse trees and scoring approximate matches.

Term variants are implicitly considered in this algorithm through the observation of the residual structure, the textual sequence spanning between two matched words. An explicit description of variation would nevertheless provide a better understanding and a better description of the types of morphosyntactic relations that are allowed, or not, for tree matching. The challenge is difficult, as will become evident in the next chapters of this book.

Another innovative approach of the study is to exploit the output of a generic natural language shallow parser that was not conceived for this precise task. The Helsinki parser has two among the major qualities that are required for an exploitation in broad-coverage information retrieval: it is robust and efficient. The counterpart is that the resulting analyses still retain some amount of ambiguity and only provide partial surface dependencies, not genuine exhaustive phrases. These limitations are acceptable in an information retrieval framework.

From my own experience, it seems that it is not necessary to build a tree structure for comparing queries and text utterances. A comparison of text windows through equality of extreme words and pattern matching of syntactic tags assigned to intermediary words might suffice to calculate an efficient measure of similarity.

2.3.9   Sparck Jones and Tait Variant Generator

Synthetic Presentation

The purpose of the variant generator presented in Sparck Jones and Tait (1984a, b) is to parse a query, extract the terms from the query, generate a rich set of variants from these base terms, and exploit these variants in document retrieval by converting them into boolean queries.

The natural language parser is a generic analyzer that applies primitive-based semantic pattern matching in conjunction with conventional syntactic analysis (Boguraev and Sparck Jones 1984). Subparts of the syntacticosemantic parse trees of the queries are extracted and constitute the initial list of terms. Semantic and syntactic variants of these terms are generated and converted into strings. Ultimately each term variant is expressed as a boolean query.

Since it relies on a knowledge-intensive parser, the term variant generator was not applied to large-scale data. A preliminary evaluation on a small set of queries shows that the essential issue is to increase both the power of the parser and the coverage of the grammar.

Term Selection and Variant Generation

The selection of terms and the generation of semantic and syntactic variants are the two contributions of this study that are most relevant to term spotting through NLP. I therefore focus on these two aspects in the remainder of the presentation.

The extraction of terms and the generation of variants rely crucially on the output of Boguraev's parser. The parse trees are syntactic structures with thematic roles highlighting

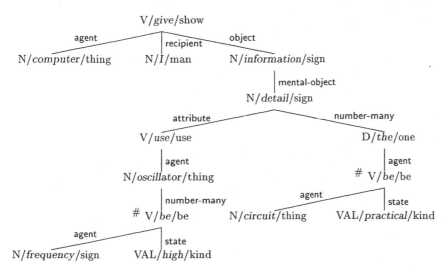

Figure 2.27
Simplified parse tree for the query *give me information about the practical circuit details of high frequency oscillators.*

the relation between a head node and its arguments. Figure 2.27 illustrates a parse tree from which superfluous features are removed. Each node is associated with a word from the query and is labeled with a triple composed of a syntactic category, a string, and a semantic label. The branches of the tree are labeled with thematic roles. The # tags indicate compound noun structures.

Term Extraction

The first step of the postprocessing of a parsed query is the selection of the multi-word candidate terms that are appropriate for retrieval purposes and that can be deduced from the semantic representation provided by the parser. The details of the mode of selections of the terms are not provided in Sparck Jones and Tait (1984a, b). The size of the candidate structure together with the semanticostructural characteristics of the parse tree seem to be the two major criteria for this selection. Parts of the query are deliberately ignored because they are expected to be irrelevant or unhelpful. (Here the part *give me information about* does not yield any candidate term.) Figure 2.28 illustrates three terms drawn from the parse tree of the sample query.

The second step of term extraction is the manipulation of candidate terms in order to obtain richer structures for variant production. For example, semantic relations are added on the

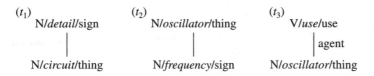

Figure 2.28
Three candidate terms extracted from the parse tree of figure 2.27.

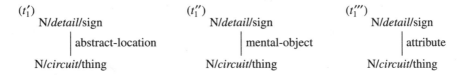

Figure 2.29
Three semantic variants of term (t_1) *circuit detail* from figure 2.28.

branches of the candidate terms that do not have one. Examples of addition of semantic labels to a candidate term are shown in figure 2.29. The approach to the reconstruction of semantic relations underlying compounds is not controlled and can lead to nonsensical results. Since these variants are matched on occurrences in documents, incorrect variants should not correspond to occurrences.

At this step more complex inferences can also be performed to prepare the generation of term variants at the next step. Inferences also include the addition of a preposition to a compound term, the link between a nominal form and a verbal one, etc.

Variant Generation

At this step the semantic representations are transformed into actual output text strings. The different syntactic methods for expressing each of the semantic variants are considered in turn. For example, *heavy components* and *components that are heavy* are generated as syntactic variants of the same unique semantic source.

The generation of syntactic variants is done in two steps. First, the semantic tree is converted into a syntactic tree with required word forms as syntactic leaves. Then the syntactic tree is converted into a word string. All the word strings corresponding to all the possible variants are collected and converted into a boolean query. The generation of syntactic variants accounts for inflectional variations, addition of definite or indefinite determiners, and even the production of synonyms. For example, the variants corresponding to the terms in figure 2.29 include *the details about the circuits*, *detail about the circuits*, *details about a circuit*, and *the detail of circuits*.

Comments

The term variant generator proposed by Sparck Jones and Tait is only evaluated on 10 queries and 11,429 abstracts, a relatively small test set. The results of the evaluation are not sufficiently convincing and are performed at a too small scale to justify investing the need for a knowledge-rich approach to information retrieval. The approach has, however, the merit to show that it is feasible to use a semanticosyntactic parser for extracting candidate terms and, then, to generate a wide range of variants of these terms. Better results would surely be obtained if a symmetric parsing of the corpus were performed, instead of generating boolean queries from term variants.

My opinion is that the technique proposed by Sparck Jones and Tait is too ambitious to be extended to a broad-domain application with large sets of documents. This approach assumes that it is feasible to provide exhaustive and complete semanticosyntactic analyses of queries and—possibly—of large corpora. To my knowledge, large-scale parsers for information extraction tend to use partial and stratified parsers dedicated to specific tasks (MUC-6 1995), instead of a huge knowledge-rich parser that covers all the constructions.

The other controversial aspect of this work is the lack of evaluation of the complexity that results from an exhaustive generation of term variations. Such an approach leads to two extreme positions, neither of which are satisfactory. If the coverage of the variants is exhaustive, the resulting volume of term variants is too huge to be computationally tractable. If, as in Sparck Jones and Tait (1984a, b), the number of variants is restricted to a set of 17 linguistic forms, then it is very unlikely that the whole range of possible variations is covered. Instead of an explicit and exhaustive generation of variants, use could be made of underspecified variations in order to limit the number of variant forms without decreasing the coverage of the generator.

2.3.10 *SPIRIT* System and Debili's Parser

This section describes a large project for the exploitation of natural language tools in information retrieval. The project includes several components derived from diverse areas of research. The focus is on one of its most novel modules, a dependency parser with an endogenous corpus-based acquisition of lexicosemantic restrictions that conflates semantically related dependencies. Before turning to the detailed description of the parser (Debili 1982), I first sketch the organization of the complete *SPIRIT* system (Andreewsky, Debili, and Fluhr 1977).

SPIRIT System

The general organization of *SPIRIT* is shown in figure 2.30. The input to the system is either a document or a natural language query. The output is a normalized text with single and multi-word weighted indexes that is passed to a retrieval engine.

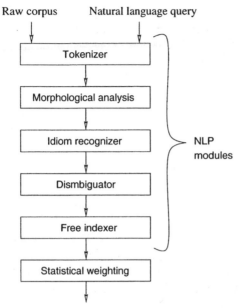

Figure 2.30
Flowchart of *SPIRIT*.

After tokenizing, each word in the text receives a noncontextual morphological analysis. The output is a list of lemmas with corresponding morphological features. For the purpose of considering morphological variants, each word is linked with the words in its derivational family. Thus *taxe* (tax) receives two analyses—a singular noun (a tax) or a verb (to tax)—and is linked to the words in the same family such as *taxation* (taxing) and *taxable* (taxable).

The third step is in charge of recognizing frozen expressions that are semantically opaque and can be considered as lexical atoms. These lexemes are mainly composed of complex prepositions such as *afin de* (so as to), complex conjunctions, and idiomatic verb phrases.

The next module contextually disambiguates the syntactic categories of words that receive multiple morphological analyses. The final natural language processor is called *compound recognition*. The purpose of this step is to highlight the significant elementary head-modifier dependencies and to extract the corresponding pairs of words. These relations are acquired through corpus-based discovery, which is described in the next section on the Debili's parser.

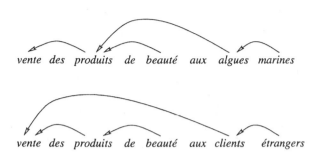

Figure 2.31
Two dependency-based representations of French noun phrases.

Finally, each index receives a weight based on its relative frequency in a given document. Weighted indexes are produced for the documents and the natural language queries. The distance between a query and a document is based on the number of common indexes, their weights, and the nature of the syntactic dependencies holding between these indexes. Let us now turn to a more detailed presentation of the final linguistic module for free indexing through the discovery of dependency relations.

Debili's Parser

Debili's (1982) parser is primarily based on Tesnière's notion of structural dependency (Tesnière 1959). In this model, words are connected by dependency relations, with each connection linking a superior word with an inferior one. A word can be simultaneously the superior word for one relation and the inferior one for another connection. Figure 2.31 shows the dependency-based representation of the sentences *vente de produits de beauté aux algues marines* (sale of beauty products from seaweed) and *vente de produits de beauté aux clients étrangers* (sale of beauty products to foreign customers).

Before calculating the dependency relations, the text is broken into syntactic chunks through finite-state filters, mainly verbal and nominal chunks. These chunks are as large as possible so as to cover as many words as possible in the parsed sentences. For example, the sentence [*Dans l'étude de toute contamination*]ₙ *il* [*convient de tenir compte*]ᵥ [*de l'importance relative de processus physico-chimiques et biologiques*]ₙ [*pouvant intervenir simultanément*]ᵥ[22] is split into two nominal and two verbal chunks and *il* (it) is the only word not covered by a chunk.

Then all the possible dependency relations in these chunks are produced by another set of filters. Each filter is specialized in the calculation of a specific type of dependency. Some are dedicated to the satellite dependencies such as the dependency between a determiner and a head word. Other filters, more important for information retrieval, generate dependencies

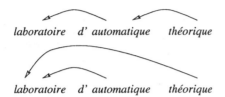

Figure 2.32
Two ambiguous dependency-based representations of the phrase *laboratoire d'automatique théorique* (laboratory of theoretical computing).

between head nouns and their modifiers such as the connection between a pre- or postnominal modifier and a head noun, the connection between several nouns in a complex noun phrase or between several verbs in a complex verb phrase. At this stage the attachments are not disambiguated if no syntactic evidence is likely to provide a clue for discarding incorrect dependencies. Thus *laboratoire d'automatique théorique* (laboratory of theoretical computing) receives an ambiguous reading in which the final adjective is linked to the two preceding nouns, although it only depends on *automatique* (computing) (figure 2.32).

The elements that are not linked to another word by dependency relations are head nouns. These are likely to be connected to a verb in the analysis of superior dependency relations.

When the production of dependency relations is achieved, words are morphologically analyzed through some kind of stemming procedure. Each word is decomposed into a stem and possible prefix and suffix. Words with the same stem are grouped into morphosemantic families, which are exploited in the next procedure.

As indicated above, the production of dependency relations yields more relations than are actually present in the text. The purpose of the last module is to discard the ambiguous relations. The technique relies on corpus-based acquisition of dependency relations and is similar to other approaches presented elsewhere in this chapter (*CLARIT* in section 2.3.1, *LEXTER* in section 2.2.3, and *TTP* in section 2.3.11). Where there is competition between two dependency relations, if one of both relations is found elsewhere in the corpus in a nonambiguous situation, the other relation is discarded. For example, if *automatique théorique* (theoretical computing) is encountered in the corpus, the dependency from *théorique* to *laboratoire* is rejected in favor of the dependency from *théorique* to *automatique*. Thus only the upper structure in figure 2.32 is retained as a valid representation of *laboratoire d'automatique théorique*.

During corpus-based learning, every time a nonambiguous situation is found, the corresponding dependency is learned. The interesting feature of Debili's corpus-based acquisition is that each learned dependency is extrapolated to the derivational family of the words found in the occurrence. For instance, if *affichage mural* (wall posting) is encountered in a

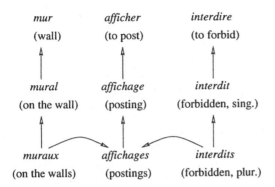

Figure 2.33
Generalized dependencies corresponding to the sentence *Les affichages sur les murs sont interdits* (postings on the walls are forbidden).

nonambiguous situation, this relation is acquired together with the relation between words in the same paradigms: *affichage sur les murs* (posting on the walls), *afficher sur les murs* (to post on the walls), etc. Figure 2.33 illustrates the double representation of a sentence along the syntagmatic axis (horizontal) and the paradigmatic axis (vertical).

Corpus-based acquisition is also a means for disambiguating polysemous words by collecting similar dependencies of synonymous words elsewhere in the corpus. Thus the sentence *le bail expire* (the lease expires) is ambiguous because *expire* means either *to exhaust*, *to die*, or *to finish*. The observation of the nonambiguous sentence *le bail cesse* (the lease stops) argues in favor of the last meaning of *to expire* in the preceding sample sentence.

Comments

The techniques proposed in *SPIRIT* and in Debili's parser are original and innovative. The approach to NLP relies on a notion of dependency instead of the now classical Chomskian notion of embedded tree structures. Several techniques that were more fully studied later are introduced in this work: for example, chunk parsing (Abney 1991), dependency-based parsing in *Constraint Grammar* (Karlsson et al. 1995), endogenous disambiguation (Strzalkowski and Vauthey 1992; Bourigault 1994), and corpus-based acquisition of selectional restrictions (Resnik 1993 sec. 5.5).

The model proposes original solutions to the various levels of NLP: morphology through stemming and recomposition of derivational families, syntax through an overgeneration of dependency links, and semantics through corpus-based disambiguation. Unfortunately, the generation of phrase indexes and their weighting schemes are not sufficiently detailed to give a precise idea of the links with the linguistic procedures.

2.3.11 *TTP* Robust Parser

Synthetic Presentation

The *TTP* parser is a robust and accurate natural language parser of English based on the Linguistic String Grammar developed by Sager (1981). The output of the parser is a normalized representation of each sentence that encompasses predicate argument relations (Strzalkowski and Vauthey 1992; Strzalkowski 1994; Strzalkowski 1995). The parser succeeds in achieving an efficient in-depth parse of the linguistic data through a skip-and-fit recovery strategy that allows it to efficiently parse ill-formed inputs or structures not covered by the grammar (Strzalkowski and Scheyen 1996). Although some alternative analysis of a sentence can be lost through this recovery process, the gain in speed and robustness of the parser greatly compensates the slight lack of completeness.

From the syntactic analysis of sentences, head-modifier pairs are extracted that are likely to be phrase indexes for the document. Ultimately head-modifier pairs are also used as contexts for computing similarities between terms and organizing them into clusters used for automatic query expansion.

The *TTP* Parser

The *TTP* Parser consists of a sequence of NLP programs that perform part-of-speech tagging, dictionary-based lemmatizing, and syntactic parsing. In addition, similarities between terms are calculated on the basis of syntactic regularities and are used for building clusters of similar terms. Only the natural language components, and more specifically the parser, are described here into detail. The general organization of the tool is shown by figure 2.34.

The first two stages of text processing by *TTP* consist of part-of-speech tagging and dictionary-based morphological analysis. The role of part-of-speech tagging is to facilitate the syntactic analysis performed by the parser by associating each word with a unique syntactic category. The role of morphological normalization is to conflate morphological variants in order to improve recall in information access. Two tasks are essentially performed during morphological normalization: (1) inflected words must be reduced to their base form (singular for nouns, infinitive for verbs), and (2) nominalized verb forms must be reduced to the root of the corresponding verb (e.g., *implementation* is reduced to *implement*). Task 2 is performed through the removal of regular suffixes and a lexical lookup for checking whether the corresponding stem is a verb in the dictionary. The output of these two steps is given in the first three lines of table 2.13.

The *TTP* parser relies on a large and comprehensive grammar of the English language, the *Linguistic String Grammar* (Sager 1981), complemented by subcategorization information extracted from the *Oxford Advanced Learner's Dictionary*. The *TTP* parser is designed to process large quantities of unrestricted text. The parser is accurate, thanks to the rich

Raw corpus

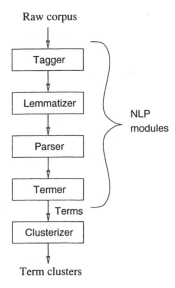

Figure 2.34
Flow-chart of *TTP*.

linguistic data exploited during the analysis. A skip-and-fit recovery mechanism allows interruption of the parse of a constituent if the parse is not achieved within a preset amount of time. When this occurs, the parser ignores fragments of the input sentence and resumes normal processing after skipping a few words.

An illustration of the recovery mechanism on the NP-*to*-VP complements associated with verbs is the verb *to urge* as in the sentence *urge* [*those flying to New York*]$_{\rm NP}$ *to* [*take*]$_{\rm VP}$. This construction is too long to parse because of the ambiguous syntactic roles of the two prepositions *to*. If the subject noun phrase *those flying* of the NP-*to*-VP is timed out, the parser jumps over the segment *those flying to New York* until it encounters the closest verb, here *to take*, an element that can serve as a starter for parsing the remaining constituent *to*-VP.

TTP Termer

The output of the parser, illustrated by the fourth layer of table 2.13, stresses the head-modifier relations. In the sample output, the two modifiers of the noun *president* are *former* and *soviet*. At the verb level, subject and complements are distinguished. The noun *tank* is the subject and *Wisconsin* is the complement of the verb *to invade*.

These head-modifier relationships are used by the termer for producing binary terms according to the following rules. A binary term is composed of one of the four pairs:

Table 2.13
A sample parse by *TTP* and corresponding index terms

Input sentence
The former Soviet president has been a local hero ever since a Russian tank invaded Wisconsin.

Tagged sentence
The/dt *former*/jj *Soviet*/jj *president*/nn *has*/vbz *been*/vbn *a*/dt *local*/jj *hero*/nn *ever*/rb *since*/in *a*/dt *Russian*/jj *tank*/nn *invaded*/vbd *Wisconsin*/np *.*/per

---

Tagged and lemmatized sentence
the/dt *former*/jj *soviet*/jj *president*/nn *have*/vbz *be*/vbn *a*/dt *local*/jj *hero*/nn *ever*/rb *since*/in *a*/dt *russian*/jj *tank*/nn *invade*/vbd *wisconsin*/np *.*/per

---

Parsed sentence
```
[assert
  [[perf [HAVE]] [[verb [BE]]
    [subject [np [n PRESIDENT] [t_pos THE]
             [adj [FORMER]] [adj [SOVIET]]]]
    [object [np [n HERO] pt_pas A] [adj [LOCAL]]]
    [adv EVER]
    [sub_ord [SINCE
             [[verb [INVADE]]
               [subject [np [n TANK] [t_pos A]
                 [adj [RUSSIAN]]]]
               [object [np [name [WISCONSIN]]]]]]]]]]]]]
```

Terms

president	*soviet*	*hero*	*hero local*
president soviet	*president former*	*tank invade*	*tank russian*
invade	*tank*	*russian*	*wisconsin*
invade wisconsin			

---

1. The head noun of a noun phrase and its left noun or adjective modifier, here *president former* and *president soviet*.

2. The head noun of a noun phrase and the head of its right adjunct, for example, *the organization of social groups and communities* produces *group organization* and *community organization*.

3. The main verb of a clause and the head of its object phrase, here *invade Wisconsin*.

4. The head of the subject phrase and the main verb, here *tank invade*.

The parser does not perform the disambiguation of noun phrase modifier attachments in case of multiple modifiers. For example, both noun phrases *natural language processing* and *dynamic information processing* receive the same analysis: a head noun with a nominal and an adjectival modifier. The structure is nevertheless syntactically and semantically ambiguous because the rightmost adjective can be attached to the nominal modifier or to the head noun. This situation is not desirable since a correct generation of terms depends on a correct disambiguation of modifier attachments. For example, from

[[*natural language*] *processing*]   (2.30)

the correctly disambiguated structure of *natural language processing*, the termer generates the two correct binary terms *natural language* and *language processing* and is prevented from generating the incorrect term *natural processing*.

Noun phrase attachments are disambiguated through a corpus-based investigation technique similar to the endogenous disambiguation proposed by Bourigault (1994) in section 2.2.3 or by Debili's Debili (1982) parser in section 2.3.10. First, all the possible subphrases of each ambiguous compound are generated. Then, distributional statistics are gathered from unambiguous noun phrases in the document and the statistically preferential constructions are selected. In the preceding example, the three subphrases *natural language*, *language processing*, and *natural processing* are generated. If the two former phrases occur more frequently in unambiguous configurations than the latter one, the correctly disambiguated structure (2.30) is proposed. (More about the structural disambiguation of noun phrases is given in section 6.2.2.)

Comments

The *TTP* parser is a fully integrated exploitation of a natural language parser in information retrieval. The task is difficult because it requires a wide-coverage grammar—sufficiently accurate to extract correct head-modifier relations from a wide variety of constructions— and an efficient parser equipped with procedures for recovering from ill-formed inputs or complex constructions that tend to slow down the processes. Through a skip-and-fit recovering procedure and the exploitation of a large grammar and a large lexicon, the parser provides an elegant trade-off between efficiency and accuracy. It belongs to the family of large-scale parsers that can cope robustly with large corpora such as *Slot Grammar* (McCord 1980, 1990), Debili's parser (Debili 1982), *Fiddicht* (Hindle 1983), or *Sextant parser* (Grefenstette 1994b).

Since the purpose of the parser is to generate relevant index terms, an approach that would retain ambiguities or that would generate all the possible variants would not be appropriate for the task at hand. The disambiguation is nevertheless not achieved during the parsing stage. An additional module for endogenous disambiguation resolves structural ambiguities with the help of nonambiguous situations. The combination of text preprocessing, parsing, and statistical disambiguation yields rich and unambiguous parse trees that can be used for automatic indexing, term acquisition, and observation of distributional regularities for the purpose of term classification. The drawback of such an integrated approach combining different techniques is its lack of insight in the linguistic mechanisms and a precise evaluation of the parser with respect to the parsing task per se.

The final results of the information retrieval experiments combine all the stages of automatic indexing and document retrieval: parsing, term generation, term weighting, document retrieval, and query expansion. They do not illustrate how the parser copes with complex sentences, whether it actually succeeds in conflating verb phrases and noun phrases whose head words belong to the same derivational family, whether it actually exploits all the dependencies in each sentence, or whether it correctly processes complex structures such as complex coordinations.

Despite this lack of linguistic evaluation, the *TTP* parser is undeniably one of the most important contributions to the exploitation of rich NLP tools in information retrieval.

2.3.12 Synthesis of Phrase Indexing

The various tools used for phrase indexing are much more heterogeneous than the tools used for term acquisition. The reason is that most natural language indexers are generic parsers that are tailored to the task of automatic indexing. The many competing traditions in natural language processing are mirrored by the diversity of tools for NLP-based automatic indexing.

Table 2.14 gives the major characteristics of the eleven indexers described in this section. The first two lines provide details about word processing: morphological analysis through dictionary lookup or stemming through suffix stripping. The third lines gives the nature of the part-of-speech disambiguator: linguistic rules or probabilistic language models. The next three lines indicate the type of structure used for grouping words with syntactic and semantic relations: labeled text chunks, dependency structures, or phrase structures. The seventh line indicates whether structural ambiguities are resolved. The last two lines of the table indicate whether term variation is taken into consideration by the indexer so as to conflate all the observed linguistic variants of each unique concept or, conversely, to generate all the possible variants of each single term.

In my opinion, the three main relevant characteristics differentiating the termers are (1) the depth of the morphological analysis, whether restricted to inflectional morphology or extended to derivational morphology, (2) the nature of the structural description, whether text fragments, interword links, or traditional phrase structures, and (3) the possible concern for term variations. These three characteristics are deeply interrelated because the nature of term conflation depends on the type of linguistic features provided by the morphological and syntactic modules.

Table 2.14
Comparative features of the different indexers

		CLARIT	COP	COPSY	Fagan	FASIT	IRENA
1	Morphological analysis	×	?		×		
2	Stemming		?	×		×	×
3	P-o-s disambiguation	Probabilities	?			Rules	
4	Chunks	×					
5	Dependency relations		×	×			×
6	Phrase structures	×	×		×		×
7	Structural disambiguation	×					
8	Variant generation						
9	Variant conflation	×		×	×	×	×
10	Language	En	En	En	En	En	En

		NPtool	Sheridan and Smeaton	Sparck Jones and Tait	SPIRIT	TTP
1	Morphological analysis	×	×	?	×	×
2	Stemming			?		
3	P-o-s disambiguation	Rules	Rules	?	Rules	Probabilities
4	Chunks				×	
5	Dependency relations	×	×		×	
6	Phrase structures		×	×		×
7	Structural disambiguation				×	×
8	Variant generation			×		
9	Variant conflation		×		×	
10	Language	En	En	En	Fr	En

The preceding table does not account for the scalability of the tools to large corpora and various domains. This issue is, however, crucial for indexers that must handle huge amounts of textual data. The overall impression is that efficiency is considered as a central issue by most studies—even by the most fundamental ones such as the *Constituent Object Parser*. The concern for efficiency certainly influences the technical choices made for designing the natural language processors used in these studies:

1. Theoretical approaches to natural language processing, such as *Generalized Phrase Structure Grammar* (*GPSG*) (Gazdar et al. 1985) or *Head Driven Phrase Structure Grammar* (*HPSG*) (Pollard and Sag 1987), are underrepresented, while efficient techniques such as tagging or shallow natural language parsing are the main stream.

2. Since stemming is quasi-systematically exploited in automatic indexing, most natural language processors for information retrieval are equipped with a rich morphological component addressing both inflectional and derivational morphology.

3. Semantic analysis is generally reduced to structural disambiguation through statistics or corpus-based acquisition. Knowledge-intensive semantic analysis is not considered as a realistic target for automatic indexing, except for Sparck Jones and Tait's (1984a, b) approach.

4. Variation appears to be much more frequently addressed in NLP for information retrieval than in other domains of NLP.

The most plausible explanation for the important role given to variation is that a variationist approach to language is a differential (or relative) description which is much more manageable for large-scale applications than absolute descriptions. Instead of providing the exact syntactic or semantic analysis of a linguistic utterance, variation-based analysis ascertains whether two occurrences are sufficiently similar to be conflated. Furthermore a variationist description facilitates a subsequent classification of the information extracted from corpora, whether for term acquisition or for automatic indexing. Variation appears to be an elegant alternative to traditional exhaustive analyses because it combines descriptive economy and computational efficiency without significant loss of accuracy.

2.4 *FASTR*, Exploiting Term Variation in Term Spotting

The remaining chapters of the book present *FASTR* which is a natural language processor designed for the recognition of terms within large corpora. The main original feature of *FASTR* is its basic mechanism for term identification: a transformational variant generator through which terms are dynamically transformed into variant structures. These partially instantiated structures are ultimately exploited for extracting occurrences of term variants from texts.

Contrary to grammar-based approaches to automatic indexing, such as the *COP* (section 2.3.2), term recognition in *FASTR* only relies on a partial and local analysis of the sentences. It is therefore efficient enough to be applied to large volumes of textual and terminological data. Contrary to dependency-based analyses, such as *COPSY* (section 2.3.3), *FASTR* offers a full-fledged unification formalism that can describe various types of constraints such as semantic features and agreement constraints. It is therefore accurate enough to accept correct variants and reject spurious occurrences through the exploitation of appropriate linguistic constraints.

Because meta-grammatical data is tuned gradually, the problem of handling the amount of linguistic information needed for the application is manageable. Contrary to full semantic analyses of variation such a Sparck Jones and Tait (1984a, b), the linguistic knowledge in *FASTR* can be gradually enriched through the progressive addition of new constraints according to the successes and failures of the parser. Thus, when compared with the studies presented in this chapter, *FASTR* proposes an original compromise of accuracy and efficiency well suited to provide high-quality results on real-world data.

The identification of term variants plays a key role in my term-spotting technique because each concept in a domain can be expressed through a wide variety of linguistic forms. Variation is not a peripheral symptom, it is a pervasive phenomenon in terminological linguistics. As will be shown in the quantitative evaluations of term variants reported in the remainder of this book, syntactic and morphosyntactic represent respectively 25 and 15% of term occurrences. This book shows that since terminological linguistics is deeply concerned with variation, it makes sense to build an indexer on a variational mechanism instead of a phrase builder.

3 Terms

In order to achieve the recognition of terms within corpora *FASTR* relies on two levels of description:

1. A terminological level in which terms are represented by syntactic structures.

2. A metaterminological level in which variations are implemented by local rules that transform term structures into term variant structures.

This chapter is dedicated to the first level. The following chapter describes term variations.

Term spotting calls for the use of various linguistic features. As outlined by Shieber (1986), a unification-based formalism offers an expressive and flexible framework for the description of complex and heterogeneous linguistic data. Following this argument, a logical representation of terminological data is used in *FASTR* and presented in section 3.1. Section 3.2 is dedicated to term morphology. Section 3.3 focuses on the representation of term syntax. Section 3.4 sums up how these two components interact in order to perform term recognition within textual data. Finally, section 3.5 details the implementation of the parser and its decomposition into specialized NLP modules.

3.1 *FASTR* Formalism

3.1.1 Grammatical Formalism

Finite-state machines are often presented as the neat solution for processing large-scale textual and lexical data (Roche and Schabes 1997b). For example, in the *INTEX* system used for compound noun recognition (Silberztein 1993), single words and compound words are represented by transducers. Various techniques allow for data compression and efficiency optimization of these machines; this makes them very attractive for industrial applications of NLP (Mohri 1997). Finite-state machines can also be used for implementing simple grammars, which are based on a notion of syntactic dependency between a head noun and its modifiers. For example, Tapanainen and Järvinen (1994) propose a parser for the *Constraint Grammar* of Karlsson (1990) based on finite-state automata. Such a computational framework is well adapted for (pre-)industrial systems for which only a slight amount of tuning is necessary.

In the case of term extraction, I am working in a domain for which few linguistic studies are available. What are the linguistic patterns for term variations? What is the scope of the dependencies? What are the relevant features for variant recognition? Since many questions of this sort remain open, it is important to design a flexible a tool. *FASTR* was first designed as a finite-state automaton. The constant evolution of the tool in response to the demands of handling more complex linguistic phenomena led me to the rewriting of *FASTR* in a unification-based framework. The formalism *PATR-II* of Shieber (1986) and the parser

OLMES for compound adverb analysis of Habert (1991) were two sources of inspiration for the transformation of *FASTR* into a unification-based grammar.

The major drawback to the use of a descriptively powerful unification-based formalism is its computational inefficiency. The unification of two feature structures with disjunction is an $\mathcal{NP}$-complete problem (Kasper and Rounds 1986). Another disadvantage of unification grammars is their lack of modularity. The writing of a unification grammar with recursive rules can result in a complex architecture, a house of cards in which the modification of one of the rules can have unpredictable consequences on the balance of the whole parser. However, a grammar of terms is very shallow grammar with few or no recursive dependencies between terms. Therefore a grammar of terms can be written in a unification-based formalism without suffering from the maintainability problems associated with deep recursive grammars. My desire to handle large volumes of textual and terminological data makes efficiency a crucial factor. Therefore my efforts have focused of the optimization of the parser so that I can simultaneously enjoy the "descriptive felicity" and not suffer from the "innate inefficiency" of unification. These goals will allow me to tackle the problem of optimizing the parser in section 3.5.4.

3.1.2   A Two-Level Feature-Based Formalism

The major application of term spotting within corpora is automatic indexing. This application is typically more concerned with the conceptual content of text utterances than with their actual linguistic form. In order to conflate the various forms of a concept, each concept is made to correspond with a unique linguistic form, and all the other linguistic utterances that denote the same concept are taken as variants of the original term. (My descriptive organization is thus similar to the separation between concept identifiers and linguistic forms which is used in thesauri such as *UMLS* 1995.)

As stated at the start of chapter 1, definition 1.1, syntactic, morphosyntactic, and semantic variations are sufficient for a proper filtering of correct variants.[23] I do not need to rely on an exhaustive semantic description of terms and their constituents. Following Habert (1982), I can decompose the description of variants at the *paradigmatic* and *syntagmatic* *levels*. Structural transformations are described at the syntagmatic level. Morphological and semantic relationships between lemmas are provided at the paradigmatic level. No absolute semantic description is required. My approach to term variation is differential are relies solely on the combination of structural transformation with lexical relationships. These two descriptive dimensions are embedded in metarules which generate term variants from term rules. The set of metarules for a given language build up the *metagrammar* of this language.

Metarules operate on term rules which build up the *grammar* corresponding to a given controlled vocabulary. These terminological data are divided into a single-word rules and a multi-word term rules. The formal specification of the information system described in this chapter and the following one is given with the Z formalism (Diller 1994; Spivey 1994) in Jacquemin (1997b, app. A).

I now turn to the description of the formal language used for describing grammatical data in *FASTR*. Then some additional details about the mathematical grounding will be provided.

Formal Language

The language used by *FASTR* for representing term rules is inspired by *PATR-II* (Shieber 1986), in which grammar rules are composed of a *context-free skeleton* that denotes the constituent structure of the terms and *logical constraints* that denote the information linked to the constituents (feature structures).

The following rules (3.1) and (3.2) describe respectively the single noun *artery* and the term *Umbilical artery*. In rule (3.2), the context-free skeleton of the term rule is restricted to *immediate dependency*. Trees of depth greater than 1, however, can also be described in this framework (see below rule 3.4). The equations between paths following the context-free skeleton are descriptions of feature structures, which are the key component of unification-based formalisms (Carpenter 1992). Feature structures are represented straightforwardly by *directed acyclic graphs* such as the one shown in figure 3.1.

Word *'arter'*: $\qquad\qquad$ (3.1)

$\langle cat \rangle \doteq \text{`}N\text{'}$

$\langle inflection \rangle \doteq 2.$

Rule $N_1 \rightarrow A_2\ N_3$: $\qquad\qquad$ (3.2)

$\langle N_1\ lexicalization \rangle \doteq N_3$

$\langle A_3\ lemma \rangle \doteq \text{`umbilical'}$

$\langle A_3\ inflection \rangle \doteq 1$

$\langle N_3\ lemma \rangle \doteq \text{`arter'}$

$\langle N_2\ inflection \rangle \doteq 2$

$\langle N_1\ agreement \rangle \doteq \langle N_3\ agreement \rangle.$

Rule (3.1) describes the noun *artery* whose canonical root is *arter* and whose inflectional paradigm is 2. The construction of the inflections of this noun from its lemma and its inflection number are described in section 3.2.1.

Rule (3.2) describes an Adjective-Noun term, whose syntactic head N_1 share the *agreement* features with the head noun N_3. The identification of the lemmas building this term relies on a key composed of the values of the three features *cat*,[24] *lemma*,[25] and *inflection*:

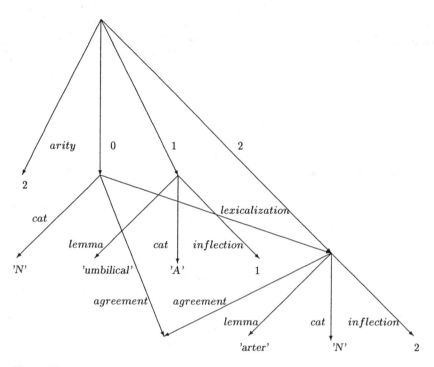

Figure 3.1
Graphical representation of rule (3.2).

each lemma is identified uniquely by a triple composed of the values of these three features. (See the specification of *FASTR* in Jacquemin 1997b, app. A, and the link between feature structures and *n*-ary relations in Véronis 1992.)

By the constraints for single-word and term rules, each rule is associated with a feature structure. The feature structure of single-word rules is attached to the root of the rules, whereas the feature structures of term rules are distributed over their syntactic structure. In order to represent these feature-enriched syntactic structures, I use the notation of Shieber (1992). Any rule of *arity n* is converted into a unique description by adding the features $0, 1, \ldots, n$ and a feature *arity*. The feature structure linked to the root node of the term structure is the value of the feature 0; the features of the *n* constituents are the values of the arcs labeled 1 to *n*. The graph shown in figure 3.1 represents the least specific feature structure denoted by rule (3.2) of *Umbilical artery*. The corresponding *attribute-value matrix* is given by figure 3.2. The nodes shared by more than one arc are indicated by boxed numerical tags.

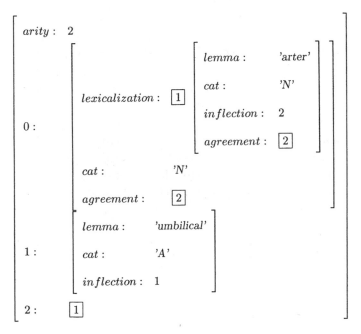

Figure 3.2
Matrix representing the feature structure of rule (3.2).

Mathematical Grounding

The description of feature structures in *PATR-II* is based on two types of equalities: $path \doteq value$ or $path \doteq path$ (Shieber 1992). A graph satisfies an equation $path \doteq path$ if and only if the node reached by traversing the arcs of the first path is identical to the node reached by traversing the arcs of the second path. Similarly an equation $path \doteq value$ is satisfied if and only if the node reached by this path is labeled by this value. For example, the equation $\langle N_1\ agreement \rangle \doteq \langle N_3\ agreement \rangle$ of rule (3.2) is denoted by a unique node at the end of paths $\langle 0\ agreement \rangle$ and $\langle 2\ agreement \rangle$ in figure 3.1.

The feature structure denoted by a set of logical formulas such as rule (3.2) is the minimal structure (with respect to subsumption) satisfying these constraints. This logical model and its interpretation by graphs (or automata) are developed in Rounds and Kasper (1986). The model is extended to describe hierarchical typed feature by Kasper (1993). In this way, together with negation and implication, these formalisms are brought closer to terminological logics, and thus, the descriptive framework becomes more open and flexible. An overview of the main recent trends in constraint-based formalisms is reported in Rupp, Rosner, and Johnson (1994).

Feature Propagation

The agreement constraint $\langle N_1 \; agreement \rangle \; \doteq \; \langle N_3 \; agreement \rangle$ is used for sharing (head) features between the lexical head N_1 and its projection N_3 (Pollard and Sag 1987 p. 58). By this constraint the syntactic phrase *Umbilical artery* is analyzed as a nominal phrase whose agreement features are equal to the agreement features of *artery*. In the structure *stenosis of the [umbilical artery]*, the bracketed term is considered as a singular noun phrase.

This mechanism of automatic feature percolation is a common characteristic of the classical unification-based formalisms such as *GPSG* (Gazdar et al. 1985) or *HPSG* (Pollard and Sag 1987). However, in deverbal compounds such as *Pull-in*, *Take off*, or *Nose bleed*, the categorial endocentricity is lost: the head noun is a verb, whereas the phrase is nominal. Since feature percolation cannot be performed automatically, it is desirable to offer a framework in which the dependency between a head and its projection is explicitly stated (Barbaud 1994).

3.1.3   Formalism with Disjunction and Negation

In tuning the metagrammar to variations in English, the formalism of *FASTR* takes advantage of two additional facilities: disjunction and negation.

Disjunction

Disjunctions in *FASTR* can be expressed in both parts of a rule: its context-free skeleton or its feature structure. When formulated within a feature structure, disjunction must be restricted to values. (This restriction of disjunction is common in unification-based formalisms; see Kasper 1993.) Rule (3.3), for example, is a compact representation of a word with two alternative inflectional paradigms, 1 or 6. This rule corresponds to the word *formula*, which accepts two plural forms *formulas* and *formulæ*. Disjunction in context-free skeletons amounts to the formulation of alternate phrase structures; each is tried in turn by the parser. Rule (3.4) is a condensed description of both terms *Regulation of temperature* and *Regulation of [blood pressure]*.

Word *'formula'*:   (3.3)

$\langle cat \rangle \; \doteq \; 'N'$

$\langle inflection \rangle \; \doteq \; 1 \mid 6.$

Rule $N_1 \rightarrow N_2 \; P_3 \; (N_4 = (N_5 + (N_6 \rightarrow N_7 \; N_8)))$:   (3.4)

$\langle N_1 \; lexicalization \rangle \; \doteq \; N_2$

$\langle N_2 \; lemma \rangle \; \doteq \; 'regulation'$

$\langle N_2 \; inflection \rangle \; \doteq \; 1$

$\langle P_3 \; lemma \rangle \; \doteq \; 'of'$

$\langle N_5 \; lemma \rangle \; \doteq \; \textit{`temperature'}$

$\langle N_5 \; inflection \rangle \; \doteq \; 1$

$\langle N_7 \; lemma \rangle \; \doteq \; \textit{`blood'}$

$\langle N_7 \; inflection \rangle \; \doteq \; 1$

$\langle N_8 \; lemma \rangle \; \doteq \; \textit{`pressure'}$

$\langle N_8 \; inflection \rangle \; \doteq \; 1$

$\langle N_1 \; agreement \rangle \; \doteq \; \langle N_2 \; agreement \rangle$

$\langle N_4 \; agreement \rangle \; \doteq \; \langle N_5 \; agreement \rangle \; \doteq \; \langle N_6 \; agreement \rangle \; \doteq \; \langle N_8 \; agreement \rangle.$

Any rule containing disjunctions is equivalent to a set of rules without disjunction. This set is calculated by transforming the feature structure into a disjunctive form with all the disjunctions on the root node. Consequently disjunction does not increase the descriptive power of a formalism; it only allows the writing of more concise grammars. The suppression of disjunction would significantly increase the size of the metagrammar and would eventually result in an unmaintainable set of metarules.

Negation

Negation is an additional facility of *FASTR* that allows for the expression of negative constraints such as the rejection of some words in the description of a variation (see section 5.4). However, the property of *monotonicity* is lost through the addition of negation to the logical description of feature structures (Carpenter 1992, p. 56). The notion of monotonicity is that if a feature structure satisfies a description, then adding more information results in a feature structure that still satisfies the description. To take an example of the lost of monotonicity through negation, consider a feature structure S with an undefined feature *cat* that satisfies the inequality $\phi : \neg(cat \doteq \textit{`A'})$. Now consider a feature structure, $S'$ subsumed by $S$, whose feature *cat* is equal to *`A'*. The structure S' does not satisfy ϕ.

In NLP it can be assumed that there are a finite number of paths and that these paths only have finite sets of values. In this case the inequality $\neg(path \doteq value)$ is interpreted as a disjunction of equalities with all the possible values of *path*, excluding *value*. In the context of *Constraint Logic Programming* (Colmerauer 1984), this means that *path* cannot be equal to *value*, no matter what unification is performed. Of course, several negations can be stated for the same path in the same set of equations; a conjunction of negations is interpreted as a negation of a disjunction.

Negation can be formally defined through typed feature structures (Carpenter 1992, ch. 7). Types are associated with features through the notion of *appropriateness*, which amounts to specifying features that are appropriate for each type and providing enforced restrictions for their values. The negation of typed features defined by Carpenter (1992) is called *abbreviatory negation.* Where there are inequalities between paths and values, abbreviatory negation can be interpreted as a disjunction of inequalities (through the transformation into a disjunctive normal form where all the disjunctions are at the top level). Paths associated with inequalities can receive any value accepted by the corresponding type except those stated in the inequalities (Kasper 1993). Where the set of associated values is large, it is indeed faster to enumerate a few rejected values than a large set of licensed ones—this is the motivation for naming this negation "abbreviatory."

For the implementation of *FASTR*, a method similar to that found in Colmerauer (1984) was chosen. Some features such as *lemma* are too large to be explicitly enumerated in case of negation. It suffices to memorize the set of disallowed values for each node affected by negation. Subsequent unifications are successful only if these nodes never become equal to one of the unlicensed values.

3.2   Morphology

Although inflectional and derivational morphology can be fully described through metarules (Jacquemin 1997b, sec. IV.2.d), I adopt here a presentation that mirrors the actual implementation in *FASTR*.

3.2.1   Inflectional Morphology

The morphological model of *FASTR* is a concatenative morphology enriched with feature structures similar to the rule-based description of Alshawi (1992) or Anick and Artemieff (1992). The basic notion is the concept of *inflectional paradigm*: a set of words sharing the same suffixes for the same set of declensions. An inflectional paradigm is defined as a unique pair composed of a syntactic category and an inflectional number. Morphological analysis is built on the following data (more explicitly stated in Jacquemin 1997b, app. A):

1. Lexical rules describing lemmas, such as rule (3.1) of *artery*.

2. Inflectional feature structures associated with each inflected lexical category, as in (3.5) for nouns.

3. Lists of suffixes associated with each inflectional paradigm, as in (3.6) for nouns of inflectional numbers 1, 2, 3, 4, 5, and 6.

Savoy (1993) uses a similar description for French in morphologically based stemming. The aim here is more complex than stemming. Morphological data are collected through morphological analysis for later use in syntactic analysis. Thus the feature structures delivered by the morphological step are fully compatible with the features used by the syntactic step, and they interact with them in order to ensure a proper synergy between morphology and syntax. Recent versions of *FASTR* demonstrate that the morphological step can be skipped if the corpus is morphologically analyzed and each word is associated with a feature structure (Jacquemin, Klavans, and Tzoukermann 1997; see also chapter 7).

Let us illustrate the three preceding sets of data for the lemma *artery*: rule (3.1) describes a nominal lemma whose *canonical root* is *arter* and whose inflectional number is 2. The canonical root is the string from which inflections are built through the concatenation of appropriate suffixes.[26] The alternative approach in concatenative morphology is to use *reference roots* with which inflections are built through affix stripping followed by affix addition (Silberztein 1993). An implementation through canonical roots is chosen in *FASTR* because it is more efficient. The full procedure is described in section 3.5.

The feature structures corresponding to the two inflections of nouns in English are given by

Inflected category N(2)   (3.5)

N[1]⟨*agreement number*⟩ ≐ *'singular'*.

N[2]⟨*agreement number*⟩ ≐ *'plural'*.

The different declensional paradigms of nouns are given by concatenating the suffixes of (3.6) and the canonical roots. The first line is a comment, and the second one corresponds to the inflectional paradigm of nouns whose inflectional number is 1: nouns whose singular is equal to the canonical root and whose plural is built by adding an inflectional suffix *s*:

Suffixes N   (3.6)

"dog / dogs"

N[1]   0   *s*

"accuracy / accuracies"

N[2]   *y   ies*

"approach / approaches"

N[3]   0   *es*

"linguistics / linguistics"

N[4]   0   *

"mouse / mice"

N[5]   0   ?1

"formula / formulae"

N[6]   0   *e*

Since its inflectional number is 2, the suffix list of N[2] is used to build the inflections of the canonical root *arter*. The string of its plural is *arter-ies* (the feature of the path $\langle string \rangle$); the corresponding feature structure is obtained by unifying the feature structure of the lemma and the second feature structure of (3.5). The attribute-value matrix of the resulting inflected word is illustrated by

$$
0 : \begin{bmatrix} \begin{bmatrix} lemma : & \text{'arter'} \\ string : & \text{'arteries'} \\ cat : & \text{'N'} \\ inflection : & 2 \\ agreement : & [number : \text{'plural'}] \end{bmatrix} \end{bmatrix}
\tag{3.7}
$$

Four metacharacters are available for describing inflectional paradigms:

0 stands for the empty suffix.

! indicates a reduplication of the last letter of the root.

∗ is used to mark unrealized inflections.

? stands in front of an integer n to use the nth auxiliary root instead of the canonical root.

As an illustration of the meta-character ∗, the fourth declensional paradigm of nouns correspond to nouns without plural. This restriction can also be formulated by adding a feature

$\langle agreement\ number \rangle \ \doteq\ $ 'singular'

to the rule of the corresponding lemmas in order to make unification fail for the plural inflection. Nouns, whose inflectional number is 5, have their plural equal to their first auxiliary root. Words with irregular declensions are grouped into specific paradigms, and auxiliary root(s) are linked to their lemma through the feature *auxiliary_root*. *Mouse* belongs to this paradigm because its canonical root would be reduced to the string *m* without the call for an auxiliary root. This mechanism appears to be particularly useful for languages with a rich declensional morphology such as French or Spanish (Tzoukermann and Liberman 1990). The rule for *mouse* is given by

Word *'mouse'*:   (3.8)

$\langle cat \rangle \ \doteq\ $ 'N'

$\langle auxiliary_root \rangle \ \doteq\ $ ('mice')

$\langle inflection \rangle \ \doteq\ 5.$

3.2.2 Derivational Morphology

After Bauer (1983), the derivation is the morphological process that results in the formation of new lexemes through affixation. In English the two main modes of affixation are suffixing and prefixing.

In *FASTR* there are two ways for describing derivational morphology: a *dynamic* method that is very similar to inflectional morphology and a *static* method in which derivational links are explicitly stated in the single word lexicon and a list of suffixes is used to derive inflected forms from stems.

Dynamic Derivational Morphology

A *derivational paradigm* is a family of words with similar derivational constructions. The description of derivational morphology consists of lexical rules in which words with derivatives have a feature *derivation* (see the following rule 3.9 for the verb *compensate*), derivational feature structures (see features in 3.10 for some verbal derivations), and a list of suffixes associated with each derivational paradigm (see list in 3.11).

Word *'compens'*: (3.9)

$\langle cat \rangle \doteq$ 'V'

$\langle inflection \rangle \doteq 5$

$\langle derivation \rangle \doteq 1.$

Derived category V(1) (3.10)

V[1]

$\langle cat \rangle \doteq$ 'N'.

$\langle agreement\ number \rangle \doteq$ 'singular'.

$\langle history \rangle \doteq$ 'ation'.

V[2]

$\langle cat \rangle \doteq$ 'N'.

$\langle agreement\ number \rangle \doteq$ 'plural'.

$\langle history \rangle \doteq$ 'ation'.

Derivation suffixes V (3.11)

*"alienate → alienation/alienations/alienable/ * "*

V[1] *ation   ations   able   *

"decide → decision/decisions/decidable/decisive"

V[2] *sion   sions   dable   sive*

"*depress* → *depression/depressions/depressible/depressive*"

V[3] *ion   ions   ible   ive*

Derived words such as *compensation* are built by concatenating a stem (here *compens-ate*) and a suffix (here *-ation*). The feature structure of the derived word is the unification of the feature structures of the stem and the associated suffix. Here the resulting feature of the word *compensation* is given by

$$
0: \begin{bmatrix} \begin{bmatrix} string: & 'compensation' \\ cat: & 'N' \\ root: & \begin{bmatrix} cat: & 'V' \\ lemma: & 'compens' \\ inflection: & 5 \\ derivation: & 1 \end{bmatrix} \\ agreement: & [\, number: \ 'singular' \,] \\ history: & 'ation' \end{bmatrix} \end{bmatrix} \qquad (3.12)
$$

Static Derivational Morphology
The alternate approach to morphological relations amounts to expressing static links between words and their stems in the single word lexicon. The following rule indicates that the stem of *compensation* is *compensate*:

Word *'compensation'*:   (3.13)

⟨*cat*⟩ $\doteq$ '*N*'

⟨*inflection*⟩ $\doteq$ 1

⟨*root cat*⟩ $\doteq$ '*V'*

⟨*root lemma*⟩ $\doteq$ '*compens*'

⟨*history*⟩ $\doteq$ '*ation*'.

Even though it has a slightly different form, the resulting feature structure contains the same morphological information as in (3.12):

$$
0: \begin{bmatrix} \begin{bmatrix} string: & 'compensation' \\ lemma: & 'compensation' \\ cat: & 'N' \\ inflection: & 1 \\ root: & \begin{bmatrix} cat: & 'V' \\ lemma: & 'compens' \end{bmatrix} \\ agreement: & [\, number: \ 'singular' \,] \\ history: & 'ation' \end{bmatrix} \end{bmatrix} \qquad (3.14)
$$

3.3 Extended Domain of Locality and Lexicalization

I now turn to the syntax of terms and the way it is represented in *FASTR*.

As was shown in chapter 2, NLP tools are used in information access for two main purposes: *free indexing* and *controlled indexing*. The latter is a special case of the former in which the list of possible indexes is predefined. Both methods must account for the various linguistic forms that can be used to express a concept: they must take term variation into account. *Term normalization* is a linguistically and conceptually motivated process that aims at conflating all the term occurrences with the same conceptual meaning.

In order to cope with term variability, a parser must have access to the lexical and syntactic properties of terms. It is therefore necessary to build lexicons of single and multi-word entries that provide linguistic information about terms, proper nouns, and acronyms (Amsler 1989). In multi-word entries, two characteristics must be accounted for:

1. The syntactic structure of these entries.

2. The possible variations of this structure when encountered within text corpora.

These two preceding features are interdependent: variations are due both to the syntax of multi-word entries and the interaction of this syntax with general syntax (Jacquemin 1994a). This section describes two additional facilities of *FASTR* that provide a formalism in which syntax and lexicon are interwoven: the notions of *extended domain of locality* and *lexicalization*.

3.3.1 Extended Domain of Locality

The notion of *extended domain of locality* is taken from *Tree-Adjoining Grammars* (*TAG*s), in which a grammar is a set of syntactic trees linked to lexical items. The major innovation of this formalism is to present a grammar as a unique and cohesive system including and relating lexical and grammatical information (Joshi 1987). Before turning to the notion of extended domain of locality which is inherent to this formalism, let us first briefly recall the main features of *TAG*s.

A *TAG* is a set of *elementary trees* that are combined through the operations of *adjunction* and *substitution*. I only consider substitution here because the metarules described in chapter 4 are used to implement constructions that are accounted for through adjunction in *TAG*s. An example of substitution in a *TAG* is illustrated by figure 3.3. The elementary tree α_2 is substituted into the tree α_1 because one of the frontier nodes of α_1 has the same label A as the root node of α_2. (This node is intentionally marked for substitution by a $\downarrow$.) The substitution of α_2 in α_1 yields the tree β.

Because of the possibility of multi-word lexical entries in *TAG*, the same structure can be directly given as an elementary tree α. Roughly speaking, the constructed tree β of *magnetic*

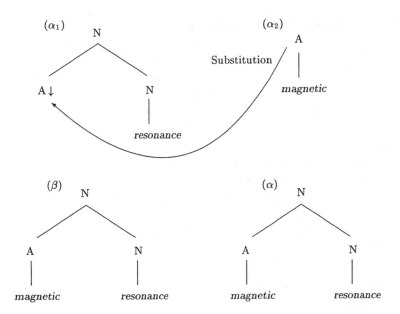

Figure 3.3
Substitution in a *TAG*.

resonance should be considered as a variation of *resonance*, whereas the elementary tree α represents the multi-word term *Magnetic resonance*. In the first case, the linguistic utterance is referring to the concept *RESONANCE*, through a semantic composition with *magnetic*. In the second case, the concept referred to by *magnetic resonance* is a specific concept *MAGNETIC_RESONANCE*, different from *RESONANCE* (obviously a hypernym). Such ambiguous analyses also exist in nontechnical languages where frozen expressions like *to hit the papers* can be remotivated and analyzed literally (Abeillé 1991).

The possibility of multiple derivations in *TAGs* is due to their specific method of derivation. Contrary to *context-free grammars* (*CFGs*), in which rewriting is performed on strings, rewriting is performed on trees in *TAGs*. In a *CFG* the *syntactic tree* of a well-formed structure is also its *derivation tree*; that is, the history of the rules that have been employed for deriving the string. For example, the derived tree β of figure 3.3 can only result form the application of the following three context-free rules:

N → A N

A → *magnetic*

N → *resonance*

Conversely, in the case of a *TAG*, the same derived tree β can result from two different derivations: from the substitution of α_2 in α_1 or from the unique tree α.

One of the major ideas used in the application of *TAGs* to the representation of lexical data is the *extended domain of locality*. In this way, within a single elementary structure, the grammatical dependencies between the nodes of a complex lexical entry can be expressed, whatever their mutual distance. Such a facility is not available in context-free formalisms, where the rules are restricted to *immediate dependency*—links between nodes within a tree of depth 1. In such a framework it is necessary to call for feature propagation in order to express longer dependencies.

3.3.2 Lexicalization

Apart from it expressiveness, extended domain of locality is also useful for *lexicalization*. Since multiple lexical entries are expressed by single trees, all their lexical items are present on their frontier nodes and are available for anchoring these rule to single words. A *TAG* is said to be lexicalized if and only if every rule is linked to a lexical item (or possibly several in a multiple entry) (Abeillé and Schabes 1989). Lexicalization is a linguistically motivated relation between lexical items and grammar rules that follows the principle that the syntax of a lexical item—here the variations of a term—is the result of the interaction of generic and idiosyncratic rules. Because of their lexical specificity, grammar rules are linked to the corresponding lexical items, called their *lexical anchors*.

According to the preceding criterion of lexicalization, the grammar equal to $\{\alpha_1, \alpha_2, \alpha\}$ is lexicalized in the example shown in figure 3.3. The rule α_1 is anchored to *resonance*, α_2 is linked to *magnetic* and α to *magnetic resonance*.

The descriptive capacity of *TAGs* was first studied for English by Kroch (1987). An application of *LTAG* (Schabes, Abeillé, and Joshi 1988) to the description of French was presented in Abeillé (1991). Through the description of French compound verbs, this study outlines the advantages of both notions of extended domain of locality and lexicalization. However, these two distinctive features of *LTAGs* are not only interesting for their linguistic appropriateness; lexicalization is also a crucial characteristic for the optimization of the parser (Schabes 1990; Schabes and Joshi 1990). I will come back to this application of lexicalization in section 3.5.

3.3.3 Expressing a *LTAG* within a Unification-Based Framework

FASTR can be geared toward the expression of a lexicalized tree grammar by embedding *LTAGs* into the descriptive paradigm of unification-based grammars. The transcription is straightforward: the nodes of the grammar trees are decorated with feature structures, and the context-free skeletons of rules are not restricted to immediate dependency (Vijay-Shanker 1992). Rule (3.15) is expressed in this formalism; it represents the term *Measure of [arterial pressure]* with an embedded structure *arterial pressure*:

Rule $N_1 \rightarrow N_2 P_3 (N_4 \rightarrow A_5 N_6)$:   (3.15)

$\langle N_1 \; \textit{lexicalization} \rangle \; \doteq \; N_2$

$\langle N_2 \; \textit{lemma} \rangle \; \doteq \; \textit{'measure'}$

$\langle N_2 \; \textit{inflection} \rangle \; \doteq \; 1$

$\langle P_3 \; \textit{lemma} \rangle \; \doteq \; \textit{'of'}$

$\langle A_5 \; \textit{lemma} \rangle \; \doteq \; \textit{'arterial'}$

$\langle A_5 \; \textit{inflection} \rangle \; \doteq \; 1$

$\langle N_6 \; \textit{lemma} \rangle \; \doteq \; \textit{'pressure'}$

$\langle N_6 \; \textit{inflection} \rangle \; \doteq \; 1$

$\langle N_1 \; \textit{agreement} \rangle \; \doteq \; \langle N_2 \; \textit{agreement} \rangle$

$\langle N_4 \; \textit{agreement} \rangle \; \doteq \; \langle N_6 \; \textit{agreement} \rangle.$

Rule (3.15) is adequately represented by the feature structure of figure 3.4.

3.4   Derivation within *FASTR*

To give a more precise description of term spotting by *FASTR*, I now turn to the analysis of a multi-word term with an embedded structure. I need to consider the occurrence *measure of arterial pressure* and a grammar composed of rules (3.16) and (3.17). Rule (3.16) denotes the term *Measure of* $N_{\text{measurable}}$ and rule (3.17) the term *Arterial pressure*. $N_{\text{measurable}}$ stands for any nominal construction referring to a measurable quantity. Since the term *Arterial pressure* possesses this feature, its substitution into the tree of rule (3.16) is allowed.

Rule $N_1 \rightarrow N_2 P_3 N_4$:   (3.16)

$\langle N_1 \; \textit{lexicalization} \rangle \; \doteq \; N_2$

$\langle N_2 \; \textit{lemma} \rangle \; \doteq \; \textit{'measure'}$

$\langle N_2 \; \textit{inflection} \rangle \; \doteq \; 1$

$\langle P_3 \; \textit{lemma} \rangle \; \doteq \; \textit{'of'}$

$\langle N_4 \; \textit{agreement sem} \rangle \; \doteq \; \textit{'measurable'}$

$\langle N_1 \; \textit{agreement} \rangle \; \doteq \; \langle N_2 \; \textit{agreement} \rangle.$

Rule $N_1 \rightarrow A_2 N_3$:   (3.17)

$\langle N_1 \; \textit{lexicalization} \rangle \; \doteq \; N_2$

$\langle A_2 \; \textit{lemma} \rangle \; \doteq \; \textit{'arterial'}$

$\langle A_2 \; \textit{inflection} \rangle \; \doteq \; 1$

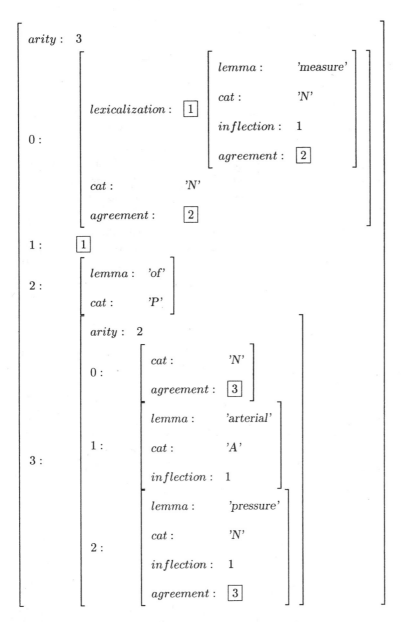

Figure 3.4
Feature structure of the term *Measure of* [*arterial pressure*].

$\langle N_3 \; lemma \rangle \; \doteq \; 'pressure'$

$\langle N_3 \; inflection \rangle \; \doteq \; 1$

$\langle N_3 \; agreement \; sem \rangle \; \doteq \; 'measurable'$

$\langle N_1 \; agreement \rangle \; \doteq \; \langle N_3 \; agreement \rangle.$

This grammar produces two analyses of the string *measure of arterial pressure*: One analysis covers the whole sequence and exploits both rules. The other analysis only needs rule (3.17) and only analyzes *arterial pressure*. If the noun *pressure* carries the feature $\langle agreement \; sem \rangle \; \doteq \; 'measurable'$, or if this feature is unbounded, a third parse is built, *measure of pressure*, through rule (3.16). In the third analysis, the noun *pressure* is successfully substituted on the node N_4 because noun phrases and single nouns share the same syntactic tag N.[27]

The preceding rules must be supplemented with the rules corresponding to the single words found in the terms (*measure*, *of*, *arterial*, and *pressure*). I only illustrate the rule (3.18) of the noun *measure*:

Word *'measure'*:   (3.18)

$\langle cat \rangle \; \doteq \; 'N'$

$\langle inflection \rangle \; \doteq \; 1.$

The inflections of the noun *measure*, whose inflectional paradigm is 1, are given by concatenating its canonical root and one of both suffixes of line N[1] in formula (3.6). The suffix used for producing the inflected word *measure* is the first one: 0, the empty string. The corresponding feature structure of the inflected word is calculated by unifying the feature structure of the lemma (rule 3.18) and the feature structure attached to the inflectional suffix (the first one, indicated by N[1] in formula 3.5). The resulting feature structure of the inflected word *measure* is

$$
\begin{bmatrix}
lemma: & 'measure' \\
cat: & 'N' \\
inflection: & 1 \\
agreement: & [\, number: \;\; 'singular'\,] \\
string: & 'measure'
\end{bmatrix}
\tag{3.19}
$$

The features of all the other inflected words are calculated similarly. In the case of a large lexicon, words may share *homographs*: words with common inflected strings (here the value of the feature $string$). The string *measure* can also be any person of the present of the verb *to measure* but the third person of singular. This ambiguity is a source of inaccuracy in parsing. In recent versions *FASTR* has been coupled with a part-of-speech tagger in order

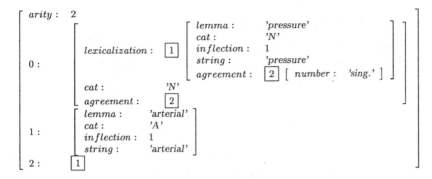

Figure 3.5
Feature structure of the inflected string *arterial pressure*.

to take advantage of the disambiguation performed by the tagger (Jacquemin, Klavans, and Tzoukermann 1997).

Each of the inflected words *arterial* and *pressure* can be substituted into one of the leaf nodes of rule (3.17) because their respective feature structures can be unified. (In the present case the possibility of unification amounts to a verification that the common features share common values.) The feature structure resulting from these unifications is given in figure 3.5.

The resulting feature structure can in turn be substituted in the tree of rule (3.16), together with the feature structures of the inflected words *measure* and *of*. The resulting feature structure is shown in figure 3.6. These successful unifications yield a terminal-derived tree because all its frontier nodes are inflected words. The string that is analyzed by this tree is the concatenation of the values of the feature *string* of the all the frontier nodes collected by a depth-first traversal of the tree. The features of the root node indicate that this structure is analyzed as a singular noun phrase.

In section 3.1.1 I showed that unification formalisms are known to result in inefficient parsers and that the building of such machines requires important optimizations. The following section describes the grammar and provides more detail about its implementation in *FASTR*.

3.5 Parsing with *FASTR*

Analysis in *FASTR* is organized according to the traditional stratified scheme of NLP applications: a morphological step followed by a syntactic step (Alshawi 1992). In addition two new components are necessary for dealing with term extraction: (1) a term preprocessor

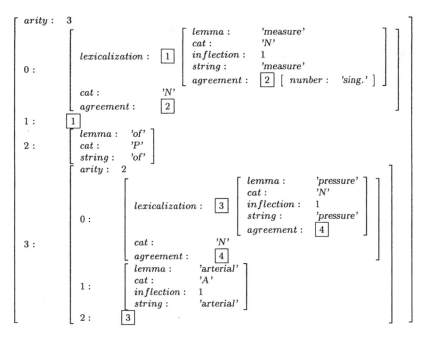

Figure 3.6
Feature structure of the inflected string *measure of* [*arterial pressure*].

that allows for the recycling of terms into the grammar and (2) a term variant generator that enriches the term grammar by transforming term rules into term variant rules through the application of metarules. The data flow in *FASTR* is described by figure 3.7.

3.5.1   Term Recycling

In the experiments reported in this book, two main sources of terms have been used: terms lists exploited in manual indexing (Jacquemin and Royauté 1994) and terms acquired automatically. In the second case, two main possibilities exist: either terms are obtained through a massive initial acquisition (Jacquemin, Klavans, and Tzoukermann 1997), or terms are incrementally acquired through term enrichment from variation (chapter 6).

First, terms in the initial list are morphologically analyzed, and each word belonging to a term receives a set of possibly ambiguous morphological features. Then, terms are syntactically disambiguated according to a generic noun phrase grammar, yielding unambiguously analyzed terms. For example, through this process, out of the two possible taggings of the term *Arterial pressure*, Adjective-Verb and Adjective-Noun, the second one is chosen and represented as A_1 N_1H. This structure indicates that the term has an Adjective-Noun

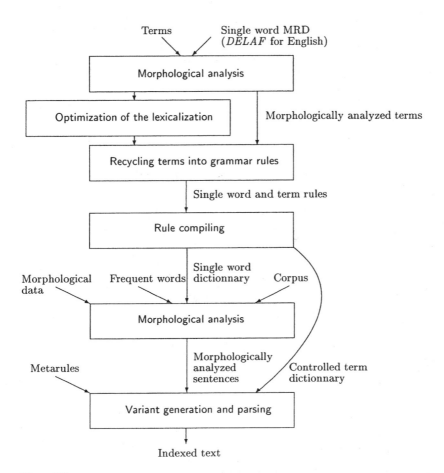

Figure 3.7
Data flow and processes in *FASTR*

structure, that the head word of the structure is the second word, and that the inflectional paradigms are respectively 1 for the adjective[28] and 1 for the head noun.[29]

Finally, these term structures, together with the lemmas of the words, are used to generate the final single word and term rules that will be compiled in the application (see rules 3.1 and 3.2 for examples of such rules).

3.5.2 Morphological Analysis

The second step is morphological analysis of text corpora, which is subdivided into the following procedures (figure 3.8):

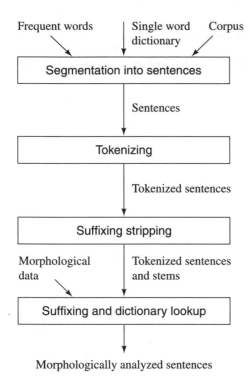

Figure 3.8
Data flow and processes of morphological analysis.

1. Segmentation of input text into sentences.

2. Tokenizing, or the segmentation of sentences into words and typographical normalization (a feature *form* keeps a record of the written form of the initial words: uppercase letters, word followed by a special character such as hyphen, quote, etc.).

3. Morphological analysis and transformation of each word into a lemma with a feature structure. This procedure is decomposed into the following subprocesses:

a. The *suffix stripping* phase removes from the inflected word all the possible suffixes.

b. The *dictionary lookup* phase considers each remaining stem and checks whether it is a root or an auxiliary root of the lexicon; then, each actual (auxiliary) root is suffixed in order to search for the inflections that are equal to the current inflected word.

Suffix stripping is performed by comparing the inverted word with the *trie* (de la Briandais 1959; Fredkin 1960) built from the inverted suffixes known for the inflectional system of

English. Through suffix stripping, the English word *housing* produces the two candidate stems *housing* and *hous* because *ing* is a correct suffix in English. Since *hous* and *housing* are both correct lexical roots, the inflected word *housing* is analyzed ambiguously as the singular of the noun *housing* and the gerund of the verb *to house*.

3.5.3 Syntactic Analysis

The step following morphological analysis is syntactic analysis. Active rules are parsed according to the following two procedures:

1. **Recursive descent.** Each rule is analyzed through a depth-first recursive descent. The parser backtracks in case of parse failure or in case of disjunctive values (Aho, Sethi, and Ullman 1986 p. 208). During this step all the features except the feature *lemma* are ignored.

2. **Unification.** The feature structures—linked to the single words of the corpus and to the nodes of the term rules—are only taken into consideration if the parse of the rule skeleton is achieved successfully. Unification is performed wherever substitution takes place: either between a leaf node and a substituted root node or between a leaf node and an inflected word. If unification succeeds, the corresponding term is reported as output.

First, active rules are analyzed without transformation; then, each possible variant of the rule is generated and transmitted to the parser.

Unification is performed independently from recursive descent in the name of efficiency. Unification rarely fails when recursive descent succeeds: when parsing the corpus [Medic] with the term list [Pascal] of *INIST/CNRS*, only 0.8% of unifications fail, whereas 20.9% of the rule skeleton parses cannot be achieved. The contrast is even more striking when considering the analysis of the variants: only 1.0% of the variants have their syntactic skeleton in the input sentence, but 73.0% of these successful syntactic parses are subsequently confirmed by a successful unification. Because of the high success rate of final unification, it would be inefficient to perform unification, an expensive algorithm, during the descent.

3.5.4 Bottom-up Filtering and Optimization of the Lexicalization

In *FASTR* the grammar is composed of numerous rules, each rule contains one or more lexical items, and rules are not recursive. Because of such large volume of lexical and grammatical data, it is necessary to check that all the word composing a rule are found in the current sentence before parsing it: in indexing the corpus [Medic] (1.6 million words), parsing succeeds for 78.9% of the rules selected through this criterion.

Schabes and Joshi (1990) propose a two-step parsing method for *LTAGs*—a special type of lexicalized grammar;

1. **Filtering.** A subset of the grammar is selected by rejecting all the rules whose lexical items are not in the input sentence.

2. **Parsing.** The input sentence is parsed with this relevant subset of the grammar.

This filtering method can be extended to term spotting in *FASTR*, because the grammars that I use for term spotting are lexicalized through the feature *lexicalization*.

Since each rule in *FASTR* is only linked to one lexical item, filtering is performed in two steps. First, all the rules whose unique lexical anchor is in the input sentence are activated. Then, a second filter checks that all the remaining lexical items are present in the processed input. Through the application of this cascaded bottom-up filtering, 78.9% of the activated rules are successfully parsed. Comparatively, a baseline measure in which rules are activated if only one lexical anchor is found in the current input yields 34 times more active rules.

For optimal efficiency it is desirable that the lexicalization does not link single words to too many terms. Given a weighting scheme that assigns a weight to any single word as a function of its links with terms, optimizing a lexicalization amounts to searching for the best solution among all the possible ones: the solution(s) whose sum of weights is the lowest one. In Jacquemin (1994b), it is shown that this problem, called *lexicalization of a grammar (LG)*, is $\mathcal{NP}$-complete because the classical $\mathcal{NP}$-complete problem of bin packing can be polynomially reduced to *LG*. A suboptimal solution relying on a weakly polynomial algorithm is proposed and experiments on both natural and artificially generated data confirm the quality of the suboptimal solution. Optimizing the lexicalization of the grammar leads to a more even distribution of terms on single words and to a higher load of rare words: it multiplies the parsing speed by a factor greater than 2.

3.6 Summary

This chapter has presented the basics of *FASTR*: the formalism for representing the lexical and grammatical data, the combination of these data in the analysis of multi-word terms, and the implementation of the parsing algorithm through NLP modules.

The formalism of *FASTR* is a unification-based formalism inspired by *PATR-II*. It is consistently used for representing morphological, lexical, syntactic data and, in the next chapter, metagrammatical data. In this formalism, information is embedded in nontyped feature structures enriched with negation and disjunction.

More precisely, single-word rules are represented by a string (a canonical root), a part-of-speech category, and additional features such as an inflection number that denotes the inflectional paradigm. Term rules are composed of a context-free skeleton that represents the constituent structure of the term and a set of feature structures attached to the nodes of the context-free skeleton.

Inflectional morphology and derivational morphology are fully described through morphological paradigms composed of a list of feature structures and an associated list of suffixes. Morphological analysis is based on the concatenation of candidate stems and suffixes associated with their inflection number. In recent applications of *FASTR*, morphological analysis has sometimes been performed by external modules prior to term extraction. In these cases *FASTR* takes as input a morphologically analyzed—and generally disambiguated—corpus.

For the purpose of term extraction through *FASTR*, initial terminological data—whether collected automatically or extracted from thesauri—are transformed into lexicalized grammar rules. Each rule is linked with one lexical item that serves to optimize the parse through bottom-up filtering. For each parsed sentence, words are morphologically analyzed, and only term rules linked with at least one lexical item in the current sentence are activated.

Each rule is analyzed through a depth-first recursive descent. If the parse of the rule skeleton is achieved successfully, the feature structures linked with the words in the corpus and with the nodes of the term rules are unified. If unification succeeds, the text occurrence is reported as output together with the reference of the corresponding term.

In a second step, each possible variant of each term rule is generated and transmitted to the parser. The next chapter presents the metagrammar used for term variant generation.

4 Variations

The observation of technical terms within corpora or through a Web crawler reveals that a single concept may have several linguistic expressions. For a proper automatic indexing of documents, the large range of term variations that are likely to be encountered must be taken into account. Term variations burden and confuse indexers that only rely on string recognition. Two main families of variations must be accounted for: variations that alter the string of a term such as adjectival modification, or variations that modify words in terms such as morphological transformations or semantic expansions. For instance, *generation of regular languages*, *generate each context-free language*, and *language generated* are three variants of *Language generation* which cannot be identified without an explicit model of term variation. The last two variants involve the morphological transformation of the head word *generation*, which is replaced by the verb *generate*.

The specificity of *FASTR* is to focus on the recognition of term variants without calling for exhaustive sentence parsing. In *FASTR* variations are described through local grammar transformations implemented by metarules. Section 4.1 shows how the transformational theory of Harris (1968) reveals the linguistic characteristics of term transformations. Section 4.2, covers the description of term variations by metarules; they complement the grammatical and morphological data presented in chapter 3. Details on the implementation of metarules are given in section 4.3.

4.1 Linguistic Analysis of Term Variations

From Harris's model, I adopt two key concepts: the concept of *transformation*, which parallels the notion of term variation, and the concept of *sublanguage*, which motivates my empirical approach to the tuning of metarules.

4.1.1 Transformations

Harris (1968, chs. 3–4) describes a language as composed of *phrase schemata* and *transformations*. The transformations operate on the basic schema in order to generate the observed constructions. In this model words are grouped into distributional classes; the words in the same class belong to the same phrase schemata which constitute their prototypical environment. In Harrisian linguistics a *transformation* is a device that groups various phrases stemming from the same schema into an equivalence class; this mechanism is used for building language structures based on primary phrases. All the transformations result from the composition of a few elementary *operations* that are not language-specific (as opposed to transformations).

Harrisian linguistics has been applied to the analysis of medical texts in Harris et al. (1989). In this study each sentence in the text was transformed into phrase schemata

Table 4.1
Eight sentences with identical informational content $A\,V_p\,C_z$

	Sentences
1	*Les plasmocytes sont producteurs d'anticorps*
2	*Les plasmocytes produisent des anticorps*
3	*Des anticorps sont produits par les plasmocytes*
4	*Des anticorps sont produits dans les plasmocytes*
5	*La production plasmocytaire d'anticorps a été établie*
6	*La production d'anticorps par les plasmocytes a été établie*
7	*La production d'anticorps qu'on observe dans les plasmocytes, a été établie*
8	*L'origine plasmocytaire de la production d'anticorps a été établie*

Source: From Harris et al. 1989, p. 176.

composed of an *operator* and its *arguments*. These schemata are assumed to represent the bulk of information in the document. For instance, the sentences 1 to 8 of table 4.1, taken from Harris et al. (1989, p. 176), have an equivalent informational content $A\,V_p\,C_z$. V_p is an operator denoting *production* (production). The subject argument of this operator is A *anticorps* (antibodies) and the object argument is C_z *plasmocytes* (plasmocytes), a subclass of C *cells* (cellules). V_p is, in turn, a subclass of the operator V denoting a *response*. Despite its distributional regularity, V_p is expressed by a large variety of lexemes such as *formation* (development), *production* (production), *synthèse* (synthesis), *résultat* (result), and *multiplication* (multiplication).

The transformational approach of Harris is well adapted to the description of term variation because term variants are paraphrastic language utterances that correspond to the same basic conceptual interpretation. In such a framework each term variation is obtained from a unique basic term through the application of elementary operations. However, for efficiency purposes I will not consider elementary operations but complex transformations that are the composition of several elementary operations.

4.1.2 Sublanguages

Harris (1968, sec. 5.9) introduces the notion of *sublanguage*: a subset of language in which only a part of the available operators are used. Some sentences that would be syntactically correct in general language, such as *hydrochloric acid was washed in polypeptids*, are not acceptable in a specialized context. In biology the reverse construction is the correct one: *polypeptids were washed in hydrochloric acid*.

Thus the correct sentences of a sublanguage are characterized by a restriction on the possible combinations of operators and arguments. Conversely, since the selection restrictions in sublanguages are more numerous than in general language and the combinations between classes of words more complex, the grammar of a sublanguage is said to be "richer" than the grammar of general language. General language and sublanguages overlap only partially; both contain sentences that are not acceptable for the other.

The Harrisian approach has led to several applications in NLP that are geared toward specialized corpora and large-scale parsing. A number of these applications are collected in Kittredge and Lehrberger (1982) and Grishman and Kittredge (1986). The techniques used belong to two complementary and interdependent domains: large-scale parsers with fine-grained distributional data (Sager 1986) and tools for acquiring distributional information through the observation of distributional regularities (Hirschman 1986). Both the correlation of parsing and acquisition and the high number of syntactic idiosyncrasies in sublanguages influence the *FASTR* approach.

Interdependence of Parsing and Knowledge Acquisition

Since a parser for a sublanguage requires some linguistic knowledge about the selection restrictions in this domain, it must be provided with a minimal set of lexicosyntactic patterns. Since knowledge acquisition is best performed on a parsed corpus, it must be bootstrapped with a manual tagging of text corpora. Consequently approaches to parsing that rely purely on human knowledge are weaker than those in which knowledge exploitation and knowledge discovery reinforce each other.

FASTR has been designed to interweave recognition and acquisition so that the incremental extraction of term variants can provide the parser with an ever-increasing set of terminological data. The parser is bootstrapped with an initial list of terms, and it subsequently updates the knowledge for term extraction.

Error Recovery

The linguistic description of sublanguages involves the addition of specific rules, because some of the constructions of specialized languages are considered incorrect for general language. For instance, some "telegraphic" styles used in technical notes systematically omit determiners (Lehrberger 1986). Because of the idiosyncrasies of specialized languages, it is necessary to devise methods for recovering from errors due to an incorrectly or partially specified grammar.

The two main approaches to error recovery are *recuperation* and *redefinition*. Recuperation is based on the normative assumption that deviant forms must be forced to match correct structures. For this purpose Weischedel (1983) uses metarules for transforming rejected utterances into accepted ones.

Although it also relies on metarules, the *FASTR* approach belongs to redefinition approaches, as it modifies the grammatical data when utterances are rejected by the parser. A similar approach to the processing of *ill-formed inputs* has been illustrated by Fitzpatrick, Bachenko, and Hindle (1986). By the redefinition approach to ill-formedness, unexpected occurrences can lead to a full revision of the grammar. In short, language is treated as an evolving system that may undergo grammatical enrichment and obsolescence. Conversely, recuperation assumes that parsing failure causes temporary damage that can be repaired with peripheral changes that do not involve a redefinition of the grammar.

The redefinition approach adopted in *FASTR* is a dynamic one that calls for a constant update of the metarules. Chapter 5 illustrates the experimental tuning of the grammar on English data.

4.1.3 Knowledge Maintenance

FASTR is designed to recognize occurrences of terms and variants. The requirements for the term recognition procedure are simpler than for a generation procedure. For instance, an analyzer of term variants must reject *blood and cell* as a variant of *Blood cell* but should accept *blood and bone marrow cell*. In comparison, a generation procedure must possess a much finer knowledge of the semantic restrictions involved in the construction of variants. For instance, *dorsal and cervical spine* is a correct coordination built from *Dorsal spine*. This term can also be coordinated with other A *spine* (A = adjective) structures such as *Lumbar spine* or *Lumbosacral spine*. But all the A *spine* terms in which *spine* does not refer to a nervous spine such as *Fish spine* or *Hedgehog spine* cannot be coordinated with *Dorsal spine*.

Thus, in generation, the constraint of *semantic isotopy* between coordinated terms with a common head must be considered, whereas it can be ignored in analysis: it is not likely for an occurrence such as *hedgehog or dorsal spine* to be encountered in a real-world corpus. The relative easiness of term analysis compared with term generation justifies the use of a pure syntactic method for the filtering of correct term variants. The author's first technique for describing term variations was based on *acceptability* (Jacquemin 1991). However, since for human experts determining acceptability is time-consuming and still does not meet the strict requirements of redefinition techniques, acceptability definition has been replaced by experimental tuning.

Acceptability

The first attempt to filter correct variants (presented in Jacquemin 1991) was based on a description of acceptabilities: for each term the acceptable transformations were listed exhaustively (see table 4.2). This approach is an extension of the methodology of *lexicon-grammars* to terminology. Lexicon-grammars, developed at *LADL* (University of Paris 7) (Gross 1975; 1986b; Silberztein 1990), consist of tables in which each line corresponds to a single lexeme and describes the list of the acceptable syntactic structures for the lexeme.

Table 4.2
Acceptabilities of some variants of *Commande à distance* (remote control) and *Roue à aubes* (paddle wheel)

Term	Noun modifier		Coor-dination	Deverbal V *à* N	Adjectivi-zation	Insertion N A&N *à* D N
	1st	2nd				
commande à distance	+	−	+	+	−	−
roue à aubes	−	+	+	−	−	?

The transformations associated with terms in Jacquemin (1991) are inspired by Gross (1988). In Gross' transformations the variability of the compound nouns was characterized by the acceptability of variations. Similarly Jacquemin (1991) proposed that terms can accept or reject a variant depending on several linguistic features. The symbol + in the top left cell of table 4.2 indicates that the term *Commande à distance* (remote control) accepts an adjectival postmodification of the head noun *commande* such as *commande automatique à distance* (automatic remote control) or *commande de robot à distance* (remote control for a robot). Not all of the variations proposed by Gross (1988) apply to automatic term spotting, and conversely, some have been refined and divided into more accurate transformations for use in automatic indexing.

The descriptive method of determining acceptabilities has been abandoned, however. It has been replaced by a loose definition of variants that is progressively tuned through experimental observation. Altogether there are a number of reasons for this methodological choice:

1. Defining acceptability is a time-consuming task, since it requires expert editing of each cell in a table.

2. Acceptability does not provide an absolute measure. The same syntactic construction has different acceptabilities depending on the lexical items involved in the construction (see the preceding examples of coordination with *spine*). It is therefore misleading to believe that acceptabilities suffice to describe term variations. A better understanding of the semantics of compounding is needed for a correct description of variations; see, for example, Wasow, Sag, and Nunberg (1984, p. 109), Nunberg, Sag, and Wasow (1994), and Ruwet (1991).

3. It is not clear how to determine the acceptability of the composition of one or more variations. (An analysis of compositions of variations is provided in section 5.2 which discusses the acceptability of nonelementary variations.)

4. Term variations in corpora show that expected variants may not be encountered in a corpus, whereas some of the observed variants might be judged a priori as unacceptable.

Acceptability is difficult to evaluate due to the sparseness of term variation experience (80% of the terms have 0 or 1 variants in the 1.6 million word corpus [Medic]). The expert linguist, therefore, cannot rely on personal experience for judging the acceptability of a given construction. (See also Habert 1991 for similar comments about adverbs of domain.)

5. Variation is closely related to term creation. Term embedding is a specific type of term variation that creates new terms. Because of this interdependency between acceptability and lexicality, it is difficult to define the acceptability of a construction involved in term creation.

In sum, the introspective evaluation of term variation is not a valid information source for extracting variants from texts. A technique that is sensitive to the variations observed in corpora is more appropriate because sublanguages have a large variety of terms variations that are very difficult to predict.

Experimental Tuning

Instead of choosing among an exhaustive description of terms and their acceptable variants, automatic indexing with *FASTR* is based on an initial set of relaxed metarules, where each metarule is experimentally tuned and progressively refined.

The initial variations are deliberately underconstrained. They are designed to accept all the possible variants plus some errors (high recall, low precision). The initial metarules simply check the presence of the items composing a complex term within a text window without controlling the syntactic structure in play between these words. Step by step, these variations are enriched with filtering constraints that are expected to rule out spurious variants without rejecting correct ones. More details are provided on the tuning of certain metarules through experimentation in chapter 5 and in Jacquemin and Royauté (1994).

4.2   Description of Variations through Metarules

Section 4.1 drew a parallel between the observation of terms and variations and the core relations and transformations of Harrisian linguistics. Since terms are described by grammar rules, it would be appropriate to devise a generic mechanism that relates terms to variants by transforming term rules into variant rules. The search for a mechanism that transforms, for instance, active verbs into passive ones has led Gazdar et al. (1985) to include a metagrammar in *GPSG*. Similarly, in *FASTR*, metarules are responsible for transforming rules of controlled terms into new rules that will be used for extracting term variants from texts.

Before presenting the metagrammar of *FASTR*, I need to review the definition of metarules in *GPSG* and in *Feature-Based Lexicalized Tree-Adjoining Grammar* (*FB-LTAG*) of Srinivas et al. (1994). *GPSG* is the formalism in computational linguistics that has most emphasized the role of metarules and most clearly elaborated the advantages of this technique.

4.2.1 Metarules in *GPSG*

This section summarizes metarules of *GPSG* as described in Gazdar et al. (1985, ch. 4); the knowledgeable reader can safely skip this description.

The following rule (4.1) of *GPSG* describes verbs with two complements such as *give something to someone*:

$$VP \rightarrow H[2], \ NP, \ PP['to'] \tag{4.1}$$

Similarly verbs with only one direct complement, such as *eat*, are described by

$$VP \rightarrow H[3], \ NP \tag{4.2}$$

Both rules (4.1) and (4.2) describe the active form of verbs with subcategorization classes 2 and 3. In order to extend the coverage of this grammar to the passive voice of these same words, the first and noneconomical solution is to reformulate two new rules such as

$$VP[PAS] \rightarrow H[3], \ PP['to'], \ (PP['by']) \tag{4.3}$$

$$VP[PAS] \rightarrow H[2], \ (PP['by']) \tag{4.4}$$

More preferable would be a mechanism that would account for the transformation of active verbs into passive ones. It must state that the subject is transformed into an optional indirect object introduced by *by*. (Optional arguments in *GPSG* are written within parentheses.) Metarule (4.5) satisfies this requirement; it is a function transforming grammar rules of active verbs into grammar rules of passive ones. Through (4.5), (4.1) is associated with (4.3) and (4.2) with (4.4):

$$VP \rightarrow W, \ NP \tag{4.5}$$
$$\Downarrow$$
$$VP[PAS] \rightarrow W, \ (PP['by'])$$

The meaning of this metarule is the following:

Any (active) phrase rule, with a direct object NP and a set of constituents W, is associated with a passive verb phrase whose constituents are the constituents of W and an optional prepositional phrase with the preposition *by*.

This metarule introduces a new metalinguistic object W that represents a multi-set of constituents, possibly empty. However, it does not state explicitly that the optional prepositional phrase of the passive form is identical to the subject of the active form.

In *GPSG* the mechanism of the production of transformed rules through metarules is the following:

1. A metarule is composed of a right-hand side (its source) and a left-hand side (its target). The source contains the abbreviatory variable W and, at most, one other constituent C. The target also includes W, possibly C, and as many other constituents as necessary.

2. The first step of the transformation of a rule by a metarule is the *matching* of the source of the metarule and the grammar rule. If the constituent C appears in the source of the metarule, it matches the constituent of the same category in the rule. The pairing succeeds only if the description of the constituent C in the rule is richer than or equal to the constituent C in the metarule.

3. The categories and variables in the target are determined by the values of categories and variables in the source and in the initial rule. Once this determination is made, the transformed rule is created from a copy of the target structure. All the categories bound to W and all the categories of the target construction different from C are copied in the transformed rule. The output category C', corresponding to C in the source, is unified with C, except that when C and C' disagree over the value of some feature, C' dominates.

A recapitulation of the different steps is illustrated on the following metarule (4.6) said *subject-aux inversion*. This metarule transforms an incorrect utterance such as *Max always asks whether are there any problems* into *Max always asks whether there are any problems*.

$$V^2[- - \text{SUBJ}] \rightarrow W \tag{4.6}$$

$$\Downarrow$$

$$V^2[+\text{INV}, +\text{SUBJ}] \rightarrow W, \ N^2$$

This metarule transforms the simplified rule (4.7) into the rule (4.8):

$$V^2[+\text{AUX}, - - \text{SUBJ}] \rightarrow H^0[46], \ V^2[+\text{AUX}, - - \text{SUBJ}] \tag{4.7}$$

$$V^2[+\text{AUX}, +\text{INV}, +\text{SUBJ}] \rightarrow H^0[46], \ V^2[+\text{AUX}, - - \text{SUBJ}], \ N^2 \tag{4.8}$$

This computation outlines two important characteristics of metarules in *GPSG*. First, the features of the category C which are not specified in the metarule (here the feature +AUX of V^2) are implicitly transferred from the source to the target. Second, the features of C (here the feature -SUBJ of V^2) can have different values in the source and the target of the metarule. This possibility introduces a discontinuity in the transmission of feature values which is incompatible with the unification framework. As mentioned in section 3.1, because I have chosen to work in a unification formalism, the method for building transformed

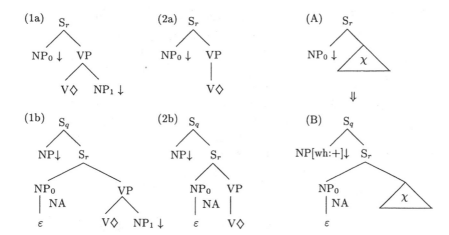

Figure 4.1
Two metarules in *FB-LTAG*, after Srinivas et al. (1994).

rules through metarules in *GPSG* is not compatible with my choice for reason of its nonmonotonicity.

4.2.2 Metarules in *FB-LTAG*

The concept of metarule appears in other formalisms, especially when it is necessary to reduce the size of the grammar. This is particularly true of lexicalized formalisms. In these formalisms, syntactic features are linked to lexical items, and the size of the grammar is proportional to the size of the lexicon.

One of these lexicalized formalisms is *FB-LTAG* (Srinivas et al. 1994). In *FB-LTAG*, source metarules are used for calculating an extended set of trees associated with each lexical entry. As in *GPSG*, metarules are used for linking a passive form or a *wh*-question with the active form of the same verb. Metarules are formally defined in Becker (1994a, b) as rewrite rules, and they are therefore not monotonous. Metarules in *FB-LTAG* are restricted to one application through a notion of finite closure. The modeling of recursive phenomena, such as adjectival modifiers, is left to the operation of adjunction.

Figure 4.1 illustrates one metarule in *FB-LTAG* for *wh*-movement of the subject. The source of the metarule is A and its target is B. The transformation of verb rules by this metarule is shown for two different families of verbs. The pair 1a/1b corresponds to transitive verbs such as *eat*; it associates a rule generating *John eats the cake* with a rule for *Who ε eats the cake*. The pair 2a/2b corresponds to verbs without complements, such as *sleep*.

Both *FB-LTAG* and *FASTR* are restricted to transformations inside an extended domain of locality: the transformation of an initial tree by a metarule always yields an initial tree (a tree describing the extended domain of locality of its lexical anchor). In *FB-LTAG* there is a clear separation between the phenomena that are accounted for by adjunction and these that are modeled by metarules. This division of competence does not exist in *FASTR*, since this formalism does not have adjunction. Instead of adjunction, extended dependencies are described in *FASTR* by complex metarules which are the result of the composition of several elementary metarules. In section 5.3 extended variations are calculated as compositions of elementary transformations. A more linguistically oriented account of the interaction of microvariations is given in Daille et al. (1996).

4.2.3 Metarules in *FASTR*

As in *GPSG* and *FB-LTAG*, metarules in *FASTR* are functions that map the rules of the grammar onto new grammar rules. They are built from a source that is paired with the original rule, and a target that produces the transformed rule. Contrary to *GPSG*, the pairing is performed through the unification of the feature structure denoted by the original rule (see section 3.1.2) with the feature structure denoted by the source of the metarule. If unification succeeds, the transformed rule is equal to the target structure of the metarule; otherwise, no transformed structure is produced.

As an illustration, let us consider the following rule denoting the term *Umbilical artery*, already given earlier in rule (3.2):

Rule $N_1 \rightarrow A_2 N_3$: $\qquad\qquad\qquad\qquad\qquad\qquad\qquad\qquad\qquad\qquad\qquad$ (4.9)

$\langle N_1$ *lexicalization* $\rangle \doteq N_3$

$\langle A_3$ *lemma* $\rangle \doteq$ *'umbilical'*

$\langle A_3$ *inflection* $\rangle \doteq 1$

$\langle N_3$ *lemma* $\rangle \doteq$ *'arter'*

$\langle N_2$ *inflection* $\rangle \doteq 2$

$\langle N_1$ *agreement* $\rangle \doteq \langle N_3$ *agreement* $\rangle$.

This term accepts coordination variations such as *umbilical or carotid artery*. Let us design a metarule that transforms this term rule into a variation pattern, recognizing the preceding utterance as a correct variant. This metarule ought to be generic enough to accept any Adjective-Noun term and to produce a correct variation pattern.

The source and the target patterns of this metarule are underspecified phrase descriptions such as

Metarule Coor($N_1 \rightarrow A_2 N_3$) $\equiv N_1 \rightarrow A_2 C_4 A_5 N_3$: . $\qquad\qquad\qquad\qquad\qquad$ (4.10)

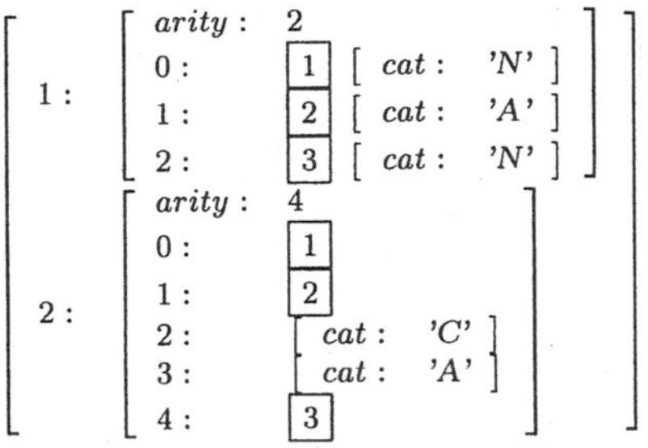

$$\begin{bmatrix} 1: & \begin{bmatrix} arity: & 2 \\ 0: & \boxed{1} \; [\; cat: \quad 'N' \;] \\ 1: & \boxed{2} \; [\; cat: \quad 'A' \;] \\ 2: & \boxed{3} \; [\; cat: \quad 'N' \;] \end{bmatrix} \\ 2: & \begin{bmatrix} arity: & 4 \\ 0: & \boxed{1} \\ 1: & \boxed{2} \\ 2: & \begin{bmatrix} cat: & 'C' \\ cat: & 'A' \end{bmatrix} \\ 3: & \\ 4: & \boxed{3} \end{bmatrix} \end{bmatrix}$$

Figure 4.2
Feature structure of the coordination metarule (4.10).

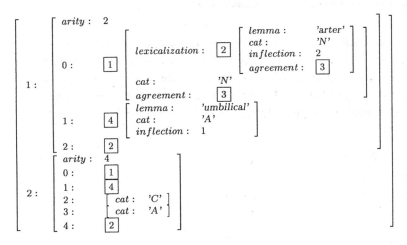

Figure 4.3
Feature structure of the coordination metarule (4.10) after unification of its source with rule (4.9).

The feature structure denoted by this metarule is shown in figure 4.2. Its root node has two daughters, labeled $\langle 1 \rangle$ and $\langle 2 \rangle$, corresponding respectively to the source and the target. Of course, the constituents with the same identifiers are equated. For instance, the equality of N_3 in the left- and the right-hand sides is denoted by the equality of the paths $\langle 1 \; 2 \rangle$ (second constituent of the source) and $\langle 2 \; 4 \rangle$ (fourth constituent of the target) indicated by the label $\boxed{3}$.

In order to calculate the transformed rule, the feature structure denoted by rule (4.9) is unified with the feature structure of the source of the metarule (the value of the path $\langle 1 \rangle$ stemming from the root). Figure 4.3 represents the feature structure of metarule (4.10) after this unification.

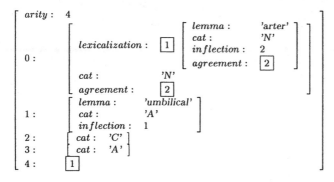

Figure 4.4
Feature structure of the transformation of rule (4.9) by metarule (4.10).

After unification, the feature structure of the transformed rule is the same as the feature structure of the target of the metarule. It is equal to the value of the path ⟨2⟩ stemming from the root. To isolate this value—through a copy, for instance—it is necessary to take in consideration the possibility of shared values between the source and the target. The feature structure of the transformed rule is given by figure 4.4. The corresponding equational form is given by

Rule $N_1 \rightarrow A_2\ C_4\ A_5\ N_3$:   (4.11)

⟨N_1 *lexicalization*⟩ $\doteq N_3$

⟨A_2 *lemma*⟩ $\doteq$ *'umbilical'*

⟨A_2 *inflection*⟩ $\doteq 1$

⟨N_3 *lemma*⟩ $\doteq$ *'arter'*

⟨N_3 *inflection*⟩ $\doteq 2$

⟨N_1 *agreement*⟩ $\doteq$ ⟨N_3 *agreement*⟩.

Regular Expressions in Metarules

Metarule (4.10) does not account for all the configurations of argument coordination of Adjective-Noun terms. More generally, not only an adjective but a whole noun modifier can be coordinated with *umbilical*. For example, *middle cerebral* and *umbilical* are coordinated in *umbilical and middle cerebral artery*. In order to handle these larger structures, the formalism of *FASTR* is equipped with a compiler and an interpreter of regular expressions. To account for more general coordinations, the preceding metarule (4.10) is reformulated as follows:

Metarule Coor($N_1 \rightarrow A_2\ N_3$) $\equiv$ $N_1 \rightarrow A_2$ $\langle$C $\{A \mid N \mid A_{pp}\}^{1-3}\rangle$ N_3: . $\qquad$ (4.12)

The intermediate regular expression between angle brackets states that the adjective and the noun of the initial term can be separated by a coordinating conjunction followed by one to three words of the three following categories: adjective, noun, or adjectival past participle. This metarule correctly recognizes *umbilical*$_A$ *and*$_C$ *middle*$_A$ *cerebral*$_A$ *artery*$_N$ as a variant of *Umbilical artery*.

The usual operators of regular expressions are available in *FASTR*: concatenation, alternative, Kleene star, bounded repetition, and optionality. The syntax of regular expressions in *FASTR* is suggested by the following simplified context-free grammar in which all the terminal strings are quoted:

Reg_expr $\rightarrow$ '$\langle$'Seq'$\rangle$' $\qquad$ Fact $\rightarrow$ '{'Alt'}'

$\qquad$ Seq $\rightarrow$ Fact_oper Seq $\quad$ Fact $\rightarrow$ Term

$\qquad$ Seq $\rightarrow$ Fact_oper $\qquad$ Fact $\rightarrow$ Reg_expr

Fact_oper $\rightarrow$ Fact '*' $\qquad$ Alt $\rightarrow$ Term '|' Alt

Fact_oper $\rightarrow$ Fact '+' $\qquad$ Alt $\rightarrow$ Term $\qquad\qquad$ (4.13)

Fact_oper $\rightarrow$ Fact '?' $\qquad$ Term $\rightarrow$ 'A' | 'N' | 'C' ...

Fact_oper $\rightarrow$ Fact^{Nb}'-'^{Nb} $\qquad$ Nb $\rightarrow$ '0' Nb | ... | '9' Nb

Fact_oper $\rightarrow$ Fact $\qquad\qquad$ Nb $\rightarrow$ '0' | ... | '9'

Constraints in Metarules

Apart from the possibility of regular expressions, the formalism of metarules has the same characteristics as the formalism of rules. In particular, constraints, whether positive or negative, can be added to a metarule in order to improve the quality of the resulting transformed rules.

Let us illustrate the usefulness of such additional constraints by presenting a metarule for argument coordinations of Noun-Noun terms. A Noun-Noun term, such as *Tumor cell*, accepts coordination variants in which the modifier *tumor* is coordinated with a noun modifier. For instance, (... *the damage of*) *tumor*$_N$ *or*$_C$ *nontumorous*$_A$ *hepatic*$_A$ *cells*$_N$ is a correct variant of *Tumor cell*. In order to filter out incorrect variants, an additional negative constraint states that the argument noun, here *tumor*, cannot be plural. The resulting metarule is

Metarule Coor($N_1 \rightarrow N_2\ N_3$) $\equiv$ $N_1 \rightarrow N_2$ $\langle$C $\{A \mid N \mid A_{pp}\}^{1-3}\rangle$ N_3: $\qquad$ (4.14)

$\neg(\langle N_2$ *agreement number*$\rangle$ $\doteq$ '*plural*').

The negative constraint allows for the correct ruling out of spurious variations of *Tumor cell* such as (. . . *but failed to lyse*) *tumors or K562 cells*. Chapter 5 presents some of the methods for experimentally discovering such constraints, whether positive or negative.

Morphological and Semantic Links in Metarules

Among the positive constraints that can accompany a metarule, some can describe morphological links. Two words are morphologically related if they belong to the same derivational family (constructed from the same stem). For instance, *enzymopathy*, *enzymatic*, *enzymic*, and *enzymatically* are morphologically related because they are all built from the stem *enzyme*. The stem *enzyme* itself also belongs to this family.

In a metarule the membership of two words in the same morphological family is expressed by stating that they share a common root. This value is associated with the paths ⟨*root*⟩ (see the feature structures 3.12 and 3.14). Thus, in the following metarule, the noun N_2 and the adjective A_4 are expected to be morphologically related:

Metarule NountoAdj($N_1 \rightarrow N_2\ N_3$) ≡ $N_1 \rightarrow A_4\ N_3$:   (4.15)

⟨N_2 *root*⟩ $\doteq$ ⟨A_4 *root*⟩.

Metarule (4.15) extracts adjectivization variants from corpora such as *enzymatic*$_A$ *activity*$_N$, a variant of *enzyme activity*, or *enzymatic*$_A$ *system*$_N$, a variant of *enzyme system*. This metarule functions no matter what the mode of calculus of derivative morphology, whether dynamic or static.

Similarly semantic links are another type of lexical relationships that can be expressed through positive constraints on metarules. The semantic relationship between two words is formulated by expressing that their semantic paths share a common value. For instance, in metarule (4.16), the two nominal modifiers N_2 and N_4 must be semantically related:

Metarule SemArg($N_1 \rightarrow N_2\ N_3$) ≡ $N_1 \rightarrow N_4\ N_3$:   (4.16)

⟨N_2 *syn*⟩ $\doteq$ ⟨N_4 *syn*⟩.

Metarule (4.16) extracts semantic variants from corpora such as *hard lens*, a variant of *rigid lens*, because of the synonymous relationship of *hard* and *rigid*. This representation of semantic relationships corresponds to class-based descriptions such as *synsets* in *WordNet*.

Since the presentation of metarules in *FASTR* has been introduced in relation to the metarules in *GPSG*, I now conclude this introduction to the metagrammar of *FASTR* with a contrast between the two formalisms.

Comparison with *GPSG*

A metarule in *FASTR* is defined as a pair of rules—a source and a target—and the construction of a transformed rule relies solely on the mechanism of unification. The parallel between metarules in *FASTR* and in *GPSG* is as follows:

1. The matching of the pattern and an input rule in *GPSG* corresponds to the unification of the initial rule and the left part of the metarule in *FASTR*.

2. The determination of the target variables and categories in *GPSG* implicitly results from the variables shared by the source and the target of a metarule in *FASTR*.

In *GPSG*, if the source and the target disagree over the value of some feature, the generation of the transformed rule succeeds and the target structure wins. Conversely, such a situation in *FASTR* results in an unproductive metarule because the initial unification between the rule and the source fails. (Although it concerns only the left part of the metarule, the unification algorithm checks whether the whole set of constraints of the metarule yields a correct feature structure.)

The definition of metarules in *FASTR* through unification is related to the study of Busemann and Hauenschild (1988), which detailed the efficient implementation of principle-based grammars such as *GPSG* in a unification-based framework. In this study all the idiosyncratic nonmonotonic mechanisms of *GPSG* were replaced by a progressive specification of categories through unification. Busemann and Hauenschild did not use metarules in the course of parsing—they treated them as a preprocessing component. The metarules mechanism, as implemented in *FASTR*, naturally complements the unification-based implementation of a principle-based grammar proposed in Busemann and Hauenschild (1988) by adding a unification-based metagrammar.

The second discrepancy between *GPSG* and *FASTR* is the absence, in *FASTR*, of an abbreviatory variable *W* that contains multi-sets of categories. I did not find it useful to implement this facility on *FASTR* because the variety of term structures is much narrower than the variety of verb subcategorizations. Each term structure has its own idiosyncratic variations, and these structures are in a small enough number to allow special case description.

To sum up, the metarules in *FASTR* are more generic than those in *GPSG*, for they are based on unification which is a generic calculus. Conversely, since *FASTR* is a task-oriented tool, namely in performing term and variant extraction, the metarules in *FASTR* do not need to provide some of the facilities proposed by *GPSG*, such as abbreviatory variables and the transformation of underspecified rules, the lexical rules. Some confusion may occur in *GPSG* because the definitions of lexical rules and metarules cover similar descriptions (the various subcategorizations of a lexeme). This has led some authors to replace metarules by a more constrained device that does not interfere with lexical rules (Shieber et al. 1983; Kilbury 1986). No such problem exists in *FASTR* where rules represent terms and metarules represent variations.

4.3   A Constructive View of Metarules

This section complements the presentation of the parser given in section 3.5; it describes the generation of term variants by metarules.

4.3.1   Compile-Time and Run-Time Applications

The main issue in implementing a generation of transformed rules is to choose the time when it should be performed. There are two possible ways to apply metarules, with the following consequences (Weisweber and Preuß 1992):

Compile-time application. The transformed rules are calculated only once during the pre-processing step. A large set of initial data is produced which is stored and then used during the parsing process. This approach spares the computational cost of recalculating transformed rules when they are needed, but it requires a large storage capacity and efficient techniques for accessing the precompiled data.

Run-time application. The transformed rules are dynamically calculated during the parsing process. Only the rules whose transformations are likely to have successful parses are transformed. This choice does not require much storage capacity, but it has an extra computational cost due to the dynamic calculation of transformed rules. This solution implicitly requires the ability to distinguish among the grammar rules the rules that are relevant for parsing the current input.

The relative merits of these two approaches have been discussed for *GPSG*. The same conclusions apply *FASTR* or any formalism in which a core set of rules is expanded through a transformational process. Thompson (1983) argued for the compile-time application because it reduces the computational load of the parser. His arguments are discussed further by Weisweber and Preuß (1992) who meticulously analyzed the effective computational cost of the run-time application. They contradicted Thompson's arguments and showed that the computational overload of the run-time application is moderate. They also indicated that the compile-time application of metarules generates a huge set of data because of the combinatory effect between rules and metarules. Therefore the management of this large data set of transformed rules, in addition to requiring large storage capacities, also requires nonnegligible extra computation for retrieving and accessing data during parsing.

These arguments for choosing run-time application in *FASTR* are supported by the following two remarks. The first comment is about the actual size of the data used by *FASTR*: the size of the compiled term list is approximately 10 Mbytes (for 100,000 terms and 30,000 single words). A pre-compiling of the transformed term rules would multiply by a factor greater than 25 the size of the terminological data. (On average, 28 metarules apply to each term and generate transformed rules that are greater than the initial rules.) The resulting size of the pre-compiled dictionary would be over 250 Mbytes and therefore would be accessed more slowly.

The second and main comment is about the experimental tuning of metarules when using *FASTR* (see chapter 5). The experimental tuning of metarules is performed by successive trials of different set of metarules on the same set of rules and the same corpus. A compile-time application of metarules would force the experimenter to repeatedly recompile the transformed rules after each modification of the metagrammar. By comparison, a run-time application allows for instantaneous runs after every modification of the metagrammar.

4.3.2 Transformational Analysis

In the diagram presented earlier in figure 3.7, the generation of transformed rules and their exploitation in parsing is shown as the last step of the computation. The process takes as input a lemmatized text, a compiled dictionary of single words and terms, and a metagrammar, and outputs an indexed text.

For each parsed sentence all the rules that are linked to the inflected words of the sentence by the feature *lexicalization* are activated. Each active rule is loaded in turn by the parser. If the parse succeeds, the corresponding term occurrence is reported. Otherwise, all the successive transformations of this rule are generated and applied until one succeeds or until all the transformations have been generated.[30] If a transformed rule is successfully analyzed, the corresponding variant is reported in the index file.

Through this method only 2.1 transformed rules are built, on average, for each activated rule, although terms have, on average, 28 possible transformations. When indexing the corpus [Medic], with the term list [Pascal] and a set of 115 metarules, on a Pentium (300 MHz), 32 Mbytes main memory running Linux, the average parsing speed is 25,000 words/min. Of course, the parsing speed is a function of the size of the terminological and transformational data. With a set of terms 10 times smaller, the parsing speed is 6 times higher. The required memory size also depends on the size of the term list: an approximative size of 10 Mbytes is necessary for a controlled list of 100,000 terms.

Clearly, my decision to use a rich and convenient formalism, a unification-based grammar, has not resulted in poor computational performance. It has included a very cautious implementation of *FASTR*, optimizations for accessing the data (Jacquemin 1994b), and optimizations for parsing the sentences (e.g., unification is delayed until all the lexical items of a term or a variant are recognized).

The next chapter illustrates the practical use of *FASTR* for tuning the metagrammar in English. The flexible unification-based grammar allows for a convenient incremental refinement of the transformational data through feature additions.

4.4 Summary

This chapter has presented the metagrammar of *FASTR* that operates on top of the lexical and terminological data. The metagrammar is a device motivated by a transformational description of term variation that stems from Harrisian linguistics. In Harris's theory, sentences are described as combined transformations of core phrase schemata composed of an operator and its arguments. In *FASTR*, phrase schemata correspond to basic term structures and transformations to variations. This theory is all the more appropriate because it pays particular attention to sublanguages, languages attached to specialized domains such as medicine or physics.

In accordance with linguistic analysis, this chapter has proposed an implementation of variations through metarules that transform term rules into term variant rules. The description of metarules follows the guidelines of rules in the preceding chapter. The metarules consist of a double context-free skeleton—the input and the output structures— and a set of equations expressing constraints on the nodes of these two skeletons.

The formalism of *FASTR* is closely compared with *GPSG* and *FB-LTAG*, two other concurrent approaches to metarules in unification-based formalisms. Two facilities are added to the standard formalism for metarules. First, the syntactic structure of the output context-free skeleton can contain regular expressions in order to permit the expression of complex target structures. Second, morphological and semantic links are expressed in metarules by links that connect words in the source structure and words in the target structure that share the same root or belong to the same semantic class.

During the process of term spotting by *FASTR*, term variant extraction comes after nonvariant extraction presented in the preceding chapter. Variant rules are dynamically generated by transforming each active term rule through metarules. Each variant rule is then parsed by *FASTR*, and the corresponding text occurrences are reported if the parse succeeds. The metarule that has produced the recognized term variant serves as a linguistic link between the basic controlled term and the variant occurrence retrieved from the parsed text.

5 Experimental Tuning

This chapter is dedicated to the building, the tuning, and the evaluation of metarules for describing syntactic term variations in English.[31]

After a description of metarules for binary terms in section 5.1 and for *n*-ary terms in section 5.2, a general presentation of compositions of metarules is given in section 5.3. These variations are prone to errors because they do not contain any constraints on the categories and the features of their components. The experimental tuning of metarules for variant detection in untagged corpora is described in section 5.4. Based on the preliminary structure of nonfiltering variations, filtering variation are defined through progressive corpus-based additions of linguistic constraints. Finally, section 5.5 provides a qualitative and a quantitative evaluation of term and variant spotting.

5.1 Elementary Variations of Binary Terms

The approach to term spotting that is chosen in *FASTR* is a generative approach. All the possible variants that are likely to be encountered within corpora are generated through compositions of elementary variations on core word dependencies given by controlled terms. This section presents the four main families of elementary term variations in English: permutations, modifications/substitutions, coordinations, and elisions.

Permutations and modifications were reported in Dunham (1986) and modifications/substitutions were considered in the studies on free indexing by Fagan (1987) and Metzler and Haas (1989). Some of the variations described in Dunham (1986) are not elementary and correspond to compositions of variations that will be studied in section 5.3. Other variants exemplified in Dunham (1986) are typical oral expressions (e.g., the postposition of the final adjective in *inflammation with mesothelial reaction, visceral*). Since the discussion here focuses on the indexing of technical and scientific written documents, such oral-specific variations are not presented here.

5.1.1 Permutation

The first family of variations is *permutation*, which captures the link between a term that is a compound noun such as *Tooth root* and a noun phrase with the same meaning, here *the root of a lower premolar tooth*:

Definition 5.1 (Permutation) A permutation is a transformation that associates a term containing a nominal left-hand modifier N with a noun phrase containing a right-hand prepositional phrase whose head is N.

The unconstrained expression of a permutation metarule is given by

$$\text{Metarule Perm}(X_1 \rightarrow X_2\ X_3) \equiv X_1 \rightarrow X_3\ P_4\ X_2 : . \tag{5.1}$$

In cognitive linguistics Langacker (1987, pp. 295–97) compares the semantics of a compound such as *Corn kernel* and the corresponding noun phrase construction *kernel of corn.* Langacker shows that these two utterances are not semantically equivalent: *Corn kernel* designates a single grain that is representative of a larger mass, whereas a *kernel of corn* identifies a single individual kernel with its own characteristics. Such a distinction can be too finely grained for applications in automatic indexing; the role of the preposition in the meaning of permutation variants is more distinctive (*cell of blood* as opposed to *cell from blood*).

In [Medic] 65.3% of the permutations are built with the preposition *of*, 11.1% with the preposition *in*, and the remaining permutations are built with other various prepositions such as *from, for, on, with,* and *to.* Thus the majority of permutations observed in the corpus are built with *of*, a *colorless* preposition that does not entail an important difference of interpretation between the compound and the noun phrase (despite the subtle shades of meaning revealed by cognitive studies). However, permutations built with colored prepositions such as *from* are not necessarily equivalent to the controlled term. For instance, when encountering the utterance *T cells from the peripheral blood of six patients*, two interpretations are possible. The first is that *T cells* are a type of *blood cells*; the second is that *T cells* can be found within *blood* but are not a type of *blood cells.* Only the former case corresponds to a genuine variant.

Table 5.1 shows the first 20 permutations extracted from [Medic] by the nonfiltering metarule (5.1).

Errors
Only nominal modifiers can be permuted with the head noun so as to preserve the dependency between the words of the original term. For instance, a permutation of the term *Molecular form*, such as *soluble forms of the two molecular species*, is not a correct variant of this term. Apart from adjectives, some other modifiers are not likely to be involved in a permutation. For instance, the modifier *beta* in *Beta effect* is not appropriate for a permutation: the occurrence *effects of beta*, extracted from the utterance *The effects of beta adrenoceptor blockade, (. . .) were studied . . .* , is not a variant of *Beta effect.* In table 5.1, the examples associated with terms whose argument is neither an adjective nor the word *beta* are correct. A manual observation of the full sentences in which these occurrences are found confirms their acceptability.

Coverage
Metarule (5.1) nevertheless does not cover all the possible permutation variations. There are three following reasons for this:

1. Variants of *n*-ary terms with $n \geq 2$ are not produced by metarule (5.1).

Table 5.1
Unfiltered permutations from [Medic]

Controlled term	Variant	Number of occurrences	Correct variant
Autoimmune disease	*diseases with autoimmune*	1	−
Basal area	*area of basal*	1	−
Basal layer	*layer of basal*	1	−
Beta distribution	*distribution of beta*	3	−
Beta distribution	*distributions from beta*	1	−
Beta effect	*effect between beta*	1	−
Beta effect	*effect on beta*	1	−
Beta effect	*effects of beta*	2	−
Beta-structure	*structure of beta*	1	−
Biological method	*method in biological*	1	−
Birth date	*date of birth*	1	+
Birth place	*place of birth*	1	+
Blood cell	*cells from blood*	1	+
Blood cell	*cells in blood*	2	+
Blood culture	*cultures of blood*	3	+
Blood dissemination	*dissemination in blood*	1	?
Blood flow	*flow of blood*	1	+
Blood group	*group of blood*	1	+
Blood volume	*volume of blood*	2	+
Body image	*images of body*	1	+

2. Permutation variations that are not the result of decompounding do not conform to the pattern of metarule (5.1). For instance, *the Philadelphia chromosome (Ph1)* is a correct variant of *Ph1 chromosome* even though it not accepted by this metarule because the inserted word is an opening parenthesis, not a preposition.

3. Some genuine permutations are not accepted by metarule (5.1) because the distance between the head word of the term and the head word of the prepositional phrase is too important. This distance arises from the composition of an elementary permutation with some other transformation, generally a modification. For instance, the permutation of *Light effect* yields *effect of light*, which can be, in turn, transformed by a modification into *effects of ultraviolet light*. This latter variant is not recognized by metarule (5.1). Such compositions of elementary variations are studied in section 5.2.

5.1.2 Modification and Substitution

In Fagan (1987, pp. 78–81, 89–90), complex noun phrases such as *automatic document retrieval* are systematically reduced to binary noun phrases (here *automatic retrieval* and *document retrieval*). Binary noun phrases allow for the pairing of text utterances corresponding to identical dependencies with various linguistic expressions. In *FASTR* the dual transformation is called *modification* or *substitution*, and this amounts to the insertion of an additional dependency into an elementary one.

Definition 5.2 (Modification or substitution)   A modification or a substitution is a transformation that associates a term with a variant in which the head word or one of its argument has an additional modifier.

In definition 1.1 because of restriction 4 only modifications or substitutions that insert words within the term string are considered. For instance, *blood mononuclear cell* is a modification/substitution variant of *Blood cell*, whereas *red blood cells* is not considered to be a variant because *red* is an external modifier.

According to Daille (1994, sec. 2.2.2), two types of modifications should be distinguished:

• If the inserted modifier builds a term with the head word of the original term, the variation is a substitution. Thus *myeloid hematopoietic cell* is a substitution variant of *Myeloid cell* because *Hematopoietic cell* belongs to the controlled term list [Pascal]. The construction of a substitution variant is modeled by the aggregation of two terms in section 5.2.3.

• Otherwise, the variation is a genuine *modification* if the inserted modifier is not involved in a lexicalized (or conceptualized) construction with the head word of the term. For instance, *myeloid leukemia cell* is a modification of *Myeloid cell* because *leukemia cell* is not a controlled term. Contrary to substitutions, the modeling of modifications only involves one term.

The distinction between these two types of variation relies on membership in a controlled term list, which is extralinguistic knowledge. This membership is the determining criterion for deciding whether the variant can be used for term acquisition (see chapter 6).

The basic form of a nonfiltering metarule for a modification/substitution that inserts a single word into a 2-word term is given by

Metarule Modif$(X_1 \rightarrow X_2\,X_3) \equiv X_1 \rightarrow X_2\,X_4\,X_3 :\ .$ (5.2)

The first twenty variations extracted by metarule (5.2) are displayed in table 5.2.

Errors
This nonfiltering metarule is not selective enough since an utterance such as *acids and electrolytes* could be incorrectly accepted as a variant of *Acid electrolyte* (as in . . . *contains glucose, amino acids and electrolytes*). There are at least two good reasons for rejecting this variant: the modifier *acid* cannot be plural and the inserted modifier cannot be a

Table 5.2
Unfiltered modifications/substitutions from [Medic]

Controlled term	Variant	Number of occurrences	Correct variant
Abelson leukemia	*Abelson murine leukemia*	2	+
Abnormal chromosome	*abnormal X chromosome*	3	+
Absolute value	*absolute CA125 values*	1	+
Absorbed dose	*absorbed radiation dose*	1	+
Acid electrolyte	*acids and electrolytes*	1	−
Acid reaction	*acid Schiff reaction*	1	+
Acidic protein	*acidic bili protein*	1	+
Acidic protein	*acidic epidermal protein*	1	+
Acoustic cavitation	*acoustic and cavitation*	1	−
Active site	*active secondary site*	1	+
Addison disease	*addison's disease*	1	+
Adductor muscle	*adductor pollicis muscle*	2	+
Adenosquamous carcinoma	*adenosquamous lung carcinoma*	1	+
Adenovirus 5	*adenovirus type 5*	1	+
Adenovirus 12	*adenovirus type 12*	1	+
Adoptive transfer	*adoptive cell transfer*	1	+
Adrenal artery	*adrenal middle artery*	1	+
Adult animal	*adult experimental animals*	1	+
Adult animal	*adult obese animals*	1	+
Adult animal	*adult transgenic animals*	1	+

coordinating conjunction. The addition of selective constraints that address this sort of problem is presented in section 5.4.

Structural Ambiguity

The ternary variants extracted by metarule (5.2) have two possible structures: $X_2 [X_4 X_3]$ and $[X_2 X_4] X_3$. Only the former structure respects the constraint 3 of definition 1.1 about having all the dependency relations of the original term preserved in the variant. In the latter structure, X_2 depends on X_4 whereas it depends on X_3 in the original term.

Although formally incorrect, the $[X_2 X_4] X_3$ variants of $X_2 X_3$ terms are generally genuine conceptual variants. For instance, [*sunflower seed*] *oil* is a genuine variant of *Sunflower oil*, but it does not correspond to my *a priori* definition of variants. Indeed, what is called here a *variant* (*sunflower seed oil*) corresponds to the full expression of the term. Reciprocally, what is called an *original term* (*Sunflower oil*) is an elliptic variant.

Reduced forms are used as controlled terms for the pragmatic reasons of economy and cognitive salience. First, the shortest linguistic expression of a concept is frequently fixed in usage if this form is not ambiguous (Sager 1990, sec. 4.2.1). Second, the salient feature of *sunflower seed oil* is not the part of the plant from which the *oil* is extracted (the *seeds* and not the *roots* or the *leaves*) but the plant itself (*sunflower*). It is common pragmatic knowledge that *Sunflower oil* is obtained from the *seeds* of *sunflower*: the *seeds* are the *active zone* (Langacker 1987, sec. 7.3.4) of *sunflower*—its prominent aspect—as far as *oil* is concerned. The implicit knowledge involved in the meaning of *sunflower* N compounds depends on semantic features of the head noun N and their coactivations with the features of the argument *sunflower*. In a related example, a *bunch of sunflowers*, the *flowers* are the active aspect of the plant.

The possibility of omitting linguistic elements corresponding to implicit pragmatic knowledge is called *integrated metonymy* after Kleiber (1989, p. 127). The abbreviated linguistic expression of the term is used as its reference form because the extended expression is not likely to be encountered within corpora. Because of its rarity the expanded form is considered a variant.

5.1.3   Coordination

Coordination also stems from a principle of economy: coordinations of terms avoid the repetition of identical lexemes with similar meaning. Thus *aortic valve or mitral valve* is combined as *aortic or mitral valve* because *valve* names the same part of a mammal's heart in both terms. Because coordination is a variation with strong semantic constraints, it is exploited in linguistic studies for confirming the similarity of interpretative schemata of two or more compounds (Cadiot 1992, p. 222).

Coordination gives clues about the selection restrictions of the different entries of polysemous words. For instance, none of both terms *Aortic valve* and *Mitral valve* can be coordinated with terms in which *valve* refers to another concept such as *Safety valve* or *Tire valve*. The shift of meaning of *valve* in these terms can be seen clearly in the corresponding translations in French: *valve* is translated *valvule* in *Aortic valve*, *soupape* in *Safety valve*, and *valve* in *Tire valve*.[32] Semantic disambiguation is, however, not necessary for term extraction because it concerns parsing and not generation.

The syntactic definition of a coordination without reference to its interpretation is

Definition 5.3 (Coordination)   A coordination is a transformation that associates a pair of terms with a composite variant such that one of the two following conditions is fulfilled:

1. The head word of one term is coordinated with the head word of the other term, and both terms have identical arguments.

2. One of the arguments of one term is coordinated with one of the arguments of the other term, and both terms have identical head words.

The first condition corresponds to *head coordinations* and the second one to *argument coordinations*. Head coordination is described by metarule (5.3) and is illustrated by *axiliary artery and vein*; argument coordination is modeled by metarule (5.4) and associated with variants such as *intercostal and bronchial arteries*.

$$\text{Metarule } \text{Coor}(X_1 \to X_2\, X_3) \;\equiv\; X_1 \to X_2\, X_4\, C_5\, X_3 : . \tag{5.3}$$

$$\text{Metarule } \text{Coor}(X_1 \to X_2\, X_3) \;\equiv\; X_1 \to X_2\, C_4\, X_5\, X_3 : . \tag{5.4}$$

The first ten variants of table 5.3 are extracted by metarule (5.3) and the last ten variants by metarule (5.4).

Errors

Despite the absence of filtering constraints in metarule (5.4), the argument coordinations shown in table 5.3 are of a surprisingly good quality. This impression is confirmed by systematic evaluations reported in section 5.5.1. Both forms of coordinations are encountered

Table 5.3
Unfiltered argument coordinations (the first ten) and head coordinations (the last ten) from [Medic]

Controlled term	Variant	Number of occurrences	Correct variant
Agonist antagonist	*agonist bromocriptine and antagonist*	1	−
Aortic coarctation	*aortic arch or coarctation*	1	−
Axillary vein	*axillary artery and vein*	1	+
Blood plasma	*blood flow and plasma*	1	−
Blood plasma	*blood GPX and plasma*	1	−
Blood plasma	*blood hemoglobin and plasma*	1	−
Blood plasma	*blood serum and plasma*	1	+
Body composition	*body weight and composition*	1	+
Body surface	*body imaginer and surface*	1	−
Caudate nucleus	*caudate putamen and nucleus*	1	+
Abdominal wall	*abdominal and chest wall*	1	+
Activity coefficient	*activity and variation coefficient*	1	+
Adipose tissue	*adipose and muscle tissue*	1	+
Adipose tissue	*adipose or fibroadipose tissue*	1	+
Age distribution	*age and sex distribution*	1	+
Air transportation	*air and ground transportation*	1	+
Alpha interferon	*alpha and beta interferons*	1	+
Alpha-thalassemia	*alpha and delta thalassemias*	1	+
Amplitude modulation	*amplitude and frequency modulations*	1	+
Anal sphincter	*anal and urethral sphincters*	1	+

in the [Medic] corpus. Coordinations are hence distributed on the two metarules: on the training corpus [Medic], 15% are extracted by metarule (5.3) and 85% by metarule (5.4).

Constraints on the Coordinated Term

As for modification/substitution, the construction of a coordination involves a second term that either does or does not belong to the controlled list. For instance, *white and gray matter* is a coordination variant of *White matter* that involves *Gray matter*, another controlled term. In comparison, *mechanical and infectious factors*, a variant of *Mechanical factors*, the coordinated structure, *infectious factors*, does not belong to the controlled vocabulary. Such constructions, in which the coordinated structure does not belong to the term list, are somewhat abnormal. A coordinated term is generally a correct term (here *infectious factors*). This fact is explored in section 6.3 in the discussion on acquiring candidate terms from coordination variants.

Terms with arguments of different syntactic categories can be coordinated. In particular, the coordination of a nominal argument with an adjectival one is acceptable as long as semantic compatibility is respected (Martinet 1985, p. 112). For instance, *fat and caloric content* is a correct coordination variant of *Fat content* because both *fat* and *caloric* denote the physicochemical composition of a food. On the contrary, a post-posed argument cannot be coordinated with an ante-posed one without repeating the head word. Thus the correct coordinations of *Angle of incidence* with *Rotation angle* are *the angle of incidence and the rotation angle*, *angles of incidence and rotation*, or *incidence and rotation angles*.

5.1.4   Elliptic Anaphor

I now move to the abbreviatory expression of multi-word terms through elliptic references. For instance, the second reference to *Chromosome 17* is *chromosome* in the following utterance:

The p53 gene is a tumor suppressor gene located on <u>chromosome 17</u>.   (5.5)
Deletions of this <u>chromosome</u> (. . .) have been implicated in . . .

I first review some linguistic studies on anaphoric references of compound nouns, and then I consider the automatic extraction of such variants by *FASTR*.

Linguistic Background

Anaphor is a topic in discourse linguistics. The successive references to a common concept consist of a *first* or *initial mention* followed by *subsequent mentions* (Fraurud 1990) that generally contain only a subpart of the lexemes found in the initial mention. The anaphoric reference is frequent enough to be an important issue in automatic indexing. Liddy et al.

(1987) indicate a rate of 3.67 anaphora per abstract across a set of 600 abstracts (and abstracts contain typically less anaphora than articles or books).

Fraurud (1990) evaluates the distribution of noun phrase (NP) structures across initial and subsequent mentions. The study reveals that 75.1% of multi-word NPs are initial mentions: the multi-word NPs represent 41.2% of initial mentions and only 20.7% of subsequent mentions. In other words, the reference to multi-word NPs is made with single words one time out of every two. The single word used for referring to a multi-word NP is not necessarily the head of the NP.

Kister (1993) studies the different forms of anaphoric reference to N_1 *de* $D N_2$ terms in the French language. In French N_1 *de* $D N_2$ terms, N_1 is the head word and *de* $D N_2$ is a post-posed prepositional modifier. She shows that N_2 is used for anaphoric reference to NPs with nominal determiners (Gross 1986a, pp. 49–54, 59–67): *une foule d'ouvriers est venue à l'usine* . . . (a crowd of workers came to the factory) is followed by a subsequent mention such as *les ouvriers sont entrés* (the workers have walked in). Noncompositional compound nouns, such as *Pied de table* (leg of table) are generally referred to by using the whole NP. On the contrary, compositional noun phrases with a head noun that is also the semantic head of the NP are referred to by the head word N_1 (see example 5.5 above).

The subsequent mentions of complex terms containing n content words, with n greater than or equal to 2, are NPs built with 1 to n of these content words. These references are built according to a principle of economy: concepts are referred to by incomplete linguistic expressions provided that the elliptic expression is not ambiguous and that the full meaning can be contextually or pragmatically recovered. In support of this principle, Sager (1990, pp. 66, 108, 215) remarks that terms can have more that one elliptic expression. For instance, *spark plug* and *plug* are two elliptic references to *14 mm spark plug*.

Elliptic Variants

The processing of elliptic anaphor by *FASTR* is not straightforward because of the noncontextuality of its parsing approach. For example, there are 96 controlled terms in [Pascal] with *cell* as head word. Without knowledge of the context, how can be determined which of these 96 terms is the correct initial mention of *cell* in *Cells were preconditioned by growing in cobalamin-deficient media for six weeks*? The clue to the solution is found two sentences earlier in the same abstract: *The conversion of cyanocobalamin to adenosyl- and methyl-cobalamin is impaired in cobalamin-deficient cultured human glial cells*. Because of its noncontextuality, *FASTR* can only relate nonambiguous occurrences with their correct initial references. Other coreferences through pronouns or single words, such as *cell* in the preceding example, are too ambiguous for a noncontextual identification.

Therefore only mentions with two or more words are likely to be extracted by *FASTR*. These represent only 19.3% of the subsequent mentions of multi-word terms according to Fraurud (1990). This subset of the anaphora to multi-word terms is defined as follows:

Definition 5.4 (Elliptic anaphor)   An elliptic anaphor is a transformation of a term into a noun phrase with the same head noun and with a nonempty subset of its initial arguments.

The preceding definition can only apply to terms with at least three content words: a head word and at least two arguments. It is implemented by the following two metarules for three-word terms:

$$\text{Metarule Elis}(X_1 \rightarrow X_2\ X_3\ X_4) \equiv X_1 \rightarrow X_2\ X_4 : . \tag{5.6}$$

$$\text{Metarule Elis}(X_1 \rightarrow X_2\ X_3\ X_4) \equiv X_1 \rightarrow X_3\ X_4 : . \tag{5.7}$$

Errors

The structural ambiguity of ternary terms is the first cause of errors when using these metarules for the extraction of anaphoric variants. For instance, *bone cell* is an incorrect variant of [*Bone marrow*] *cell* because the dependency of *marrow* on *cell* in the controlled term is transformed into a dependency of *bone* on *cell* in the variant. This change of dependency does not respect the constraint 3 of definition 1.1. Metarule (5.6) only behaves properly in retrieving variants of X_2 [$X_3\ X_4$] terms such as *analytical microscopy*, a variant of *Analytical* [*electron microscopy*].

The second and main cause of error is due to the noncontextuality of *FASTR*. Despite the restriction of the extraction to a small family of anaphoric variations, the evaluations given in section 5.5 reveal a very poor precision. For a correct extraction of anaphoric variations, *FASTR* should be extended with the following two additional capabilities: a parsing memory for remembering the initial mentions of multi-word terms and a context detection for defining the scope of these initial mentions.

5.1.5   Other Term Structures

The metarules corresponding to the preceding types of variations described in sections 5.1.1 to 5.1.4 are devised for terms with a compound structure. However, an exhaustive description of term variations should consider the whole variety of term structures. More specifically, terms with an NP structure, such as *Analysis of variance*, or deverbal terms, such as *Build up*, should also be taken into consideration.

The description of the metarules for noncompound terms such as the two preceding ones is not given here due to their low frequency: they represent only 458 terms of the 71,623 terms of the [Pascal] base. Furthermore the variations of terms with an NP structure are identical to the variations composed with permutations described in section 5.3.

5.2   Elementary Variations of *n*-ary Terms

The metarules given in the preceding section are restricted to binary compound terms (for permutation, modification/substitution, and coordination) and to ternary compound terms (for elliptic anaphor). However, definition 1.1 describes a larger set of variations. An exhaustive approach to variation should take them all into consideration. The two possibilities for extending metarules describing term variations are the following:

Extension to n-ary terms with n > 2. For instance, metarule (5.1) does not describe argument coordinations of ternary terms such as *superior or inferior mesenteric artery* or *superior mesenteric or coeliac arteries*, two variants of *Superior mesenteric artery*.

Compositions of elementary variations. The four preceding types of variations can be composed to produce nonelementary variations. For instance, *volume of shed blood* is a variant of *Blood volume* which is obtained by composing a permutation, yielding *volume of blood*, with a modification/substitution producing the observed variant.

This section and the two following ones present an extended set of metarules. In this section the metarules for the binary terms of the preceding section are generalized to *n*-ary terms with *n* > 2. In section 5.3 the variations thus obtained are used to define nonelementary variations. Since metarules defined so far are context-free skeletons without filtering constraints, the third task, described in section 5.4, is to enrich nonfiltering metarules with constraints in order to increase their accuracy.

5.2.1   Structure of *n*-ary Terms

Apart from their size, ternary terms differ from binary terms in their structural ambiguity: their head or argument constituents can be unary or binary structures. Figure 5.1 illustrates the three possible structures $(\star)$, α_1, and α_2 of a ternary term.

   Most ternary terms are built from binary structures and thereby belong to one of the two structures α_1 or α_2. For instance, the structures of *White* [*blood cell*] and [*Blood cell*] *count* are respectively α_1 and α_2 because *Blood cell* belongs to the controlled term list, while the competing associations, *white blood* and *blood count*, do not. There are two alternatives for recognizing variants of structured terms: (1) find a method for automatically calculating the structure of ternary terms or (2) describe all the combinations of flat term variants corresponding to the various possibilities of structures. Since the structure of a term influences the structure of its variants, an incorrect term structuring will disturb a procedure for term variant extraction. I therefore prefer to choose the second alternative and calculate the strings corresponding to the linear projections of term structures. Evaluations described

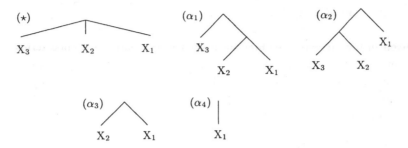

Figure 5.1
The structures of ternary, binary, and unary terms.

in section 5.5 show that this approximation does not degrade the accuracy of term variant extraction.[33]

5.2.2 Coordinations of *n*-ary Terms

All the possible coordinations of ternary terms of structure α_1 and α_2 with ternary terms of the same structures or with binary terms of structure α_3 are shown in tables 5.4 to 5.7. These coordinations are divided into head and argument coordinations. The different tree structures α_1, α_2, and α_3 are given in figure 5.1 and the different types of coordinations are illustrated by figure 5.2.

There are two alternatives for building coordinations: both coordinated terms share a common constituent, or they do not (figure 5.2). In either case the coordinations can be further separated into head and argument coordination depending on the syntactic function of the coordinated constituents. In the following tables, head coordinations are index H and argument coordinations are index A.

In order to define precisely each coordination, a second index makes explicit the coordinated constituent of the original term. This index is composed of two numbers separated by an hyphen. These numbers give the lowest and highest ranks of the contiguous words building up the coordinated constituent in the original term. The relative position of both coordinated constituents is provided by the third index of these transformations. This index states whether the coordinated constituent is located to the right (index R) or to the left (index L) of the constituent of the original term.

For instance, the first coordination in table 5.4, named $C_{A,1-2,R}(\alpha_1,\alpha_1)$, is an argument coordination of two α_1 structures. The coordinated argument $[X'_3 \, X'_2]$ is located to the right of the argument of the controlled term, which consists of the first two words of this term $[X_3 \, X_2]$. If the coordination is built at the level of the substructure of the controlled term,

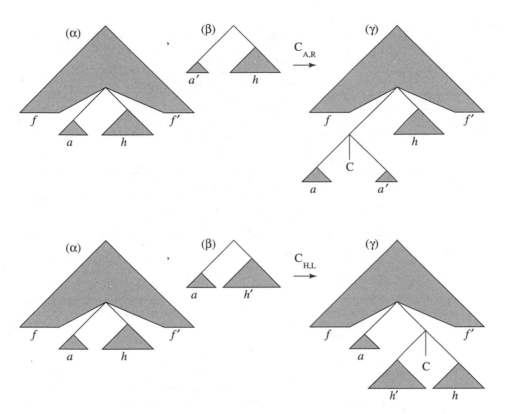

Figure 5.2
A right argument coordination and a left head coordination with a common constituent.

its identifier is C', with similar conventions for the indexes indicated above. Thus the last coordination of table 5.4, identified by $C'_{A,1-1,L}(\alpha_1, \alpha_1)$, is an argument coordination of the substructure $[X_3 X_2]$ and the ternary term $[X'_3 X'_2] X_2$. The coordinated argument $[X'_3 X'_2]$ is located on the left of the argument of the substructure X_3.

Tables 5.4 to 5.9 illustrate in turn the various coordinations of ternary, binary, and unary terms.

Coordinations of Ternary Terms with a Common Constituent

I first consider the coordinations that are built from two terms with a common constituent. Tables 5.4 to 5.7 show all the possible coordinations of ternary terms of structures α_1 and α_2 with ternary terms of the same structures or with binary terms of structure α_3. The coordinations that do not modify the string of the original term are not considered here

Table 5.4
Coordinations of two ternary terms (structure α_1) with a common constituent.

Identifier	Transformation and example from [Medic]
$C_{A,1-2,R}(\alpha_1,\alpha_1)$	$[X_3 X_2] X_1, [X'_3 X'_2] X_1 \to$ (a) $[[X_3 X_2] C [X'_3 X'_2]] X_1$ *basal cell <u>and squamous cell</u> carcinoma*
$C_{A,1-2,L}(\alpha_1,\alpha_1)$	$[X_3 X_2] X_1, [X'_3 X'_2] X_1 \to$ (*) $[[X'_3 X'_2] C [X_3 X_2]] X_1$
$C_{A,1-1,R}(\alpha_1,\alpha_1)$	$[X_3 X_2] X_1, [X'_3 X_2] X_1 \to$ (b) $[[X_3 C X'_3] X_2] X_1$ *unmatched in* [Medic]
$C_{A,1-1,L}(\alpha_1,\alpha_1)$	$[X_3 X_2] X_1, [X'_3 X_2] X_1 \to$ (*) $[[X'_3 C X_3] X_2] X_1$
$C_{H,3-3,R}(\alpha_1,\alpha_1)$	$[X_3 X_2] X_1, [X_3 X_2] X'_1 \to$ (c) $[X_3 X_2] [X'_1 C X_1]$ *squamous cell <u>papillomas or</u> carcinomas*
$C_{H,3-3,L}(\alpha_1,\alpha_1)$	$[X_3 X_2] X_1, [X_3 X_2] X'_1 \to$ (*) $[X_3 X_2] [X_1 C X'_1]$
$C_{H,2-2,R}(\alpha_1,\alpha_1)$	$[X_3 X_2] X_1, [X_3 X'_2] X_1 \to$ (d) $[X_3 [X_2 C X'_2]] X_1$ *procallogen N <u>and C</u> proteinases*
$C_{H,2-2,L}(\alpha_1,\alpha_1)$	$[X_3 X_2] X_1, [X_3 X'_2] X_1 \to$ (e) $[X_3 [X'_2 C X_2]] X_1$ *hepatitis <u>B and</u> C viruses*
$C'_{A,1-1,R}(\alpha_1,\alpha_1)$	$[X_3 X_2] X_1, [X'_3 X'_2] X_2 \to$ (f) $[[X_3 C [X'_3 X'_2]] X_2] X_1$ *unmatched in* [Medic]
$C'_{A,1-1,L}(\alpha_1,\alpha_1)$	$[X_3 X_2] X_1, [X'_3 X'_2] X_2 \to$ (*) $[[[X'_3 X'_2] C X_3] X_2] X_1$

because they do not respect the constraint 4 of definition 1.1. They are marked with an asterisk sign (*).

Coordinations of Ternary Terms without Common Constituent

These coordinations are built from one term and another structure without common constituent. Table 5.8 illustrates all the possible coordinations of ternary terms of structures α_1 and α_2 with a unary structure α_4. External coordinations are also marked with an asterisk sign (*).

Coordinations of Binary Terms

The variations of coordination of binary terms are shown in table 5.9: the coordinations of a binary term with another binary term (with or without a common constituent) and the coordinations of a binary term with a unary term.

Table 5.5
Coordinations of two ternary terms (structure α_2) with a common constituent.

Identifier	Transformation and example from [Medic]
$C_{A,1-1,R}(\alpha_2,\alpha_2)$	$X_3\,[X_2\,X_1],\,X_3'\,[X_2\,X_1] \rightarrow$ (b) $[X_3\,C\,X_3']\,[X_2\,X_1]$ *Duchene _or Becker_ muscular distrophy*
$C_{A,1-1,L}(\alpha_2,\alpha_2)$	$X_3\,[X_2\,X_1],\,X_3'\,[X_2\,X_1] \rightarrow$ (*) $[X_3'\,C\,X_3]\,[X_2\,X_1]$
$C_{A,2-2,R}(\alpha_2,\alpha_2)$	$X_3\,[X_2\,X_1],\,X_3\,[X_2'\,X_1] \rightarrow$ (d) $X_3\,[[X_2\,C\,X_2']\,X_1]$ *central venous _or oesophageal_ pressure*
$C_{A,2-2,L}(\alpha_2,\alpha_2)$	$X_3\,[X_2\,X_1],\,X_3\,[X_2'\,X_1] \rightarrow$ (e) $X_3\,[[X_2'\,C\,X_2]\,X_1]$ *zygomaticus _major and_ minor muscle*
$C_{H,2-3,R}(\alpha_2,\alpha_2)$	$X_3\,[X_2\,X_1],\,X_3\,[X_2'\,X_1'] \rightarrow$ (*) $X_3\,[[X_2\,X_1]\,C\,[X_2'\,X_1']]$
$C_{H,2-3,L}(\alpha_2,\alpha_2)$	$X_3\,[X_2\,X_1],\,X_3\,[X_2'\,X_1'] \rightarrow$ (g) $X_3\,[[X_2'\,X_1']\,C\,[X_2\,X_1]]$ *chronic _myeloic leukemia or_ lymphocytic leukemia*
$C_{H,3-3,R}(\alpha_2,\alpha_2)$	$X_3\,[X_2\,X_1],\,X_3\,[X_2\,X_1'] \rightarrow$ (*) $X_3\,[X_2\,[X_1\,C\,X_1']]$
$C_{H,3-3,L}(\alpha_2,\alpha_2)$	$X_3\,[X_2\,X_1],\,X_3\,[X_2\,X_1'] \rightarrow$ (c) $X_3\,[X_2\,[X_1'\,C\,X_1]]$ *unmatched in* [Medic]
$C'_{H,3-3,R}(\alpha_2,\alpha_2)$	$X_3\,[X_2\,X_1],\,X_2\,[X_2'\,X_1'] \rightarrow$ (*) $X_3\,[X_2\,[X_1\,C\,[X_2'\,X_1']]]$
$C'_{H,3-3,L}(\alpha_2,\alpha_2)$	$X_3\,[X_2\,X_1],\,X_2\,[X_2'\,X_1'] \rightarrow$ (h) $X_3\,[X_2\,[[X_2'\,X_1']\,C\,X_1]]$ *unmatched in* [Medic]

Remarks on Coordinations without Common Constituent

Head and argument coordinations of terms without common constituents are illustrated in figure 5.3. These coordinations are built by associating a constituent of the controlled term (head or argument) with a structure Θ of the same syntactic category. Contrary to the case of coordinations with a common constituent, the number of possible configurations does not depend on the size of the coordinated structure. Only coordinations of ternary terms and a one-word structure are shown in table 5.8. Coordinations of ternary terms and *n*-ary structures are inferred from these ones by replacing the one-word structure by a larger one.

Metarules for Ternary Term Variations

Metarules describing coordinations of ternary terms are inferred from the transformations given in tables 5.4 to 5.8 by calculating the corresponding strings. For this purpose, the structures built in tables 5.4 to 5.8 are labeled from *a* to *h*, each label corresponding to a different string. These coordinations must be completed by considering the coordinations of

Table 5.6
Coordinations of a ternary term (structure α_1) and a ternary term (structure α_2) with a common constituent

Identifier	Transformation and example from [Medic]
$C_{A,1-1,R}(\alpha_1,\alpha_2)$	$[X_3\,X_2]\,X_1,\,X_3'\,[X_2'\,X_1] \rightarrow$ (d) $X_3'[[[X_3\,X_2]\,C\,X_2']\,X_1]$ *unmatched in* [Medic]
$C_{A,1-1,L}(\alpha_1,\alpha_2)$	$[X_3\,X_2]\,X_1,\,X_3'\,[X_2'\,X_1] \rightarrow$ ($*$) $X_3'[[X_2'\,C\,[X_3\,X_2]]\,X_1]$
$C_{H,3-3,R}(\alpha_1,\alpha_2)$	$[X_3\,X_2]\,X_1,\,X_3\,[X_2'\,X_1'] \rightarrow$ (a) $[X_3\,[X_2\,C\,[X_2'\,X_1']]]\,X_1$ *unmatched in* [Medic]
$C_{H,3-3,L}(\alpha_1,\alpha_2)$	$[X_3\,X_2]\,X_1,\,X_3\,[X_2'\,X_1'] \rightarrow$ (g) $[X_3\,[[X_2'\,X_1']\,C\,X_2]]\,X_1$ *unmatched in* [Medic]
$C_{A,2-2,R}(\alpha_2,\alpha_1)$	$X_3\,[X_2\,X_1],\,[X_3',X_2']\,X_1 \rightarrow$ (a) $X_3\,[[X_2\,C\,[X_2'\,X_1']]\,X_1]$ *unmatched in* [Medic]
$C_{A,2-2,L}(\alpha_2,\alpha_1)$	$X_3\,[X_2\,X_1],\,[X_3',X_2']\,X_1 \rightarrow$ (g) $X_3\,[[[X_2'\,X_1']\,C\,X_2]\,X_1]$ *unmatched in* [Medic]
$C_{H,2-3,R}(\alpha_2,\alpha_1)$	$X_3\,[X_2\,X_1],\,[X_3,X_2']\,X_1' \rightarrow$ (e) $[X_3\,[X_2'\,C\,[X_2\,X_1]]]\,X_1'$ *unmatched in* [Medic]
$C_{H,2-3,L}(\alpha_2,\alpha_1)$	$X_3\,[X_2\,X_1],\,[X_3,X_2']\,X_1 \rightarrow$ ($*$) $[X_3\,[[X_2\,X_1]\,C\,X_2']]\,X_1'$

ternary terms and 2- or 3-word structures without common constituent, $(1+2) \times 16 = 48$ new transformations. These transformations yield four complementary string rewriting rules which insert a coordinating conjunction preceded or followed by three single words. They are labeled from *i* to *l*. Thus the $54 + 48 = 102$ combinations of a ternary terms with a term or a structure containing from 1 to 3 words only produce 12 string-rewriting rules as illustrated in table 5.10.

Most string-rewriting rules given in table 5.10 are ambiguous because they correspond to more than one structural construction. They result either from the combination of two ternary terms with the same structure or from the combination of a ternary term with another structure. An analysis of the coordinations of ternary terms extracted from [Medic] shows that 52% are built from two parallel ternary terms, 8% are built with a binary term, and 40% with a single word. (Of course these measures are directly related to the completeness of the initial term list.) Most coordinations with a unary term seem to be coordinations with another ternary term in which the ternary term is not a member of the controlled list. Thus *cervical or thoracic spinal cord* is a variant of *Cervical spinal cord*, which is interpreted as a coordination with the single word *thoracic* because *thoracic spinal cord* is not a controlled

Table 5.7
Coordinations of a ternary term (structure α_1 or α_2) and a binary term (structure α_3) with a common constituent

Identifier	Transformation and example from [Medic]
$C_{A,1-2,R}(\alpha_1,\alpha_3)$	$[X_3\,X_2]\,X_1,\,X'_2\,X_1 \to$ (d) $[[X_3\,X_2]\,C\,X'_2]\,X_1$ *dark field <u>and electron</u> microscopy*
$C_{A,1-2,L}(\alpha_1,\alpha_3)$	$[X_3\,X_2]\,X_1,\,X'_2\,X_1 \to$ (*) $[X'_2\,C\,[X_3\,X_2]]\,X_1$
$C_{A,1-1,R}(\alpha_1,\alpha_3)$	$[X_3\,X_2]\,X_1,\,X'_2\,X_2 \to$ (b) $[[X_3\,C\,X'_2]\,X_2]\,X_1$ *unmatched in* [Medic]
$C_{A,1-1,L}(\alpha_1,\alpha_3)$	$[X_3\,X_2]\,X_1,\,X'_2\,X_2 \to$ (*) $[[X'_2\,C\,X_3]\,X_2]\,X_1$
$C_{H,2-2,R}(\alpha_1,\alpha_3)$	$[X_3\,X_2]\,X_1,\,X_3\,X'_1 \to$ (d) $[X_3\,[X_2\,C\,X'_1]]\,X_1$ *unmatched in* [Medic]
$C_{H,2-2,L}(\alpha_1,\alpha_3)$	$[X_3\,X_2]\,X_1,\,X_3\,X'_1 \to$ (e) $[X_3\,[X'_1\,C\,X_2]]\,X_1$ *unmatched in* [Medic]
$C_{A,2-2,R}(\alpha_2,\alpha_3)$	$X_3\,[X_2\,X_1],\,X'_2\,X_1 \to$ (d) $X_3\,[[X_2\,C\,X'_2]\,X_1]$ *superior mesenteric <u>and coeliac</u> artery*
$C_{A,2-2,L}(\alpha_2,\alpha_3)$	$X_3\,[X_2\,X_1],\,X'_2\,X_1 \to$ (e) $X_3\,[[X'_2\,C\,X_2]\,X_1]$ *unmatched in* [Medic]
$C_{H,2-3,R}(\alpha_2,\alpha_3)$	$X_3\,[X_2\,X_1],\,X_3\,X'_1 \to$ (*) $X_3\,[[X_2\,X_1]\,C\,X'_1]$
$C_{H,2-3,L}(\alpha_2,\alpha_3)$	$X_3\,[X_2\,X_1],\,X_3\,X'_1 \to$ (e) $X_3\,[X'_1\,C\,[X_2\,X_1]]$ *unmatched in* [Medic]
$C_{H,3-3,R}(\alpha_2,\alpha_3)$	$X_3\,[X_2\,X_1],\,X_2\,X'_1 \to$ (*) $X_3\,[X_2\,[X_1\,C\,X'_1]]$
$C_{H,3-3,L}(\alpha_2,\alpha_3)$	$X_3\,[X_2\,X_1],\,X_2\,X'_1 \to$ (c) $X_3\,[X_2\,[X'_1\,C\,X_1]]$ *unmatched in* [Medic]

term. This fact is surprising, however, and suggests that *thoracic spinal cord* is a good candidate for being added to the terminology (see section 6.3).

The description of coordinations of ternary terms made so far can be simplified in order to describe coordinations of binary terms. The corresponding transformations are given in table 5.9. The associated four string-rewriting rules are in table 5.11.

Generalization to *n*-ary Terms

The string-rewriting variations proposed in tables 5.10 and 5.11 were developed manually in order to explicitly capture the diversity of structural combinations observed in the constructions of coordinations. I now propose a more generic approach to this description

Table 5.8
Coordinations of a ternary term (structure α_1 or α_2) and a unary term or a single word (structure α_4) without common constituent

Identifier	Transformation and example from [Medic]
$C_{A,1-2,R}(\alpha_1,\alpha_4)$	$[X_3 X_2] X_1, X_1' \rightarrow$ (d) $[[X_3 X_2] C X_1'] X_1$ *pentose phosphate <u>and glycolytic</u> pathways*
$C_{A,1-2,L}(\alpha_1,\alpha_4)$	$[X_3 X_2] X_1, X_1' \rightarrow$ (*) $[X_1' C [X_3 X_2]] X_1$
$C_{A,1-1,R}(\alpha_1,\alpha_4)$	$[X_3 X_2] X_1, X_1' \rightarrow$ (b) $[[X_3 C X_1'] X_2] X_1$ *unmatched in* [Medic]
$C_{A,1-1,L}(\alpha_1,\alpha_4)$	$[X_3 X_2] X_1, X_1' \rightarrow$ (*) $[[X_1' C X_3] X_2] X_1$
$C_{H,2-2,R}(\alpha_1,\alpha_4)$	$[X_3 X_2] X_1, X_1' \rightarrow$ (d) $[X_3 [X_2 C X_1']] X_1$ *procollagen n <u>and c</u> proteinases*
$C_{H,2-2,L}(\alpha_1,\alpha_4)$	$[X_3 X_2] X_1, X_1' \rightarrow$ (e) $[X_3 [X_1' C X_2]] X_1$ *unmatched in* [Medic]
$C_{H,3-3,R}(\alpha_1,\alpha_4)$	$[X_3 X_2] X_1, X_1' \rightarrow$ (*) $[X_3 X_2] [X_1 C X_1']$
$C_{H,3-3,L}(\alpha_1,\alpha_4)$	$[X_3 X_2] X_1, X_1' \rightarrow$ (c) $[X_3 X_2] [X_1' C X_1]$ *spinal cord <u>ischemia or</u> infarction*
$C_{A,1-1,R}(\alpha_2,\alpha_4)$	$X_3 [X_2 X_1], X_1' \rightarrow$ (b) $[X_3 C X_1'] [X_2 X_1]$ *cervical <u>or thoracic</u> spinal cord*
$C_{A,1-1,L}(\alpha_2,\alpha_4)$	$X_3 [X_2 X_1], X_1' \rightarrow$ (*) $[X_1' C X_3] [X_2 X_1]$
$C_{A,2-2,R}(\alpha_2,\alpha_4)$	$X_3 [X_2 X_1], X_1' \rightarrow$ (d) $X_3 [[X_2 C X_1'] X_1]$ *scanning electron <u>and light</u> microscopy*
$C_{A,2-2,L}(\alpha_2,\alpha_4)$	$X_3 [X_2 X_1], X_1' \rightarrow$ (e) $X_3 [[X_1' C X_2] X_1]$ *unmatched in* [Medic]
$C_{H,2-3,R}(\alpha_2,\alpha_4)$	$X_3 [X_2 X_1], X_1' \rightarrow$ (*) $X_3 [[X_2 X_1] C X_1']$
$C_{H,2-3,L}(\alpha_2,\alpha_4)$	$X_3 [X_2 X_1], X_1' \rightarrow$ (e) $X_3 [X_1' C [X_2 X_1]]$ *unmatched in* [Medic]
$C_{H,3-3,R}(\alpha_2,\alpha_4)$	$X_3 [X_2 X_1], X_1' \rightarrow$ (*) $X_3 [X_2 [X_1 C X_1']]$
$C_{H,3-3,L}(\alpha_2,\alpha_4)$	$X_3 [X_2 X_1], X_1' \rightarrow$ (c) $X_3 [X_2 [X_1' C X_1]]$ *unmatched in* [Medic]

Table 5.9
Coordinations of two binary terms (structure α_3) and coordination of a binary terms (structure α_3) a unary term or a single word (structure α_4)

Identifier	Transformation and example from [Medic]
$C_{A,1-1,R}(\alpha_3,\alpha_3)$	$X_2\,X_1, X_2'\,X_1 \to$ (m) $[X_2\,C\,X_2']\,X_1$ *monoclonal or polyclonal antibodies*
$C_{A,1-1,L}(\alpha_3,\alpha_3)$	$X_2\,X_1, X_2'\,X_1 \to$ (*) $[X_2'\,C\,X_2]\,X_1$
$C_{H,2-2,R}(\alpha_3,\alpha_3)$	$X_2\,X_1, X_2\,X_1' \to$ (*) $X_2\,[X_1\,C\,X_1']$
$C_{H,2-2,L}(\alpha_3,\alpha_3)$	$X_2\,X_1, X_2\,X_1' \to$ (n) $X_2\,[X_1'\,C\,X_1]$ *spinal cord or nerve*
$C_{A,1-1,R}'(\alpha_3,\alpha_3)$	$X_2\,X_1, X_2'\,X_1' \to$ (o) $[X_2\,C\,[X_2'\,X_1']]\,X_1$ *endothelial and smooth muscle cell*
$C_{A,1-1,L}'(\alpha_3,\alpha_3)$	$X_2\,X_1, X_2'\,X_1' \to$ (*) $[[X_2'\,X_1']\,C\,X_2]\,X_1$
$C_{H,2-2,R}'(\alpha_3,\alpha_3)$	$X_2\,X_1, X_2'\,X_1' \to$ (*) $X_2\,[X_1\,C\,[X_2'\,X_1']]$
$C_{H,2-2,L}'(\alpha_3,\alpha_3)$	$X_2\,X_1, X_2'\,X_1' \to$ (p) $X_2\,[[X_2'\,X_1']\,C\,X_1]$ *image cytometric analysis and evaluation*
$C_{A,1-1,R}(\alpha_3,\alpha_4)$	$X_2\,X_1, X_2'\,X_1 \to$ (m) $[X_2\,C\,X_2']\,X_1$ *topical and systematic administration*
$C_{A,1-1,L}(\alpha_3,\alpha_4)$	$X_2\,X_1, X_2'\,X_1 \to$ (*) $[X_2'\,C\,X_2]\,X_1$
$C_{H,2-2,R}(\alpha_3,\alpha_4)$	$X_2\,X_1, X_2\,X_1' \to$ (*) $X_2\,[X_1\,C\,X_1']$
$C_{H,2-2,L}(\alpha_3,\alpha_4)$	$X_2\,X_1, X_2\,X_1' \to$ (n) $X_2\,[X_1'\,C\,X_1]$ *cell metabolism and proliferation*

which relies on the general mode of construction of coordination illustrated by figures 5.2 and 5.3.[34]

So far in this book only the central results of the calculus of generic transformations have been seen. The reader who is interested in learning more such as about the proof of Theorem 5.1 should refer to Jacquemin (1997b, pp. 111–17). The following theorem gives the general expression of a coordination of an n-ary and a p-ary term.

Theorem 5.1 (Coordination) Let α be the tree of a controlled term t and γ the tree of a coordination variant of t. Their frontiers $f(\alpha)$ and $f(\gamma)$ satisfy the following properties:

1. The frontier $f(\gamma)$ of γ is composed as follows:

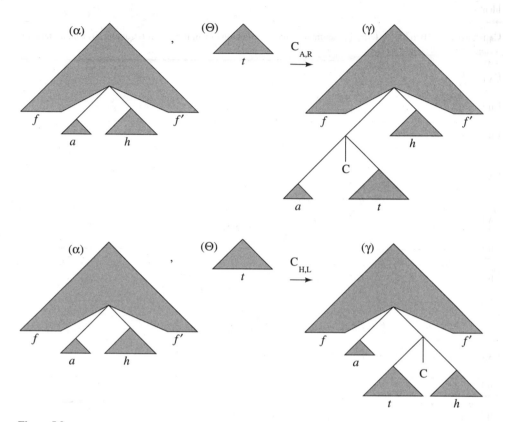

Figure 5.3
A right argument coordination and a left head coordination without common constituent.

$$\exists c_1, c_2 \in \mathcal{C}^\star, \ \exists c_3 \in \mathcal{C}^+, \ [(f(\alpha) = c_1 \cdot c_2) \wedge (|c_1 \cdot c_2| \geq 2)$$
$$\wedge \ ((c_1 \neq \varepsilon \ \wedge \ f(\gamma) = c_1 \cdot \mathrm{C} \cdot c_3 \cdot c_2)$$
$$\vee \ (c_2 \neq \varepsilon \ \wedge \ f(\gamma) = c_1 \cdot c_3 \cdot \mathrm{C} \cdot c_2))]$$

2. Let $n = |c_1 \cdot c_2|$ be the size of the controlled term, p the size of the coordinated structure, and $k = |c_3|$ the size of the inserted string, it follows that

$$(1 \leq k \leq p - 1) \ \wedge \ (k \geq p - n + 1)$$

Notations: $\mathcal{C}$ is the set of the syntactic categories, C is the category of coordinating conjunctions, ε is the empty string, and $|c|$ is the length of string c.

Table 5.10
String-rewriting expression of coordinations of ternary terms with single words and with unary, binary, and ternary terms

Identifier	String-rewriting rule
a	$X_3 X_2 X_1 \Rightarrow X_3 X_2 \mathbf{C} \mathbf{X_4} \mathbf{X_5} X_1$
b	$X_3 X_2 X_1 \Rightarrow X_3 \mathbf{C} \mathbf{X_4} X_2 X_1$
c	$X_3 X_2 X_1 \Rightarrow X_3 X_2 \mathbf{X_4} \mathbf{C} X_1$
d	$X_3 X_2 X_1 \Rightarrow X_3 X_2 \mathbf{C} \mathbf{X_4} X_1$
e	$X_3 X_2 X_1 \Rightarrow X_3 \mathbf{X_4} \mathbf{C} X_2 X_1$
f	$X_3 X_2 X_1 \Rightarrow X_3 \mathbf{C} \mathbf{X_4} \mathbf{X_5} X_2 X_1$
g	$X_3 X_2 X_1 \Rightarrow X_3 \mathbf{X_4} \mathbf{X_5} \mathbf{C} X_2 X_1$
h	$X_3 X_2 X_1 \Rightarrow X_3 X_2 \mathbf{X_4} \mathbf{X_5} \mathbf{C} X_1$
i	$X_3 X_2 X_1 \Rightarrow X_3 \mathbf{C} \mathbf{X_4} \mathbf{X_5} \mathbf{X_6} X_2 X_1$
j	$X_3 X_2 X_1 \Rightarrow X_3 X_2 \mathbf{C} \mathbf{X_4} \mathbf{X_5} \mathbf{X_6} X_1$
k	$X_3 X_2 X_1 \Rightarrow X_3 \mathbf{X_4} \mathbf{X_5} \mathbf{X_6} \mathbf{C} X_2 X_1$
l	$X_3 X_2 X_1 \Rightarrow X_3 X_2 \mathbf{X_4} \mathbf{X_5} \mathbf{X_6} \mathbf{C} X_1$

Table 5.11
String-rewriting expression of coordinations of binary terms with single words and with unary and binary terms

Identifier	String-rewriting rule
m	$X_2 X_1 \Rightarrow X_2 \mathbf{C} \mathbf{X_3} X_1$
n	$X_2 X_1 \Rightarrow X_2 \mathbf{X_3} \mathbf{C} X_1$
o	$X_2 X_1 \Rightarrow X_2 \mathbf{C} \mathbf{X_3} \mathbf{X_4} X_1$
p	$X_2 X_1 \Rightarrow X_2 \mathbf{X_3} \mathbf{X_4} \mathbf{C} X_1$

It is straightforward to verify that this theorem correctly describes the variations of ternary and binary terms which have been manually produced so far.

The guidelines for building up a coordination variation are now deduced from this theorem. Only nonexternal variations are taken into consideration: these are the variations in which neither c_1 nor c_2 is the empty string.

Construction Rule 5.1 (Coordination) The string-rewriting expression of the coordination of an *n*-word term with a *p*-word term, which satisfies definition 1.1, is an insertion of 1 to *p* words if $n \geq p$ or an insertion of $p - n + 1$ to *p* words if $p \geq n$. The first word or the last word of the inserted string is a coordinating conjunction. The string-rewriting expression of coordinations is given by

Table 5.12
String-rewriting expression of coordinations of ternary terms with quaternary terms

Identifier	String-rewriting rule
a	$X_3 X_2 X_1 \Rightarrow X_3 X_2 \mathbf{C X_4 X_5} X_1$
f	$X_3 X_2 X_1 \Rightarrow X_3 \mathbf{C X_4 X_5} X_2 X_1$
g	$X_3 X_2 X_1 \Rightarrow X_3 \mathbf{X_4 X_5 C} X_2 X_1$
h	$X_3 X_2 X_1 \Rightarrow X_3 X_2 \mathbf{X_4 X_5 C} X_1$
i	$X_3 X_2 X_1 \Rightarrow X_3 \mathbf{C X_4 X_5 X_6} X_2 X_1$
j	$X_3 X_2 X_1 \Rightarrow X_3 X_2 \mathbf{C X_4 X_5 X_6} X_1$
k	$X_3 X_2 X_1 \Rightarrow X_3 \mathbf{X_4 X_5 X_6 C} X_2 X_1$
l	$X_3 X_2 X_1 \Rightarrow X_3 X_2 \mathbf{X_4 X_5 X_6 C} X_1$
q	$X_3 X_2 X_1 \Rightarrow X_3 \mathbf{C X_4 X_5 X_6 X_7} X_2 X_1$
r	$X_3 X_2 X_1 \Rightarrow X_3 X_2 \mathbf{C X_4 X_5 X_6 X_7} X_1$
s	$X_3 X_2 X_1 \Rightarrow X_3 \mathbf{X_4 X_5 X_6 X_7 C} X_2 X_1$
t	$X_3 X_2 X_1 \Rightarrow X_3 X_2 \mathbf{X_4 X_5 X_6 X_7 C} X_1$

$$\alpha \cdot \beta \ \rightarrow \ \alpha \cdot \mathrm{C} \cdot \gamma \cdot \beta \ ; \ \alpha, \beta, \gamma \in \mathcal{C}^+ \tag{5.8}$$

$$\alpha \cdot \beta \ \rightarrow \ \alpha \cdot \gamma \cdot \mathrm{C} \cdot \beta \ ; \ \alpha, \beta, \gamma \in \mathcal{C}^+ \tag{5.9}$$

Let us illustrate the preceding rule on the coordination of a quaternary term with a ternary term. For instance, *cell cell and cell extracellular matrix interaction* is an argument coordination of the ternary term *Cell cell interaction* with the term *Cell extracellular matrix interaction*. It is illustrated by

$$C_{A,12,D}(\alpha_1, \alpha_5): \ [X_3 X_2] X_1, \ [X'_4[X'_3 X'_2]] X_1 \ \rightarrow \ [[X_3 X_2] \mathrm{C} [X'_4[X'_3 X'_2]]] X_1 \tag{5.10}$$

The corresponding string-rewriting rule

$$X_3 X_2 X_1 \ \rightarrow \ X_3 X_2 \mathrm{C} X'_4 X'_3 X'_2 X_1$$

is an instantiation of formula (5.8) (from construction rule 5.1). It is an insertion of a 4-word string beginning with a coordinating conjunction inside the 3-word term; it corresponds to the string-rewriting rule j in table 5.12.

Both formulas (5.8) and (5.9) in construction rule 5.1 define the whole set of string-rewriting rules describing the coordinations of 3-word terms with 4-word terms. These 12 string-rewriting rules are given in table 5.12. The 12 variants extracted from the corpus [Medic] through the transformations of table 5.12 are shown in table 5.13.

Construction rule 5.1 is used to create a first set of metarules, which are called *paradigmatic metarules* because they lack filtering constraints. Appendix A.1 provides a list of paradigmatic metarules for binary terms in English. These coordinations correspond to

Table 5.13
Unfiltered coordinations of a ternary term with a quaternary term from [Medic]

Controlled term	Variant	Correct
Visual evoked potential	*visual and brainstem auditory evoked potential*	+
Somatosensory evoked potential	*somatosensory and brainstem auditory evoked potentials*	+
Circumflex coronary artery	*(to the) circumflex or the right coronary artery*	+
Pursuit eye movement	*pursuit and vestibular smooth eye movements*	+
Controlled mechanical ventilation	*(during) controlled and assisted modes of mechanical ventilation*	+
Cell adhesion molecule	*cells and the distribution of adhesion molecules*	−
Circumflex coronary artery	*circumflex and left anterior descending coronary arteries*	+
Squamous cell carcinoma	*(11 lesions were) squamous cell and [2 lesions were] basal cell carcinomas*	+
Von Hippel Lindau disease	*von Hippel-Lindau and von Hippel disease*	+
Cell-cell interaction	*cell-cell and cell-extracellular matrix interactions*	+
Natural killer cell	*natural killer and lymphocyte activated killer cells*	+

the identifier `Coor`. In section 5.4 these metarules will be transformed into more accurate metarules, called *filtering metarules*, through the addition of filtering constraints.

5.2.3   Other Variations of *n*-ary Terms

Now the study of the preceding section is extended to three remaining families of variations: modifications/substitutions, elisions, and permutations.

Modifications/Substitutions
These two constructions are illustrated in figure 5.4. The string-rewriting rule corresponding to these variations is an insertion of a string inside the controlled term. Coordinations also amount to the insertion of a string, but in this case the first word must be a coordinating conjunction. With nontagged corpora, constraints on the categories can only apply to the categories of frequent words (function words, e.g., conjunctions, determiners, prepositions). Here modifications/substitutions are distinguished from coordinations through the constraint that none of the inserted words is a coordinating conjunction. In the case of a tagged corpus, it is more efficient to state that all the inserted words are content words (adjectives, nouns, or verb participles). The patterns of syntactic categories inside term variants are described in chapters 7 and 8 and embedded in metarules of appendixes A.4 and A.5. In these descriptions the formalism of *FASTR* is enriched with regular expressions, and input data are tagged corpora.

In an indexing process, only the first successful variation is produced, *FASTR* successively applies all the metarules to a given term according to their rank in the metarule file.

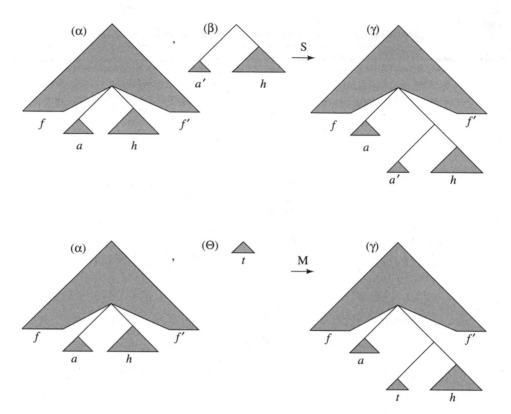

Figure 5.4
Substitution and modification of a compound term.

In appendix A.1, modification/substitution variations (identifier `Modif`) are therefore systematically placed **after** the coordination variations because modifications/substitutions are less specific than coordinations. In the case of a tagged corpus, there is no subsumption relation between coordinations and modifications/substitutions, and their relative position is of no importance.

Construction Rule 5.2 (Modification/substitution)   The string-rewriting expression of the modification/substitution of an n-word term with a p-word term, which satisfies definition 1.1, is an insertion of 1 to p words. No word in the inserted string is a coordinating conjunction:

$$\alpha \cdot \beta \ \rightarrow \ \alpha \cdot \gamma \cdot \beta \ ; \ \alpha, \beta \in \mathcal{C}^+ \ \wedge \ \gamma \in (\mathcal{C} \setminus \{C\})^+ \tag{5.11}$$

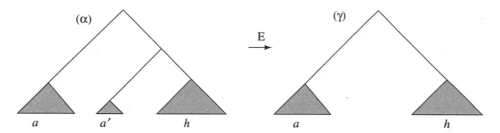

Figure 5.5
Elision of a compound term.

Elisions

Elisions, represented in figure 5.5, are variations that amount to the deletion of arguments. The rewriting rules for elisions of ternary terms are given in section 5.1.4; the general construction rule is as follows:

Construction Rule 5.3 (Elision)   The string-rewriting expression of the elision of an *n*-word term, which satisfies definition 1.1, is a deletion of 1 to $n - 1$ arguments:

$$\alpha \cdot \beta \cdot \gamma \ \rightarrow \ \alpha \cdot \gamma \ ; \ \alpha, \beta, \gamma \in C^{\star} \ \wedge \ \beta, \gamma \neq \varepsilon \tag{5.12}$$

String-rewriting expressions of elisions are not used in term extraction because of their poor precision (see section 5.5).

Permutations

The permutation variation is the transformation of a compound structure (argument(s) followed by a head word) into a phrase structure (head word followed by preposition phrase(s)). It is illustrated by figure 5.6, and the corresponding construction rule is as follows:

Construction Rule 5.4 (Permutation)   The string-rewriting expression of the permutation of an *n*-word term, which satisfies definition 1.1, is the permutation of two nonempty strings and the insertion of a preposition at the pivot of the permutation:

$$\alpha \cdot \beta \cdot \gamma \cdot \delta \ \rightarrow \ \alpha \cdot \gamma \cdot P \cdot \beta \cdot \delta \ ; \ \alpha, \beta, \gamma, \delta \in C^{\star} \ \wedge \ \beta, \gamma \neq \varepsilon \tag{5.13}$$

Only the first paradigmatic permutation variation (identifier Perm) in appendix A.1 is built according to this rule. For a two-word term the only instantiation of formula (5.13) corresponds to $\alpha = \varepsilon$, $\beta = X_2$, $\gamma = X_1$, and $\delta = \varepsilon$. These inequalities entail that the only permutation of $X_2 X_1$ be $X_1 P X_2$.

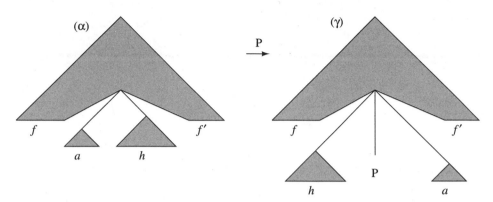

Figure 5.6
Permutation of a compound term.

All the remaining `Perm` metarules in appendix A.1 correspond to the composition of a permutation and modifications/substitutions. The purpose of the following section is to account for those compositions of elementary variations that are likely to provide new string-rewriting rules.

5.3 Compositions of Elementary Variations

Let us illustrate the composition of two variations by analyzing *expression of lymphokine gene*, a variant of *Gene expression*. This variant cannot be obtained by transforming the controlled term by one of the elementary variations studied in sections 5.1 and 5.2. An analysis of this variant requires a composition of elementary transformations such as

Metarule $\text{Perm}(X_1 \rightarrow X_2\,X_3) \equiv X_1 \rightarrow X_3\,P_4\,X_2 : .$ (5.14)

Metarule $\text{Modif}(X_1 \rightarrow X_3\,P_4\,X_2) \equiv X_1 \rightarrow X_3\,P_4\,X_5\,X_2 : .$ (5.15)

gene expression

$\xrightarrow{\text{Perm}}$ *expression of gene*

$\xrightarrow{\text{Modif}}$ *expression of lymphokine gene*

In fact another transformational path produces this variant: *expression of lymphokine gene* is also the result of the composition of a modification/substitution with a permutation:

Metarule Modif$(X_1 \rightarrow X_2 \, X_3) \equiv X_1 \rightarrow X_5 \, X_2 \, X_3 : \;.$ (5.16)

Metarule Perm$(X_1 \rightarrow X_5 \, X_2 \, X_3) \equiv X_1 \rightarrow X_3 \, P_4 \, X_5 \, X_2 : \;.$ (5.17)

gene expression

$\xrightarrow{\text{Modif}}$ *lymphokine gene expression*

$\xrightarrow{\text{Perm}}$ *expression of lymphokine gene*

In this section two topics related to the composition of variations are briefly recalled. First, the composition of elementary string modifications in approximate string matching and the composition of metarules in generative unification grammars is described in section (5.3.1). Afterward, in section (5.3.2), the compositions of previously presented elementary variations is detailed.

5.3.1 Related Topics

Approximate String Matching

The conflation of term variations can be regarded as a special method for approximately matching strings (Hall and Dowling 1980). Techniques for approximate string matching have two main areas of application: misspelling corrections and classifications of approximate items in information access. Hall and Dowling (1980) propose for this purpose a distance, called the *Damerau-Levensthein metric* which consists of a measure and a minimization algorithm. The distance between two strings depends on the sequence of elementary changes (single omissions, insertions, substitutions, and reversals) that is necessary to transform the misspelled string into the correct one (Damerau 1964). A dynamic programming algorithm is used for finding the shortest path among the different possible sequences (Levenshtein 1966) .

A systematic study of compositions of term variations would be much more complicated than sequences of elementary transformations considered in Hall and Dowling (1980). (A sketch of the combinatorial study of the compositions of variations in French is presented in Jacquemin 1991, pp. 122–26.) In order to avoid facing the exhaustive combination of variations when calculating transformational sequences, I now consider some related works on transformational paths which propose restrictive constraints on combinations of metarules.

Transformational Paths

There has been much in the literature of transformational grammar about ordering and constraints on the successive applications of transformations on a single sentence (Bach 1974, sec. 6.3). However, transformations in transformational grammars describe associations between a surface structure and a deep structure, in scope very different from the term variations studied here which associate two syntactic structures.

On the the other hand, the metarules in *GPSG* have closer similarities with the mechanism of term variation. They correspond to reorganizations of the syntactic structure which associate various modes such as negation, interrogation, and relativization with a core affirmative construction. Because metarules in *GPSG* correspond to irrevocable modifications of a sentence, their application is governed by the principle of *finite closure* (Gazdar et al. 1985, p. 72; after Thompson 1983). Under this restriction, metarules can transform the same structure only once; the grammar generated by applying sequences of metarules on grammar rules is thereby finite.

A major difference between *GPSG* and *FASTR* is that the same syntactic phenomena are represented by different means. Among the three families of term variations studied so far—coordinations, modifications/substitutions, and permutations—only permutations would be represented by metarules in *GPSG* because only permutations are irreversible transformations of noun phrases. In contrast, coordinations and modifications/substitutions would be implemented in *GPSG* by immediate domination rules for the former and rule schemata for the latter, both mechanisms allowing for iterative application.

As coordinations and modifications/substitutions are recursive, they can be found more than once inside a sequence of variations. Symmetrically, permutations that are typically nonrecursive can only be encountered at most once in a sequence. In any case the number of metarules in a sequence is necessarily lower than the size of the analyzed occurrence, because all the elementary variations of *n*-ary terms described so far increase the length of the variant by at least one word. For instance, *digital intraoral radiographic system* is produced by the application of at most two metarules on a binary term. Actually the successive application of two modifications/substitutions that insert one word into the term results in the observed variant.

The following observations about the nonrecursiveness of permutations and the limit of the size of a sequence lead to the following rule:

Construction Rule 5.5 (Composition of variations) Assuming that the metagrammar only contains variations that increase the length of a structure, any term variant results from the application of a *finite* sequence of elementary variations. This composition contains at most one permutation, which is the first transformation in the sequence. The other variations in the sequence are coordinations and modifications/substitutions.

I now turn to the actual compositions of variations in order to motivate their final structure (see appendix A.1).

5.3.2 Calculus of Compositions of Variations

The composition of variations can be separated into two different families: *homogeneous compositions* built from only one type of variation (either coordinations or modifications/substitutions) and *heterogeneous compositions* built from any of the three types of elementary variations studied so far. Only the string-rewriting form of the compositions for binary terms will be considered, since binary terms represent approximately 90% of the observed variants (see table 5.25). A deeper study of the compositions of variations can be found for English in Daille et al. (1996, sec. 6) and for French in Jacquemin (1991, pp. 122–26, 163–66).

Homogeneous Compositions

The string-rewriting form of the composition of n coordinations is the result of n insertions of a string (of two or more words) beginning with or ending with a conjunction (see construction rule 5.1). The construction rule of a sequence of coordinations is given by formula (5.18), in which some of the strings β_i will be empty if the corresponding coordination inserts a string inside another string inserted at a preceding step:

Construction Rule 5.6 (Composition of coordinations) The string-rewriting expression of the composition of n coordinations is the insertion, inside the string of the controlled term, of p strings that begin and/or end with a coordinating conjunction such that n coordinating conjunctions are inserted in all:

$$\alpha_1 \cdot \alpha_2 \cdots \alpha_{p+1} \rightarrow \alpha_1 \cdot \beta_1 \cdot \alpha_2 \cdot \beta_2 \cdots \alpha_p \cdot \beta_p \cdot \alpha_{p+1} ;$$

$$\alpha_1, \alpha_2, \ldots, \alpha_{p+1}, \beta_1, \beta_2, \ldots, \beta_p \in \mathcal{C}^+ \ \wedge \ p \leq n$$

$$\wedge \ \sum_{i=1}^{p} |\beta_i|_{\mathrm{C}} = n \ \wedge \ \beta_1, \beta_2, \ldots, \beta_p \in (\mathrm{C} \ (\mathcal{C} \setminus \{\mathrm{C}\})^+)^\star \ ((\mathcal{C} \setminus \{\mathrm{C}\})^+ \ \mathrm{C})^\star$$

(5.18)

Notation: $|\alpha|_{\mathrm{C}}$ is the number of categories C in the string α.

The last constraint in the formula above stipulates that the composition of coordinations cannot produce a string with two or more successive coordinations. A conjunction is always inserted inside a well-formed constituent that neither begins nor ends with a coordinating conjunction (the comma is considered as a coordinating conjunction here).

Compositions of coordinations represent 3.8% of the coordinations extracted from [Medic] (23 out of 603). They are all shown in table 5.14 and are divided into *enumerations*—variations 1 to 21—and *cross-coordinations*—variations 22 and 23. Most enumerations—variations 1 to 19 and 21—are argument coordinations. Variation 21 is

Table 5.14
Compositions of coordinations from [Medic]

	Controlled term	Variant
		$[[X_2 \ \mathbf{C} \ \mathbf{X'_2}] \ \mathbf{C} \ \mathbf{X''_2}] \ X_1$
(1)	*Water content*	*water and Na and K contents*
(2)	*Southern blotting*	*southern, northern and western blotting*
(3)	*Temporal lobe*	*temporal, parietal and occipital lobes*
(4)	*Cardiovascular disease*	*cardiovascular, cerebrovascular and malignant disease*
(5)	*Mechanical properties*	*mechanical, thermal and spectroscopic properties*
(6)	*Textile industry*	*textile, clothing and footwear industries*
(7)	*Latent phase*	*latent, subclinical and early phases*
(8)	*Nickel compound*	*nickel, beryllium and cadmium compounds*
(9)	*Protein content*	*protein, RNA and DNA contents*
(10)	*Rapid technique*	*rapid, inexpensive and efficient technique*
(11)	*Leather industry*	*leather, gelatine and food industries*
(12)	*Clinical investigation*	*clinical, genetic and dystrophin investigations*
(13)	*Positive reinforcement*	*positive, differential and negative reinforcement*
(14)	*Age distribution*	*age, sex and race distribution*
(15)	*Systolic pressure*	*systolic, diastolic and mean pressure*
(16)	*Thyroid gland*	*thyroid, lymphoid or salivary gland*
(17)	*High intensity*	*high, low or intermediate intensity*
		$[[X_3 \ \mathbf{C} \ \mathbf{X'_3}] \ \mathbf{C} \ \mathbf{X''_3}] \ [X_2 \ X_1]$
(18)	*Anterior cerebral artery*	*anterior, middle and posterior cerebral arteries*
(19)	*Somatosensory evoked potential*	*somatosensory, visual and auditory evoked potentials*
		$X_2 \ [\mathbf{X'_1} \ \mathbf{C} \ [\mathbf{X''_1} \ \mathbf{C} \ X_1]]$
(20)	*Magnetic measurement*	*magnetic noise, number or measurement*
		$[[[X_3 \ \mathbf{C} \ \mathbf{X'_3}] \ \mathbf{X_2}] \ \mathbf{C} \ [\ \mathbf{X''_3} \ \mathbf{X_2}]] \ X_1$
(21)	*Squamous cell carcinoma*	*squamous and small cell and large cell carcinomas*
		$[X_2 \ \mathbf{C} \ \mathbf{X'_2}] \ [\mathbf{X'_1} \ \mathbf{C} \ X_1]$
(22)	*Animal fat*	*animal and vegetable oils and fat*
		$[X_2 \ \mathbf{C} \ \mathbf{X'_2}] \ [[\mathbf{X''_2} \ \mathbf{X'_1}] \ \mathbf{C} \ X_1]$
(23)	*Arterial blood*	*arterial and venous acid base and blood*

Table 5.15
History of four compositions of coordinations from [Medic]

Controlled term	Successive variants	Inserted string(s)
Water content	water *and Na* contents	*and Na*
	(1) water *and Na and K* contents	*and K*
Magnetic measurement	magnetic *number or* measurement	*number or*
	(20) magnetic *noise, number or* measurement	*noise,*
Squamous cell carcinoma	squamous *and large* cell carcinomas	*and large*
	(21) squamous *and small cell and large* cell carcinomas	*and small cell*
Animal fat	animal *and vegetable* fat	*and vegetable*
	(22) animal *and vegetable oils and* fat	*oils and*

a two-level argument coordination. Cross-coordinations are double coordinations; they are simultaneously head and argument coordinations.

Enumerations have interested researchers with a concern for knowledge acquisition because they frequently participate in linguistic patterns that reveal conceptual relations such as hyponymy. They have been studied in English by Hearst (1992) and in French by Morin (1997, 1999). In both studies enumerations are represented by finite-state techniques.

In the case of binary terms $X_2 X_1$, the preceding formula (5.18) can be simplified because $\alpha_1 = X_2$, $\alpha_p = X_1$, and $\alpha_2, \alpha_3, \ldots \alpha_p$ are empty strings. Then formula (5.18) implies that

$$X_2\, X_1 \;\to\; X_2 \cdot \beta \cdot X_1 \;;\; \beta \in \mathcal{C}^+ \;\wedge\; |\beta|_C = n$$
$$\wedge \;\; \beta \in (C\, (\mathcal{C} \setminus \{C\})^+)^\star \; ((\mathcal{C} \setminus \{C\})^+\, C)^\star \tag{5.19}$$

Table 5.15 gives the history of the construction of the four compositions of coordinations from [Medic] shown in table 5.14.

As in the compositions of coordinations, the compositions of modifications/substitutions amount to successive insertions of strings that *a contrario* neither begin nor end with a coordinating conjunction. They are described by:

Construction Rule 5.7 (compositions of modifications/substitutions) The string-rewriting expression of the composition of n modifications/substitutions is the insertion, inside the string of the controlled term, of n strings that do not contain a coordinating conjunction:

Table 5.16
Compositions of modifications/substitutions among 100 random modifications/substitutions variants from [Medic]

	Controlled term	Variant
		$X_2 [\mathbf{X_2'} [\mathbf{X_2''} X_1]]$
(1)	*Environmental factor*	*environmental <u>behavioral</u> <u>high</u> <u>risk</u> factors*
(2)	*Mean value*	*mean <u>arterial</u> <u>blood</u> <u>pressure</u> value*
(3)	*Magnetic measurement*	*magnetic <u>resonance</u> <u>microimaging</u> measurements*
(4)	*Minimum time*	*minimum <u>recommended</u> <u>disinfection</u> times*
(5)	*Lingual gland*	*lingual <u>mandibular</u> <u>salivary</u> gland*
(6)	*Pulsed echo*	*pulsed <u>gradient</u> <u>spin</u> echo*
(7)	*Gradient method*	*gradient <u>spin</u> <u>echo</u> <u>imaging</u> methods*
(8)	*Malignant tumor*	*malignant <u>mouse</u> <u>skin</u> tumors*
(9)	*Rapid technique*	*rapid <u>multiple</u> <u>indicator</u> <u>dilution</u> technique*
		$X_2 [[\mathbf{X_2'}\, \mathbf{X_2''}]\, X_1]$
(10)	*Digital system*	*digital <u>image</u> <u>analyzing</u> system*
		$[X_2\, \mathbf{X_2'}]\, [\mathbf{X_2''}\, X_1]$
(11)	*Enzyme immunoassay*	*enzyme <u>linked</u> <u>sandwich</u> immunoassays*
(12)	*Population survey*	*population <u>based</u> <u>prevalence</u> survey*
		$X_2\, \mathbf{X_2'}\, \mathbf{X_2''}\, X_1$
(13)	*Glucose dehydrogenase*	*glucose <u>6</u> <u>phosphate</u> dehydrogenase*
(10)	*Xanthine oxidase*	*xanthine <u>plus</u> <u>xanthine</u> oxidase*
(*a*)	*Papillary carcinoma*	*papillary [<u>transitional</u> <u>cell</u> carcinoma]*
(*b*)	*Cell factor*	*cell [<u>growth</u> <u>inhibitory</u> factor]*
(*c*)	*Automatic system*	*automatic [<u>image</u> <u>analysis</u>] system*

$$\alpha_1 \cdot \alpha_2 \cdots \alpha_{p+1} \;\rightarrow\; \alpha_1 \cdot \beta_1 \cdot \alpha_2 \cdot \beta_2 \cdots \alpha_p \cdot \beta_p \cdot \alpha_{p+1}$$

$$\alpha_1, \alpha_2, \dots, \alpha_{p+1} \in \mathcal{C}^+ \;\wedge\; \beta_1, \beta_2, \dots, \beta_p \in (\mathcal{C} \setminus \{C\})^+ \;\wedge\; p \leq n \tag{5.20}$$

For the purpose of illustrating compositions of modifications/substitutions, 100 modification/substitution variants from [Medic] were randomly chosen. Only 14 of these variants are nonelementary; they are given in table 5.16. The modifications/substitutions *a* to *c* are elementary even though the inserted string is longer than one word. Actually *a* and *b* are elementary substitutions because the bracketed string is a term of the [Pascal] list; *c* is an elementary modification because the inserted string is also a controlled term. The subpart of a variant that corresponds to a term from the authority list [Pascal] is marked with square brackets in table 5.16.

Formula (5.20) simplifies as follows for binary terms:

$$X_2 X_1 \;\rightarrow\; X_2 \cdot \beta \cdot X_1 \;;\; \beta \in (\mathcal{C} \setminus \{C\})^+ \tag{5.21}$$

This formula is identical to (5.11) given for elementary modifications/substitutions.

This simplification does not hold for n-ary terms with $n \geq 3$ because, in this case, a string can be inserted in more than one position (and not only between the two words X_2 and X_1 as in the case of binary terms). There are only two such modifications/substitutions in the corpus [Medic]: *vitamin $\underline{D}$ resistant $\underline{hypophosphataemic}$ rickets*, a variant of *Vitamin resistant rickets*, and *gas $\underline{chromatography}$ thermal $\underline{energy}$ analysis*, a variant of *Gas thermal analysis*. With such a low frequency, it is legitimate to confuse compositions of modifications/substitutions and elementary modifications/substitutions.

Heterogeneous Compositions

In order to take into consideration all the possibilities of heterogeneous combinations of variations, I first look at the compositions of coordinations and modifications/substitutions, and then I turn to the composition of these variations with permutations.

A sequence of n coordinations and modifications/substitutions is the successive insertion of n strings, some of which begin or end with a coordinating conjunction. The construction rule 5.8 for these sequences is obtained by combining construction rules 5.6 and 5.7.

Construction Rule 5.8 (Coordinations and modifications/substitutions) The string-rewriting expression of the composition of n' coordinations and $n - n'$ modifications/substitutions is the insertion, inside the string of the controlled term, of p strings that possibly contain coordinating conjunctions such that n' coordinating conjunctions are inserted:

$$\alpha_1 \cdot \alpha_2 \cdots \alpha_{p+1} \;\rightarrow\; \alpha_1 \cdot \beta_1 \cdot \alpha_2 \cdot \beta_2 \cdots \alpha_p \cdot \beta_p \cdot \alpha_{p+1} \;;$$
$$\alpha_1, \alpha_2, \ldots, \alpha_{p+1}, \beta_1, \beta_2, \ldots, \beta_p \in \mathcal{C}^+ \;\wedge\; p \leq n$$
$$\wedge\; \beta_1, \beta_2, \ldots, \beta_p \in (\mathcal{C} \setminus \{C\})^\star \, (C \, (\mathcal{C} \setminus \{C\})^+)^\star \tag{5.22}$$
$$((\mathcal{C} \setminus \{C\})^+ \, C)^\star \, (\mathcal{C} \setminus \{C\})^\star \;\wedge\; \textstyle\sum_{i=1}^p |\beta_i|_C = n'$$

The two following examples illustrate such compositions, in which the inserted string is underlined:

induced bronchoconstriction

$\xrightarrow{\;C\;}$ *induced $\underline{vasodilatation\ and}$ bronchoconstriction*

$\xrightarrow{\;M/S\;}$ *induced $\underline{nasal}$ vasodilatation and bronchoconstriction*

$\xrightarrow{\;C\;}$ *induced nasal $\underline{and\ bronchial}$ vasodilatation and bronchoconstriction* *partial deletion*

$\xrightarrow{\text{C}}$ *partial and complete deletion*

$\xrightarrow{\text{M/S}}$ *partial and complete homozygous deletion*

$\xrightarrow{\text{C}}$ *partial and complete homozygous or hemizygous deletions*

The order of the variations in the sequence is not unique. However, when a coordination involves an inserted structure, it is necessary to apply the corresponding modification/substitution before the coordination.

The remaining cases of heterogeneous compositions are compositions of one permutation and one or more coordinations, compositions of one permutation and one or more modifications/substitutions, and compositions of one permutation and one or more coordinations and modifications/substitutions. I only consider the latter possibility, henceforth *generalized composition*. (Both remaining compositions are simply particular cases of generalized composition.)

Construction Rule 5.9 (Generalized composition)   The string-rewriting expression of the composition of one permutation, n' coordinations, and $n - n'$ modifications/substitutions is built as follows:

1. The permutation of two nonempty strings and the insertion of a preposition at the pivot of the permutation.

2. The insertion, inside the string of the controlled term, of p strings which may contain coordinating conjunctions:

$$\alpha_1 \cdot \alpha_2 \cdots \alpha_p \rightarrow \alpha_1 \cdot \beta_1 \cdots \alpha_{k-1} \cdot \beta_{k-1} \cdot \alpha_l \cdot \beta_l \cdots \alpha_{m-1} \cdot \beta_{m-1}$$
$$\cdot P \cdot \beta_k \cdot \alpha_k \cdots \beta_{l-1} \cdot \alpha_{l-1} \cdot \beta_m \cdot \alpha_m \cdots \cdot \beta_p \cdot \alpha_p$$

$$1 \le k < l < m \le p + 1 \ \wedge \ 2 \le p \le n$$

$$\wedge \ \alpha_1, \alpha_2, \ldots, \alpha_p \in \mathcal{C}^+$$

$$\wedge \ \forall i \in \{1, \ldots, n\} \setminus \{k-1, k, m-1, m\} (\beta_i \in \mathcal{C}^+)$$

$$\wedge \ \forall i \in \{k-1, k, m-1, m\} \ (\beta_i \in \mathcal{C}^\star)$$

$$\wedge \ \beta_1, \beta_2, \ldots, \beta_p \in (\mathcal{C} \setminus \{\text{C}\})^\star \ (\text{C} \ (\mathcal{C} \setminus \{\text{C}\})^+)^\star$$

$$((\mathcal{C} \setminus \{\text{C}\})^+ \ \text{C})^\star \ (\mathcal{C} \setminus \{\text{C}\})^\star$$

$$\wedge \ \sum_{i=1}^{p} |\beta_i|_{\text{C}} = n' \tag{5.23}$$

In formula (5.23), $\alpha_l \ldots \alpha_{m-1}$ and $\alpha_k \ldots \alpha_{l-1}$ are the two strings that are permuted by the initial transformation. In the case of a binary term $X_2 X_1$, the preceding formula simplifies because $k = 1$, $l = 2$, $m = 3$, $n = 2$, and the only nonempty α_i strings are $\alpha_2 = X_1$ and $\alpha_1 = X_2$:

$$X_2 X_1 \rightarrow X_1 \cdot \beta_2 \cdot P \cdot \beta_1 \cdot X_2 \; ; \; \beta_1, \beta_2 \in \mathcal{C}^\star \wedge \beta_1, \beta_2 \in (\mathcal{C} \setminus \{C\})^\star \, (C \, (\mathcal{C} \setminus \{C\})^+)^\star$$

$$((\mathcal{C} \setminus \{C\})^+ \, C)^\star \, (\mathcal{C} \setminus \{C\})^\star \tag{5.24}$$

For simplicity formulas (5.22), (5.23), and (5.24) are underspecified. They do not state that modifications/substitutions can only insert a string into a phrase before the head of a term or a substructure. Consequently in formula (5.24) the string β_2 either begins with a coordinating conjunction (and corresponds to a coordination) or is a very specific case of modification/substitution such as a parenthesized precision. There are only two such examples in the training corpus: *temperature _and strain rates pertinent_ to hot rolling*, a variant of *Rolling temperature*, and *temperature _(up to 1,000 K)_ of the surface*, a variant of *Surface temperature*. The weak productivity of the insertions in the position β_2 has led us to assert only metarules Perm with $\beta_2 = \varepsilon$ (see appendix A.2). For ternary variants, the possibilities of insertion are more numerous; they are detailed in section 6.3.4 for term acquisition.

To conclude this section, let us illustrate the case of generalized variation through a variant which involves the three families of variations:

cell transformation

$\xrightarrow{\text{P}}$ *transformation _of_ cells*

$\xrightarrow{\text{M/S}}$ *transformation of _endothelial_ cells*

$\xrightarrow{\text{M/S}}$ *transformation of _capillary_ endothelial cells*

$\xrightarrow{\text{C}}$ *transformation of capillary _and venous_ endothelial cells*

This variant corresponds to $\beta_2 = \varepsilon$ and $\beta_1 = $ *capillary and venous endothelial* in formula (5.24). The order of the composition is not unique, but the following two principles must be respected:

Principle 1 Permutation must be the first variation in the sequence.

Principle 2 One of both modifiers in the coordination (*capillary* or *venous*) must be inserted by a modification/substitution before the coordination.

Principle 1 is expressed in construction rule 5.5. Principle 2 is stated after the examples following construction rule 5.8.

The elementary variations and their compositions are described in appendix A.2:

1. Coordinations, compositions of coordinations, and compositions of coordinations and modifications/substitutions are identified as `Coor`.

2. Modifications/substitutions and compositions of modifications/substitutions correspond to the `Modif` metarules.

3. Permutations and compositions of permutations with coordinations and/or modifications/substitutions are associated with the identifiers `Perm` and `NPerm`.

These metarules are complemented with metarules `ExtC`, `ExtM`, `ExtP`, and `NExtP` that span a larger text window in order to validate the size of the windows chosen for the regular metarules.

The metarules designed so far rely on a study of the structures of variations and their transformations into string-rewriting rules. However, these metarules lack categorial and morphological constraints and allow for the extraction of numerous spurious structures that are not likely to represent term variations. For this reason these metarules are called *paradigmatic metarules*. The purpose of the next section is to enrich these metarules with constraints in order to improve their precision. The hence modified metarules are called *filtering metarules*.

5.4   Refining Metarules

The technique used so far for designing paradigmatic metarules is a top-down approach in which string-rewriting rules are inferred from a linguistic model of structural combinations. I now shift to an empirical tuning of the paradigmatic metarules through a manual observation of occurrences which are collected automatically from the training corpus [Medic] through paradigmatic metarules. Correct examples and counterexamples are used for deducing additional constraints on metarules in order to enhance the quality of the extraction.

5.4.1   Three Shallow Parsers for Term Extraction

The tool developed for this study, *FASTR*, belongs to a family of shallow parsers that are now commonly used in different domains of application for large-scale NLP techniques such as information extraction (*FASTUS*; Hobbs et al. 1997), part-of-speech tagging (*Constraint Grammar*; Karlsson et al. 1995), or term extraction (*LEXTER*; Bourigault 1994). These parsers are generally modular; they are composed of several independent and cooperative modules, each dedicated to a specific task.

In order to present the organization of *FASTR*, its architecture is compared with two other parsers intended for noun phrase extraction or term extraction: *NPtool* implemented with *Constraint Grammar* (Voutilainen 1993) and *LEXTER* (Bourigault 1994). The three

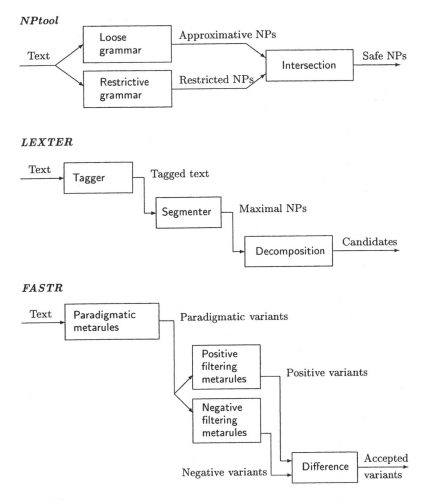

Figure 5.7
Simplified flow-charts of processes and communications *NPtool*, *LEXTER*, and *FASTR*.

tools are represented in figure 5.7 using a *SADT*-like formalism of *actigrams* where boxes correspond to processes and links to data flows (Marca and McGowan 1988).

As the flowchart shows, the *LEXTER* method is sequential; each step refines the data produced by the preceding one; this is also the organization of *FASTUS*, another parser composed of piped finite-state transducers. In comparison, *NPtool* is organized in a parallel fashion. The input text is analyzed by two concurrent modules. The output of these two modules is intersected in order to select only the data that are accepted by both modules. One module uses a loose NP grammar, whereas the other uses a more restricted grammar.

In *FASTR* the detection of variants involves both sequential and concurrent methods. On one hand, the successive use of paradigmatic and filtering metarules is sequential. On the other hand, the selective filtering of the second step is performed in a concurrent fashion. The second step outputs the difference between the positive and the negative filters so as to reject, among the positively accepted variants, the incorrect ones detected by negative metarules.

5.4.2   Experimental Tuning

The tuning of the metagrammar is based on an observation of the occurrences extracted from the training corpus through paradigmatic metarules. Three modes of enrichment of paradigmatic metarules are used for transforming them into filtering metarules:

1. *Specification.* The addition of constraints to a paradigmatic metarule restricts the set of accepted variants by increasing its selectivity.

2. *Specialization.* If a paradigmatic metarule covers several different linguistic phenomena, several filtering metarules are generated from this single paradigmatic metarule with possibly incompatible linguistic constraints.

3. *Duality.* Some descriptions are more easily stated by specifying both acceptable and unacceptable criteria. The corresponding filtering metarules are the *positive* and *negative metarules*.

I now turn to the illustration of these modes of refinement on some examples.

Specification of a Head Coordination
The paradigmatic metarule (5.25) is refined into a filtering metarule (5.26):

$$\text{Metarule Coor}(X_1 \rightarrow X_2\,X_3) \equiv X_1 \rightarrow X_2\,X_5\,C_4\,X_3 : . \tag{5.25}$$

$$\text{Metarule Coor}(X_1 \rightarrow X_2\,X_3) \equiv X_1 \rightarrow X_2\,X_5\,C_4\,X_3 : \tag{5.26}$$
$$\neg(\langle X_5\ cat\rangle \doteq \text{`Pu'})$$
$$\neg(\langle X_2\ cat\rangle \doteq \text{`P'}).$$

The additional constraints are motivated by the observation of incorrect occurrences retrieved by the paradigmatic metarule:

• Constraint $\neg(\langle X_5\ cat\rangle \doteq \text{`Pu'})$. X_5 is an argument and cannot be a function word such as a punctuation marker. For instance, *genes, and expression* from:

Vanadate did not increase MRNA corresponding to PODC or RB <u>genes, and expression</u> of c-sis and c-fes genes was undetectable whether vanadium was present or not.

is not a correct variant of *Gene expression*.

• Constraint $\neg(\langle X_2\ cat\rangle \doteq \ 'P')$. The category of X_2 cannot be preposition because terms with a Preposition-Noun structure are too much frozen for being involved in a coordination. Thus *in water and direct* is not a variant of *In direct* in

There was an association between the presence of limescale <u>in</u> <u>water and direct</u> culture for amoebae . . .

No constraint is stated on the number of the argument X_2, although it is expected to be a singular adjectival modifier. First, no incorrect variant with a plural X_2 is observed in the training corpus. Second, there are some correct coordinations with a plural noun X_2; they correspond to argument coordinations of right-headed terms such as *chromosomes 5 and 6*, a variant of *Chromosome 6*. (There are several left-headed binary terms in the [Pascal-Metal] term list, such as *Chromosome 5*, *Year 1970*, or *Vitamin D*.) However, an observation of the other types of coordination variants in the next paragraph shows that this constraint is mandatory for argument coordination metarules.

Observations of paradigmatic variants have also led us not to assert that both coordinated heads must agree in number. For instance, *vegetable oils and fat* from

. . . food workers involved in the extraction of animal and <u>vegetable</u> <u>oils and fat</u> . . .

is a correct head coordination of the plural term <u>vegetable oils</u> and the singular term <u>vegetable fat</u>. The first paradigmatic variants accepted and rejected by metarule (5.26) are given in table 5.17.

Table 5.17
Acceptation and rejection of head coordinations from [Medic]

Document	Controlled term	Paradigmatic variant accepted by (5.26)
000025	*Chromosome 6*	*chromosomes 5 and 6*
000039	*Renal function*	*renal hemodynamics and function*
000115	*Cell differentiation*	*cell growth and differentiation*
000295	*Crystal growth*	*crystal nucleation and growth*
000456	*Endolymphatic sac*	*endolymphatic duct and sac*

Document	Controlled term	Paradigmatic variant rejected by (5.26)
003940	*Language perception*	*language, and perception*
011901	*In direct*	*in water and direct*
013108	*Cell surface*	*cells, and surface*
013859	*Gene expression*	*genes, and expression*
015525	*Pattern analysis*	*patterns, and analysis*

The metarules defined here are intended for an untagged corpus. Because of their small number and their lack of ambiguity, punctuations, conjunctions, and prepositions are good indications for accepting or rejecting variants in such a framework. In chapters 7 and 8 the input texts are tagged with unambiguous part-of-speech categories. There the categories of content words (nouns, adjectives, and verbs) are used for defining syntactic patterns in the design of filtering metarules.

Remaining Errors   The only incorrect variant extracted by metarule (5.26) from the training corpus [Medic] is *agonist bromocriptine and antagonist* from

The effects of the dopamine <u>agonist bromocriptine and antagonist</u> haloperidol on . . .

This error is due to the presence of an adjectival term in the controlled term list, *Agonist antagonist*. This term is not adapted to a description of its variations by such a metarule.

Specialization of an Argument Coordination
Contrary to the preceding example in which one paradigmatic metarule produces only one filtering metarule, metarule (5.27) is split into two filtering metarules (5.28) and (5.29), each of which describes a different type of coordination:

Metarule $Coor(X_1 \rightarrow X_2 X_3) \equiv X_1 \rightarrow X_2 C_4 X_5 X_3 : .$ (5.27)

Metarule $Coor(X_1 \rightarrow X_2 X_3) \equiv X_1 \rightarrow X_2 C_4 Pp_5 X_3 :$ (5.28)
$\langle X_2 \text{ } number \rangle \doteq \langle Pp_5 \text{ } number \rangle.$

Metarule $Coor(X_1 \rightarrow X_2 X_3) \equiv X_1 \rightarrow X_2 C_4 X_5 X_3 :$ (5.29)
   $\neg(\langle X_2 \text{ } number \rangle \doteq \text{ 'plural'})$
   $\neg(\langle X_5 \text{ } number \rangle \doteq \text{ 'plural'})$
   $\neg(\langle X_5 \text{ } cat \rangle \doteq \text{ 'Pp'})$
   $\neg(\langle X_5 \text{ } cat \rangle \doteq \text{ 'D'}).$

Metarule (5.28) is intended for coordinations with a possessive pronoun. All the variants extracted by this metarule from the training corpus are shown in table 5.18. The only constraint in this metarule states that the pronoun Pp_5 must agree in number with the following noun X_3.

   Metarule (5.29) completes the preceding one and describes the coordinations of two nonpronominal arguments and bears the following constraints:

• Constraints $\neg(\langle X_2 \text{ } number \rangle \doteq \text{ 'plural'})$ and $\neg(\langle X_5 \text{ } number \rangle \doteq \text{ 'plural'})$. Left-headed binary terms, such as *Chromosome 5*, cannot accept head coordinations such as *chromosome*

Table 5.18
Acceptance of pseudoargument coordinations from [Medic]

Document	Controlled term	Paradigmatic variant accepted by (5.28)
009160	*Gene expression*	*genes and their expression*
016388	*Frequency shift*	*frequency and its shift*
016968	*Cell subpopulation*	*cells and their subpopulations*

Table 5.19
Acceptance and rejection of genuine argument coordinations from [Medic]

Document	Controlled term	Paradigmatic variant accepted by (5.29)
000074	*Apical membrane*	*apical and basolateral membrane*
000078	*Food intake*	*food and water intake*
000106	*Neutral lipid*	*neutral and acidic lipid*
000108	*B cell*	*B and T cells*
000265	*Low field*	*low and intermediate field*

Document	Controlled term	Rejected paradigmatic variant
000751	*Tumor cell*	*tumors or K562 cells*
000817	*Cell culture*	*cells or fetal cultures*
002347	*Cell culture*	*cells or after culture*
003424	*Cell structure*	*cells or biliary structures*
004256	*Test method*	*tests and conventional methods*

and gene 5. Only right-headed terms are likely to be transformed by metarule (5.29). Thus both X_2 and X_5 are singular adjectival arguments. These constraints force the filtering metarule to reject incorrect occurrences such as *cells or biliary structures*, which is a spurious variant of *Cell structure* in

No obvious damage to hepatic parenchymal cells or biliary structures was observed . . .

• Constraint $\neg(\langle X_5 \; cat \rangle \; \doteq \; `D')$. In this case similar reasons motivate the rejection of a co-ordinated function word (here a determiner). The only corresponding incorrect occurrence in [Medic] is *tissue or a factor*, an incorrect variant of *tissue factor*.

• Constraint $\neg(\langle X_5 \; cat \rangle \; \doteq \; `Pp')$. In order to avoid a conflict between metarules (5.28) and (5.29), metarule (5.29) is constrained so as not to accept coordinations with a pronominal pronoun.

The first examples of variations filtered by these metarules are given in table 5.19.

Remaining Errors   Some incorrect variants remain among the variants filtered by (5.29) which cannot be rejected on pure syntactic criteria. For instance *tube and ventral wall* is not a variant of *Tube wall* in

Sonography showed associated anomalies, including neural <u>tube and ventral wall</u> defects.

As indicated in section 5.1.3, the difference of categories between the two coordinated arguments observed in this variant is not a criterion of rejection. For instance, *fat or caloric content* is a correct coordination of an adjectival argument with a nominal one.

Specialization and Duality of a Permutation

An analysis of the paradigmatic permutation metarules observed in [Medic] show that they can be classified along three different types:

1. *Genuine permutations.* These variations correspond to the model of permutation around the prepositional pivot mentioned in section 5.1.1. For binary terms $X_2 X_3$, such a permutation can only occur if X_2 is a substantive. The variants in the top panel of table 5.20 are such genuine permutations.

2. *Attributive constructions.* In these permutations the pivot is the verb *to be*. Unlike genuine permutations, the permuted argument must be an adjective or a past participle. Examples of such permutations are shown in the central panel of table 5.20.

3. *Deverbal structures.* The last family of variations belongs to morphosyntactic variations which are studied in chapter 7. These variations correspond to a *conversion*: a change of syntactic category without change of form (Bauer 1983, p. 32). Upon 88 such variants encountered in [Medic], 78 are built from the controlled term *Hypothesis test*; more examples are given in the bottom panel of table 5.20.

These three families of variations are described by specializing a common metarule (5.30) and splitting it into three filtering metarules (5.31), (5.33), and (5.35). For keeping track of the rejected variants and for avoiding lengthy disjunction, each filtering metarule is accompanied by a negative metarule building the three following pairs: (5.31)–(5.32), (5.33)–(5.34), and (5.35)–(5.36). Negative metarules are expected to retain only spurious variants. Negative metarules (5.32) and (5.34) assert that X_2 is a not substantive by accepting any variant in which the category of X_2 is not noun or gerund. Negative metarule (5.34) attracts any variant for which the verb is not *to be*. In the metarules given in appendix A.2, each negative metarule is placed before its companion positive metarule so that the negative filter catches the spurious variants before the associated positive filter detects the correct variants among the remaining occurrences.

Table 5.20
Acceptation and rejection of permutations from [Medic]

Document	Controlled term	Variant accepted by (5.31), not by (5.32)
000010	*Cell fraction*	*fractions of cells*
000023	*Transmission mode*	*mode of transmission*
000160	*Distribution volume*	*volumes of distribution*
000233	*Perception threshold*	*thresholds for perception*
000265	*Variance analysis*	*analysis of variance*

Document	Controlled term	Paradigmatic variant rejected by (5.32)
000045	*Embryonic development*	*development of embryonic*
000051	*Infected cell*	*cells of infected*
000067	*Electrochemical method*	*method with electrochemical*
000163	*Dynamic response*	*response to dynamic*
000906	*Sequential analysis*	*analysis of sequential*

Document	Controlled term	Variant accepted by (5.33), not by (5.34)
000686	*Isolated cell*	*cells were isolated*
001056	*Still disease*	*disease is still*
001937	*Low intensity*	*intensities were low*
002177	*Benign neoplasm*	*neoplasms were benign*
002533	*Double contrast*	*contrast was double*

Document	Controlled term	Paradigmatic variant rejected by (5.34)
000025	*Chromosome translocation*	*translocations involving chromosome*
001106	*Statistical model*	*model showed statistical*
001992	*Pituitary hormone*	*hormone secreting pituitary*
003998	*Degenerative disease*	*disease show degenerative*
005405	*Morphological analysis*	*analysis defines morphological*

Document	Controlled term	Variant accepted by (5.35), not by (5.34)
000016	*Impact study*	*study the impact*
000532	*Hypothesis test*	*test this hypothesis*
000648	*Medium containing*	*containing the medium*
001643	*Hypothesis test*	*test the hypothesis*
002003	*Hypothesis test*	*test this hypothesis*

Metarule Perm$(X_1 \rightarrow X_2 X_3) \equiv X_1 \rightarrow X_3 X_4 X_2 :\ .$ (5.30)

Metarule Perm$(X_1 \rightarrow X_2 X_3) \equiv X_1 \rightarrow X_3 P_4 X_2 :\ .$ (5.31)

Metarule NPerm$(X_1 \rightarrow X_2 X_3) \equiv X_1 \rightarrow X_3 P_4 X_2 :$ (5.32)

$\neg(\langle X_2\ tense \rangle \doteq\ 'gerund')$

$\neg(\langle X_2\ cat \rangle \doteq\ 'N').$

Metarule Perm$(X_1 \rightarrow X_2 X_3) \equiv X_1 \rightarrow X_3 V_4 X_2 :$ (5.33)

$\langle X_3\ number \rangle \doteq \langle V_4\ number \rangle.$

Metarule NPerm$(X_1 \rightarrow X_2 X_3) \equiv X_1 \rightarrow X_3 V_4 X_2 :$ (5.34)

$\neg(\langle V_4\ lemma \rangle \doteq\ 'be').$

Metarule Perm$(X_1 \rightarrow X_2 X_3) \equiv X_1 \rightarrow X_3 D_4 X_2 :\ .$ (5.35)

Metarule NPerm$(X_1 \rightarrow X_2 X_3) \equiv X_1 \rightarrow X_3 D_4 X_2 :$ (5.36)

$\neg(\langle X_2\ tense \rangle \doteq\ 'gerund')$

$\neg(\langle X_2\ cat \rangle \doteq\ 'N').$

Remaining Errors   As will be shown in the evaluation of section 5.5, these metarules are less precise, although more complex than coordination or modification/substitution metarules. The main reason is that permutation variants—as opposed to coordinations and modifications/substitutions—are not compound nouns and would be more easily detected if the corpus was tagged with part-of-speech categories. In the absence of unambiguous syntactic tags, most errors are due to ambiguities of grammatical categories:

1. *False positives.* Gerunds can be either substantives or adjectives, depending on the context. (In [Pascal], 101 binary terms have a gerund head and 114 have a gerund argument.) If X_2 is a gerund with an adjectival role, the occurrence extracted by metarule (5.31) is not a correct variant. For instance, *systems of operating* in

The intense illumination <u>systems of operating</u> microscopes . . .

is not a variant of *Operating system* because *operating* is an adjectival modifier of *microscope* in the current sentence.

2. *False negatives.* Metarule (5.34) rejects irrelevantly some correct $X_{1,\text{subject}}$ $X_{3,\text{verb}}$ $X_{2,\text{object}}$ variants in which $X_{3,\text{verb}}$ is not *to be*. Thus *translocations involving chromosome* is definitely a variant of *Chromosome translocation* in

<u>Translocations involving chromosome</u> 4 were observed in three cell lines.

Table 5.21
Implicitly rejected permutations from [Medic]

Document	Controlled term	Rejected paradigmatic variant
000111	*Specific identification*	*identification or specific*
000454	*Screw plate*	*plates and screws*
000584	*Mononuclear cell*	*cells and mononuclear*
000619	*Supplemented diet*	*diet, supplemented*
000624	*Reduced rate*	*rate, reduced*

3. *False drops.* In some cases the insertion of a colon character between the permuted constituents of a term can correspond to a correct variation such as *design: randomized*, a variant of *Randomized design* in

Design: randomized, double-blind, placebo-controlled study.

No specific metarule is dedicated to this construction, because it would retrieve more incorrect variants than correct ones.

Table 5.20 shows, for each positive metarule, the first five matched variants and, for the negative metarules (5.32) and (5.34), the first five accepted variants (which are ultimately rejected according to the *FASTR* flowchart given in figure 5.7). No rejected variation by metarule (5.36) is displayed because this variation does not filter out any variation from [Medic]. Table 5.21 displays the five first rejected paradigmatic variations of permutation which are accepted neither by a positive metarule nor by a negative one.

Refinement of Other Variations

As is demonstrated by the examples in this section, the empirical tuning of a metagrammar is the progressive modification of a linguistic model through the observation of examples from a corpus. It took me approximately one month each to tune the metagrammar of French and English. Ongoing experiments on other languages are indicated in section 8.2.1. It takes approximatively the same time for tuning a metagrammar of these languages at the same level of granularity. However, some languages, such as German and Japanese, raise novel issues such as the agglutination of compounds (German) or the lack of word boundaries (Japanese).

The metarules corresponding to the three families of variations and their compositions are given in appendix A.2 for binary terms. Despite their tuning on the [Medic] corpus, these metarules do not achieve a 100% rate of precision and recall on this corpus.

On the one hand, some cases are deliberately ignored because they depend too much on the domain of the training corpus.[35] On the other hand, some variations are discarded because they retrieve an equal number of correct and spurious variants and because their improvement calls for techniques such as part-of-speech tagging. The use of part-of-speech tagging is intentionally avoided in this chapter so as to demonstrate that accurate results can be obtained without calling for this technique. On the contrary, in the chapters 7 and 8 on the extraction of morphosyntactic and semantic variants, it is mandatory to preprocess the texts with a part-of-speech tagger for obtaining good quality results.

Section 5.5 is devoted to evaluating the quality of these variations on a test corpus in a different domain (metallurgy). Beforehand, the use of an intermediate formalism for the description of terms and their variants is justified.

5.4.3 *FASTR*: An Intermediate Formalism

As noted by Fagan (1987, p. 75), the text analysis for information retrieval must rely on an approach "that is intermediate between the most complex and simplest approaches." For the purpose of free indexing, Fagan uses a syntactic parser, focuses on noun phrases, and decomposes the noun phrases into elementary descriptors composed basically of a head word and an argument.

Unlike Fagan (1987) the purpose of *FASTR* is controlled indexing. The process of building a list of potential descriptors is clearly separated from the process of indexing. Indexing with *FASTR* amounts to extracting occurrences of terms or variants with the help of transformations that produce variation patterns from terms.

The formalism of *FASTR* is called *intermediate* because it is intermediary between two extreme solutions that each produce similar results with different level of descriptions: transducers or combinations of tree structures. The transformations performed by metarules could be implemented through transducers as described in Kay (1983). The transducers resulting from these metarules could ultimately be composed, determinized, and minimized into a single, compact, and efficient machine (Mohri 1994). Apart from their optimization, transducers also have the quality of being reversible: they can both analyze and generate term variations.

I did not chose this level of description because of its lack of readability and because the exploitation of feature structures in finite-state machines leads to a dramatic expansion of their size (Kiraz 1997). The human tuning of the metarules can take advantage of a more readable formalism such as the declarative metagrammar of *FASTR* (inspired from *PATR-II*; Shieber 1986). Unification-based formalisms offer the flexibility of accepting any new feature without reconsidering the architecture of the application and without any significant change in performance.

The formalism of *FASTR* could also be represented as complex structural combinations of elementary tree structures. I have deliberately chosen to simplify this description into string-rewriting rules with constraints (see sections 5.1, 5.2, and 5.3) in order to make the implementation of *FASTR* more efficient.

5.5 Evaluating Syntactic Metarules

The tuning of the syntactic metarules for English was performed on a training corpus [Medic] and a training term list [Pascal] (presented in appendix C). The evaluation of these metarules was made on a test corpus [Metal] and a test term list [Pascal-Metal]. Both corpora are a raw untagged corpora. The term lists were tagged by Jean Royauté (*INIST/CNRS*) with the help of the lexical database *DELAF* of the *LADL* laboratory (University Paris 7) (Royauté and Jacquemin 1993).

From each tagged term list, a lexicon of all the single words appearing in the terms and a grammar of all the terms are created (excerpts of these two files are shown in appendix D). Every single word has a category, a lemma, and an inflection number. Every term rule asserts the same features for all of its single words plus a unique *label* and a lexical anchor denoted by the feature *lexicalization*.

The evaluation described in this section was performed on 113 filtering metarules. The metarules for two-word terms are described in appendix A.2. The size of the complete metagrammar is shown in table 5.22.

The results are evaluated on the indexing of the test corpus [Metal] indexed with the test term list [Pascal-Metal] through the metagrammar tuned on the training corpus and term list. As indicated in the following indexed sentence, each index is composed of a sentence reference, a term string, an occurrence or a variant, and a variation reference (0 denotes nonvariant occurrences):

Table 5.22
Size of the filtering metagrammar

	Coor	Modif	Perm	Total
Metarules for 2-word terms	7	5	7 positive, 6 negative	25
Metarules for 3-word terms	12	7	10 positive, 8 negative	37
Metarules for 4-word terms	18	9	12 positive, 12 negative	51
Total	37	21	29 positive, 26 negative	113

```
Preparation of copper-rhodium alloy single crystals by
the vertical Bridgman method is described in this paper.
000095   rhodium alloy    rhodium alloy           0
000095   copper alloy     copper rhodium alloy    XX,9,Modif
000095   single crystal   single crystals         0
```

5.5.1 Qualitative Evaluation

The qualitative evaluation of the controlled indexing in English relies on the human scanning of three sets of data:

1. The *filtered variants* are the occurrences to be evaluated. They are produced by filtering metarules (section 5.4 and appendix A.2).

2. The *paradigmatic variants*, produced by paradigmatic metarules (sections 5.1, 5.2, and 5.3, and appendix A.1), are not evaluated per se. They are used to check that they do not contain any good variant that is not retrieved by any of the filtering metarules. Paradigmatic variants are a superset of filtered variants because filtering metarules are built from paradigmatic metarules through the addition of constraints.

3. The *co-occurrences*, as defined by the following definition 5.5, are used as baseline for the measure of recall. Co-occurrences are a superset of paradigmatic variants.

Definition 5.5 (Co-occurrence)   A co-occurrence is an n-word window containing all the content words of a controlled term.

The parameter n is chosen to include all the correct variants contained within a set of documents. For the English language, $n = 20$ is used; a human scanning of 200 randomly chosen co-occurrences within a window of 21 to 30 words has not revealed any additional correct variants.

Co-occurrences are separated into two classes: *insertion co-occurrences* if the order of the words in the window is the same as the order of the words within the controlled term, and *permutation co-occurrences* otherwise.

Filtered variants are a subset of paradigmatic variants, which are, in turn, a subset of co-occurrences (see points 2 and 3 above). Inclusion of paradigmatic variants into filtered variants is strict; for instance, *oxygen atom concentration, ion* is a paradigmatic variant of *Oxygen ion*, which is not accepted by a filtering metarule of modification/substitution. (A punctuation cannot be inserted into a modification/substitution.) Similarly *parameters b(0), b(1), b(2) and is exact to order* is a permutation co-occurrence of *Order parameter*, which is not a paradigmatic variant because it spans too a large window. (This co-occurrence spans 20 words because punctuation markers are counted each as one word.)

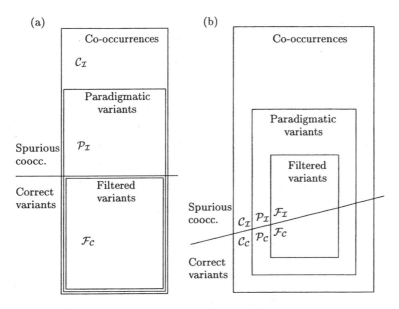

Figure 5.8
Co-occurrences, paradigmatic and filtered variants: in (a) the ideal case and in (b) the actual situation.

The output of *FASTR* is correct if filtered variants only contain correct variants and contain them all (see figure 5.8a). Thus paradigmatic variants and co-occurrences should only consist of fortuitous co-occurrences that do not satisfy definition 1.1 of correct variants. However, a human observation shows that some paradigmatic variants and some co-occurrences that do not belong to filtered variants are correct and that, conversely, some of the filtered variants are incorrect (see figure 5.8b).

The actual overlap between correct variants, and the three sets of data defined above, leads to the partition of co-occurrences into six nonoverlapping sets:

- $\mathcal{F}_C$, the correct variants among filtered variants; $\mathcal{P}_C$, the correct variants among paradigmatic variants that are not filtered variants; and $\mathcal{C}_C$, the correct variants among co-occurrences that are not paradigmatic variants,

- $\mathcal{F}_I$, $\mathcal{P}_I$, and $\mathcal{C}_I$, the incorrect variants among the same sets as above.

The sizes of these sets for controlled indexing of the test corpus are given in table 5.23. Paradigmatic and filtered variants are subdivided according to the three families of metarules; co-occurrences are divided into insertions (representing coordinations and insertions) and permutations.[36]

Table 5.23
Number of variants on [Metal] (indexes denote the arity of the controlled term)

	Coor_2	Modif_2	Modif_3	$\text{Modif}_{\geq 4}$	Perm_2	Perm_3	$\text{Perm}_{\geq 4}$	**Total**
$|\mathcal{C}_\mathcal{C}|$		47	5	0	29	4	0	**85**
$|\mathcal{C}_\mathcal{I}|$		147	11	0	147	33	2	**340**
$|\mathcal{P}_\mathcal{C}|$	0	30	1	0	32	3	0	**66**
$|\mathcal{P}_\mathcal{I}|$	2	75	1	0	157	6	0	**241**
$|\mathcal{F}_\mathcal{C}|$	51	197	21	3	3	88	4	**367**
$|\mathcal{F}_\mathcal{I}|$	0	12	0	0	0	9	0	**21**
Total		561	39	3	368	143	6	**1,120**

Measure of Quality

As seen in section 2.1.5, the evaluations used in information retrieval can be extended to automatic indexing. The expressions of these measures rely on the sizes of the sets $\mathcal{F}_\mathcal{C}$, $\mathcal{P}_\mathcal{C}$, $\mathcal{C}_\mathcal{C}$, $\mathcal{F}_\mathcal{I}$, $\mathcal{P}_\mathcal{I}$, and $\mathcal{C}_\mathcal{I}$ introduced above. The precision is the ratio of correct variants among filtered variants:

$$P = \frac{|\mathcal{F}_\mathcal{C}|}{|\mathcal{F}_\mathcal{C} \cup \mathcal{F}_\mathcal{I}|} \tag{5.37}$$

Two expressions of recall are given depending on whether the baseline is the set of correct variants among paradigmatic variants (R_p) or the set of correct variants among co-occurrences (R_c):

$$R_p = \frac{|\mathcal{F}_\mathcal{C}|}{|\mathcal{F}_\mathcal{C} \cup \mathcal{P}_\mathcal{C}|}, \quad R_c = \frac{|\mathcal{F}_\mathcal{C}|}{|\mathcal{F}_\mathcal{C} \cup \mathcal{P}_\mathcal{C} \cup \mathcal{C}_\mathcal{C}|} \tag{5.38}$$

Similarly the two expressions for precision of fallout are

$$\Pi_p = \frac{|\mathcal{P}_\mathcal{I}|}{|\mathcal{F}_\mathcal{I} \cup \mathcal{P}_\mathcal{I}|}, \quad \Pi_c = \frac{|\mathcal{P}_\mathcal{I} \cup \mathcal{C}_\mathcal{I}|}{|\mathcal{F}_\mathcal{I} \cup \mathcal{P}_\mathcal{I} \cup \mathcal{C}_\mathcal{I}|} \tag{5.39}$$

The measured values of these five measures for the different families of variations are given in table 5.24.

Comments on the Measure of Quality

Despite the use of a noncontextual parser and the difficulty of the task, the results obtained on the test corpus are very good: the total precision is 94.5%. The high value of the precision of

Table 5.24
Qualitative evaluation of term extraction on [Metal]

	Coor	Modif	Perm	**Total**
P	100%	94.8%	91.1%	**94.5%**
R_p	100%	87.7%	72.4%	84.7%
R_c	76.6%		57.5%	**70.7%**
Π_p	100%	86.4%	94.8%	92.0%
Π_c	95.1%		97.4%	**96.5%**

fallout (96.5%) indicates that the vast majority of the spurious co-occurrences are discarded by filtering metarules. The weak point of the approach is recall (70.7%); it is due partly to the fact that precision has been preferred over recall when designing metarules in order to avoid burdening the user with an excessive number of spurious indexes.

As with the different families of variations, the quality of coordination variants is higher than the quality of modifications/substitutions, which are, in turn, of a better quality than permutations. The lower quality of permutations is due to the syntactic structure of the variants: permutation variants are noun phrases, while other type of variants are compound nouns. Such a structure would be better analyzed with a contextual parser that accounts for a larger scope of transformations. However, the quality of the results confirm the relevance of the *FASTR* approach to term extraction based on shallow and robust techniques of transformational local grammars.

I will now report on a few examples of noise and silence in the extraction of term variants:

• *Noise in modification/substitution.* Noise in modification/substitution is due to structural ambiguity. For instance, *high-resolution electron energy* is not a correct variant of *High energy* in

... *has been studied using <u>high resolution electron energy</u> loss spectroscopy (HREELS).*

The variant is incorrect because its structure is [[A N$_3$] [[N$_2$ N$_1$] N$_4$] N$_5$] [[*high resolution*] [[*electron energy*] *loss*] *spectroscopy*], and therefore the dependency between *high* and *energy* in the controlled term is lost in the variant. The metarule producing this incorrect variant is however correctly applied because there is only one incorrect variant among the 36 occurrences extracted from test corpus by this metarule. A way of recovering from such errors is to disambiguate the resulting variants through corpus statistics (see Strzalkowski and Vauthey 1992, and section 6.2.2).

• *Silence in modification/substitution.* Silence in modification/substitution is due to specific variations. *FCC structure of the crystals* is an example of incorrectly rejected correct modification/substitution variant of *FCC crystal* in

The <u>FCC structure of the crystals</u> is retained after annealing . . .

It is rejected by the filtering metarules because it contains a preposition. The criteria of definition 1.1 are too strong because they reject variations in which the head of the term (here *crystal*) is different from the head of the variant (here *structure*). This variation corresponds to the association of a typifying property—here a structure—with objects having these property—here a crystal. However, the corresponding filtering criterion (the rejection of insertions of a preposition) is correctly applied because it correctly rejects 26 spurious variants and discards only 5 correct variants.

• *Noise in permutation.* Noise in permutation is due to structural ambiguity. *Alloys of the copper* is not a correct variation of *Copper alloy* in

On <u>alloys of the copper</u> palladium cobalt system an investigation is made . . .

In this example *copper* depends on *system*, while it depends on *alloy* in the original term. Here too the corresponding metarule should not be removed: it only retrieves 4 incorrect variants out of 37. A remedy to this problem could be to use *FASTR* on a corpus bracketed by a noun phrase extractor such as *NPtool* (Voutilainen 1993). By requiring that the occurrences do not include an argument (here *copper*) without the corresponding head word (here *system*), a spurious variant, such as the preceding one, would not be extracted.

• *Silence in permutation.* Silence in permutation is due to noisy variations. In the absence of additional linguistic knowledge, some variations patterns are noisy and are therefore discarded. For instance, *orientations observed in the crystal* is rejected as variant of *Crystal orientation*, although correct, because a word is inserted between the head noun and the preposition (here *observed*). Using the metarule allowing such an insertion on the test corpus would actually retrieve four additional correct variants including the preceding one, but it would also extract four more spurious variants. In an approach favoring recall, this metarule could, however, be included in the metagrammar.

The Case of Elision

In section 5.2.3 elision is presented as a possible term variation, but no metarule in appendix A.2 mirrors this variation. The reason is that *FASTR* is not appropriate for extracting these variants. The following set of metarules is used to evaluate the extraction of elisions by *FASTR* on the test corpus:

Metarule Elis($X_1 \rightarrow X_2\ X_3\ X_4$) $\equiv$ $X_1 \rightarrow X_2 X_4$: . (5.40)

Metarule Elis($X_1 \rightarrow X_2\ X_3\ X_4$) $\equiv$ $X_1 \rightarrow X_3\ X_4$: . (5.41)

Metarule Elis($X_1 \rightarrow X_2\ X_3\ X_4\ X_5$) $\equiv$ $X_1 \rightarrow X_3\ X_4\ X_5$: . (5.42)

Metarule Elis($X_1 \rightarrow X_2\ X_3\ X_4\ X_5$) $\equiv$ $X_1 \rightarrow X_2\ X_4\ X_5$: . (5.43)

Metarule Elis($X_1 \rightarrow X_2\ X_3\ X_4\ X_5$) $\equiv$ $X_1 \rightarrow X_2\ X_3\ X_5$: . (5.44)

Metarule Elis($X_1 \rightarrow X_2\ X_3\ X_4\ X_5$) $\equiv$ $X_1 \rightarrow X_4\ X_5$: . (5.45)

Metarule Elis($X_1 \rightarrow X_2\ X_3\ X_4\ X_5$) $\equiv$ $X_1 \rightarrow X_2\ X_5$: . (5.46)

Metarule Elis($X_1 \rightarrow X_2\ X_3\ X_4\ X_5$) $\equiv$ $X_1 \rightarrow X_3\ X_5$: . (5.47)

Metarules (5.40) and (5.41), for 3-word terms, were previously given as metarules (5.6) and (5.7). It is mentioned there that only terms of three or more words are likely to have elliptic variants extracted by metarules. The remaining metarules (5.42) to (5.47) are intended for 4-word terms; they are built according to construction rule 5.3.

The exploitation of these metarules on the test corpus yields very poor results. The 107 first variants are all incorrect; they are all produced by metarules (5.41) and (5.45) which remove external (leftmost) modifier(s). Let us illustrate the output of these rules on the following sample sentence:

```
. . . have been investigated experimentally by a combination of conven-
tional and high resolution transmission electron microscopy.
```

```
000008   transmission electron microscopy
         transmission electron microscopy   0
000008   secondary electron microscopy
         electron microscopy                XXX,2,Elis
000008   high voltage electron microscopy
         electron microscopy                XXXX,4,Elis
000008   field electron microscopy
         electron microscopy                XXX,2,Elis
000008   scanning electron microscopy
         electron microscopy                XXX,2,Elis
```

Through this indexing, *electron microscopy* appears as an elliptic variant of three 3-word terms (*secondary electron microscopy*, *field electron microscopy*, and *scanning electron microscopy*) and one 4-word term (*high-voltage electron microscopy*) even though this

Table 5.25
Absolute text coverage of terms and variants on [Metal]

| | Term occurrences | | | Term variants | | |
Term arity	2	3	4	2	3	4
Surface	5,108	861	24	2,146	216	15
Ratio	4.3%	0.7%	0.0%	1.8%	0.2%	0.0%
Ratio of total surface		5.0%			2.0%	

Table 5.26
Relative text coverage of terms and variants on [Metal]

| | Term occurrences | | | Term variants | | |
Term arity	2	3	4	2	3	4
Surface	5,108	861	24	2,146	216	15
Ratio	61.0%	10.3%	0.3%	25.6%	2.6%	0.2%
Total distribution		71.6%			28.4%	

sentence contains a genuine occurrence of *Transmission electron microscopy*. This sentence and the corresponding indexes justify that metarules (5.41) and (5.45) cannot be used in the metagrammar because they conflate all the ternary or quaternary terms sharing the same two rightmost words (*Transmission electron microscopy*, *Secondary electron microscopy*, *High-voltage electron microscopy*, etc.).

Unfortunately, the remaining metarules do not achieve a more correct extraction of elliptic variants: out of 155 variants extracted on the test corpus by metarules (5.40), (5.42) to (5.44) and (5.46) to (5.47), only 53 of them are correct. The correct variants generally correspond to terms with an integrated metonymy (see section 5.1.2). For instance, the term *Kerr magnetooptical effect* is frequently encountered as *Kerr effect* because, in this domain, a shared pragmatic knowledge implicitly attributes the characteristic *magnetooptical* to the concept denoted by the linguistic utterance *Kerr effect*.

The poor results of *FASTR* on elliptic variants have led us to give up the description of these variations. A correct processing of referential sequences to multi-word terms might be achieved successfully through a memorization of full term occurrences and a segmentation of texts into coherent passages.

5.5.2   Quantitative Evaluation

This section is concerned with the description of the volumes of texts covered by controlled terms and their variants. Two complementary aspects of coverage are measured: the absolute coverage (table 5.25) and the relative coverage (table 5.26). The volumes are measured on

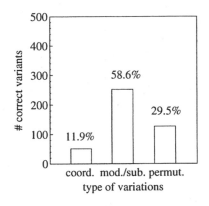 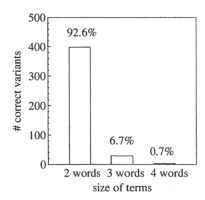

Figure 5.9
Distributions of correct variants among types of variations and sizes of terms in [Metal].

the manually checked term and variant occurrences extracted from the test corpus [Metal] with the test term list [Pascal-Metal].

Terms and their variants cover approximately 7% of the test corpus. Inside this *conceptual surface*, terms represent 72% of the surface and variants occupy the remaining 28%. The large numbers of variants reveal that variation is a central issue for achieving correct coverage of the conceptual surface of a text through indexing. It justifies, a posteriori, the necessity of describing term variations in the process of automatic indexing.

Figure 5.9 shows the relative importance of the different types of variations and the different sizes of terms. The distribution among the different types of variations depends on the language under study: for instance, permutation is pervasive in English and marginal in French. Figure 5.9 also depicts the volume of variations for 2-, 3-, and 4-word terms. Three facts should be taken into account for the tuning of a metagrammar:

1. As indicated by this figure, an order of magnitude separates the volumes of n-term variants from $n + 1$-term variants. There are approximately 10 times fewer 3-word term variants than 2-word term variants and 100 times fewer 4-word term variants than 2-word term variants.

2. The number of metarules is proportional to the size of the terms by a factor of 1.5 (see table 5.22). Thus the complexity of a metagrammar increases with the size of the terms, and thereby its efficiency decreases when it is designed for larger terms.

3. The quality of the variations increases with the size of the controlled term: the larger the controlled term, the more original words are included in the variant and the smaller is the possibility of having a spurious co-occurrence.

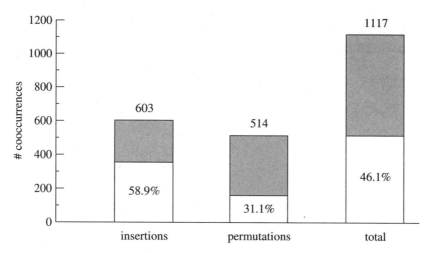

Figure 5.10
Rate of correct variants among co-occurrences in [Metal].

The combination of these remarks suggests that it is a waste of effort to tune a metagrammar for terms of 4 or more words. On the contrary, it is essential to conceive the metarules of 2-word terms with great care. The metarules for 3-word terms require less attention because they extract approximately ten times fewer variants than metarules for 2-word terms. Furthermore, since they contain three content words, these variations are "naturally" accurate and require less effort for human tuning.

Figures 5.10 and 5.11 indicate the rate of correct variations among the different types of co-occurrences and paradigmatic variations. According to definition 5.5, a co-occurrence is a text window containing all the content words of a multi-word term. Figure 5.10 reveals that only 46.1% of the co-occurrences actually correspond to a term variant. This weak value indicates that there is an important discrepancy between co-occurrences and lexicosyntactic relations. Even after the application of an additional shallow filter, such as the filter of paradigmatic variants, the proportion of nonvariants among collocations remains high: figure 5.11 shows that 38.6% of the paradigmatic variants are not correct term variants.

Early work on statistical word associations such as term associations in information retrieval (Stiles 1961; Choueka 1988) or lexical associations for lexicographic purposes (Church and Hanks 1990) assumes that recurring adjacencies correspond to linguistic relations. Even though this assumption is statistically relevant, a closer inspection of these associations shows that many of them correspond to fortuitous co-occurrences. The shortcomings of pure statistical approaches to the recognition of lexical associations has led some authors to build hybrid systems relying on both linguistic filtering and statistical selection, such as Smadja(1993b) or Daille (1996) described in sections 2.2.6 and 2.2.1.

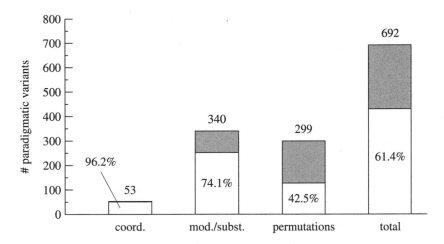

Figure 5.11
Rate of correct variants among paradigmatic variations in [Metal].

Figure 5.12 shows that variation is not an homogeneous modification of terms: only a small number of terms have a high number of variations. The pattern of the number of terms as a function of their number of variations has the same hyperbolic behavior as Zipf's law. The uneven distribution of term variability suggests that variation might be an indication of the informational content of a term.

According to Polanco, Grivel, and Royauté (1995) there is a correlation between the variability of a term and its belonging to an active domain. This observation is correlated with the use of overcomposition through term substitution for building *n*-ary terms from binary terms such as *Blood cell + Mononuclear cell → blood [mononuclear cell]*. Since modifications/substitutions represent 58.6% of term variants and variants of binary terms represent 92.6% of term variants (figure 5.9), it is very likely that a term with an important variability participates in lexical creativity (Guilbert 1965). Further studies should confirm the correlation of variation and term creation in order to conceive tools for tracking term creation through the observation of variations. Such tools could be applied to the survey of emergent technologies through the detection of novel terms.

5.6 Summary

This chapter has presented the design of a metagrammar of syntactic variations for the French language. In the first step of this process, paradigmatic metarules are created according to the standard syntactic structures of noun phrases and their combination into

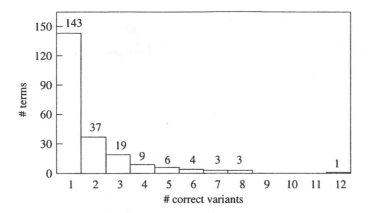

Figure 5.12
Distribution of terms along their number of variants in [Metal].

variations. In the second step, the paradigmatic variations are experimentally tuned and enriched through the progressive addition of constraints.

Four types of elementary variations are defined for binary terms: coordinations, permutations, modifications/substitutions, and elisions. They all transform terms into term variants that are semantically close to the original terms. These transformations depend on the structure of the original terms and are specific to the English language.

The four types of elementary variations are then extended to n-ary terms which are multi-word terms with more than two content words. Unlike binary terms, n-ary terms with $n > 2$ are structurally ambiguous. The different possible structures and all their combinations are taken into account for the design of the associated elementary variations. The calculation of n-ary term variations is detailed for coordinations, the hardest case, and then generalized to the other types of elementary variations.

The final generalization of elementary variations is the composition of variations. Composition amounts to applying iteratively elementary variations to basic term structures. The sequence of variations is reflected by a transformational path. If the path contains a permutation, it contains only one permutation, and the permutation is the first variation in the path. Homogeneous and heterogeneous compositions of variations are calculated and these formulas are then exploited in the design of paradigmatic metarules.

Three complementary techniques are used for refining the paradigmatic metarules resulting from the structural analysis of variations and their compositions:

1. Specification is the addition of constraints for the purpose of rejecting spurious variants.

2. Specialization is the splitting of a single metarule into specialized metarules dedicated to single linguistic phenomena.

3. Duality is the addition of negative metarules that are in charge of intercepting incorrect variants. Thus these variants are "stolen" from the positive metarules that would otherwise incorrectly accept them.

These refinements are performed through the addition of constraints deduced from human investigations of corpora. The corresponding metarules called filtering metarules are used by *FASTR* for extracting syntactic variants.

A qualitative evaluation of variant extraction through measures of information retrieval adapted to term extraction indicates a precision of 95% and a recall of 71%. Coordinations, modifications, and permutation are extracted by *FASTR* with high recall and good precision. Thus *FASTR* is a tool that is well adapted to the task for which it was designed. The only poor results of *FASTR* concern elisions and have led us to give up the description of these variations. A quantitative analysis of the manually checked data shows that variation is an important phenomenon because it represents 28% of multi-word term occurrences. Taking variation into account is not only a means for improving a term spotter, it is also an opportunity for acquiring terminological and conceptual knowledge from corpora, as shown in the next chapter.

This chapter has described the different syntactic variants that can be produced from a controlled vocabulary. The next chapter explores the reverse activity which consists of inferring basic terms from observed syntactic variants.

6 Term Enrichment

To the constant evolution of sciences or technologies corresponds an evolution of the associated languages and their terminologies. Any NLP system that relies on the controlled terminology of a domain must therefore be fed with updated terminological data in order to avoid becoming obsolete. Recent terms are generally scattered, unstable, and subject to variations. Their detection is not straightforward because they may contain unknown words or unusual morphological phenomena, and they may look misleadingly when they consist of nondenominative phrases such as *General paralysis* (Rey 1995 sec. 4.1).

Corpus-based term acquisition is an appropriate technique for discovering new terms because specialists constantly employ terms that have not yet undergone standardization processes. In order to provide any term-based process such as controlled indexing, machine translation, or information extraction with a tool for corpus-based term acquisition, I consider a technique for incremental term enrichment that relies on the analysis of corpora with the help of a set of seed terms. The results of the methods are twofold: first, a set of new candidates is extracted, and second, links between these candidates and controlled terms are highlighted, which allow for the construction of partial ontologies.

The original aspect of this method is that it focuses on term enrichment—the addition and the anchoring of terms to an existing base—instead of initial term acquisition from scratch.

This chapter is organized as follows: In section 6.1 some methods for automatic thesaurus construction are reviewed. Then a statistical technique for acquiring terms from variants and for structurally disambiguating them is proposed in section 6.2. Finally, the core analytic technique for incremental term enrichment is proposed in section 6.3.

6.1 Automatic Thesaurus Acquisition

The techniques for term acquisition are presented in section 2.2 of this book. They share some common features:

• They are *massive* because they extract large amounts of terms. They leave to a (generally human) postprocessor the task of filtering and organizing the collected candidates.

• They are *definitive* because they do not rerun the acquisition algorithm with the help of the newly acquired data.

• They are *unstructured* since they do not furnish conceptual links between candidates.

In order to structure a term base, two complementary solutions are proposed in the information retrieval literature: *concept formation* or *term classification*, and *acquisition of conceptual links*. Both activities are generically named *thesaurus acquisition*. Concept formation is the construction of classes of semantically related terms, while acquisition of conceptual links is the acquisition of semantic relationships between terms.

6.1.1 Concept Formation

Co-occurrence Analysis

A very classical technique for automatic term classification relies on the observation of co-occurrences. Terms that tend to be found more frequently in co-occurrence than in isolation should be put in the same class. The exploitation of statistical associations in building thesauri for information retrieval was studied from the start of automatic information retrieval. Early publications were not looking to evaluate the precise effects of statistical grouping on the performance of automatic information retrieval. On the contrary, Sparck Jones's seminal book (1971) studied explicitly the impact of thesaurus construction on information access. In this study a relatively simple measure of similarity between terms is used that is based on Tanimoto's coefficient. The similarity of two terms is the ratio of co-occurrences to independent occurrences:

$$S(t, t') = \frac{f(t, t')}{f(t) + f(t') - f(t, t')}$$

in which $f(t, t')$ is the number of co-occurrences of t and t', and $f(t)$ and $f(t')$ are the number of occurrences of t and t'. The main focus of Sparck Jones's study is to evaluate precisely the effects of clustering on information retrieval through a systematic comparison of precision, recall, and fallout in a test collection.

In addition to co-occurrences in texts, co-occurrences in metadata can be also used to build term clusters. In Aizawa and Kageura (1998), bilingual keyword clusters are generated from bilingual keyword lists (Japanese and English) assigned to academic papers. In a first step, a graph is derived from a bilingual keyword corpus and links are weighted according to the frequencies of co-occurrence. In a second step, the graph is partitioned in bilingual clusters based on a minimal edge cut. When partitioning succeeds, each cluster is composed of semantically equivalent Japanese and English keywords.

A second method for automatic term classification in information retrieval relies on the *discrimination values* of terms, their ability to discriminate between relevant and nonrelevant documents in a collection (Crouch 1990). In this study a thesaurus class consists of terms with similar discrimination values or, in other words, with close informational content with respect to a collection of documents. A class is made of terms that can be substituted one to another without altering significantly the spatial distribution of the collection.

The simplest measure of the discrimination value of terms is inversely proportional to the frequency of co-occurrence within a collection of documents. Thesauri are manually constructed through the measure of *statistical co-occurrences* within the vector space model of *SMART* (Salton and Lesk 1971; Salton 1971). The more the terms co-occur within documents, the more they can be replaced one by another without changing the representation of the documents. In Crouch (1990), the discrimination value of a term is obtained by calculating the density of the document space with and without this term as index. A good discriminator is a term that decreases the space density when it is assigned to a document.

Other measures for automatic thesaurus construction are presented in Srinivasan (1992); they rely mainly on statistical similarities of terms. In order to increase the similarity between word forms, stemming algorithms are used for conflating words which belong to the same morphological family such as *medicine*, *medicines*, *medical*, and *medication* (see section 2.1.3). Another way of increasing term/term similarity consists of first clustering a collection of documents and then calculating the co-occurrences of terms in document clusters (Crouch 1990; Crouch and Yang 1992). Since such methods fail to correctly group generic and polysemous words such as *application* or *tool*, they can be fruitfully associated with phrase extraction techniques which narrow the meanings of terms (Lewis and Croft 1990).

In information retrieval automatically built thesauri are used for broadening the indexing vocabulary or the query vocabulary. The terms in a query or a document are replaced by thesaurus classes in order to increase recall.

There is a parallel between the statistical techniques for automatic thesaurus construction and measures of word associations used in lexicography and presented in section 2.1.4 (Church and Hanks 1990). All these techniques are labeled as *first-order word affinities* by (Grefenstette 1994a) because they group together words that are recurrently found close one to another.

Context Analysis

In contrast, *second-order word affinities* group words with similar contexts. The corresponding approach in NLP is Harrisian linguistics, which assumes that semantically close words tend to fulfill similar syntactic roles and, thereby, tend to have similar contexts. (An introduction to Harrisian linguistics is given in section 4.1.) The application to NLP of this theory has inspired early experiments in corpus linguistics of Sager and her colleagues (Hirschman, Grishman, and Sager 1975; Sager 1981; Grishman and Kittredge 1986). Through massive text analysis, classes of words are extracted that correspond to words with similar grammatical contexts. For instance, Hirschman, Grishman, and Sager (1975) build classes of words such as Na^+, *glucose*, *ion*, *sodium*, and *calcium* and classes of verbs such as *influence*, *stimulate*, *concentrate*, *affect*, and *inhibit* through the automatic classification of words with similar distributions. While first-order word affinities rely on document co-occurrences that focus on the informational role of a word, linguistic features and, more precisely, subcategorization frames play a central role in second-order word affinities because they group words with similar subjects, objects, or modifiers.

Research in concept formation from context similarities is still active. Hindle (1990) calculates noun similarities from the output of a robust parser. In this approach words that are the subject or object of similar sets of verbs are similar. Grefenstette (1994b) also relies on syntactic contexts for calculating similarities. In addition to verb/arguments relations, he considers narrower contexts corresponding to head/modifier relations inside noun phrases (such contexts are also used by Ruge 1991). Instead of building word classes, Grefenstette and Hindle provide lists of words associated with polysemous words. In Hindle (1990) the words closest to *boat* are: *ship*, *plane*, *bus*, *jet*, *vessel*, *truck*, *car*, *helicopter*, and *man*. When using closer contexts in Grefenstette (1994b), antonym pairs are often extracted such as *small/large*, *high/low*, and *long/short*.

In Charniak (1993, pp. 144–45) such term grouping methods are criticized because they do not perform well on scattered words and because they produce apparently weird relations such as a word and its antonym. In my opinion, the first remark effectively corresponds to a weakness of the method. The symbolic method for calculating word similarities in section 6.3, which is not sensitive to the volume of occurrences, is proposed here in order to address this issue. The second remark of Charniak does not undermine the quality of the results: such antonym pairs are given in psycholinguistics experiments on *free associations* of words (Deese 1964, cited in Grefenstette 1994b, pp. 70–75).

The clustering of words with similar graphical contexts, proposed in Schütze (1993), is a nonlinguistic approach for calculating word similarities that also produces antonyms or "complementary" words such as *kid* and *dad*. The common capability of low- and high-level techniques in the detection of complementary words is underlined in Justeson and Katz (1991). In this study antonymous adjectives are extracted concurrently by co-occurrence measures and syntactic analysis: on the one hand, co-occurrences of antonym adjectives are remarkably high, and on the other hand, parallel syntactic constructions also frequently highlight such antonym adjectives as in . . . *he must work for long hours in the hot sun and cold rain*.

Although generally finer than first-order relations, second-order word affinities need to be further refined into smaller classes.

Refinement of Context Analysis

There are several techniques for refining or subclassifying classes produced through context observations.

A first mode of subclassification is proposed by Grefenstette (1994a) as *third-order word affinities*. It consists of a further exploitation of the context of the words composing a class in order to derive finer subclasses. Since the similarity produced by second-order techniques is not symmetric, it is enhanced by giving higher similarity scores to pairs of words which are reciprocally close.

A different extension of second-order techniques is proposed by Hatzivassiloglou and McKeown (1993) who combine positive and negative distributional criteria for the construction of adjectival semantic classes. The negative criterion used in conjunction with contextual similarity is that two adjectives modifying simultaneously the same word cannot belong to the same class. Another refinement of the contexts is proposed in Hatzivassiloglou (1997), who considers only conjunctions as valid co-occurrences.

Second-order techniques can be seen as an extension of first-order affinities because they exploit classes of syntactic contexts instead of co-occurrence contexts. This generalization is further improved by Resnik (1993, pp. 18–21) who exploits contexts of semantic classes instead of contexts of words through the use of *WordNet* (Miller et al. 1990). By replacing words by their *WordNet* classes, Resnik calculates semantic selection restrictions of verbs: the classes of *WordNet* that are most likely to be the class of their object noun. Thus polysemous nouns can be disambiguated by exploiting the selection restrictions of verbs. For instance, *hit*, *play*, and *watch* respectively select the meanings of *baseball* corresponding to *OBJECT*, *GAME*, and *DIVERSION* (Resnik 1993 p. 65).

In very specialized domains in which semantic classes are not available, it is possible to rely on a fine-grained classification of nouns based on the observation of all their modifiers within noun phrases. The observation of geometrical constraints on the graph built by nouns sharing common modifiers has led Habert, Naulleau, and Nazarenko (1996) to the construction of fine-grained corpus-dependent word relations. This technique yields nonlabeled links between words.

There is a limit to the quality of links that can be achieved by pure automatic domain-independent processing techniques without human tuning of the favorable linguistic contexts. In order to build a final terminological knowledge base, Condamines and Rebeyrolles (1998) propose linguistic techniques to define nonambiguous linguistic markers of relationships adapted to a corpus. A similar approach is advocated by the designers of *DocKMan*, a knowledge extraction tool for the semi-automatic extraction of knowledge-rich contexts (Davidson et al. 1998). *DocKMan* is composed of two parts: a text analyzer based on an incremental refinement of linguistic patterns and a knowledge base manager that helps the user capture and organize information. These works introduce the final subtheme of automatic thesaurus acquisition, the extraction of links between words, as developed in the following section.

6.1.2 Conceptual Links

Two main directions of research are found for the acquisition of conceptual links:

• *An information extraction-like technique.* Conceptual links are extracted from sentences in which predicates are explicitly uttered through predicative lexemes.

• *A information retrieval-like technique.* Links are extracted from a sentence in which no lexeme materializes the associated predicate.

Both techniques rely on the detection of significant syntactic patterns. They generally do not call for statistical filtering because each occurrence can be considered as a valid occurrence and because occurrences are much less numerous than they are in the techniques for automatic classification studied in the preceding section.

Predicative Links

Corpus-based techniques for the acquisition of predicative links through the extraction and the interpretation of predicative pattern call for exhaustive dictionaries covering all the possible significant linguistic forms. An alternative solution for extracting genuine predicative links is advocated by Fox et al. (1988) who analyze a machine-readable dictionary with the *LSP* parser of Sager (1981). From the definitions of *sheep*, *wool*, *ram*, *ewe*, and *lamb*, they infer the relations *wool PART-OF sheep*, *sheep IS-A animal*, *ewe FEMALE-OF sheep*, etc. It is not certain whether such a dictionary-centered approach can be applied to large-scale or specialized domains. Furthermore the authors do not really address the now well-known problems of inconsistencies in machine-readable dictionaries such as circularity, incoherence, and incompleteness.

Other authors work on full-text documents with the help of an application-tailored dictionary, whether manually defined (Robison 1970), (semi-)automatically acquired from pre-tagged corpora (Riloff 1993), or fully acquired from training corpora for the MUC-6 evaluation (Fisher et al. 1995). Lexicosyntactic patterns of Robison (1970) are attached to one meaning of a predicate. For instance, *admission* has two senses. The first is "being admitted into something" and corresponds to the patterns *admission of S into S* or *admission of S to S* (*S* is a noun phrase). The second is "confession" and corresponds to the patterns *admission of S (that) clause* or *admission by S (that) clause*. Riloff's patterns are more closely related to a specific domain and are automatically detected by spotting specific syntactic patterns such as ⟨*subj*⟩ *passive-verb*. In the MUC-4 terrorism domain corpus, the corresponding instances are ⟨*subj*⟩ *exploded*, ⟨*subj*⟩ *was murdered*, etc. This model of linguistic information through lexical selections is closely related to the lexicon-centered description of language in linguistics such as the *lexical functions* of Mel'čuk (1984).

In Velardi, Pazienza, and Fasolo (1991), automatic acquisition of predicative patterns from corpora is improved by exploiting concept hierarchies. By replacing the instances of a syncategorematic pattern by semantic types, instantiated patterns automatically acquired from corpora are generalized. Thus from the instance *farming in greenhouse*, a first semantic relation is inferred: [AGRICULTURAL ACTIVITY] → (LOCATION) → [BUILDING FOR CULTIVATION]. Then a coarser-grained relation is built by traversing the taxonomy: [ACTIVITY] → (LOCATION) → [PLACE]. The problem with this approach and some other work on lexical acquisition, such as Basili, Pazienza, and Velardi (1994), is the lack of benchmarks against which the outcoming semantic tags and relations can be evaluated. On the contrary, Agarwal (1995) proposes a technique for lexical acquisition in which validation plays a central role. In Agarwal (1995) nouns and verbs are classified according to the similarity of their syntactic contexts. Validation is performed through the reference to an external semantic thesaurus and through expert evaluation: only classes belonging to a *WordNet* synset are kept. These classes are ultimately validated by a human expert.

More ambitious work in extraction of information from corpora envisions a complete definition of a domain-oriented lexical semantics. The semantic model of the *generative lexicon* seems to be flexible enough for corpus-based semantics whether focusing on acquisition (Pustejovsky, Bergler, and Anick 1993) or interpretation (Fabre 1996). Another framework for the definition of semantic primitives is proposed by Pugeault, Saint-Dizier, and Monteil (1994) who use Jackendorf's predicate argument structures for representing and acquiring knowledge from technical texts. Such in-depth approaches relying on a complete semantic interpretation have to date been restricted to small-scale examples. It is uncertain whether these techniques can be extended to large-scale data such as the ones used for the MUC conferences.

I now turn to nonpredicative conceptual relations which are also relevant in extraction of conceptual links from corpora. They correspond to hierarchical links such as hypernymy or meronymy.

Implicit Links

Hyponymy and meronymy can be classified as implicit links because the corresponding predicate (*IS-A* or *PART-OF*) is not embodied in the semantics of one of the lexemes occurring in the context from which these relations are extracted.[37]

Hearst (1992) automatically detects hyponymy relations within a tagged corpus through finite-state techniques. She exploits six patterns based on lexicosyntactic categories which denote hyponymy. For instance, NP(,)$^?$ *especially* (NP,)*(*or*|*and*) NP extracts the occurrence *most European countries, especially France, England, and Spain* and yields an hyponymy relation from *European country* to *France, England*, and *Spain*. An algorithm allowing for the automatic detection of such patterns in corpora is given in Morin (1999). It relies on the classification of the lexicosyntactic patterns in which hyponym relationships from a reference thesaurus are encountered. The process is incremental, and newly acquired conceptual pairs can be used for further acquisition of other relevant linguistic patterns.

Machine-readable dictionaries are another source of acquisition of hyponyms. Dictionary definitions (e.g., *oxygen*) generally consist of a "genus" that relates the current meaning to an hypernym (e.g., *is a colorless gas*) and a "differentia" that illustrates the specificities of the current instance (e.g., *that exists in large quantities in the air*). Chodorow, Byrd, and Heidorn (1985) automatically extract genus relations from dictionary definitions through a shallow parser based on heuristics tuned to dictionary definitions. From the preceding definition, a relation between *oxygen* and *gas* is extracted. Amsler (1980) shows that the hierarchies encountered in dictionaries are *tangled hierarchies* because they do not have the neat tree structure of specialized thesauri such as *UMLS* (1995). Despite the presence of multiple inheritance and cyclic constructions, dictionary-based hierarchies can nevertheless be used for the construction of partial taxonomies with the help of an expert of the domain (Byrd et al. 1988). Another solution to the improvement of dictionary-based hierarchies is to combine multiple sources of evidence by working simultaneously with several dictionaries (Véronis and Ide 1991).

This section complements section 2.2 in providing an overview of some techniques in term acquisition and automatic thesaurus construction. The remainder of this chapter is dedicated to these two themes with a focus on term variation. In section 6.2 a statistical filter is proposed for selecting good candidate terms among term variants. In section 6.3 a local analysis is used for extracting candidate terms from variants of controlled terms. Conceptual links are discovered along with the candidate terms; they are exploited in the construction of partial taxonomies.

6.2 Statistical Acquisition from Variations

Statistical analysis of terms is divided into two parts. Section 6.2.1 describes a technique for the statistical ranking of ternary candidate terms based on variants extracted by *FASTR*. This approach is consistent with some work in domain surveys that show term variation to be a good indicator in the creation of new terms (Polanco, Grivel, and Royauté 1995; Ibekwe-SanJuan 1998). Section 6.2.2 presents a method for the structural disambiguation of ternary terms in order to prepare the way for a semantic analysis of the candidate terms.

6.2.1 Statistical Acquisition of Candidates from Variants

In a probabilistic analysis of the extraction of variants by *FASTR*, the probabilistic space consists of term variants. The low frequencies of variants and their linguistic form make them similar to the linguistically filtered n-grams of Su, Wu, and Jing-Shin (1994) used for compound acquisition. Therefore I first present this work and then motivate the technical choices of a two-step algorithm for variant acquisition with respect to this study.

The hybrid technique for compound noun extraction of Su, Wu, and Jing-Shin (1994) relies on an indicator of compound nouns. Each bi- or tri-gram is associated with a ternary vector composed of a Mutual Information measure, a relative frequency measure, and a boolean value denoting whether or not the part-of-speech pattern of the n-gram respects some syntactic constraints. Before performing the proper statistical filtering, n-grams occurring only once or twice are rejected and not considered for further estimations. Then the parameters of the compound model are estimated on a training set composed of compound and noncompound clusters. Finally, the n-grams of the test set are sorted according to their log-likelihood function.

Variant Rejection

A frequency cutoff similar to Su, Wu, and Jing-Shin (1994) is used to keep only reliable candidates: the variants extracted by *FASTR* with less than three occurrences are rejected. This constraint discards 3,702 single-occurring variants and 293 twice-occurring ones. In all, 94.5% of the distinct variants (tokens) extracted by *FASTR* from [Medic] are excluded. There remains 233 variants that appear three or more times in the corpus and are preserved for the second step of the filtering.

A quick linguistic analysis of these variants reveals that some of them denote the same concept as the original term. Such variants should not be kept for further filtering because they are not likely to provide new candidate terms. They distribute as follows:

• *Coordinations (5.6%)*. *Arterial and venous blood* is a variant of *Arterial blood* which does not denote a different concept. The introduced concept, *venous blood*, represents only a part of the variant; this type of acquisition is studied in following section 6.3.

• *Abbreviations (7.3%)*. *Human papilomavirus (HPV) 16* is a variant of *Human papilo-mavirus 16* introducing the acronym *HPV* without conceptual shift.

• *Genitives (18.0%)*. Terms with a proper name as modifier, such as *Bloom's syndrome*, are registered in the lexicon without the graphical mark of the genitive (here *Bloom syndrome*). Because of this graphical discrepancy, most occurrences of these terms are incorrectly considered as variants although being mere plain occurrences.

• *Permutations (15.0%)*. As shown in section 5.1.1, elementary permutations introduce only very light semantic shifts. For instance, *analysis of data* is almost synonym of the original term *Data analysis*. The introduction of a determiner also does not alter the conceptual meaning of a term, even though it may change its referential value. Thus *expression of this gene* in

The DCC gene (. . .) codes for a potential tumor suppressor gene (. . .). We investigated the <u>*expression of this gene*</u> . . .

refers to *DCC gene* in the preceding sentence.

The rejection of the synonymous variants leads to 126 remaining variants: 4 compositions of permutations and modifications/substitutions, and 122 modifications (97%).

Statistical Analysis

Ninety-eight of the 126 variants remaining after step 1 (78%) are produced by the modification metarule (5.2), which is repeated below:

Metarule Modif$(X_1 \rightarrow X_2\ X_3) \equiv X_1 \rightarrow X_2\ \mathbf{X_4}\ X_3$: .

Table 6.1
Variations from [Medic] ($\neq$ (5.2) and frequency > 3): Part 1

Number	$\mathrm{Modif}(X_1 \to X_2\, X_3) \equiv X_1 \to X_2\, \mathbf{X_4}\, \mathbf{X_5}\, X_3$	
3	*Dopamine receptor*	*dopamine <u>D 1</u> receptor*
3	*Performance analysis*	*performance <u>liquid chromatographic</u> analysis*
4	*Serum protein*	*serum <u>C reactive</u> protein*
6	*Vitamin deficiency*	*vitamin <u>B 12</u> deficiency*
12	*Glucose dehydrogenase*	*glucose <u>6 phosphate</u> dehydrogenase*
28	*Platelet factor*	*platelet <u>derived growth</u> factor*

Number	$\mathrm{Modif}(X_1 \to X_2\, X_3\, X_4) \equiv X_1 \to X_2\, X_3\, \mathbf{X_5}\, X_4$	
3	*Lambert Eaton syndrome*	*Lambert Eaton <u>myasthenic</u> syndrome*
3	*Low affinity site*	*low affinity <u>binding</u> sites*

Number	$\mathrm{Modif}(X_1 \to X_2\, X_3) \equiv X_1 \to X_2\, \mathbf{X_4}\, \mathbf{X_5}\, \mathbf{X_6}\, X_3$	
3	*Serum factor*	*serum <u>insulin like growth</u> factor*
7	*Reverse reaction*	*reverse <u>transcriptase polymerase chain</u> reaction*

Number	$\mathrm{Modif}(X_1 \to X_2\, X_3\, X_4) \equiv X_1 \to X_2\, \mathbf{X_5}\, X_3\, X_4$	
3	*Acute lymphocytic leukemia*	*acute <u>non</u> lymphocytic leukemia*
3	*Angiotensin converting enzyme*	*angiotensin <u>I</u> converting enzyme*
3	*Pulmonary wedge pressure*	*pulmonary <u>capillary</u> wedge pressure*
5	*Left coronary artery*	*left <u>circumflex</u> coronary artery*
6	*Left coronary artery*	*left <u>main</u> coronary artery*
16	*Regional blood flow*	*regional <u>cerebral</u> blood flow*

Number	$\mathrm{Modif}(X_1 \to X_2\, X_3\, X_4) \equiv X_1 \to X_2\, X_3\, \mathbf{X_5}\, X_4$	
4	*High affinity site*	*high affinity <u>binding</u> sites*
6	*High-frequency ventilation*	*high-frequency <u>jet</u> ventilation*
6	*Human papillomavirus 16*	*human papillomavirus <u>type</u> 16*
6	*T cell receptor*	*T cell <u>antigen</u> receptor*
6	*Two-dimensional electrophoresis*	*two-dimensional <u>gel</u> electrophoresis*
8	*Pulsed field electrophoresis*	*pulsed field <u>gel</u> electrophoresis*

Number	$\mathrm{Modif}(X_1 \to X_2\, X_3\, X_4) \equiv X_1 \to X_2\, \mathbf{X_5}\, \mathbf{X_6}\, X_3\, X_4$	
22	*Left coronary artery*	*left <u>anterior descending</u> coronary artery*

Table 6.2
Variations from [Medic] ($\neq$ (5.2) and frequency > 3): Part 2

Number	$\text{Modif}(X_1 \rightarrow X_2 X_3 X_4 X_5) \equiv X_1 \rightarrow X_2 X_3 X_4 \mathbf{X_6} X_5$	
3	*Premature rupture of membrane*	*premature rupture of <u>fetal</u> membranes*

Number	$\text{Perm}(X_1 \rightarrow X_2 X_3) \equiv X_1 \rightarrow X_3 \mathbf{P_4} \mathbf{X_5} X_2$	
3	*Pressure effect*	*effects <u>on blood</u> pressure*
4	*Blood cell*	*cells <u>from peripheral</u> blood*
11	*Control center*	*centers <u>for disease</u> control*

Number	$\text{Perm}(X_1 \rightarrow X_2 X_3) \equiv X_1 \rightarrow X_3 \mathbf{P_4} \mathbf{X_5} \mathbf{X_6} X_2$	
4	*Blood cell*	*cells <u>in the peripheral</u> blood*

The nine remaining classes only possess from one to six variants; they are shown in tables 6.1 and 6.2. Such small frequencies do not motivate the use of statistical filters.

The only large class C of variants contains 98 different variants; it corresponds to metarule (5.2). These variants are ranked according to an *association ratio a*, which is the average value of Mutual Information I and relative frequency f_r:

$$a(w_1 \ w_2 \ w_3) = 0.5 \times \frac{I(w_1 \ w_2 \ w_3)}{I_M - I_m} + 0.5 \times \frac{f_r(w_1 \ w_2 \ w_3)}{f_M - f_m} \tag{6.1}$$

with

$$\begin{cases} I_M = \max_{w_1 \ w_2 \ w_3 \in C} I, & I_m = \min_{w_1 \ w_2 \ w_3 \in C} I, \\ f_M = \max_{w_1 \ w_2 \ w_3 \in C} f_r, & f_m = \min_{w_1 \ w_2 \ w_3 \in C} f_r \end{cases}$$

Mutual Information $I(w_1, w_2)$ measures the information on w_2 carried by w_1 (see formula 2.8). Relative frequency $f_r(w_1 \ w_2 \ w_3)$ measures the rate of repetition of the variant $w_1 \ w_2 \ w_3$ in the corpus. The weighting parameters of both measures are chosen equal to 0.5. They cannot be optimized through machine learning techniques here because the number of variants is too low. Statistical training would require working on a corpus at least ten times larger than the [Medic] corpus (a 1.2-million word corpus) in order to possess a training set of at least 1,000 terms.

Table 6.3 shows the first 40 candidates produced by metarule (5.2) and ranked by decreasing value of association ratio a. Although *test-retest reliability* may seem incorrect, it is indeed a good candidate as shown by

In 58 subjects with stable asthma, good short term <u>test-retest reliability</u> was demonstrated with . . .

Table 6.3
Variations from [Medic] (metarule 5.2 and frequency > 3), ranked by decreasing association ratio a.

a	I	f_r	Candidate
0.60	−7.45	63.0	*blood mononuclear cell*
0.58	−6.75	54.0	*protein kinase C*
0.57	−8.76	70.0	*case control study*
0.51	−6.58	44.0	*inflammatory bowel disease*
0.50	−2.06	3.0	*Trypanosoma brucei rhodesiense*
0.45	−2.90	3.0	*shear elastic modulus*
0.43	−4.30	13.0	*sodium dodecyl sulfate*
0.43	−3.18	3.0	*hypoxanthine guanine phosphoribosyltransferase*
0.39	−5.42	18.0	*pulsed dye laser*
0.39	−4.49	10.0	*malignant fibrous histiocytoma*
0.39	−3.77	3.0	*Chediak-Higashi syndrome*
0.38	−4.07	4.0	*potassium titanyl phosphate*
0.38	−3.98	3.0	*inflatable penile prosthesis*
0.37	−6.18	21.0	*platelet activating factor*
0.37	−4.04	3.0	*semiconductor diode laser*
0.36	−7.03	27.0	*systolic blood pressure*
0.35	−4.85	7.0	*digital subtraction angiography*
0.35	−4.79	6.0	*labial salivary gland*
0.35	−4.33	3.0	*Lowe oculocerebrorenal syndrome*
0.34	−4.67	4.0	*neutron capture therapy*
0.33	−7.50	28.0	*arterial blood pressure*
0.33	−4.98	5.0	*nicotinic acetylcholine receptor*
0.32	−5.03	4.0	*dorsal root ganglion*
0.32	−4.80	3.0	*test retest reliability*
0.30	−6.35	13.0	*enzyme linked immunoassay*
0.30	−5.19	3.0	*malignant pleural mesothelioma*
0.29	−5.99	9.0	*thyroid stimulating hormone*
0.29	−5.91	8.0	*delayed type hypersensitivity*
0.29	−5.51	5.0	*temporal cilioretinal artery*
0.29	−5.46	4.0	*stratified random sample*
0.29	−5.39	4.0	*descending thoracic aorta*
0.29	−5.24	3.0	*proton beam irradiation*
0.28	−5.76	5.0	*neonatal respiratory distress*
0.28	−5.61	5.0	*carotid cavernous sinus*
0.27	−5.68	3.0	*gas liquid chromatography*
0.27	−5.55	3.0	*artificial urinary sphincter*
0.26	−7.13	15.0	*diastolic blood pressure*
0.26	−6.39	9.0	*somatic cell hybrid*
0.26	−6.28	8.0	*hematopoietic progenitor cell*
0.26	−6.17	6.0	*facial nerve paralysis*

The conceptual link between candidate term—a modification/substitution variant—and the controlled term that has produced the variant falls mainly into one of the two following linguistic classes:

1. *Metonymy links*. These variants result from the addition of a modifier that corresponds to pragmatically omitted information. Such modifiers do not modify the meaning of the initial term (see *integrated metonymy* in section 5.1.2). For some terms, such as *Health system*, the omitted modifier is unique and obvious: *health care system*. For some other terms, such as *Capillary flow*, there could be several possible modifiers, but in a given context such as the medical domain, only one is encountered: *capillary blood flow*. In all these cases the variant and the controlled term can be conceptually conflated as a unique concept.

If, even in a limited domain, there exist more than one possibility for extending a term through metonymy, it is necessary to consider the two variants and the original term as three separate concepts. Thus *Sudden death* and its two metonymic variants *sudden cardiac death* and *sudden infant death* denote three separate concepts: a generic one (*sudden death*) and two specific ones denoted by the two variants. This particular situation actually belongs to the following case denoting hyponymy relations.

2. *Hyponymy links*. In most cases the modification/substitution variant of a term is an hyponym of the original term: a term denoting a more specific concept. For instance, *penetrating cardiac injury* is a specific case of *Penetrating injury* concerning heart injuries.

The conceptual discrepancy between the two preceding cases is mirrored by a structural difference: left-branching structures for metonymic variants (the first two words are bracketed together as for [*health care*] *system*) and right branching structures for hyponymy relations (e.g., *penetrating* [*cardiac injury*]). In order to more easily interpret a term variant proposed as a candidate, it is preferable to provide a means for disambiguating its structure. The following section proposes a decision algorithm relying on measures of statistical preference for the disambiguation of these candidates. It focuses on the class of metarule (5.2) variants which is, by far, the one with the highest number of candidates.

6.2.2 Structural Disambiguation

This section presents a technique for disambiguating ternary candidates that relies on the observation of subdependencies within a corpus. Given a ternary compound $X_3 X_2 X_1$, the purpose of structural disambiguation is to decide on its structure among the three possibilities illustrated by figure 6.1.

The technique proposed in this section is inspired by Lauer (1995) who convincingly describes a new approach and shows its superiority over previously proposed techniques. Contrary to Lauer's study, I will count actual occurrences of pairs of words instead of *conceptual*

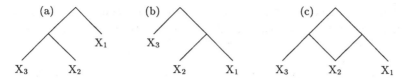

Figure 6.1
The three possible structures of a ternary term.

associations (Resnik and Hearst 1993). Conceptual associations are co-occurrences of groups of words, words with the same categories in the *Roget's Thesaurus*. In a very specialized domain, such as medicine, conceptual word grouping is not as straightforward as in a generic domain to which *Roget*'s categories apply.

Adjacency and Dependency Ratios

Lauer (1995) presents two previously proposed techniques for structural disambiguation: the *adjacency model* versus the *dependency model*. The former compares the associations $X_3 X_2$ and $X_2 X_1$. It is illustrated by R_{adj} in

$$R_{adj} = \frac{|X_3 X_2|}{|X_2 X_1|}, \quad R_{dep} = \frac{|X_3 X_2|}{|X_3 X_1|} \qquad (6.2)$$

It reflects the "classical" method introduced by Marcus (1980, app. A): the structure a of figure 6.1 is chosen if $X_2 X_1$ is not semantically acceptable or if $X_3 X_2$ is semantically preferable over $X_2 X_1$, and structure b is chosen otherwise. This technique is extended to corpus-based linguistics by Resnik (1993, sec. 5.5) who replaces semantic acceptability by corpus-based selectional associations.

The search for head-modifier structures of Strzalkowski and Vauthey (1992) and the *endogenous* disambiguation technique of Bourigault (1993, sec. IV.2) are also adjacency corpus-based techniques that rely on the presence of one of the two possible substructures $X_3 X_2$ or $X_2 X_1$ in the disambiguated corpus. Bourigault's technique is incremental because it takes advantage of disambiguated occurrences for extracting more accurately the remaining ones. The structure remains ambiguous if no evidence of a disambiguated substructure is found in the corpus. This technique is therefore better suited for homogeneous corpora, which are more likely to provide repeated structures.

The dependency model proposed by Lauer (1994) compares the associations $X_3 X_2$ and $X_3 X_1$ and corresponds to the ratio R_{dep} of formula (6.2). If $X_3 X_1$ is more acceptable than $X_3 X_2$, the structure b of figure 6.1 is chosen; otherwise, structure a is built.

In both ratios of formula (6.2), $|m \; m'|$ is the number of occurrences of the pair of words, except the occurrences in the ambiguous structure. More precisely, if $m'' \; m \; m' \; m'''$ is the

Table 6.4
Structural disambiguation of two ternary terms through the adjacency and the dependency model

	Blood cell count	White blood cell
$|X_3 X_2|$	88	1
$|X_2 X_1|$	18	74
$|X_3 X_1|$	4	6
R_{adj}	$4.9 > 1$	$0.013 < 1$
R_{dep}	$22 > 1$	$0.17 < 1$
Structure	$[X_3 X_2] X_1$	$X_3 [X_2 X_1]$

text sequence containing $m\, m'$, it is considered as a valid occurrence of the pair $m\, m'$ if and only if neither $m''\, m\, m'$ nor $m\, m'\, m'''$ is the ambiguous term. The purpose of this restriction, also stated by Bourigault (1993), is to avoid considering the ambiguous form for its own disambiguation.

Each of both models (adjacency and dependency) uses its respective ratio for disambiguating compound nouns: if the ratio is lower than 1, the structure b of figure 6.1 is chosen; otherwise, structure a is selected. These two techniques are illustrated on two ambiguous structures in table 6.4. The results provided on the corpus [Medic] by both techniques correspond to the actual linguistic structure.

Lauer (1995) compares both models and shows that the dependency model performs better than the adjacency model. He also stresses that the exploitation of categories from a thesaurus (Resnik and Hearst 1993) always outperforms the basic techniques based on actual co-occurrences.

The preceding disambiguation techniques do not deal with terms of four or more content words. This restriction is not problematic because these terms represent only 3,998 of the 50,073 complex terms in [Pascal] (about 8%). For such terms, more sophisticated algorithms such as connectionist techniques can be used for disambiguation (Wermter 1995ch. 5).

Algorithm of Disambiguation

I now turn to the description of a disambiguation algorithm for the candidates with a $X_3\, \mathbf{X_2}\, X_1$ structure resulting from the modification of an $X_3\, X_1$ structure. The algorithm relies on lexicon-based information—the presence of the substructures $X_3 X_2$ and $X_2 X_1$ in the controlled term list—and on corpus-based information—the values of the adjacency and dependency ratios. Lexicon-based information prevails over corpus-based information.

1. If exactly one of both subterms $X_3 X_2$ or $X_2 X_1$ belongs to the controlled vocabulary, the corresponding substructure is built. For instance, since *Facial nerve* is a controlled term

and not *nerve paralysis*, the structure of *facial nerve paralysis* is [*facial nerve*] *paralysis* (figure 6.1a).

2. If both subterms $X_3 X_2$ and $X_2 X_1$ are in the controlled term list, the structure of the term is a *directed acyclic graph* with $X_3 X_2$ and $X_2 X_1$ as substructures (figure 6.1c). Thus the structure of *arterial blood pressure* is [$_1$ *arterial* [$_2$ *blood*]$_1$ *pressure*]$_2$ because both *Blood pressure* and *Arterial blood* are in [Pascal].

3. If neither of the two substructures $X_3 X_2$ or $X_2 X_1$ is found in the controlled vocabulary, the decision is made according to a function that is based on the adjacency and dependency ratios.

Decision Function

The decision function presented here relies on the log values of the ratios $l R_{adj}$ and $l R_{dep}$ given in formula (6.2), and is calculated on the 98 candidate terms acquired from the corpus [Medic]. In order to tune the decision function, all the 98 candidates are used, even though, for some of them, one of the two substructures $X_3 X_2$ or $X_2 X_1$ is found in the controlled term list. Among these 98 terms, tables 6.5 and 6.6 show the 55 terms for which at least one of the two ratios is defined together with the possible subterms found in the controlled base [Pascal] (fifth column).

The *statistical adjacency structure* (resp. *statistical dependency structure*) is defined as the substructure inferred from the value of the adjacency ratio (resp. the dependency ratio). For instance, the statistical adjacency structure of $X_3 X_2 X_1$ with $l R_{adj} < 0$ is $X_3 [X_2 X_1]$. Similarly the *statistical anti-structure* is the structure inferred from the log of the inverse ratio.

The observation of the log-adjacency and log-dependency ratios of 39 ternary candidate terms with at least one subterm in the controlled vocabulary [Pascal] leads to the following conclusions:

1. For the 12 candidates such that $l R_{adj}$ and $l R_{dep}$ have the same sign, the common statistical substructure belongs to the controlled list. The statistical anti-structure of two of these candidates also belongs to the base, they have the cross-structure c of figure 6.1: [*arterial* [*blood*] *pressure*] and [*gas* [*liquid*] *chromatography*]. (Their statistical structure is $X_3 [X_2 X_1]$.)

2. The 5 candidates with opposite signs for $l R_{adj}$ and $l R_{dep}$ have their statistical adjacency structure in [Pascal]. For instance, *cell volume density* has a positive adjacency log-ratio, a negative dependency log-ratio, and its statistical adjacency substructure *Cell volume* is a controlled term.

3. There remain 9 candidates for which only one of both log-ratios $l R_{adj}$ or $l R_{dep}$ is defined. For 4 of them, the corresponding statistical substructure belongs to the controlled list.

Table 6.5
Adjacency and dependency ratios and possible subterms of candidate terms (part 1: both lR_{adj} and lR_{dep} are defined)

lR_{adj}	lR_{dep}	Number	Term and statistical structure	Subterm(s) from [Pascal]
1.85	1.57	9	[*T cell*] *antigen*	—
1.41	0.94	5	[*health care*] *system*	—
0.73	1.03	6	[*facial nerve*] *paralysis*	*facial nerve*
0.70	0.10	70	[*case control*] *study*	—
0.52	−0.15	3	[*cell volume*] *density*	*cell volume*
0.43	0.90	9	[*somatic cell*] *hybrid*	—
0.39	0.83	6	[*myeloid leukemia*] *cell*	—
0.30	0.30	8	[*delayed type*] *hypersensitivity*	—
0.30	−0.30	21	*platelet* [*activating factor*]	—
0.22	−0.86	44	[*inflammatory bowel*] *disease*	—
0.02	0.88	4	[*blood glucose*] *concentration*	—
−0.11	−0.63	9	*thyroid* [*stimulating hormone*]	—
−0.15	0.37	7	*central* [*retinal vein*]	—
−0.22	−0.45	8	*hematopoietic* [*progenitor cell*]	—
−0.30	−0.18	18	*pulsed* [*dye laser*]	*dye laser*
−0.30	−0.48	3	*malignant* [*pleural mesothelioma*]	—
−0.30	−0.70	3	*multiple* [*motor system*]	—
−0.44	0.60	3	*plasma* [*volume expansion*]	*plasma volume, volume expansion*
−0.48	−0.60	3	*penetrating* [*cardiac injury*]	—
−0.57	0.30	3	*nuclear* [*matrix protein*]	—
−0.65	−0.30	5	*medullary* [*thyroid carcinoma*]	—
−0.80	−0.15	3	*protein* [*gene product*]	*gene product*
−0.83	0.74	9	*congenital* [*heart disease*]	*heart disease*
−0.88	−0.50	11	*high* [*signal intensity*]	—
−1.00	−0.70	4	*descending* [*thoracic aorta*]	*thoracic aorta*
−1.04	−1.11	9	*positive* [*airway pressure*]	—
−1.07	−0.52	28	*arterial* [*blood pressure*]	*arterial blood, blood pressure*
−1.20	0.56	6	*cell* [*growth factor*]	*growth factor*
−1.40	−1.04	3	*gas* [*liquid chromatography*]	*gas liquid, liquid chromatography*
−1.71	−0.90	6	*low* [*signal intensity*]	—
−1.84	−2.03	63	*blood* [*mononuclear cell*]	*mononuclear cell*
−1.87	−1.23	5	*systolic* [*arterial pressure*]	*arterial pressure*
−1.99	−0.43	15	*diastolic* [*blood pressure*]	*blood pressure*
−2.11	−1.33	3	*blood* [*T cell*]	—
−2.17	−0.90	11	*high* [*blood pressure*]	*blood pressure*
−2.18	0.30	4	*capillary* [*blood flow*]	*capillary blood, blood flow*
−2.33	−0.56	7	*helper* [*T cell*]	—
−2.41	−1.20	3	*transformed* [*B cell*]	*B cell*

Table 6.6
Adjacency and dependency ratios and possible subterms of candidate terms (part 2: only one of both lR_{adj} and lR_{dep} is defined)

lR_{adj}	lR_{dep}	Number	Term and statistical structure	Subterm(s) from [Pascal]
0.65	—	7	*[digital subtraction] angiography*	—
0.60	—	3	*[outflow tract] obstruction*	—
0.51	—	4	*[duodenal ulcer] disease*	—
−0.06	—	10	*giant [cell tumor]*	*giant cell*
−0.07	—	3	*organic [acid analysis]*	*organic acid*
−0.11	—	3	*beta [cell function]*	*cell function*
−0.30	—	3	*proton [beam irradiation]*	*proton beam*
−0.44	—	5	*carotid [cavernous sinus]*	*cavernous sinus*

lR_{adj}	lR_{dep}	Number	Term and statistical structure	Subterm(s) from [Pascal]
—	1.88	3	*[nervous system] tissue*	*nervous system*
—	1.04	5	*[long term] bone*	*long term*
—	0.60	13	*[sodium dodecyl] sulfate*	—
—	0.60	3	*[hypoxanthine guanine] phosphoribosyl*	—
—	0.54	3	*[cerebral artery] infarction*	*cerebral artery*
—	0.33	13	*enzyme [linked immunoassay]*	—
—	−0.02	54	*protein [kinase C]*	*protein kinase*
—	−0.30	6	*recurrent [laryngeal nerve]*	*laryngeal nerve*
—	−0.70	3	*degenerative [disk disease]*	—

Among the remaining 5 terms, 4 have a log-ratio with an absolute value lower than 0.1. Only *proton beam irradiation* has an absolute log-ratio greater than 0.1; its statistical substructure, *proton beam*, is not in [Pascal], whereas *Beam irradiation* is a term of [Pascal].

From the preceding observations, the following decision function is built:

Decision Function 6.1 (Ternary term disambiguation) The statistical disambiguation of a ternary term $X_3 X_2 X_1$, for which at least one of both log-ratios lR_{adj} and lR_{dep} is defined, is performed according to the following heuristics:

1. If both log-ratios lR_{adj} and lR_{dep} are defined, the sign of the adjacency ratio prevails over the sign of the dependency ratio. The structure is the statistical structure corresponding to the prevailing ratio.[38]

2. When only one of both ratios is defined, the structure is the statistical structure corresponding to this ratio. If the absolute value of this ratio is lower than 0.1, the decision is unsure.

Table 6.7
Evaluation of the algorithm for disambiguating ternary terms

Decision	Correct	Incorrect	Ratio of correct decisions
$R_{adj} > 1$	12	10	54.5%
$R_{adj} < 1$	49	5	90.7%
Total R_{adj}	61	15	80.3%
Total R_{dep}	7	1	87.5%
Total	68	16	81.0%

Evaluation

The algorithm cannot be evaluated on the [Metal] corpus, as it yields too few candidate terms. The evaluation is performed on an artificially built set of candidate terms composed of the 84 ternary terms from the [Pascal] list with at least on of their two substructures $X_3 X_2$ or $X_2 X_1$ in [Pascal], and with at least one of their adjacency or dependency ratios defined.

The results of the evaluation are shown in table 6.7. The first three lines concern the terms for which the adjacency ratio prevails, that is to say, the terms for which this ratio is defined. The fourth line corresponds to the terms for which the decision is made according to the dependency ratio. The fifth line, corresponding to the global results, indicates a 81% ratio of success.

The overall quality of the results is good because more than 80% of the ternary terms are correctly disambiguated. However, this method is not much more accurate than the blind decision which systematically chooses the right-branching structure $X_3 [X_2 X_1]$ with a success ratio of 76.2%. This is due to the poor success rate of the decision function when $R_{adj} > 1$ (54.5%). Consequently a systematic decision for a right-branching structure in this case does not significantly reduce the quality of the final results.

Resorting to the dependency ratio when $R_{adj} > 1$ does not improve performance because this ratio is either undefined or has the same sign as the adjacency ratio. On the contrary, a part-of-speech tagging of the ternary term and a systematic rejection of the $[X_3 X_2] X_1$ structures for which X_2 is an adjective improves the decision function when $R_{adj} > 1$. It allows for a correct filtering of seven errors upon ten incorrect structures such as [*central venous*] *pressure*. The success ratio of the improved decision function is 86.3%, a value significantly higher than the blind decision method.

In order to account for this additional decision in the disambiguation of ternary terms, the decision function is thus reformulated:

Decision Function 6.2 (Ternary term disambiguation—revised) The statistical disambiguation of a ternary term $X_3 X_2 X_1$, for which at least one of both log-ratios lR_{adj} and lR_{dep} is defined, is performed according to the following heuristics:

1. If both log-ratios lR_{adj} and lR_{dep} are defined, the sign of the adjacency ratio prevails over the sign of the dependency ratio.

– If $lR_{adj} > 0$ and if X_2 is an adjective, the structure is the statistical anti-structure $X_3 [X_2 X_1]$.

– Otherwise, the structure is the statistical structure corresponding to the prevailing ratio.

2. When only one of both ratios is defined, the structure is the statistical structure corresponding to this ratio. If the absolute value of this ratio is lower than 0.1, the decision is unsure.

This revised decision function is applied to the terms of tables 6.5 and 6.6, and the resulting disambiguation is indicated by square brackets in the fourth column. The only two terms for which tagging forces the choice of the statistical anti-structure are *platelet activating factor* (table 6.5) and *enzyme linked immunoassay* (table 6.6). The two errors encountered in these tables are [*inflammatory bowel*] *disease* and [*blood glucose*] *concentration* (table 6.5) which should be bracketed $X_3 [X_2 X_1]$. These errors occur at weak values of the adjacency ratio for which confidence is lower.

To sum up, this section has proposed a combined technique for the acquisition of ternary terms and their corpus-based disambiguation. The disambiguation is performed according to a decision function based on frequencies observed within the (ambiguous) corpus. Disambiguation plays an important role in term acquisition because it provides the user with information about the semantic link between a term and the corresponding candidate. Thus $X_3 [X_2 X_1]$ is an hyponym of $X_3 X_1$, while $[X_3 X_2] X_1$ has a metonymic relation with $X_3 X_1$. For instance, *congenital* [*heart disease*] is an hyponym of *Congenital disease* while the relation between [*facial nerve*] *paralysis* and *Facial paralysis* is metonymic.

The technique proposed in this section being statistical, it concerns only frequent term variants (94.5% of the variants are discarded because they have two or less occurrences). I now turn to the description of a complementary enrichment module. It is intended for rare, and nevertheless significant, variants that are likely to provide candidates through deconstruction.

6.3 Term Enrichment from Variations

"Traditional" corpus-based acquisition of terms, such as Smadja (1993a), Bourigault (1995), Justeson and Katz (1995), and Daille (1996), use a linguistic and a statistical filter for extracting relevant patterns from a tagged corpus (see section 2.2). The knowledge source is a specialized corpus, and the text miner is a noun phrase grammar dedicated to the recognition of terminological sequences. These approaches provide the user with large lists of terms, possibly ranked according to a criterion of relevance. They are well adapted to a first and initial acquisition of terms from scratch, on a new domain, in which no prior terminological knowledge is available.

In this study the framework is different: I assume that an initial list of terms is available. The issue is to build a tool for term acquisition that takes into account this initial information and tries to relate the newly acquired terminological material with the previously possessed controlled vocabulary. *Term enrichment* is the actual issue: How can a term list be enriched through corpus analysis with the help of controlled terms?

The distinctive feature of the framework is also its strength. The purpose of this research is to show how advantage can be taken from prior terminological knowledge for acquiring new terms by recognizing variants of controlled terms within the corpus. Most variants (coordinations, substitutions, their compositions, and their compositions with permutations) involve more than one term in their construction (see sections 5.1, 5.2, and 5.3). Since the terminological vocabulary is huge, it is surely incomplete, and the terms that are associated with the controlled terms in the construction of term variants may not be in the controlled vocabulary. Deconstructing observed variants in order to detect the possible associated terms is a good way to acquire new terms because it is performed in a marked linguistic context. For instance, the variant *uterine and carotid artery* of *Uterine artery* is the opportunity for discovering the term *carotid artery*. The context of acquisition shows that both terms can be coordinated, indicating that the meanings of *artery* in the original term *Uterine artery* and in the candidate term *carotid artery* are similar: a blood vessel.

6.3.1 Term Enrichment through Variant Deconstruction

Any variation involving another term is a function that transforms a pair of terms into a variant. The following formula expresses a coordination as a function relating a pair of terms to a coordination variant:

$$c : \mathcal{T} \times \mathcal{T} \to \mathcal{V} \tag{6.3}$$

$$(t_1, t_2) \mapsto c(t_1, t_2)$$

$$([\textit{uterine artery}], [\textit{carotid artery}]) \mapsto [[\textit{uterine and carotid}] \textit{ artery}]$$

$\mathcal{T}$ is the set of the terms on a domain and $\mathcal{V}$ is the set of variants that can be built from these terms or their combinations.

The descriptions of term variants, given in chapter 5, amounts to the descriptions of images of terms by variations. They are calculated by replacing the actual terms t_2 by a syntactic pattern θ (here [X N], a structure that subsumes any binary term) and by calculating the corresponding string-rewriting function γ_θ from the set of term strings $\mathcal{T}_f$ to the set of variant strings $\mathcal{V}_f$:

$$\gamma_\theta : \mathcal{T}_f \to \mathcal{V}_f \tag{6.4}$$

$$f(t) \mapsto \gamma_\theta(f(t)) = f(c(t, \theta)) = f(c(t, [\text{X N}]))$$

uterine artery $\mapsto$ *uterine* C X *artery*

f is the function that associates a syntactic tree with its frontier. The variants extracted from a corpus is the intersection of the image of $\mathcal{T}_f$ under γ_θ and the corpus. (The actual calculus of the variants is more than a mere intersection of sets because it involves unification. This level of detail is however not relevant for term acquisition.) In the preceding example, γ_θ(*uterine artery*) is equal to *uterine* C X *artery*. The function γ_θ corresponds to the metarule (5.29).

Let us now assume that a variant v_f, equal to $\gamma_\theta(f(t))$, is extracted from the corpus, for instance *uterine or carotid artery*. This variant results from the association of the controlled term t (here $t = $ *Uterine artery*) with a term t' whose syntactic structure is θ (here $t' = $ *carotid artery*). Such a discovery of the term t', which is likely to have participated to the construction of the variant, is a source of terminological enrichment. The purpose of this section is to provide the reader with a systematic method for the acquisition of candidate terms through the deconstruction of variants of controlled terms.

Formally term enrichment from a set of variations $\mathcal{V}_f$, produced through the function γ_θ, is the calculus of the term(s) t' that are likely to be associated with a term t in the construction of a variant v_f of t:

$$v_f \in \mathcal{V}_f$$

$$\Leftrightarrow \exists t, t' \in \mathcal{T}, \ v_f \in f(c(t, t'))$$

$$\Leftrightarrow \exists t, t' \in \mathcal{T}, \ c(t, t') \in f^{\sim}(\{v_f\})$$

we introduce p_2, the projection of a cartesian product on its second dimension:

$$\Rightarrow \exists t' \in \mathcal{T}, \ t' \in p_2(c^{\sim}(\{f^{\sim}(\{v_f\})\})) \tag{6.5}$$

The candidate term t' belongs to the projection on the second dimension of the image of $\mathcal{V}_f$ by $c^{\sim} f^{\sim}$. The relation $c^{\sim}$ is the inverse relation of c, the variation, and $f^{\sim}$ is the relation associating a frontier with all the corresponding trees. As shown by formula (6.5), the detection of candidate terms from variations relies mainly on the calculus on inverse relations of variations; this is the purpose of sections 6.3.2, 6.3.3, and 6.3.4. In these sections only a sketch of the technique and its main results are presented. A more detailed exposition of the calculus of inverse variations is given in Jacquemin (1998a) and in Jacquemin (1997b, secs. VI.3.b–VI.3.d).

6.3.2 Inverse Relations of Coordinations

Recall that theorem 5.1 gives a general formula for the calculus of a coordination from the string of the initial term together with constraints on the length of the strings. (The

Table 6.8
String of a candidate $f(\beta)$ as a function of the controlled term $f(\alpha)$ and its coordination variant $f(\gamma)$

$f(\gamma)$	Cutting up c_1, c_2	$f(\alpha)$	$f(\beta)$	Constraints
$c_1 \, C \, c_3 \, c_2$ $(C_{H,R})$	$c_1 = c_{11} \cdot c_{12} \cdot c_{13}$	$c_{11} \cdot c_{12}\cdot$ $c_{13} \cdot c_2$	$c_{12} \cdot c_3$	$\begin{cases} c_{12} \neq \varepsilon \\ c_{13} \neq \varepsilon \end{cases} \Rightarrow \lvert c_1 \rvert \geq 2$
$c_1 \, C \, c_3 \, c_2$ $(C_{A,R})$	$\begin{cases} c_1 = c_{11} \cdot c_{12} \\ c_2 = c_{21} \cdot c_{22} \end{cases}$	$c_{11} \cdot c_{12}\cdot$ $c_{21} \cdot c_{22}$	$c_3 \cdot c_{21}$	$\begin{cases} c_{12} \neq \varepsilon \\ c_{21} \neq \varepsilon \end{cases} \Rightarrow \begin{cases} \lvert c_1 \rvert \geq 1 \\ \lvert c_2 \rvert \geq 1 \end{cases}$
$c_1 \, c_3 \, C \, c_2$ $(C_{A,L})$	$c_2 = c_{21} \cdot c_{22} \cdot c_{23}$	$c_1 \cdot c_{21}\cdot$ $c_{22} \cdot c_{23}$	$c_3 \cdot c_{21}$	$\begin{cases} c_{21} \neq \varepsilon \\ c_{22} \neq \varepsilon \end{cases} \Rightarrow \lvert c_2 \rvert \geq 2$
$c_1 \, c_3 \, C \, c_2$ $(C_{H,L})$	$\begin{cases} c_1 = c_{11} \cdot c_{12} \\ c_2 = c_{21} \cdot c_{22} \end{cases}$	$c_{11} \cdot c_{21}\cdot$ $c_{21} \cdot c_{22}$	$c_{12} \cdot c_3$	$\begin{cases} c_{12} \neq \varepsilon \\ c_{21} \neq \varepsilon \end{cases} \Leftrightarrow \begin{cases} \lvert c_1 \rvert \geq 1 \\ \lvert c_2 \rvert \geq 1 \end{cases}$

main equations are recalled below.) The second part of the theorem and its demonstration in Jacquemin (1997b, pp. 116–17) give a method for the reciprocal calculus of a candidate term associated with a controlled term in the construction of a variant. This section shows how a candidate term is deduced from a coordination variant and a controlled term. The theme of variant decomposition is further explored in the following two sections: substitutions in section 6.3.3, and compositions of permutations and substitutions in section 6.3.4.

Earlier in figure 5.2 two of the four different configurations of coordinations were shown (they must be complemented with left argument and right head coordinations). Given a controlled term whose frontier is $f(\alpha) = f \, a \, h \, f'$, and a variant $f(\gamma)$, the calculus proposed in Jacquemin (1997b, pp. 116–17) provides the frontier(s) of the candidate(s) $f(\beta) = a' \, h'$ as a function of $f(\alpha)$ and $f(\gamma)$. The general expression of the coordination variants $f(\gamma)$ was given by construction rule 5.1, and it corresponds to the formulas (5.8) and (5.9) repeated below:

$$f(\gamma) = c_1 \, C \, c_3 \, c_2$$

$$f(\gamma) = c_1 \, c_3 \, C \, c_2$$

The pairing of these variants with the frontiers of the γ trees shown in figure 5.2 is made thanks to the chopping of the substrings c_1 and c_2 into fragments c_{ij} ($1 \leq i \leq 2$ and $1 \leq j \leq 3$). Table 6.8 sums up the different possible pairings with one of the four types of coordinations. The second item in theorem 5.1 states the following double constraint (6.6) concerning the length of the string of the variant:

$$(1 \leq \lvert c_3 \rvert \leq \lvert f(\beta) \rvert - 1) \wedge (\lvert c_3 \rvert \geq \lvert f(\beta) \rvert - \lvert f(\alpha) \rvert + 1) \tag{6.6}$$

Table 6.8 is to be used as follows: For each term α and its variant γ, given by their frontiers $f(\alpha)$ and $f(\gamma)$, the fourth column shows the frontier $f(\beta)$ of the candidate which yields

γ through the coordination with α (provided that the constraints in the fifth column and in formula 6.6 are respected).

The results of table 6.8 are given in detail for 2- and 3-word terms in appendix B (tables B.1 and B.2).[39] Let us illustrate the exploitation of these tables for the calculus of candidates from variants. The candidate corresponding to the variant *temperature and blood pressure regulation* of *Temperature regulation*, is found in the second line of table B.1: *blood pressure regulation*. This result is obtained by replacing w_1 by *temperature*, w_2 by *regulation*, C by *and*, and c_3 by *blood pressure*.

Tables B.1 and B.2 are used for designing pattern extractors that take as input a variant and output a candidate. The calculus of the pattern extractor is straightforward for binary terms because all the coordination variants of binary terms have only one possible associated candidate. On the contrary, all the variants of ternary terms are associated with two possible candidates; only one of them must be selected. There are two causes of ambiguity: variations of the same linguistic type with ambiguous structure and variations of different linguistic types. I study each in turn.

Structural Ambiguity of Variants

Lines 5 and 6 or 8 and 9 of table B.2 yield two different candidates for the same variant depending on the structural analysis of the coordinated term. (I focus here on lines 8 and 9; lines 5 and 6 would be handled similarly.) The binary candidate associated with the variant w_1 C c_3 w_2 w_3 is c_3 w_2, and the ternary candidate is c_3 w_2 w_3. For instance, *inflammatory and erosive joint disease*, a variant of *Inflammatory joint disease*, yields the binary candidate *erosive joint* and the ternary one *erosive joint disease*.

An analysis of the 21 variants w_1 C c_3 w_2 w_3 extracted from the corpus [Medic] and given in table 6.9 shows that the correct candidate is the ternary one for the following reasons:

1. For 14 of the c_3 w_2 candidates, w_2 is not a valid head word because it is not a noun. For instance, the candidate associated with *peripheral and central nervous system* is not *central nervous* because *nervous* is an adjective; the correct candidate is the ternary term *central nervous system*.

2. For the 7 remaining variants, the binary candidates are *vena cava*, *bile duct*, *electron microscopy*, and *joint disease*. Two of these candidates belong to the controlled vocabulary (*Vena cava* and *Electron microscopy*), arguing for ternary candidates, such as *inferior vena cava*, which correspond to new terms. A structural disambiguation of the remaining two ternary candidates, according to the decision function 6.1, yields a right-branching structure c_3 [w_2 w_3]. This structure also pleads for the ternary candidate c_3 w_2 w_3 that respects the statistical structure, contrary to the binary candidate c_3 w_2 which misses the head word w_3.

Consequently the correct candidate is the longest structure c_3 w_2 w_3 that corresponds to the coordination of two ternary terms with the same length and the same syntactic head.

Table 6.9
Twenty-one w_1 C c_3 w_2 w_3 coordinations of a w_1 w_2 w_3 term (from [Medic])

Number	Term $f(\alpha)$	Variant $f(\gamma)$
000617	*Duchenne muscular dystrophy*	*Duchenne or Becker muscular dystrophy*
001632	*Middle cerebral artery*	*middle and posterior cerebral arteries*
003996	*Superior vena cava*	*superior and inferior vena cava*
004131	*Peripheral nervous system*	*peripheral and central nervous system*
004203	*Intrahepatic bile duct*	*intrahepatic and extrahepatic bile ducts*
004203	*Intrahepatic bile duct*	*intrahepatic and extrahepatic bile ducts*
004401	*Visual evoked potential*	*visual and auditory evoked potentials*
004463	*Somatosensory evoked potential*	*somatosensory or visual evoked potentials*
006074	*Central nervous system*	*central and peripheral nervous system*
007047	*Cervical spinal cord*	*cervical and thoracic spinal cords*
007228	*Auditory evoked potential*	*auditory and somatosensory evoked potentials*
007329	*Duchenne muscular dystrophy*	*Duchenne and Becker muscular dystrophy*
008302	*Scanning electron microscopy*	*scanning and transmission electron microscopy*
000009	*Right pulmonary artery*	*right and left pulmonary arteries*
010515	*Right pulmonary artery*	*right and left pulmonary arteries*
011956	*Inflammatory joint disease*	*inflammatory and erosive joint disease*
014466	*Superior vena cava*	*superior and inferior vena cava*
014795	*Anterior cerebral artery*	*anterior or middle cerebral arteries*
016457	*Peripheral nervous system*	*peripheral and central nervous system*
016787	*Intrahepatic bile duct*	*intrahepatic and extrahepatic bile ducts*
017161	*Cervical spinal cord*	*cervical or thoracic spinal cord*

Similarly the preferred candidate term corresponding to lines 5 and 6 is w_1 w_2 c_3, the term that is most structurally similar to the controlled term.

Linguistic Ambiguity of Variants

In table B.2, lines 1 and 2 (w_1 w_2 C c_3 w_3) and 10 and 11 (w_1 c_3 C w_2 w_3) produce two different candidates depending on the type of linguistic variation (head or argument coordination). In both cases the candidates are smaller than the controlled term (w_1 c_3 and c_3 w_3 for the first variant, and c_3 w_3 and w_1 c_3 for the second variant). Therefore the preceding argument about the structural similarity of the controlled term and the candidate cannot hold here.

Let us observe the variants corresponding to the two structures of variation w_1 c_3 C w_2 w_3 and w_1 w_2 C c_3 w_3:

1. The 2 variants corresponding to w_1 c_3 C w_2 w_3 ($c_3 = w_4$ w_5) are *chronic myeloic leukemia or lymphocytic leukemias* and *left ventricular hemodynamics and coronary arteries*. The correct candidates are extracted from the left head coordination. Their structure is

Table 6.10
Eleven w_1 w_2 C w_4 w_3 coordinations of a w_1 w_2 w_3 term (from [Medic])

Number	Term $f(\alpha)$	Variant $f(\gamma)$
000116	*Pentose phosphate pathway*	*pentose phosphate and glycolytic pathways*
000933	*Blood cell count*	*blood cell and neutrophil counts*
002265	*Blood cell count*	*blood cell and platelet count*
003227	*Open angle glaucoma*	*open angle and exfoliative glaucoma*
006300	*Scanning electron microscopy*	*scanning electron and light microscopy*
006601	*Superior mesenteric artery*	*superior mesenteric and coeliac arteries*
007747	*Procollagen N-proteinase*	*procollagen N and C-proteinases*
008982	*Heat shock protein*	*heat shock and related proteins*
011085	*Central venous pressure*	*central venous or oesophageal pressure*
015568	*Pull out test*	*pull out and bending test*
015860	*Dark field microscopy*	*dark field and electron microscopy*

w_1 c_3: *left ventricular hemodynamics* and *chronic myeloic leukemia*. These candidates correspond to the structure that is a substring of the variant and not to the alternative structure c_3 w_3 that contains two head words.

2. The structure w_1 w_2 C c_3 w_3 ($c_3 = w_4$) yields 11 variants shown in table 6.10. For some of them, the correct candidate is c_3 w_3. For instance, the candidate associated with *dark-field and electron microscopy*, a variant of *Dark-field microscopy*, is *electron microscopy*. For some other variants, the correct candidate is w_1 c_3 w_3 with a structure that is parallel to the controlled term. For instance, the candidate corresponding to *blood cell and platelet count*, a variant of *Blood cell count*, is *blood platelet count*. This structure is, however, not proposed by the formulas given in table B.2 because it results from a coordination in which the candidate term β shares a common substructure f (or f') with the controlled term α (see figure 5.2).

To sum up, in case of structural ambiguity involving two variations of the same linguistic type, the candidate with the longest string is preferred. In case of ambiguity due to the possibility of two different coordinations, the candidate corresponding to a substring of the variation is preferred. Patterns of acquisition for coordination variants of binary terms are given in appendix A.6. Their identifier is ExtrCoor.

6.3.3 Inverse Relations of Substitutions

In figure 5.4, we saw that the general structure of a right substitution corresponds to the topmost construction. The complementary construction is a left substitution in which the substituted argument a' is located on the right side of the initial argument a.

Table 6.11
String of a candidate $f(\beta)$ as a function of the controlled term $f(\alpha)$ and its substitution variant $f(\gamma)$

Var.	$f(\gamma)$	Cutting up c_2	$f(\alpha)$	$f(\beta)$	Constraints
S_R	$c_1\ c_3\ c_2$	$c_{21} \cdot c_{22}$	$c_1 \cdot c_{21} \cdot c_{22}$	$c_3 \cdot c_{21}$	$\begin{cases} c_1 \neq \varepsilon \\ c_{21} \neq \varepsilon \end{cases} \Rightarrow \begin{cases} \lvert c_1 \rvert \geq 1 \\ \lvert c_2 \rvert \geq 1 \end{cases}$
S_L	$c_1\ c_3\ c_2$	$c_{21} \cdot c_{22} \cdot c_{23}$	$c_1 \cdot c_{21} \cdot c_{22} \cdot c_{23}$	$c_3 \cdot c_{22}$	$\begin{cases} c_1 \neq \varepsilon \\ c_{21} \neq \varepsilon \\ c_{22} \neq \varepsilon \end{cases} \Rightarrow \begin{cases} \lvert c_1 \rvert \geq 1 \\ \lvert c_2 \rvert \geq 2 \end{cases}$

The mode of calculus of a candidate term from a substitution variation is similar to the calculus of candidates from coordinations described in the preceding section. Given a controlled term $f(\alpha) = c_1\ c_2$ and its variant $f(\gamma) = c_1\ c_3\ c_2$ (see construction rule 5.2), the strings of the candidate terms $f(\beta)$ are obtained by pairing the string of the variant $f(\gamma)$ with the frontier of one of the two trees corresponding to left and right substitution. They are shown in table 6.11. The candidates extracted from variations of binary and ternary terms are given by tables B.3 and B.4 of appendix B.

As in the case of coordination variants, the problem of multiple candidates also arises for substitution variants. The lines 3, 4, and 5 in table B.4 propose three candidates for a single variant $w_1\ c_3\ w_2\ w_3$: $c_3\ w_2\ w_3$, $c_3\ w_2$, and $c_3\ w_3$. Among the 118 substitution variants of ternary terms extracted from [Medic], six correspond to the insertion of the "slash" mark (/) denoting a ratio or an alternative such as *sleep/wake cycle* or *lecithin/sphingomyelin ratio*, respectively variants of *Sleep wake cycle* and *Lecithin sphingomyelin ratio*. These variants are not likely to yield new candidate terms. The remaining 112 variants are genuine substitutions such as *regional cerebral blood flow*, a variant of *Regional blood flow*. In all these variants the inserted modifier c_3 (here *cerebral*) is more specific than the peripheral modifier w_1 (here *regional*). Consequently the correct candidate is $c_3\ w_2\ w_3$, the longest proposed structure, which includes this additional modifier c_3 and the head word w_3. The pattern extractors associated with substitution variants are described in appendix A.6. Their identifier is `ExtrModif`.

6.3.4 Inverse Relations of Compositions of Permutations and Substitutions

In addition to the elementary variations seen in the two preceding sections, the composite variations studied in section 5.3.2 are likely to yield candidate terms. Since the surface form of compositions of substitutions is the same as elementary substitutions, the patterns of acquisition of composition of substitutions is the same as the patterns of acquisitions of elementary substitutions seen in the preceding section. For similar reasons the patterns of acquisitions for compositions of coordinations and substitutions are the same as the patterns for elementary coordinations given in section 6.3.2.[40] Because of these similarities, I only

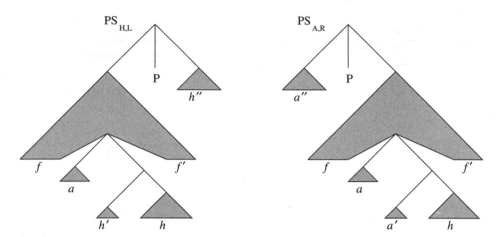

Figure 6.2
Composition of a permutation and a left head and a right argument substitution.

study the compositions of permutations and substitutions that correspond to patterns of variations that have not been studied so far.

Principle 1 of section 5.3.2, concerning the composition of heterogeneous variations, stipulates that there can only be one permutation and that the permutation must be the first transformation in the composition. Consequently the four types of compositions of a permutation and substitutions are obtained by transforming a permutation variant through a generalized substitution. Two of the four possible structures are shown in figure 6.2; they correspond to the composition of a permutation and a left head and a right argument substitution. Two other additional structures are possible: composition of a permutation and a right head or a left argument substitution.

The candidates $f(\beta)$ associated with these four families of term variations $f(\gamma)$ are given in table 6.12. As in the preceding types of variations, the candidates $f(\beta)$ are obtained by pairing the variant $f(\gamma)$ with the frontier of the tree describing the variation (see figure 6.2). The instantiations of these formulas for 2- and 3-word terms are shown in tables B.5 and B.6 of appendix B. The actual pattern extractors for variants of binary terms, corresponding to the `Perm` metarules, are given in appendix A.6. Their identifier is `ExtrPerm`. Negative metarules `NPerm`, which are not expected to retrieve correct variants, are therefore not likely to provide candidate terms.

6.3.5 Postfiltering of Candidate Terms

In the preceding three sections (6.3.2, 6.3.3, and 6.3.4), pattern extractors have been defined that take as input a variant and that output the corresponding *candidate term*. The

Table 6.12
String of a candidate $f(\beta)$ as a function of the controlled term $f(\alpha)$ and its variant $f(\gamma)$, a composition of a permutation and a substitution

$f(\gamma)$	Cutting up c_2, c_4	$f(\alpha)$	$f(\beta)$	Constraints
c_1 c_3 c_2 P c_4 (PS$_{H,L}$)	$c_2 = c_{21} \cdot c_{22}$	$c_4 \cdot c_1 \cdot$ $c_{21} \cdot c_{22}$	$c_3 \cdot c_{21}$	$\left\{ \begin{array}{l} c_1 \neq \varepsilon \\ c_{21} \neq \varepsilon \\ c_4 \neq \varepsilon \end{array} \right. \Rightarrow \left\{ \begin{array}{l} \lvert c_1 \rvert \geq 1 \\ \lvert c_2 \rvert \geq 1 \\ \lvert c_4 \rvert \geq 1 \end{array} \right.$
c_1 c_3 c_2 P c_4 (PS$_{H,R}$)	$c_2 = c_{21} \cdot$ $c_{22} \cdot c_{23}$	$c_4 \cdot c_1 \cdot c_{21} \cdot$ $c_{22} \cdot c_{23}$	$c_3 \cdot c_{22}$	$\left\{ \begin{array}{l} c_1 \neq \varepsilon \\ c_{21} \neq \varepsilon \\ c_{22} \neq \varepsilon \\ c_4 \neq \varepsilon \end{array} \right. \Rightarrow \left\{ \begin{array}{l} \lvert c_1 \rvert \geq 1 \\ \lvert c_2 \rvert \geq 2 \\ \lvert c_4 \rvert \geq 1 \end{array} \right.$
c_1 P c_2 c_3 c_4 (PS$_{A,R}$)	$c_4 = c_{41} \cdot c_{42}$	$c_2 \cdot c_{41} \cdot$ $c_{42} \cdot c_1$	$c_3 \cdot c_{41}$	$\left\{ \begin{array}{l} c_1 \neq \varepsilon \\ c_{41} \neq \varepsilon \end{array} \right. \Rightarrow \left\{ \begin{array}{l} \lvert c_1 \rvert \geq 1 \\ \lvert c_4 \rvert \geq 1 \end{array} \right.$
c_1 P c_2 c_3 c_4 (PS$_{A,L}$)	$c_4 = c_{41} \cdot$ $c_{42} \cdot c_{43}$	$c_2 \cdot c_{41} \cdot c_{42} \cdot$ $c_{43} \cdot c_1$	$c_3 \cdot c_{42}$	$\left\{ \begin{array}{l} c_1 \neq \varepsilon \\ c_{41} \neq \varepsilon \\ c_{42} \neq \varepsilon \end{array} \right. \Rightarrow \left\{ \begin{array}{l} \lvert c_1 \rvert \geq 1 \\ \lvert c_4 \rvert \geq 2 \end{array} \right.$

output is intentionally named a *candidate* because I have no confidence about the actual terminological status of the extracted linguistic sequence.

The candidates obtained through pattern extraction from coordination variants are linguistically correct and do not require any further processing. On the contrary, candidates extracted from substitutions or from compositions of permutations and substitution are incorrect if they result from modifications instead of substitutions (see section 5.1.2 and Daille 1994, sec. 2.2.2). In this case they must be postfiltered in order to discard the part of the candidates corresponding to the linguistic modifications without terminological status.

Let us illustrate the difference between modification and substitution as far as acquisition is concerned. A variant resulting from the adjunction of a determiner is clearly a modification that does not involve a second term:

cell fraction

$\overset{P}{\longrightarrow}$ *fraction of cell*

$\overset{M}{\longrightarrow}$ *fraction of these cells*

In this case the substructure produced by the pattern extractor—here *these cells*—is obviously not a candidate term.

Conversely, the addition of an adjectival modifier results in a variant which possibly involves a substitution:

image processing

$\xrightarrow{\text{P}}$ *processing of image*

$\xrightarrow{\text{M/S}}$ *processing of cardiac images*

The sequence produced by the pattern extractor—here *cardiac image*—is a valid candidate term.

The purpose of the linguistic filter proposed in this section is to discard the spurious part of the candidate terms which is due to variations of modification. The filtering is purely linguistic; it relies on linguistic clues, such as the presence of a determiner, which assert that the corresponding sequence must be rejected. Because of this necessary additional filtering, the structures produced by the pattern extractors are called *precandidate terms*.

In English compounding, the head word is the rightmost element of a compound and it is preceded by its modifiers (Giorgi and Longobardi 1991, sec. 3.5). When embedded in a noun phrase, the compound is possibly preceded by specifiers (generally a determiner) and followed by optional postmodifiers (generally prepositional phrases). The postfiltering of candidates is intended to remove the parts of a compound which do not correspond to the syntax of compounding, namely the leading specifiers. This post-filtering is illustrated on two candidates in formulas (6.3.5) and (6.3.5). In the first case, the remaining structure is a correct multi-word candidate; in the second case, there only remains a single word, which therefore is not a correct candidate. Candidates with a structure which does not respect the standard structure of nominal terms $(N|A|V)^+ (N|V)$ are discarded as well.

system performance

$\xrightarrow{\text{metarule}}$ *performance of an expert system*   [variant]

$\xrightarrow{\text{extraction}}$ *an expert system*   [precandidate]

$\xrightarrow{\text{postfiltering}}$ *expert system*   [candidate term]

gene expression

$\xrightarrow{\text{metarule}}$ *expression of these two genes*   [variant]

$\xrightarrow{\text{extraction}}$ *these two genes*   [precandidate]

$\xrightarrow{\text{postfiltering}}$ *genes*   [single word]

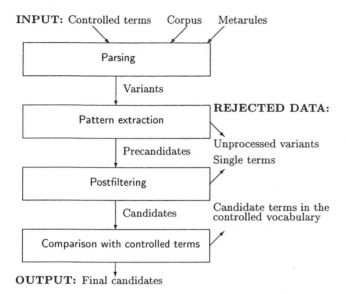

Figure 6.3
Flow-chart for term acquisition through variant deconstruction.

Postfiltering is followed by a final step: the candidate terms are compared with the controlled term list in order to reject the candidates which already belong to this list. An overview of the flowchart for automatic term acquisition through variant deconstruction is illustrated by figure 6.3.

6.3.6 Results

Tables 6.13, 6.14, and 6.15 show the first 15 candidates (in alphabetical order) acquired from the three types of variations mentioned in the preceding sections. Each candidate is accompanied by the controlled term whose variant has produced the candidate, and a mark indicating whether the candidate already belongs to the controlled list.

Ranking Candidates
In order to improve the acquisition of terms, a set of techniques for classifying candidates is now proposed.

A first method for ranking terms is to use the association ratio given for the acquisition of ternary variants in formula (6.1) (a similar formula can be easily established for binary terms). Tables 6.16 and 6.17 present the first 15 and last 15 binary and ternary terms ranked by decreasing value of association ratio. This classification only affects terms for which the

Table 6.13
Candidates extracted from coordination variants on [Medic]

Candidate	Known	Controlled term	Occurrences
abdominal aorta	×	*Thoracic aorta*	4
acidic lipid		*Neutral lipid*	1
acinic cell carcinoma		*Mucoepidermoid carcinoma*	1
acromioclavicular joint		*Sternoclavicular joint*	1
active phase		*Latent phase*	1
adrenal gland	×	*Thyroid gland*	1
affective disorder	×	*Cognitive disorder*	1
aged animal	×	*Young animal*	1
agonist bromocriptine		*Agonist antagonist*	1
air conduction	×	*Bone conduction*	1
amniotic fluid estimation		*Ratio estimation*	1
antigen presenting cell		*Accessory cell*	2
antimicrobial susceptibility test		*Identification test*	1
aortic arch	×	*Aortic coarctation*	1
aortic valve	×	*Mitral valve*	3

Table 6.14
Candidates extracted from substitution variants on [Medic]

Candidate	Known	Controlled term	Occurrences
abdominal spear injuries		*Penetrating injury*	1
ablating tool		*Cutting tool*	1
absorbed dose	×	*Radiation dose*	2
access pressure		*Blood pressure*	1
accessory nerve	. ×	*Spinal nerve*	2
accurate measurement		*Continuous measurement*	1
acetylcholine receptor		*Muscarinic receptor*	3
acetylcholine receptor		*Nicotinic receptor*	6
acetylcholinesterase molecular forms		*Soluble form*	2
acid analysis		*Organic analysis*	3
acid base disorders		*Metabolic disorder*	1
acid dehydrogenase complex		*Oxo complex*	1
acoustic wave	×	*Surface wave*	1
actin distribution		*F distribution*	1
action potential	×	*Evoked potential*	1

Table 6.15
Candidates extracted from compositions of permutations and substitutions on [Medic].

Candidate	Preposition	Known	Controlled term	Occurrences
aberrant granule	*by*		*Granule neuron*	1
accessory cell	*of*	×	*Cell proliferation*	1
activated b cells	*of*		*Cell differentiation*	1
activated rat mast cells	*from*		*Cell supernatant*	1
acute phase proteins	*of*	×	*Protein synthesis*	1
adipose tissue	*of*	×	*Tissue extract*	1
adult cells	*in*		*Cell function*	1
agarose gels	*in*		*Gel electrophoresis*	1
airway control	*of*		*Control method*	1
affected individuals confined	*of*		*Confined plasma*	1
aminotransferase levels	*of*		*Level measurement*	1
anaphylatoxin levels	*of*		*Level measurement*	1
aneuploid tumor cells	*of*		*Cell population*	1
angulated epithelioid cells	*of*		*Cell proliferation*	1
animal tolerance	*of*		*Tolerance limit*	1

Mutual Information can be computed. However, for some binary terms—it never happens for ternary terms—the denominator of the Mutual Information formula is zero because one of both words building up the candidate term only occurs in conjunction with the other one in the corpus (see formula 2.8). The first 15 terms with an "infinite" Mutual Information are shown by decreasing value of frequency in table 6.18.

Finally, the statistical ranking of the candidates is completed by a *symbolic criterion* for measuring the quality of a candidate term, which advantages the candidates resulting from the deconstruction of different types of variants. For instance, *bile duct* (third line of figure 6.19) is simultaneously acquired from a coordination and a modification/substitution variant:

pancreatic duct

$\xrightarrow{C}$ *pancreatic and bile duct*

$\xrightarrow{\text{acquisition}}$ *bile duct*

hepatic duct

$\xrightarrow{M/S}$ *hepatic bile duct*

$\xrightarrow{\text{acquisition}}$ *bile duct*

Table 6.16
First 15 and last 15 of the 2,482 binary candidates ranked by decreasing association ratio a.

a	I	f_r	Candidate
0.74	−3.75	592.0	*T cell*
0.51	−3.26	275.0	*peripheral blood*
0.51	−0.22	18.0	*varicella zoster*
0.49	−0.40	4.0	*moisture exchanger*
0.48	−1.01	44.0	*myelogenous leukemia*
0.48	−0.82	33.0	*paraffin embedded*
0.47	−1.32	57.0	*natural killer*
0.46	−2.93	183.0	*breast cancer*
0.46	−0.95	16.0	*inborn error*
0.46	−0.78	1.0	*previa percreta*
0.45	−0.97	11.0	*fibrous histiocytoma*
0.45	−0.95	1.0	*nitinol alloy*
0.45	−0.95	1.0	*chrome alloy*
0.44	−1.50	39.0	*lipid peroxidation*
0.44	−1.10	3.0	*retest reliability*
0.05	−6.37	2.0	*rat tumor*
0.05	−6.37	1.0	*cancer tumor*
0.04	−6.60	2.0	*patients data*
0.04	−6.60	1.0	*treatment control*
0.04	−6.59	1.0	*bone study*
0.04	−6.56	1.0	*tissue control*
0.04	−6.56	1.0	*normal gene*
0.04	−6.54	1.0	*control antibody*
0.04	−6.54	1.0	*B disease*
0.04	−6.52	1.0	*adult cell*
0.03	−6.69	2.0	*used cell*
0.03	−6.67	1.0	*male cell*
0.02	−6.88	1.0	*patient biopsy*
0.01	−7.01	1.0	*group study*
0.00	−7.11	1.0	*patients DNA*

Table 6.17
First 15 and last 15 of the 1,406 ternary candidates ranked by decreasing association ratio a

a	I	f_r	Candidate
0.77	−5.55	220.0	magnetic resonance imaging
0.50	−1.83	1.0	thevagal nodosal ganglion
0.50	−1.75	1.0	enterica serovar typhimurium
0.48	−5.26	86.0	restriction fragment length
0.46	−5.44	80.0	Sprague-Dawley rat
0.46	−2.47	1.0	plurihormonal mammosomatotroph adenoma
0.44	−6.19	93.0	spontaneously hypertensive rat
0.42	−3.07	2.0	ficoll hypaque gradient
0.42	−3.06	2.0	rubber bleb nevus
0.41	−3.18	1.0	plated metal alloy
0.40	−4.17	20.0	polyacrylamide gel electrophoresis
0.40	−3.39	1.0	insoluble proteinaceous deposit
0.40	−3.36	1.0	barium sulfate filler
0.39	−3.55	1.0	craniocerebral missile injury
0.38	−5.01	33.0	herpes simplex virus
0.03	−9.48	1.0	spine tumor patient
0.03	−9.48	1.0	clinical evaluation study
0.03	−9.46	1.0	cancer derived cell
0.03	−9.45	1.0	using 20 DNA
0.02	−9.75	1.0	human serum control
0.02	−9.69	1.0	virus cell DNA
0.02	−9.68	1.0	type C disease
0.02	−9.62	1.0	human bladder cell
0.01	−9.89	1.0	B cell activity
0.01	−9.87	1.0	renal tumor cell
0.01	−9.79	1.0	adult blood cell
0.01	−9.77	1.0	primary T cell
0.00	−9.98	1.0	C 6 cell
0.00	−9.97	1.0	control over cell
0.00	−10.02	1.0	blood group rat

Table 6.18
First 15 of the 137 binary candidates with an infinite Mutual Information ranked by decreasing association frequency f_r

f_r	Candidate
40.0	*deoxyribonucleic acid*
9.0	*uroepithelial cell*
6.0	*betao thalassemia*
4.0	*titanyl phosphate*
4.0	*rhabdoid tumor*
4.0	*oculocerebrorenal syndrome*
4.0	*higashi syndrome*
3.0	*tubulovillous adenoma*
3.0	*cystatin C*
3.0	*brucei rhodesiense*
3.0	*adrenocorticotropic hormone*
2.0	*vero cell*
2.0	*unsynchronised cell*
2.0	*sulphonic acid*
2.0	*submicromolar concentration*

The fact that *bile duct* is acquired simultaneously from two different types of variations indicates that it is a secure candidate term. This criterion is very selective: among the 4,228 binary candidates, only 58 of them (1.4%) are produced through the deconstruction of two different variations and only two of them result from three different variations (*T cell* and *pancreatic beta cell*). Table 6.19 shows 15 of the 60 binary candidates that result from the deconstruction of two or three types of variants. Similarly 19 ternary candidates result from more than two different variants; 15 of them are given in table 6.20.

6.3.7 Evaluating Term Acquisition

In sections 6.3.2, 6.3.3, and 6.3.4, patterns of extraction have been defined in order to extract candidates from coordinations, substitutions, and compositions of permutations and substitutions. These extractors are listed in appendix A.6. Each pattern extractor is attached to a specific metarule. From any variant detected by this metarule, the extractor outputs the corresponding precandidate term. The final candidate terms are produced by pruning the precandidate in order to remove the leading determiners (section 6.3.5). The pattern extractors were tuned on the training data [Medic] and [Pascal]; they are now evaluated on the test corpus [Metal] and on the test controlled vocabulary [Pascal-Metal].[41]

Table 6.19
First 15 of the 60 binary candidates acquired from at least two variants of different types

Candidate	Coor	Modif	Perm
basal cell		×	×
betao thalassemia	×	×	
bile duct	×	×	
blood test	×	×	
cancer cell		×	×
carotid artery	×	×	
cell DNA		×	×
clinical study	×	×	
cognitive function	×	×	
CREF cell		×	×
cultured cell		×	×
digital nerve	×	×	
epidemiological study	×	×	
fibroblast cell		×	×
genomic DNA		×	×

Table 6.20
First 15 of the 19 ternary candidates acquired from at least two variants of different types

Candidate	Coor	Modif	Perm
adult T cell		×	×
age matched control	×		×
antigen presenting cell	×		×
arterial blood pressure		×	×
B cell line	×	×	
bone marrow cell	×		×
bone marrow mononuclear cell	×		×
CD4 T cell		×	×
CD8 T cell		×	×
cerebral blood flow		×	×
common carotid artery		×	×
extracorporeal shock wave		×	×
glomerular filtration rate	×	×	
glomerular mesangial cell	×	×	
MCF 7 cell		×	×

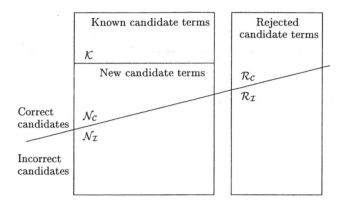

Figure 6.4
The data resulting from the evaluation of the accepted and rejected candidates.

Qualitative Evaluation

The candidates produced through pattern extraction followed by postfiltering are classified into two sets: accepted and rejected candidates $\mathcal{R}$ (candidates composed of a single word or candidate with a syntactic pattern which does not respect the standard syntax of nominal terms). Accepted candidates are then subdivided into two sets: known candidates $\mathcal{K}$—those that belong to the controlled vocabulary—and new candidates $\mathcal{N}$. As illustrated by figure 6.4, rejected and new candidates are evaluated and further divided into correct and incorrect candidates through manual scanning. A candidate is considered as correct if its structure is linguistically correct (it is a correct noun phrase) and conceptually correct (the candidate has a compositional meaning that can be calculated by combining the meanings of its components). The candidates are thus subdivided:

• Correct candidates are made of correct new candidates ($\mathcal{N}_\mathcal{C}$) that are justly accepted and correct rejected candidates ($\mathcal{R}_\mathcal{C}$) that are unjustly discarded.

• Incorrect candidates are composed of incorrect new candidates ($\mathcal{N}_\mathcal{I}$) that are unjustly accepted and incorrect rejected candidates ($\mathcal{R}_\mathcal{I}$) that are justly discarded.

The sizes of these four sets are shown by table 6.21 for the test data. Coor_2, Modif_2, Modif_3, and Perm_2 denote respectively coordinations of 2-word terms, modifications of 2- and 3-word terms, and permutations of 2-word terms. Coordinations and permutations of 3-word terms are not shown because their size is null.

For the qualitative evaluation of syntactic variants in section 5.5.1, a parallel is made between controlled indexing and information retrieval. Unfortunately, such a parallel cannot

Table 6.21
Volume of the data after evaluation of accepted and rejected candidates

	$Coor_2$	$Modif_2$	$Modif_3$	$Perm_2$	**Total**
$|\mathcal{K}|$	8	37	0	7	**52**
$|\mathcal{N}_C|$	21	106	8	30	**165**
$|\mathcal{N}_I|$	4	32	1	6	**43**
$|\mathcal{R}_C|$	0	3	0	0	**3**
$|\mathcal{R}_I|$	2	2	0	6	**10**
Total	35	180	9	49	**273**

Table 6.22
Precision of term enrichment on [Metal]

	Coor	Modif	Perm	**Total**
P	87.8%	82.1%	86.0%	**83.5%**
P'	84.0%	77.6%	83.3%	**79.3%**

be made between term enrichment and information retrieval because the set of all the candidate terms included in a corpus is very difficult to determine. I will therefore not consider recall and fallout, and focus only on precision:

$$P = \frac{|\mathcal{K} \cup \mathcal{N}_C|}{|\mathcal{K} \cup \mathcal{N}_C \cup \mathcal{N}_I|} \tag{6.7}$$

P measures the ratio of correct candidate terms to the whole set of candidates, known terms included. A more selective measure of precision P' is the ratio of correct candidates to the new candidates (exclusive of known terms):

$$P' = \frac{|\mathcal{N}_C|}{|\mathcal{N}_C \cup \mathcal{N}_I|} \tag{6.8}$$

P' is necessarily lower than or equal to P. The values of P and P' are shown in table 6.22. The most selective value of precision (P') is close to 80%. Since term enrichment cannot be thought as a purely automatic procedure without human intervention, it is legitimate to leave a certain volume of incorrect candidates among the results that will be discarded by human postfiltering.

Incorrect variants are a first source of error in term enrichment from variant deconstruction. These erroneous variants are partly filtered by pattern extraction and postfiltering, but some of them are responsible of incorrect candidate acquisition. The main other source of error is due to exotic variant structures that do not fit the pattern extractors. For instance, *lithium-containing alloy*, a modification/substitution variant of *Lithium alloy*, has an unusual structure $N_2 \, V \, N_1$ in which N_2 is the subject and N_1 the object of the verb V. This structure is not the classical right-branching structure of substitution variants which is used as a basis for term enrichment (figure 5.4). When applied to this variant, the pattern extractor incorrectly produces the candidate *containing alloy* (see table B.3 in appendix B). In fact the substitution variant observed here does not involve a second term and is not appropriate for term enrichment through variant deconstruction.

Quantative Evaluation

The two aspects of quantitative evaluation of term acquisition are, on the one hand, the measure of the correlation between the volume of variants and the volume of candidates produced from these variants and, on the other hand, the distribution of candidate terms in relation to their size or to the types of variation.

As indicated in section 6.3.5, some variants are unproductive because they only involve one term in their construction. For instance, *structure of the crystals*, a permutation variant of *Crystal structure*, does not produce a candidate term. Pure permutations (not composed with insertions) and some insertions, such as the genitive marked by *'s*, do not yield any candidate term. This type of variation is relatively frequent in the medical domain through pathologies linked to the name of a scientist, such as *Alzheimer's disease* a variant of *Alzheimer disease*. Since this variation is less frequent in the metallurgy domain, the distribution of candidates in relation to the type of variation may depend on the domain of the corpus.

Table 6.23 shows the *productivity* of each of the three families of variations (coordinations, modifications/substitutions, and compositions of permutations with modifications/substitutions). The *productivity* Pr of a family of variations is the percentage of these variations that produce a candidate; it is calculated with the following formula in which $\mathcal{K} \cup \mathcal{N}_C \cup \mathcal{R}_C$ is the set of correct candidates produced by $\mathcal{F}'$ a set of unique variants:

$$Pr = \frac{|\mathcal{K} \cup \mathcal{N}_C \cup \mathcal{R}_C|}{|\mathcal{F}'|} \tag{6.9}$$

As could be expected, the permutations and their compositions with modifications/substitutions are the least productive variations. On average, three variants in every four are productive ones.

Another loss of productivity is due to the presence of controlled terms among the candidates. In order to measure the productivity, the *renewal* ratio Re evaluates the proportion

Table 6.23
Values of productivity and renewal for term enrichment on [Metal]

	Coor	Modif	Perm	**Total**
Pr	82.9%	81.5%	75.5%	**80.6%**
Re	72.4%	76.0%	81.1%	**76.4%**

of candidates which do not belong to the controlled vocabulary:

$$Re = \frac{|\mathcal{N}_C \cup \mathcal{R}_C|}{|\mathcal{N}_C \cup \mathcal{R}_C \cup \mathcal{K}|} \tag{6.10}$$

The values of *Re* for the test corpus are listed in table 6.23. A comparison between the precisions of the variations presented in table 5.24 and the values of renewal in table 6.23 shows that the more accurate a variation, the lower is its renewal. An explanation for this observation is that high-precision variations are high-quality variations that tend to produce high-quality candidates. These candidates being of a good quality, a significant part of them are already present in the controlled vocabulary. Paradoxically variants producing better candidates tend to produce fewer candidates.

These two qualitative measures are complemented by an evaluation of the distribution of candidates in relation to the type of variations and in relation to the size of the candidates (figure 6.5). A comparison of the distributions of variants in relation to the types of variations given by figure 5.9 with the distributions of candidates in relation to the types of variations provided by figure 6.5 shows that the rate of candidates produced by permutations is lower than the ratio of permutations to the total number of variations. This discrepancy is due to the low productivity of permutations indicated in table 6.23.

6.3.8 Incremental Acquisition

This section expands on the reiteration of term enrichment: the candidates acquired through term enrichment can be used as controlled terms for a following step of acquisition. This process is iteratively repeated by considering the candidates produced at step n as controlled terms for step $n + 1$ until no new candidate is produced. The interest of this process is twofold. First, it increases the volume of acquisition. Second, since conceptual relations hold between the terms that are acquired through variant deconstruction, incremental enrichment yields conceptual networks of terms and candidates. I first formalize the process of incremental term enrichment and then apply it to the incremental building of conceptual networks.

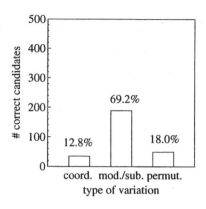 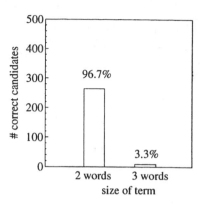

Figure 6.5
Distributions of candidates in relation to the types of variations and the sizes of terms in [Metal].

Step 1: Enrichment from the Controlled Vocabulary

The general calculus of the acquisition of a candidate term t' from a variation c and a variant v_f is given by formula (6.5). This formula is now extended so as to define the set $\mathcal{K}_1$ of all the candidates extracted at step 1 from a corpus Γ, a set of strings of controlled terms $\mathcal{T}_f$, and the strings of their variants $\mathcal{V}_f$. This latter set is the image of the controlled vocabulary $\mathcal{T}_f$ by the metarules in the metagrammmar $\mathcal{M}$. Each metarule γ is considered as a relation associating a controlled term t_f in $\mathcal{T}_f$ with a set of possible variants $\gamma(t_f)$. Hence it follows that

$$\mathcal{V}_f = \{\gamma(t_f) \,;\, (\gamma \in \mathcal{M}) \wedge (t_f \in \mathcal{T}_f) \wedge (\gamma(t_f) \subseteq \Gamma)\} \tag{6.11}$$

The calculus proposed in sections 6.3.2, 6.3.3, and 6.3.4 associates a pattern extractor $e(\gamma)$ with each metarule γ in the metagrammar $\mathcal{M}$ that corresponds to a variation involving a second term. (This constraint is expressed in the following formula by stating that γ must belong to the domain of e.) For the sake of simplicity, I assume that $e(\gamma)$ also includes the postfiltering function described in section 6.3.5. The set $\mathcal{K}_1$ of the candidates produced at step 1 is obtained by deconstructing all the variants $\gamma(t_f)$ in $\mathcal{V}_f$ which result from a metarule γ involving a second term. $\mathcal{K}_1$ is defined by the following formula in which the set of controlled terms $\mathcal{C}_1$ is introduced in order to reject the candidates that belong to the controlled vocabulary:

$$\begin{cases} \mathcal{K}_1 = \{e(\gamma)(\gamma(t_f)) \,;\, (\gamma \in \mathcal{M} \cap \mathrm{dom}(e)) \wedge (t_f \in \mathcal{T}_f) \\ \qquad \wedge (\gamma(t_f) \subseteq \Gamma)\} \setminus \mathcal{C}_1 \\ \mathcal{C}_1 = \mathcal{T}_f \end{cases} \tag{6.12}$$

This first step is now generalized to the incremental acquisition of candidates at step n from the candidates obtained at step $n - 1$.

Step n: Enrichment from Step $n - 1$

The candidates $\mathcal{K}_n$, acquired at step n, are obtained by deconstructing the variants of the candidates in $\mathcal{K}_{n-1}$, acquired at step $n - 1$. In order to retain only variants that correspond to new terms, only candidates out of the set of the known terms or candidates $\mathcal{C}_n$ are kept. $\mathcal{C}_n$ is also inductively calculated by joining $\mathcal{K}_{n-1}$, the candidates of step $n - 1$, and $\mathcal{C}_{n-1}$, the known terms or candidates from the preceding steps:

$$\left\{ \begin{array}{l} \mathcal{K}_n = \{e(\gamma)(\gamma(t_f)) \; ; \; (\gamma \in \mathcal{M} \cap \mathrm{dom}(e)) \\ \qquad \wedge (t_f \in \mathcal{K}_{n-1}) \wedge (\gamma(t_f) \subseteq \Gamma)\} \setminus \mathcal{C}_n \\ \mathcal{C}_n = \mathcal{C}_{n-1} \cup \mathcal{K}_{n-1} \end{array} \right. \tag{6.13}$$

The process is iteratively repeated until reaching a step n_0 for which $\mathcal{K}_{n_0}$ is the empty set. At this step, no new variant is extracted from the corpus Γ. The length of this computation is bounded: the algorithm necessarily terminates within a finite number of steps because a finite corpus only contains a finite number of potential candidates:

• Since the length of the corpus Γ is finite and since variants are finite substrings of the corpus, the number of potential variants in Γ is finite.

• Since candidates are—necessarily finite—substrings of variants, the number of potential candidates in Γ is finite.

The final set of candidates $\mathcal{K}$ is the union of the candidates acquired at one of the steps of the computation from 1 to n_0:

$$\mathcal{K} = \bigcup_{i=1}^{n_0} \mathcal{K}_i$$

$$= \{t \; ; \; \exists n \in \{1, \ldots, n_0\}, \; t_0 \in \mathcal{T}_f, t_1 \in \mathcal{K}_1, \ldots, t_n = t \in \mathcal{K}_n \tag{6.14}$$

$$\forall i \in \{1, \ldots, n\}, \; (\exists \gamma \in \mathcal{M} \cap \mathrm{dom}(e),$$

$$(\gamma(t_{i-1}) \subseteq \Gamma) \wedge (t_i = e(\gamma)(\gamma(t_{i-1}))))\}$$

For instance, the candidate term *crude DNA* is obtained from the controlled term *Differential technique* through the following eight steps of acquisition (C, S, and PS are respectively acquisitions from coordinations, substitutions, and compositions of permutations and substitutions):

Differential technique

$\xrightarrow{\text{S}}$ *hybridization technique*

$\xrightarrow{\text{PS}}$ *Southern blot hybridization*

$\xrightarrow{\text{S}}$ *DNA hybridization*

$\xrightarrow{\text{C}}$ *DNA amplification*

$\xrightarrow{\text{PS}}$ *target DNA*

$\xrightarrow{\text{S}}$ *tissue DNA*

$\xrightarrow{\text{C}}$ *crude DNA*

The volume of acquisition, in relation to the number of steps and the size of the initial terminological data, is shown in figure 6.6. The whole controlled vocabulary [Pascal] is not used for acquisition because only 12,717 terms have at least one variant in the [Medic] corpus. When all these terms are used, the iterative algorithm for term enrichment terminates after eleven steps and yields 3,290 candidates thus distributed among the eleven steps: 1862, 610, 255, 216, 98, 24, 50, 46, 106, 17, and 6 (see the upper curve in figure 6.7). When using only 10% of the initial seed terms, the enrichment algorithm still produces 1,034 candidates, that is to say, almost a third of the total acquisition (see the leftmost column in figure 6.6). This surprisingly good robustness to the incompleteness of the initial terminological data shows that the more incomplete the initial list, the better is the incremental completion. When using the whole initial vocabulary, the volume of term enrichment represents 40% of the initial data, whereas it represents 81% of the initial terminological data with only 10% of the seed terms.

On the contrary, the volume of term enrichment depends strongly on the type of variations exploited for acquiring candidates (see figure 6.7). Thus, when not using substitutions, only 1,638 candidates are acquired, that is to say, 50% of the total acquisition (see the *coordinations and permutations* curve in figure 6.7). Using only coordinations leads to an even more dramatic drop in the volume of acquisition: only 357 candidates are discovered (see the *coordinations* curve in figure 6.7). Because of their important volume, substitutions and compositions of permutations and substitutions are essential variations for obtaining a correct term enrichment.

The size of the corpus is also a crucial parameter for a correct term enrichment (see figure 6.8). For instance, when using 50% of the corpus, the algorithm for term enrichment produces 1,146 terms, which represent only 35% of the acquisition on the whole corpus. The sensitivity to the size of the textual data is a normal characteristic for a corpus-based

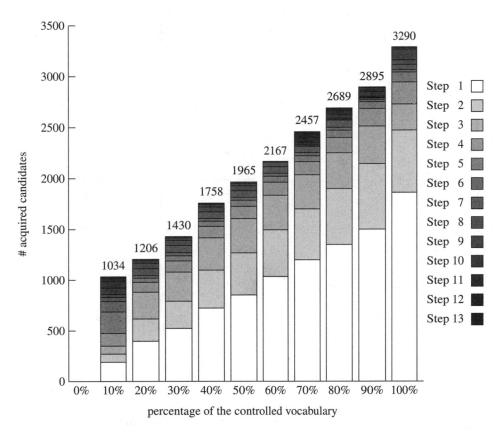

Figure 6.6
Number of candidates in relation to the percentage of the controlled vocabulary [Pascal] used for acquisition.

technique. Because of the increasing amount of electronic textual data available on-line or through the repositories for textual resources, it is reasonable to propose a technique for term enrichment that relies on such large corpora.

Conceptual Links between Candidates

The specificity of the context in which candidates are acquired—namely, term variants—induces a conceptual relation between the candidates and the original controlled terms:

• Coordination. The acquisition from an argument coordination produces a candidate that shares a common hyponym with the original term. For instance, *abdominal aorta* is acquired from *abdominal and thoracic aorta*, a coordination variant of *Thoracic aorta*. Both terms are hyponyms of *aorta* and are located at the same hierarchical level in a generic relationship.

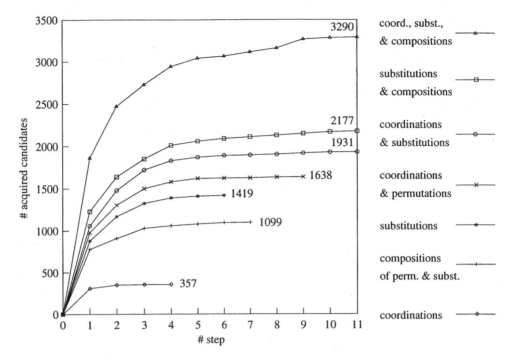

Figure 6.7
Number of candidates in relation to the type of variation used for acquisition.

• Substitution. Substitution variants yield generic links for which the candidate is more specific than the associated controlled term. For instance, the substitution variant *blood mononuclear cell* of *Blood cell* produces the candidate *mononuclear cell*. The candidate *mononuclear cell* is more specific than the controlled term *Blood cell* because the modifier *mononuclear* is closer to the head word than the modifier *blood* in the variant *blood mononuclear cell*.

These two types of conceptual relations are used for building conceptual networks composed of *co-hyponyms* resulting from acquisitions through coordinations and *partial ontologies* resulting from acquisitions through substitutions. These two types of conceptual relations parallel the notion of *synsets* (sets of synonymous words) and the generic *is-a* relation in *WordNet* (Miller et al. 1990; Fellbaum 1998).

A restricted syntactic context—terminological noun phrases—is also exploited in Habert, Naulleau, and Nazarenko (1996) and Assadi (1997) for the acquisition of conceptual knowledge. A brief description of these two works is made at the end of section 2.2.3

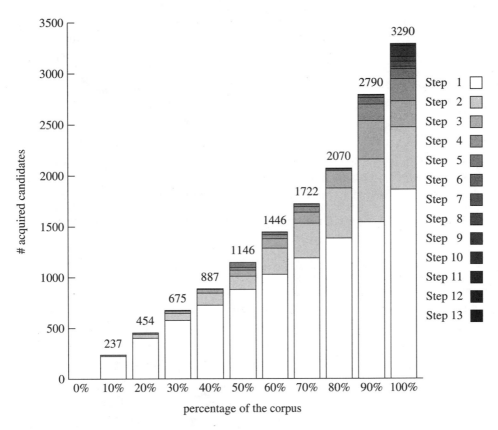

Figure 6.8
Number of candidates in relation to the percentage of the corpus [Medic] used for acquisition.

on *LEXTER*. These two studies and ours taken together stress the role of restricted and specific syntactic contexts in knowledge acquisition. The exploitation of terminological noun phrases or term variants yields conceptual relations of a finer granularity than links produced by general syntactic relations or co-occurrences. These experiments confirm the interest of studies on sublanguages for the purpose of corpus-based knowledge acquisition.

Coordination Graph
I now turn to the presentation of a visual representation of the candidate terms and their conceptual links. Coordinations are considered first because they group co-hyponyms into classes that can, in a second approach, be organized into a hierarchy through generic links resulting from acquisitions through substitutions.

A *coordination graph* is composed of *nodes* labeled by controlled or candidate terms and *directed edges*. Each edge relates a term t_f (a controlled term or a candidate produced at a preceding step) to the corresponding candidate $e(\gamma)(\gamma(t_f))$, acquired from a coordination variant of t_f (see formulas 6.12 and 6.13).

The algorithm for building up the coordination graphs extracts *indirectly connected subgraphs* G_c such that there is an undirected path from t to t' for every pair $\{t, t'\}$ of nodes in G_c. The technique for building up the network is similar to the *sprouting algorithm* of Chodorow, Byrd, and Heidorn (1985) used for user-assisted growing of a semantic tree from binary hyponym links. The algorithm computes the transitive closure of the coordination links over the set of controlled terms and candidates.

The steps for calculating a coordination graph are the following:

1. Calculate the set $\mathcal{K}$ of the candidate terms through incremental term enrichment (formula 6.3.8). It results in a set of triples:

$$\mathcal{A} = \{(t_f, e(\gamma)(\gamma(t_f)), \gamma) \, ; \, t_f \in \mathcal{C}_{n_0} \wedge \gamma \in C \cup S \cup P/S\}$$

in which t_f is a controlled or a candidate term, and in which $(t_f, e(\gamma)(\gamma(t_f)), \gamma)$ belongs to $\mathcal{A}$ if and only if $e(\gamma)(\gamma(t_f))$ is a candidate term extracted from a variant $\gamma(t_f)$ of t_f. C is the set of coordination metarules; S, the set of modification/substitution metarules; and P/S, the set of combinations of permutations and modifications/substitutions.

2. Select the subset $\mathcal{A}_C$ of $\mathcal{A}$ corresponding to the candidates extracted from coordination variants ($\gamma \in C$).

3. Calculate indirectly connected subgraphs with labeled directed edges (t, t', c) in $\mathcal{A}_C$. Given a seed term t_s, a term t belongs to the indirectly connected subgraph $G_C(t_s)$ grown from t_s:

$$t \in G_C(t_s) \Leftrightarrow \exists n \in \{1, \ldots, n_0\}, \exists t_0 = t_s, t_1, \ldots, t_n = t \in (T_f \cup \bigcup_{i=2}^{n} C_i)$$

$$\forall j \in \{1, \ldots, n\}, (\exists c \in C, \, (t_{j-1}, t_j, c) \in \mathcal{A}_C \vee \exists c' \in C, \, (t_j, t_{j-1}, c') \in \mathcal{A}_C)$$

One of the coordination graphs built from the candidates extracted from the corpus [Medic] is shown in figure 6.9. It is organized into levels: if t' is acquired from t and t is not acquired from t', t' is lower than t; otherwise, when the acquisition is reciprocal, both terms are located at the same level. In the case of cycles of more than two edges, this spatial organization may lead to the repetition of some terms.

The graph of figure 6.9 contains eleven controlled terms with a capitalized first word and eleven new candidates. All the terms denote *cells*, with the biological meaning. When head

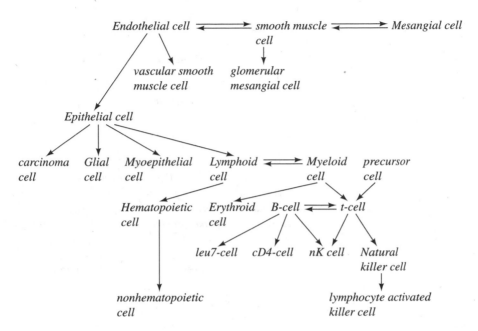

Figure 6.9
Coordination graph of *biological cells*.

coordination occurs, the head of the resulting candidate is different from the head of the original term. For example, *cell structure and function* is a variant of *cell function* which produces the candidate *cell structure* whose head *structure* is different from the head of the base term (*function*). In this case and contrary to the illustrated graph, the network is not restricted to co-hyponym terms (see the graph of *medical controls* in Jacquemin 1996a for such an heterogeneous graph). This situation is, however, exceptional; it only concerns 7% of the links in coordination graphs with three or more edges. More than 50% of these links stem from coordinations in which the common argument is *cell* such as *cell proliferation and differentiation*.

Substitution Graph
Substitution graphs are built according to the same rules as coordination graphs. They are indirectly connected subgraphs built from $\mathcal{A}_S$, the subset of $\mathcal{A}$ consisting of the candidates extracted from substitution variants ($\gamma \in S$). A substitution graph extracted from [Medic] is illustrated by figure 6.10. Some nodes represent groups of co-hyponym terms linked by coordination relations such as {*high pressure, low pressure*} and {*diastolic blood pressure, systolic blood pressure, diastolic pressure, systolic pressure*}.

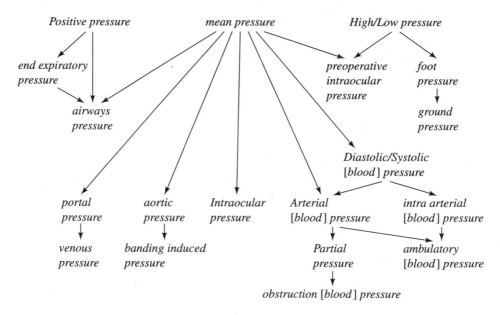

Figure 6.10
Substitution graph of *biological pressures*.

Contrary to the coordination graph, the substitution graph reveals hyponymy relations in which the topmost vertices correspond to the most generic concepts. However, the network is obviously incomplete: for instance, the generic term *high pressure* is linked to *preoperative intraocular pressure* but surprisingly not to *intraocular pressure*. The graph is in fact composed of three subgraphs: a graph of *air pressures* (left part), a graph of *blood pressures* (central part), and a graph of *ground pressures* (right part).

To sum up, the acquisition of terms through variant deconstruction proposes a limited set of high-quality candidates that are conceptually related to other candidates or to controlled terms. The proposed ontologies are incomplete; they can, however, be used as a basis for automatic thesaurus construction.

6.4 Summary

The description of term variation through the structured combination of terms into term variants, proposed in the preceding chapter, is applied directly to term enrichment in this chapter. Two techniques are exploited for this purpose: a statistical approach for the ranking and the structural disambiguation of ternary variants, and a symbolic approach through term variant deconstruction.

Techniques in automatic thesaurus construction consist of methods for automatic term acquisition (described in chapter 2) and methods for automatic enrichment of term banks. Automatic thesaurus enrichment is divided into acquisition of conceptual classes and acquisition of conceptual links. The first techniques are used for clustering terms into classes of conceptually close terms. The second ones are used for discovering automatically links between terms or classes of terms. These links are either predicative (e.g., causality links) or not (e.g., generic/specific links).

The method for automatic term acquisition is based on a statistical filtering of term variations. The method focuses on ternary modification variants, which are by far the most numerous. These variants correspond to the transformation of a binary term $X_3 X_1$ into $X_3 X_2 X_1$ through the insertion of a modifier X_2. The filtering of these candidates relies on a frequency cutoff followed by a statistical ranking. Ranking is based on an association measure which combines relative frequency and Mutual Information. An algorithm is proposed for structural disambiguation of ternary candidate terms. It relies on lexicon-based information—the presence of the substructures $X_3 X_2$ and $X_2 X_1$ in the controlled term list—and on corpus-based information—the values of ratios based on co-occurrence statistics of X_3, X_2, and X_1.

The second method presented in this chapter for term and thesaurus enrichment is a symbolic method, in comparison with the preceding one which is based on statistical measures. Among the four families of elementary term variants presented in the preceding chapter, two of them, coordinations and substitutions, result from the combination of two terms into a variant. The purpose of the automatic acquisition proposed here is to analyze these two types of multiple variants in order to extract the hidden term that was combined with the original term and produced the variant. The analysis of variants yields pattern extractors associated with the metarules that represent coordination and substitution variations. They take as input a variant and output the corresponding candidate term. Finally the candidate terms are postfiltered in order to discard the part of the candidates that correspond to the linguistic modifications without terminological status.

An evaluation of the acquisition shows that the candidate terms are acquired with a high rate of precision (79%) because they are extracted from linguistically filtered variants. This algorithm for term enrichment is incremental: the candidate terms acquired at step n can be used as original terms at step $n + 1$ for acquiring new terms. This technique is used for coping with the incompleteness of the initial terminological data.

In addition to candidate terms, the symbolic technique for term enrichment also provides the user with conceptual links between the candidates and the controlled vocabulary. The terms acquired from coordination variants share a common hypernym with the original term. Terms acquired from substitution variants are more specific than the original term. These conceptual relations are used for building conceptual networks which can serve as a basis for automatic thesaurus construction.

The next chapter explores the extraction of morphosyntactic variants. This novel type of transformations involves simultaneously syntactic modifications and morphological links.

7 Morphosyntactic Variants

Chapter 5 described the application of *FASTR* to the recognition of *syntactic variants* within untagged corpora. The current chapter expands the formalism of *FASTR* so as to cope with *morphosyntactic variants*. For instance, the variant *development of mouse embryos* is a morphosyntactic and nonsyntactic variant of *Embryonic development* because the adjective *embryonic* is transformed into the noun *embryo* in the variant. All the features of the parser presented so far are reused for this new task. To cope with more complex local syntactic analyses, the parser is enriched with finite-state machinery and is applied to tagged corpora. The resulting architecture is a new and powerful combination of local transformations with morphological links used to generate variant structures and local finite-state descriptions used to recognize morphosyntactic variations within corpora.

Section 7.1 presents the new features of the *FASTR* formalism. First, morphological links are expressed at the level of the single word lexicon, and second, regular expressions are used in metarules for the description of morphosyntactic variations. Section 7.2 describes a set of metarules on morphosyntactic variations, and their design is evaluated on the test corpus and test term list used for the evaluation of syntactic variations in chapter 5.[42]

The recognition of morphological variants is a necessary topic in the study of term variation because it expands the scope of *FASTR* to nonnominal phrase structures such as verbal, adjectival, and adverbial phrases. The studies in terminology have generally focused on noun phrases, but other categories convey important concepts in documents. In Klavans and Kan (1998) the role of verb in document analysis is outlined. Verb classes and verb phrases are used to compare article types and emphasize their differences. In the WSJ corpus, articles with communication verbs are issues, reports, opinions, and editorials; articles with motion verbs are posted earnings and announcements; articles with agreement verbs are mergers, legal cases, and opinions; etc. These results confirm that information access procedures will be more successful in categorization of documents if they are not restricted to NPs as source of information.

Currently thesauri and term banks contain mostly noun phrases. Similarly tools for automatic term acquisition yield mainly noun phrases (see section 2.2). Since *FASTR* must be provided with an initial list of terms from a thesaurus or a tool for term acquisition, the focus is on morphological variations of noun phrases: noun to verb, adjective and verb variants. In a near future, when thesauri will contain nonnominal terms and tools for term acquisition will produce verbal, adjectival, or adverbial terms, it will be possible to widen the scope of term recognition by *FASTR* to variations of nonnominal terms such as verb to noun or adjective to verb phrase variants.

7.1 Morphological Links and Regular Expressions in *FASTR*

Genuine morphosyntactic variants are variants in which at least one of the words w_1 in the original term is transformed into another word w'_1 in the variant such that w_1 and w'_1

are in the same *morphological family*. Except for Noun to Noun relations such as *tumor promotion/Tumor promoter*, morphosyntactic variations involve a deep modification of the syntactic structure because of the change of syntactic category of the morphologically transformed words. For example, the variant [*the ability*] *to treat such surfaces* is a verb phrase, while the original term *Surface treatment* is a noun phrase. These variations are called heterocategorial, and they may result in noun phrases, verb phrases, or adjective phrases. Contrary to noun phrases and adjective phrases, verb phrases have a very flexible structure—much looser than syntactic variants studied in chapters 4 and 5.

7.1.1 Regular Expressions

The metarules describing syntactic variations in chapters 4 and 5 do not make use of regular expressions. This particularity has not been problematic so far because of the weakly flexible structure of syntactic variants.

The syntactic flexibility of morphosyntactic variants has led us to the addition of regular expressions in the formulation of morphosyntactic metarules. This combination of a transformational mechanism based on phrase structures and finite-state machines has proved to be a very efficient means for describing morphosyntactic variants, as shown in the remainder of this chapter.

The formalism for expressing regular expressions in *FASTR* is presented in section 4.2.3. It offers the basic operators of Hopcroft and Ullman (1979, sec. 2.5) plus some additional descriptive facilities. The basic operators are the concatenation (denoted $e_1\,e_2$), the union (denoted $e_1 \mid e_2$), and the *Kleene closures* (denoted $e^\star$ and e^+). For idiosyncratic reasons the parenthesis corresponding to concatenation and union are respectively angle brackets ($\langle\,\rangle$) and curly brackets ($\{\,\}$).

In addition to these core operators, the formalism of regular expressions in *FASTR* also accepts bounded enumerations (denoted e^{1-5} for a concatenation from one to five occurrences of e), and optional elements (denoted $e^?$ which stands for e^{0-1}).

Thus the expression

$$\langle\, \{A \mid N \mid Np \mid V\}^{0-2}\, \{N \mid Np\}\, \langle\, PREP\, \{N \mid Np\}\,\rangle^? \,\rangle$$

describes a noun phrase pattern composed of up to two modifiers of category A, N, Np, or V, a nominal head, and an optional prepositional postmodifier composed of a preposition and a nominal head. The category of the nominal heads is either N or Np.

7.1.2 Morphological Links

The description of morphosyntactic variations, such as the conflation of *Pressure measurement* with *pressures were measured*, relies on a combination of syntactic transformations (as seen previously for syntactic variations) and morphological relations. The preceding variant can only be recognized if some metarule states the following:

1. An $N_1 N_2$ term structure can be transformed into an $N_1 V_{be} V_{pp}$ structure in which V_{be} is the verb *to be* and V_{pp} is a past participle.

2. The past participle V_{pp} in the target structure is morphologically related with the noun N_2 in the source structure.

According to the three-tier formalism proposed in *FASTR*—single words, terms, and variations—the morphological relations must be stated at the level of single words and at the level of variation metarules.

Single-Word Rules

First, the single-word file must contain information about morphological links between lexical entries. This information is embodied in a root lemma attached to the words that are morphologically derived from this lemma, as described in the paragraph about *static derivational morphology* in section 3.2.2. For instance, the following rule (7.3) indicates that the root of the noun *measurement* is the verb *to measure* which is described by rule (7.1). Lemmas with the same string and different part-of-speech categories are distinguished, as indicated by the following rule (7.2) which describes the noun *measure* that has the same root verb *to measure* as the noun *measurement*:[43]

Word *'measure'*:   (7.1)

$\langle cat \rangle \doteq$ *'V'*.

Word *'measure'*:   (7.2)

$\langle cat \rangle \doteq$ *'N'*

$\langle root\ cat \rangle \doteq$ *'V'*

$\langle root\ lemma \rangle \doteq$ *'measure'*

$\langle history \rangle \doteq$ *'-+'*.

Word *'measurement'*:   (7.3)

$\langle cat \rangle \doteq$ *'N'*

$\langle root\ cat \rangle \doteq$ *'V'*

$\langle root\ lemma \rangle \doteq$ *'measure'*

$\langle history \rangle \doteq$ *'-+ment'*.

For the English language, the links between words and their root lemma are derived from the CELEX base. The English version of the base, completed in June 1993, contains 52,446 lemmas representing 160,594 word forms. It was designed by the Dutch Center for

Lexical Information (http://www.kun.nl). This base comprises orthographic features and representations of the phonological, morphological, syntactic, and frequency properties of lemmas.[44]

The morphological links are calculated from the EML and ESL data corresponding to lemmas for English morphology and lemmas for English syntax. The output of the processing is a list of morphological families composed of a root word w_r and the lemmas that share w_r as a common root word. Take, for instance, the family of the verb *to measure* calculated from the CELEX base

commensurable/A/-+*able*	*commensurably*/ADV/-*le*+*ly*
countermeasure/N/-+	*immeasurable*/A/-+*able*
immeasurably/ADV/-*le*+*ly*	*incommensurable*/A/-+*able*
measurable/A/-*e*+*able*	*measurably*/ADV/-*le*+*ly*
measure/N/-+	*measureless*/A/-+*less*
measurement/N/-+*ment*	*mensurable*/A/-+*able*
tape-measure/N/-+	*yard-measure*/N/-+
measure/V/-+	

These data are directly converted into the formalism of *FASTR* in order to generate rules such as (7.1) to (7.3) for the verb *to measure*$_V$, the noun *measure*$_N$, and the noun *measurement*$_N$.

For the French language, no similar lexical base is publicly available, and it was necessary to create morphological families from scratch. For this purpose I used the lexical base for French inflectional morphology developed at Bell Labs (Lucent Technologies) by Evelyne Tzoukermann (Tzoukermann and Liberman 1990; Tzoukermann and Jacquemin 1997; Tzoukermann and Radev 1997). This lexical base is primarily designed for concatenative inflectional morphology, and its architecture is described in section 2.1.3.

The morphological links between words sharing the same root lemma in French are calculated from this lexical base through a stemming procedure that exploits the word stems used for inflectional morphology. The acquisition of morphological links for derivational morphology is partly deduced from inflectional allomorphs because a number of orthographic variations are common to these two morphological constructions. For instance, the construction of the inflections of the verb *envoyer* (to send) involves the word base *envoi*. This word base happens to be a noun in the same morphological family. It is therefore useful for relating the noun *envoi* (sending) with its root lemma *envoyer*. More details about the construction of morphological families in French are given in Tzoukermann and Jacquemin (1997). A concurrent approach to rule-based stemming is corpus-based stemming, which exploits corpus occurrences to refine morphological links (Jacquemin 1997a; Xu and Croft 1998).

Thus, both through automatic stemming procedures and through the exploitation of lexical databases, morphological families can be automatically calculated and used for the recognition of morphosyntactic variants.

Metarules

The second part of the formalism in which the morphological links must be expressed is the metagrammar. The morphosyntactic variations must contain the information about the involved morphological changes. For example, the metarule (7.4) describes the transformation of a Noun–Noun term $N_2 N_3$, such as *Concentration measurement,* into a verb phrase, such as [*To that end, we*] *measured extracellular K+ concentration.* The head verb V_3 of the variant is morphologically related with the head noun N_3 of the original term. This link is expressed by the equation $\langle V_3\ root \rangle \doteq \langle N_3\ root \rangle$, which requires that V_3 and N_3 share the same root. In the preceding example the common root lemma is the verb *to measure.* N_2, the noun modifier *concentration* in the original term, becomes an object of the verb in the variant and no operation of derivational morphology is involved for this word:

$$\text{Metarule NtoV}(N_1 \rightarrow N_2\ N_3) \tag{7.4}$$

$$\equiv V_1 \rightarrow V_3 \ \langle \text{ADV}^?\ \text{PREP}^? \langle \text{ART N}^?\ \text{PREP} \rangle^? \text{ART}^?\ \{ \text{A}|\text{N}|\text{V} \}^{0-3} \rangle\ N_2 :$$

$$\langle V_3\ root \rangle \doteq \langle N_3\ root \rangle.$$

Table 7.1 shows eighteen verbal variants of *Concentration measurement* extracted through this metarule from the corpus [Medic]. All these variants correspond to a textual utterance in which the first word is *measure* (the only verb in the morphological family of *measurement*), the last word is *concentration*, and the intermediate words satisfy the part-of-speech pattern expressed by the regular expression in metarule (7.4). For example, *measured extracellular K+ concentration* is tagged as a V A N N sequence which satisfies the target pattern V ADV$^?$ PREP$^?$⟨ART N$^?$ PREP⟩$^?$ ART$^?$ $\{$A|N|V$\}^{0-3}$ N, as the first four optional elements are absent and the last one is repeated twice.

FASTR is enriched to handle the extended formalism by adding a compiler that transforms regular expressions into finite-state automata.[45] An interpreter is then invoked each time a transformed rule contains a regular expression. In addition the parsing mechanism of *FASTR* is equipped with an extended lexicalization process that permits the linking of rules to morphological families instead of single lexical units. Through this extended lexicalization, when parsing a text chunk such as *measured concentrations,* the rules linked to any word in the morphological family of *measure* and any word in the morphological family of *concentrate* are loaded. Thus the rule for *Concentration measurement,* linked to the noun

Table 7.1
Eighteen verbal variants of *Concentration measurement* from the [Medic] corpus (Metarule (7.4))

Controlled term	Variant	Occurrences	Correct
Concentration measurement	*measured COHb concentrations*	1	×
Concentration measurement	*measured REE concentrations*	1	×
Concentration measurement	*measured by serum neopterin concentrations*	1	
Concentration measurement	*measured concentrations*	1	×
Concentration measurement	*measured extracellular K+ concentration*	1	×
Concentration measurement	*measured lipid concentrations*	1	×
Concentration measurement	*measured plasma concentrations*	2	×
Concentration measurement	*measured plasma histamine concentrations*	1	×
Concentration measurement	*measured the concentration*	1	×
Concentration measurement	*measured the concentrations*	4	×
Concentration measurement	*measured the endothelin-1 concentrations*	1	×
Concentration measurement	*measured the extracellular concentrations*	1	×
Concentration measurement	*measured the plasma concentration*	1	×
Concentration measurement	*measured the regional concentration*	1	×
Concentration measurement	*measured the serum concentrations*	1	×
Concentration measurement	*measuring the concentration*	1	×
Concentration measurement	*measuring the concentrations*	1	×
Concentration measurement	*measuring the ethanol concentration*	1	×

measurement, is activated because the noun *measurement* and the verb *to measure* share the same root lemma. The morphosyntactic variant *measured concentrations* of the term *Concentration measurement* is thus extracted by the appropriate metarule.

I now turn to the design of metarules describing the morphosyntactic variations for the English language. The [Medic] corpus is used as a training corpus for tuning the metarules through experimental runs. Then the quality of morphosyntactic variant extraction is evaluated on the test corpus [Metal] along the same guidelines as the evaluation of syntactic variants in section 5.5.

7.2   Evaluation of Morphosyntactic Variant Extraction

As in the case of syntactic metarules, the tuning of the morphosyntactic metarules for English was performed on a training corpus [Medic] and a training term list [Pascal] (presented in appendix C). The evaluation of these metarules was made on a test corpus [Metal] and a test term list [Pascal-Metal].

Before going into the details of evaluation, the main families of morphosyntactic variations are described. As in the case of syntactic variations, the definition of these classes does not result from introspection but rather from experiments on large and diverse corpora. The strength of the linguistic data presented in this study is their experimental grounding, as in the similar *corpus linguistics* approach for grammar tuning of Black et al. (1993).

7.2.1 Tuning Morphosyntactic Variants

The tuning of the metagrammar for morphosyntactic variations is similar to the technique for syntactic variations shown in section 5.4.2. First, paradigmatic variations are extracted through relaxed metarules. These metarules are then progressively enriched with additional constraints so as to reject spurious variations.

Contrary to syntactic variations, the paradigmatic metarules conceived for morphosyntactic variations do not call for a preliminary linguistic analysis. The paradigmatic morphosyntactic metarules are not based on partially defined syntactic structures, they instead describe *extended co-occurrences*. This conccept is defined as follows:

Definition 7.1 (Extended co-occurrence)   An extended co-occurrence is an *n*-word window containing all the content words of a controlled term or one of the words in their morphological family.

The paradigmatic metarules for extended co-occurrences are given in appendix A.3. Like the co-occurrences defined in section 5.5.1, extended co-occurrences are separated into *insertion extended co-occurrences* if the order of the words in the window is the same as the order of the words in the controlled term, and *permutation extended co-occurrences* otherwise. Thus SingDer and SingDerP metarules are charged with extracting text windows containing one word of a binary term and one word in the same morphological family as the second word of the term. The order of the words in the co-occurrence and in the term are the same for SingDer variants and are reversed for SingDerP variants. Similarly the Doub-Der and DoubDerP metarules extract variants which correspond to windows containing morphological transformations of the two words of a binary term.

For example, given a binary term $X_2\,X_3$, the following metarule:

$$\text{Metarule SingDerP}(X_1 \rightarrow X_2\,X_3) \equiv X_1 \rightarrow X_3\,\langle X^{0-9}\rangle\,X_4: \tag{7.5}$$
$$\langle X_2\,root\rangle \doteq \langle X_4\,root\rangle.$$

extracts text occurrences up to 11 words long in which the first word is X_3 and the last word X_4 belongs to the morphological family of X_2.

As in syntactic variations the list of correct variations is established by manually scanning the output of the paradigmatic variants extracted by the metarules of appendix A.3.[46] The next section presents the different classes of morphosyntactic variants that have been established through a linguistic analysis of these correct paradigmatic variants.[47]

7.2.2 Typology of Morphosyntactic Variants

The syntactic variations presented in chapter 5 are classified according to the syntactic transformation performed on the original term. In every case a syntactic variant of a nominal term is another noun phrase, and it makes sense to base the classification of syntactic variants on the target syntactic structure.

However, morphosyntactic variations produced by a single metarule can be phrases of different part-of-speech categories. Thus, among the seventeen correct variants of *Concentration measurement* shown in table 7.1, sixteen are verb phrases composed of a verb and its object and one is a noun phrase extracted from the following sentence:

To study whether serially <u>measured plasma concentrations</u> of endothelin relate to the pathophysiology of human septic shock.

Because of this diversity the classification of variations and corresponding metarules cannot rely solely on the syntactic category of the target structure. The morphosyntactic variations are therefore classified according to the type of the morphological transformation. In this framework all the variants from table 7.1 are Noun to Verb variants because the noun *measurement* is transformed into the verb *to measure*. This classification can be extended to the variations that involve more than one morphological transformations such as *rats were <u>ventilated mechanically</u>*, a variant of *Mechanical ventilation* in which the adjective *mechanical* is transformed into the adverb *mechanically* and the noun *ventilation* is transformed into the verb *to ventilate*.

7.2.3 Classification of Morphosyntactic Variants

This section lists the different families of morphosyntactic variations that are currently described in English through the metarules provided in appendix A.4. First, heterogeneous morphosyntactic variations are presented in which the source and the target categories are different. Then homogeneous variants are described in which the morphological transformation associates two words with the same categories, either two nouns or two adjectives. The former variations are called *heterocategorial variations*, the latter ones are *isocategorial variations*. Variations involving two or more morphological modifications are ignored because, as will be shown in section 7.3.1, these transformations are rare and their non-recognition does not dramatically reduce the recall rate of the extraction.

Noun to Adjective Variants

Most of these variants transform nominal modifiers into adjectival modifiers or the reverse. In the case of an Adjective to Noun variation, the nominalized adjective is either a premodifier (*<u>chromosome</u> abnormalities*) or a postmodifier embedded in a prepositional

Table 7.2
The first ten Adjective to Noun variants and the first ten Noun to Adjective variants from the corpus [Medic]

Controlled term	Variant	Occurrences	Correct
Analysis method	*analytic methods*	1	×
Analysis method	*analytical methods*	2	×
Bone defect	*bony defect*	1	×
Bone defect	*bony defects*	2	×
Bone defect	*bony resorptive defects*	1	×
Cell component	*cellular component*	1	×
Cell component	*cellular components*	2	×
Cell density	*cellular density*	3	×
Cell differentiation	*cellular differentiation*	1	×
Cell factor	*cellular adhesion factors*	1	×
Abdominal disease	*disease of the abdomen*	1	×
Abnormal chromosome	*abnormalities of chromosome*	4	×
Abnormal chromosome	*abnormalities of chromosomes*	1	·×
Abnormal chromosome	*chromosome abnormalities*	9	×
Abnormal chromosome	*chromosome abnormality*	8	×
Acidic cell	*acid in adrenocortical cells*	1	×
Acidic cell	*acid within amnion cells*	1	×
Acidic cell	*cell membrane fatty acid*	1	
Acidic cell	*cells by retinoic acid*	1	
Acidic cell	*cells transformed arachidonic acid*	1	

phrase(*abnormalities of <u>chromosome</u>*). Among the twenty examples illustrated in table 7.2, seventeen are correct variants corresponding to this type of transformation.

Apart from these modifier to modifier transformations, the metarules given in appendix A.4 for Noun to Adjective variations describe two additional types of transformations in which the nominal head of a Noun-Noun term is transformed into an adjective. The adjective in the target structure is either a modifier of a head noun, or the head of an adjective phrase. These variants are not encountered in the [Medic] corpus but occur in other corpora with head nouns built from adjectives through such suffixes as *-ness*, *-ce*, or *-cy*. For instance, the noun *sparseness* gives rise to the nominal variant *sparse data* of the nominal term *Data sparseness*. Symmetrically *error tolerant* is an adjectival variant of *Error tolerance*. These two types of Noun to Adjective variants are rare.

As in the case of syntactic variants, some of the errors in the recognition of morphosyntactic variants are due to a loss of dependency between the transformed elements of the terms. For instance, *cells transformed arachidonic acid* is not a correct variant of *Acidic cell* because *acid* is an object of the verb *transform* in the variant and not a modifier of *cell*.

Table 7.3
The first ten Noun to Verb variants from the corpus [Medic]

Controlled term	Variant	Occurrences	Correct
Acid number	*acid positions are numbered*	1	
Acid reaction	*acting at excitatory amino acid*	1	
Acid reaction	*activated deoxyribonucleic acid*	1	
Acid reaction	*counteracted by retinoic acid*	1	
Age distribution	*distributed into 3 age*	1	
Age estimation	*estimated gestational age*	3	×
Age estimation	*estimated peak age*	1	×
Age estimation	*estimating gestational age*	1	×
Amplitude distribution	*distribution of amplified*	1	
Antigen presentation	*antigen presenting*	2	

Some other errors are due to semantic discrepancies between the two morphologically related words, because some affixes modify the meaning of a constructed word too radically. For example, even though *reaction* and *actual* are morphologically related (they both have the same root verb *to act*), they share little synchronic meaning in contemporary English. Because of this semantic distance, *actual rate* is not a correct variant of *Reaction rate*.

Even for stronger semantic links, the compositional interpretation of the original term and its variant can differ in such a fashion that they denote different concepts. For example, a *Health worker* is someone working for health organizations (it is an elliptic form of *health organization worker*) whereas a *healthy worker* is a worker in good health. These two utterances cannot be regarded as variants one of another despite the obvious semantic proximity of *health* and *healthy*.

Noun to Verb Variants

Noun to verb variants are pervasive and are mainly due to nominalized verbs encountered in multi-word terms. For example, the term *Image projection* contains the noun *projection*, which a nominalization of the verb *to project*, and accepts the variant *projected images* in the utterance *The projected images demonstrated a global view of the thecal sac*. The high number of nonnominal morphosyntactic variants that have a conceptual content equivalent to nominal terms proves that a correct terminological extraction cannot solely rely on noun phrases, but must also cope with verb or adjective phrases.

Table 7.3 shows ten Noun to Verb variants extracted from the [Medic] corpus. Only three of these variants are correct. As in the case of Noun to Adjective variants, spurious Noun to Verb variants are due to incorrect morphological links or inappropriate syntactic patterns. The rate of incorrect variants is high. A refinement of the morphological families that produces a more elaborate count of errors is proposed in section 7.3.1: the variations that correspond to prefixed morphological links are counted separately. Through this filter, *acting at excitatory amino acid* is considered as a prefixed variant of *Acid reaction* because *to act* and *reaction* differ one from another with a prefix *re-*. Conversely, Noun to Verb variants corresponding to suffixal additions tend to be of very good quality as shown in table 7.1.

The noun to verb variations yield either nominal or verbal variants. In the case of nominal variants, the verb is a past participle modifying a head noun as in *differentiated squamous cell*, a variant of *Cell differentiation*. Conversely, if the variant is a verb phrase, the verbalized noun is the head word of the variant. In such a case the other noun is either the subject of the verb phrase, as in *cells proliferated* a variant of *Cell proliferation*, or the object of the verb, as in *recognized neural cells* a variant of *Cell recognition*. Some verbs, such as *to change*, can give rise to both arguments. Thus the two verb phrases *behavior changes* or *change behavior* are two equally legitimate variants of the nominal term *Behavior change*, depending on whether the change is observed (first variant) or provoked (second variant). Such verbs, called *ergative verbs*, are studied extensively in Fabre (1998) and Fabre and Jacquemin (2000) for the purpose of improving Noun to Verb variants recognition according to the target syntactic structure and the verb semantics.

Adjective to Adverb Variants

Adjective to Adverb transformations are rarely encountered in variations which involve only one morphosyntactic transformation because the transformed adverb cannot modify the head noun. They are better observed in correlation with a second morphological modification, generally a Noun to Verb transformation so that the adverb can be a modifier of the verb in the target structure. Thus *observed simultaneously* is a variant of *Simultaneous observation* that concurrently involves the transformation of the adjectival modifier *simultaneous* into the adverbial modifier *simultaneously* and the transformation of the head noun *observation* into the head verb *observed*.

In the case of variations with only one morphological transformation, an additional verb or adjective is inserted in the variant and is modified by the adverb. For example, *simultaneously obtained measurements* is a correct variant of *Simultaneous measurement* even though the dependency between *simultaneous* and *measurement* in the base term is not preserved in the variant. In this case the modification of the dependency is not problematic because the inserted verb, here *obtain*, is semantically neutral with respect to the compositional meaning of the variant. (This situation is similar to the case of *integrated metonymy* presented in section 5.1.2.) Table 7.4 shows ten Adjective to Adverb variations, six of them correct. The four remaining incorrect variations correspond to cases in which the inserted word induces a modification of the meaning and the variant denotes a concept

Table 7.4
The first ten Adjective to Adverb variants from the corpus [Medic]

Controlled term	Variant	Occurrences	Correct
Automatic system	*automatically pressurised infusor system*	1	×
Clinical form	*clinically benign form*	1	
Experimental animal	*experimentally infected animals*	2	
Experimental disease	*experimentally induced autoimmune disease*	1	×
Genetic control	*genetically matched controls*	1	×
Genetic disease	*genetically determined autoimmune disease*	1	
Genetic disease	*genetically determined neurological diseases*	1	
Genetic disease	*genetically more restricted disease*	1	×
Genetic disease	*genetically restricted disease*	1	×
Genetic variant	*genetically variant*	1	×

different from the original term. Thus a *genetically determined neurological diseases* is not a variant of a *Genetic disease* because a *Genetic disease* is not a *disease* that is *genetically determined* but a *disease* that is *due to genetic factors*.

Noun to Noun and Adjective to Adjective Variants

These two families of variants are somehow curious because they do not involve a change of syntactic category despite the presence of a morphological transformation. They correspond to orthographic alternations with the same meaning such as *analytic/analytical*, to prefixed words with different meanings such as *reaction* and *activity*, or to semantic alternations in the same syntactic category such as cause/effect (*pollution/pollutant*), means/process (*filter/filtration*), and process/result (*measurement/measure*).

Tables 7.5 and 7.6 show ten examples of each of the two types of isocategorial variations. Since the rate of incorrect variations is high, it is useful to display both correct and spurious variants in these tables.

Contrary to heterocategorial variations, such as Noun to Verb variants, correct isocategorial variants generally do not involve significant syntactic transformations. Because of the preservation of the syntactic category in the morphological transformation, the target structure of the variant is similar to the structure of a syntactic variant. In fact the structures of the correct isocategorial variants correspond mainly to modifications/substitutions presented in section 5.1.2.

Synthesis on Morphosyntactic Variations

As indicated earlier for Noun to Verb variants, prefixing rarely yields correct variations. Some of the semantic shifts due to prefixing are antonym relations (*normal/abnormal*),

Table 7.5
Five correct and five spurious Adjective to Adjective variants from the corpus [Medic]

Controlled term	Variant	Occurrences	Correct
Analytical method	*analytic methods*	1	×
Balanced diet	*well-balanced diet*	1	×
Dominant species	*predominant species*	2	×
Early stage	*earliest stage*	2	×
Early stage	*earliest stages*	1	×
Abnormal chromosome	*normal X chromosome*	1	
Active component	*reactive components*	1	
Adrenal artery	*renal arteries*	1	
Differential system	*different assay systems*	1	
Direct laryngoscopy	*indirect laryngoscopy*	1	

Table 7.6
Five correct and five spurious Noun to Noun variants from the corpus [Medic]

Controlled term	Variant	Occurrences	Correct
Age estimation	*age estimate*	1	×
Air filtration	*air ventilation filter*	1	×
Air pollution	*air pollutants*	1	×
Angular measurement	*angular measure*	1	×
Cell component	*cell composition*	1	
Acid reaction	*acid cholesterol esterase activity*	1	
Activation analysis	*reaction analysis*	2	
Bicycle ergometer	*cycle ergometer*	1	
Body movement	*body removal*	1	
Carbon dioxide	*carbon monoxide*	1	

compounds with different meanings (*dioxide/monoxide*), generic/specific relations (*magnetic/electromagnetic*), and, more generally, the lack of synchronic semantic proximity (*reaction/activity*).

As indicated in the former description of the different classes of variations, the quality of the variants crucially depends on the type of morphological modification involved in the variation. In particular, two characteristics prove to be highly significant:

• Whether or not the syntactic category is preserved through the morphological transformation.

• Whether or not the morphological modification involves the addition or the removal of a prefix.

7.3 Evaluating Morphosyntactic Metarules

This section describes the experimental evaluation of the morphosyntactic metarules on the test corpus [Metal] indexed with the test term list [Pascal-Metal]. The first part of the evaluation provides the measures of precision, recall, and precision of fallout, while the second part compares the volumes of acquisition of the different families of variations.

Both the corpus and the term list were tagged with Brill's tagger (Brill 1992). From the tagged term list, a lexicon of single words is created. It consists of the words encountered in terms and the words belonging to the same morphological family as words encountered in terms. As the evaluation of syntactic variations, a grammar of term rules is also generated from the term list.

The evaluation is performed on a set of 23 metarules for binary terms composed of a head noun preceded by a modifier. (Rules for binary terms with a Noun-Preposition-Noun structure exist, but are not used because no binary term in [Pascal-Metal] has this structure.) These metarules are reported in appendix A.4, and are distributed as follows:

AtoA	VtoN	AtoAv	AtoN	NtoA	NtoN	NtoV
2	1	1	3	3	3	6

7.3.1 Qualitative Evaluation

The evaluation of the extraction of morphosyntactic variants is performed along the same guidelines as in the case of syntactic variants proposed in section 5.5.1. The fact that paradigmatic variations are assimilated with extended co-occurrences slightly simplifies the picture. The only two sets involved in the evaluation of morphosyntactic variants are *filtered variants* extracted by filtering metarules and *extended co-occurrences*.

As in the case of syntactic variants, morphosyntactic variants divide into nonoverlapping sets corresponding to correct and incorrect variants. Thus *filtered variants* divide into correct $(\mathcal{F}_{\mathcal{C}})$ and incorrect $(\mathcal{F}_{\mathcal{I}})$ variants. Additionally filtered variants are subdivided according to the seven families of metarules plus an additional class of variations which is not described by metarules: AtoV variants.

Two subclasses compose *paradigmatic variants*: modification co-occurrences and permutation co-occurrences depending on whether or not the order of the content words is preserved. Since these two families of co-occurrences cover all the classes of filtered variants, the extended co-occurrences are divided into correct $(\mathcal{CM}_{\mathcal{C}}\ \&\ \mathcal{CP}_{\mathcal{C}})$ and incorrect

Table 7.7
Numbers of morphosyntactic variants on [Metal]

	AtoA	VtoN	AtoAv	AtoN	NtoA	NtoN	NtoV	AtoV	**Total**
$|\mathcal{CM}_\mathcal{C}|$	0	0	0	10	5	2	59	3	79
$|\mathcal{CP}_\mathcal{C}|$	0	3	0	19	14	0	44	0	80
$|\mathcal{CM}_\mathcal{I}|$					345				345
$|\mathcal{CP}_\mathcal{I}|$					364				364
$|\mathcal{F}_\mathcal{C}|$	0	0	2	80	25	31	85	0	223
$|\mathcal{F}_\mathcal{I}|$	136	2	0	29	3	53	41	0	264

($\mathcal{CM}_\mathcal{I}$ & $\mathcal{CP}_\mathcal{I}$) modification and permutation co-occurrences. The sizes of these sets for controlled indexing of the test corpus are given in table 7.7.

For a better analysis of the results, it is useful to outline the role played by prefixing in the quality and the semantics of morphosyntactic variation. A *prefixed variant* is any variant for which the morphological transformation involves the addition and/or the removal of a prefix. For example, *structural rearrangement* is a prefixed correct variant of *Structural arrangement* and *surface interaction* is a prefixed incorrect variant of *Surface reaction*.

Table 7.8 shows the volume of filtered variants that result from prefixed morphological relations. The sets $\mathcal{F}_{\mathcal{C}_p}$ and $\mathcal{F}_{\mathcal{I}_p}$ represent respectively correct and incorrect prefixed filtered variants: the subsets of $\mathcal{F}_\mathcal{C}$ and $\mathcal{F}_\mathcal{I}$ which involve prefixing. In order to characterize the incorrect prefixed variants, a more detailed typology is proposed by highlighting the variants that are antonyms $\mathcal{A}$ or hyper/hyponyms $\mathcal{HH}$ of the original terms. Again, a difference is made between prefixed antonyms or hyper/hyponyms ($\mathcal{A}_p$ and $\mathcal{HH}_p$) and nonprefixed ones ($\mathcal{A}_{\neg p}$ and $\mathcal{HH}_{\neg p}$). As shown in table 7.8, $\mathcal{A}_{\neg p} = \mathcal{HH}_{\neg p} = \emptyset$: all the variants in these two semantic classes are prefixed variants.

Measure of Quality
The quality of extraction is measured with the three measures of information retrieval adapted to term extraction and provided by formulas (5.37), (5.38), and (5.39) for syntactic variants. At the level of morphosyntactic variations, the reference sets used for calculating these measures are slightly different. The basic value of precision is defined by the same measure:

$$P = \frac{|\mathcal{F}_\mathcal{C}|}{|\mathcal{F}_\mathcal{C} \cup \mathcal{F}_\mathcal{I}|} \tag{7.6}$$

Table 7.8
Prefixed morphosyntactic variants on [Metal]

	AtoA	VtoN	AtoAv	AtoN	NtoA	NtoN	NtoV	AtoV	**Total**
$\left\|\mathcal{F}_{\mathcal{C}_p}\right\|$	0	0	0	2	0	9	0	0	11
$\left\|\mathcal{F}_{\mathcal{I}_p}\right\|$	134	2	0	7	2	51	15	0	211
$\left\|\mathcal{A}_{\neg p}\right\|$	0	0	0	0	0	0	0	0	0
$\left\|\mathcal{A}_p\right\|$	3	0	0	2	0	5	0	0	10
$\left\|\mathcal{H}\mathcal{H}_{\neg p}\right\|$	0	0	0	0	0	0	0	0	0
$\left\|\mathcal{H}\mathcal{H}_p\right\|$	131	0	0	2	0	7	0	0	140

Table 7.9
Precision of morphosyntactic term extraction on [Metal]

	AtoA	VtoN	AtoAv	AtoN	NtoA	NtoN	NtoV	AtoV	**Total**
P	0%	0%	100.0%	73.4%	89.3%	36.9%	67.5%	–	45.8%
$P_{\neg p}$	0%	–	100.0%	78.0%	96.2%	30.1%	91.7%	–	80.0%
$P_{\mathcal{A}/\mathcal{H}\mathcal{H}}$	98.5%	0%	100.0%	74.3%	89.3%	44.8%	67.5%	–	74.3%

It is complemented with a measure of precision $P_{\neg p}$ in which only nonprefixed variants are accounted for and a measure of precision $P_{\mathcal{A}/\mathcal{H}\mathcal{H}}$ with prefixed variants in which antonyms or hyper/hyponyms are considered as correct:

$$P_{\neg p} = \frac{\left|\mathcal{F}_{\mathcal{C}} \setminus \mathcal{F}_{\mathcal{C}_p}\right|}{\left|(\mathcal{F}_{\mathcal{C}} \cup \mathcal{F}_{\mathcal{I}}) \setminus (\mathcal{F}_{\mathcal{C}_p} \cup \mathcal{F}_{\mathcal{I}_p})\right|} \qquad P_{\mathcal{A}/\mathcal{H}\mathcal{H}} = \frac{|\mathcal{F}_{\mathcal{C}} \cup \mathcal{A} \cup \mathcal{H}\mathcal{H}|}{|\mathcal{F}_{\mathcal{C}} \cup \mathcal{F}_{\mathcal{I}}|} \qquad (7.7)$$

The values of these three measures of precision for the different classes of morphosyntactic variants are shown in table 7.9.

The expressions of recall and precision of fallout are adapted from formulas (5.38) and (5.39). Since incorrect variants cannot be distributed among the different classes of morphosyntactic variants, only global measures of recall and precision of recall are provided. In addition complementary values without prefixed variants and with antonyms and hyper/hyponyms are also computed:

$$R = \frac{|\mathcal{F}_C|}{|\mathcal{F}_C \cup \mathcal{CM}_C \cup \mathcal{CP}_C|} \tag{7.8}$$

$$R_{\neg p} = \frac{\left|\mathcal{F}_C \setminus \mathcal{F}_{C_p}\right|}{\left|(\mathcal{F}_C \cup \mathcal{CM}_C \cup \mathcal{CP}_C) \setminus (\mathcal{F}_{C_p} \cup \mathcal{CM}_{C_p} \cup \mathcal{CP}_{C_p})\right|} \tag{7.9}$$

$$R_{A/\mathcal{HH}} = \frac{|\mathcal{F}_C \cup \mathcal{A} \cup \mathcal{HH}|}{|\mathcal{F}_C \cup \mathcal{CM}_C \cup \mathcal{CP}_C \cup \mathcal{A} \cup \mathcal{HH}|} \tag{7.10}$$

$$\Pi = \frac{|\mathcal{CM}_{\mathcal{I}} \cup \mathcal{CP}_{\mathcal{I}}|}{|\mathcal{CM}_{\mathcal{I}} \cup \mathcal{CP}_{\mathcal{I}} \cup \mathcal{F}_{\mathcal{I}}|} \tag{7.11}$$

$$\Pi_{\neg p} = \frac{\left|(\mathcal{CM}_{\mathcal{I}} \cup \mathcal{CP}_{\mathcal{I}}) \setminus (\mathcal{CM}_{\mathcal{I}_p} \cup \mathcal{CP}_{\mathcal{I}_p})\right|}{\left|(\mathcal{CM}_{\mathcal{I}} \cup \mathcal{CP}_{\mathcal{I}} \cup \mathcal{F}_{\mathcal{I}}) \setminus (\mathcal{CM}_{\mathcal{I}_p} \cup \mathcal{CP}_{\mathcal{I}_p} \cup \mathcal{F}_{\mathcal{I}_p})\right|} \tag{7.12}$$

$$\Pi_{A/\mathcal{HH}} = \frac{|\mathcal{CM}_{\mathcal{I}} \cup \mathcal{CP}_{\mathcal{I}} \cup \mathcal{A} \cup \mathcal{HH}|}{|\mathcal{CM}_{\mathcal{I}} \cup \mathcal{CP}_{\mathcal{I}} \cup \mathcal{F}_{\mathcal{I}} \cup \mathcal{A} \cup \mathcal{HH}|} \tag{7.13}$$

The values of these six measures on the test corpus [Metal] make use of the number of correct and incorrect extended co-occurrences that involve prefixing. For modification co-occurrences the values are $\mathcal{CM}_{C_p} = 2$ and $\mathcal{CM}_{\mathcal{I}_p} = 98$, and for permutation co-occurrences $\mathcal{CP}_{C_p} = 1$ and $\mathcal{CP}_{\mathcal{I}_p} = 82$.

$$R = \frac{223}{382} = 58.4\% \quad R_{\neg p} = \frac{212}{368} = 57.6\% \quad R_{A/\mathcal{HH}} = \frac{373}{532} = 70.1\% \tag{7.14}$$

$$\Pi = \frac{709}{973} = 72.9\% \quad \Pi_{\neg p} = \frac{529}{563} = 90.9\% \quad \Pi_{A/\mathcal{HH}} = \frac{859}{1123} = 76.5\% \tag{7.15}$$

Comments on the Measure of Quality

Basic precision and recall values ($P = 45.8\%$ and $R = 58.4\%$) for the extraction of morphosyntactic variants are disappointing results. One of the reasons for this relatively poor performance is that the intended task is much more difficult than the task of syntactic variant extraction proposed in chapter 5. A second and more specific cause of error is the exploitation of prefixing in the morphological links. Most prefixed co-occurrences ($391/405 = 96.5\%$) are incorrect variations and should be discarded unless they convey some interesting conceptual link.

In order to observe and isolate the specificity of prefixed variations, the volume of prefixed variations is detailed in table 7.8. Interestingly a high proportion of the incorrect prefixed filtered variants correspond either to generic/specific relations between hyper- and hyponyms such as *Electromagnetic field/magnetic field* (140/211 = 66.3%) or to antonym relations such as *Continuous precipitation/discontinuous precipitation* (10/211 = 4.7%). These two semantic relations are not explicitly rejected by definition 1.1, but they do not correspond to the classical synonymy link between a variant and a controlled term observed so far. This is the reason these variants are considered separately.

There are two possibilities for not considering the majority of nonsynonym prefixed variants as incorrect: either prefixed variants are systematically rejected or hypo/hypernyms and antonym variants are considered as correct and, in this second case, prefixed variants are not discarded. The values of precision, recall, and precision of fallout corresponding to these two possibilities are given in table 7.9 and in formulas (7.14) and (7.15). As indicated above, the values indexed with "$\neg p$" correspond to the results without prefixed variants and the values indexed "$\mathcal{A}/\mathcal{H}\mathcal{H}$" correspond to the results with prefixed variants in which antonyms and hyper/hyponyms are considered as correct. Obviously variant extraction without prefixed variants is more accurate ($P_{\neg p} = 80.0\%$), but recall is not improved ($R_{\neg p} = 57.6\%$). On the contrary, if both prefixed variants are conserved and antonyms and generic/specific relations are accepted as correct variants, both recall and precision are satisfactory ($P_{\mathcal{A}/\mathcal{H}\mathcal{H}} = 74.3\%$ and $R_{\mathcal{A}/\mathcal{H}\mathcal{H}} = 70.1\%$).

Thus this technique for extracting morphosyntactic variations offers satisfactory performance if the extraction is not restricted to synonymous links. This additional constraint is not problematic because nonsynonymous links can be easily separated from the bulk of the variants and classified into antonyms (prefixes *dis-*, *de-*, and *in-*) and hyper/hyponyms (all the remaining prefixes).

In addition to the sources of syntactic errors that are reported in section 5.5.1 for syntactic variants, some specific errors are due to incorrect morphological relations:

• *Irrelevant morphosemantic links*. These are due to the synchronic evolution of language or to polysemous roots. For example, *different adsorbate systems* is not a variant of *Differential systems* because *differential* is much more specific than *different*. *Differential* only refers to a technical meaning in mathematics, physics, or economy, whereas *different* belong to both general and technical languages. Similarly the morphological family of *form* contains weakly semantically related words such as *conform, formalism, formation, malformation, nonconformism, reform, transformation, uniform, formula, formidable,* and *conformity* that are likely to produce incorrect variants.

• *Irrelevant morphosemantic compound links*. The irrelevancy here is due to the complexity of compounding semantics. According to (Corbin 1992; Corbin 1997) words such as *monoxide* or *dioxide* are compounds composed of two morphemes and the construction of the meaning is a composition of both meanings. On the contrary, the meaning of suffixed or prefixed words results from the modification of the root through a regular operation attached to the prefix or the suffix. According to this simplified semantic differentiation, the semantic link between two compounds sharing a morpheme (in the same head position) is looser than two prefixed and/or suffixed words sharing the same root. For this reason *carbon monoxide* is not a variant of *Carbon dioxide*.

The Case of Double Morphological Transformations

Double morphosyntactic variations, such as *studied with photoemission experiments* a variant of *Experimental study*, bring into play two morphological relations, here a Noun to Verb relation (*study/studied*) and an Adjective to Noun relation (*experimental/experiment*).[48] A priori the possible combinations of morphological relations is high: since eight different morphological transformations are encountered in single morphosyntactic variants (see table 7.7), there are 64 possible different binary associations of morphological transformations in double morphosyntactic variants.

For the purpose of determining the actual binary variations encountered in the corpus, a set of metarules is defined for catching extended co-occurrences of binary terms with two morphological links. For example, the following DoubDerP metarule describes a double variation with crossing morphological links in a window of at most eleven words. Such a metarule permits the extraction of *studied experimentally*, a variant of *Experimental study*.

$$\text{Metarule DoubDerP}(X_1 \rightarrow X_2\,X_3) \equiv X_1 \rightarrow X_5\,\langle X^{0-9} \rangle\,X_4: \tag{7.16}$$

$\langle X_3\ root \rangle \doteq \langle X_5\ root \rangle$

$\langle X_2\ root \rangle \doteq \langle X_4\ root \rangle.$

Surprisingly the actual number of binary morphological links is lower than 64, the number of theoretically possible combinations. Only ten associations are encountered in the [Metal] corpus. Since the observation is made on a relatively small corpus, these results should be considered as preliminary investigations. More systematic investigations are necessary for determining the actual range of possible double transformations. Table 7.10 shows the different types of double variations together with examples and counts from the [Metal] corpus. As in the case of single morphological links, these variations divide into modifications and permutations. The counts provided in the table cumulate both types of occurrences.

The next section gives another view of the experimental results collected by *FASTR* through the extraction of morphosyntactic variants. The number of syntactic variants extracted from [Metal] are compared with the numbers of term occurrences and the numbers of syntactic variants given in section 5.5.2.

Table 7.10
Double morphosyntactic variations on [Metal]

Type	Controlled term	Variant	Occurrences
A–N/N–V	*Atomic arrangement*	*atoms arranged*	15
A–Av/N–V	*Rapid solidification*	*rapidly solidified*	13
N–V/N–V	*Comparison measurement*	*measured spectrum is compared*	3
N–N/N–V	*Pressure test*	*tested in compression*	3
A–Av/N–A	*Chemical reaction*	*chemically active*	1
N–V/N–A	*Measurement accuracy*	*measured phonon frequencies accurately*	1
A–N/N–N	*Atomic arrangement*	*atom rearrangements*	7
A–N/N–A	*Atomic structure*	*structural relaxation of the atoms*	1
N–V/N–Av	*Measurement accuracy*	*accurately measured*	2
V–N/N–V	*Ionized radiation*	*irradiated with argon ions*	1

Table 7.11
Absolute and relative text coverage of terms and variants on [Metal]

	Term occurrences	Syntactic variants	Morphosyntactic variants	Total
Surface	5,993	2,377	1,373	9,743
Ratio of total surface	5.0%	2.0$	1.1%	7.1%
Relative ratio of conceptual surface	61.5%	24.4%	14.1%	100.0%

7.3.2 Quantitative Evaluation

Table 7.11 shows the absolute and the relative text coverage of morphosyntactic variants. As with syntactic variations, the numbers are measured on the manually checked term and variant occurrences extracted from the test corpus [Metal] with the test term list [Pascal-Metal]. Morphosyntactic variants are composed of correct variants plus antonyms and hyper/hyponyms.

The recognition of morphosyntactic variants changes the composition of the text coverage of terms and variants when compared with tables 5.25 and 5.26. Morphosyntactic variants cover an additional 1% of the text. They represent 14% of the surface covered by terms and syntactic and morphosyntactic variants. This evaluation also shows that morphosyntactic variants represent 36.6% of the variants identified so far by *FASTR*. For a correct identification of terms in a document, it is necessary to cope with these variants which contain a significant ratio of the concepts encountered in a document.

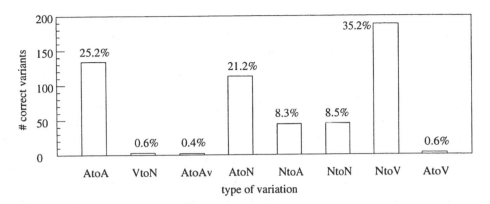

Figure 7.1
Distributions of correct morpho-syntactic variants among types of variations in [Metal].

The comparison between the number of extended co-occurrences and the number correct morphosyntactic variants shows that only 532 of the 1,355 extended co-occurrences are correct variants. Thus the percentage of correct extended co-occurrences is 39.2%, a ratio lower than 46.1%, the ratio of correct co-occurrences reported in section 5.5.2. This observation reinforces the claim that a proper term recognition cannot be performed on pure surface observation; it calls for sophisticated linguistic modules that can differentiate spurious co-occurrences from correct variants. The low rate of correct variants among co-occurrences also justifies a posteriori that the quality of extraction is lower for morphosyntactic variant than for syntactic variants.

As shown in figure 7.1, variations are not distributed evenly among the different families of morphosyntactic transformations. The three main families of variants are Adjective to Adjective variants (25.2%), Adjective to Noun variants (21.3%), and Noun to Verb variants (35.3%), which represent more than a third of the observed syntactic variants. From this distribution it can be deduced that focusing on these three families should improve the metagrammar of English. These results are difficult to predict without experimental observation. For example, the fact that there are 2.5 times more Adjective to Noun variations than Noun to Adjective variations is counterintuitive because there are 2.7 times fewer Adjective–Noun terms than Noun–Noun terms in the controlled term list [Pascal-Metal].

7.4 Summary

This chapter has investigated techniques for the recognition of morphosyntactic variants. These variants cover structural and morphological transformations of terms such as *abused intravenous drugs*, a variant of *Drug abuse* in which both types of changes are observed. The noun *abuse* is transformed into a past participle and the syntactic structure of the term is modified: a noun phrase with a Noun–Noun structure is transformed into a verb phrase with a Verb–Object structure. The enhanced version of *FASTR* proposed for extracting this new type of variant relies on a powerful combination of a feature-based formalism, a transformation mechanism, and a finite-state mechanism. These expansions to *FASTR* are an extension of the developments presented in the preceding chapters and introduce semantic variation developed in the next chapter.

The features for the recognition of morphosyntactic variants are expressed at two levels of the formalism of *FASTR*:

• *At the single-word level*. The root of morphologically structured lexical entries is expressed in their feature structure. Entries for which no root is given are considered to be their own root. The assumption underlying this representation is that each word has only one root. Thus the lexicon of single words can be organized into morphological families of words sharing the same root. Two different techniques are presented for the construction of these families. The first one, for the English language, uses the CELEX database in which the morphological structure of words including roots, prefixes, and suffixes is provided. The second one, for the French language, relies on a stemming algorithm based on graphical word endings and inflection paradigms.

• *At the metarule level*. The fact that a word can be morphologically transformed in a term variation is expressed by stating that the word in the original term and the word in the variant share the same root. This expression can be formulated for more than one word, thus allowing multiple morphological transformations in morphosyntactic variations.

These two enhancements of the formalisms are accompanied by modifications of the parser in order to support these new morphological links. The concept of lexicalization exploited in the optimizing of the application for the extraction of syntactic variants is replaced by a concept of extended lexicalization in this new framework: rules are linked to morphological families instead of single lexical entries.

Because of the syntactic flexibility of morphosyntactic variations, the formalism had to be enriched with regular expressions and accordingly, to provide the parser with a compiler of regular expressions into finite-state automata. The combination of a unification-based formalism for a rich linguistic description of the frontier words and a finite-state machine for a shallow representation of syntactic structures results in an efficient transformational analyzer. The tool is appropriate for the task at hand, the description of variable linguistic expressions of concepts in technical documents.

These new features of *FASTR* are used for devising a metagrammar of morphosyntactic variations in English on a medical corpus. The work presented in this chapter is restricted to variations of binary terms involving only one morphological transformation. Five main families of term variations are studied: three families of heterocategorial variants composed of Noun to Adjective and Adjective to Noun variants, Noun to Verb and Verb to Noun variants, and Adjective to Adverb variants, and two families of isocategorial variants, Noun to Noun and Adjective to Adjective variants. Each type of variation is associated with a set of metarules empirically tuned through experiments on the [Medic] corpus with the [Pascal] term list. The strength of the linguistic analysis performed on these types of variants is its solid experimental grounding. This makes the approach directly usable in real-world natural language processing.

The final part of this chapter is devoted to the evaluation of the metagrammar and the morphological families on [Metal], a test corpus in a different technical domain. Quality and size of extractions are reported. As in the case of syntactic variants, the quality of morphosyntactic term extraction is measured with precision, recall, and precision of fallout. As for the size of the extraction, I measure the textual coverage of texts by terms and variants. I also report in detail the relative importance of the different families of term variations.

These measures show that the extraction of morphosyntactic variations is a challenging task because it highlights an unexplored domain of corpus terminology, the nonnominal term occurrences. The numbers of morphosyntactic variants are important and cannot be detected through simplistic co-occurrence observations. The extension of *FASTR* devised for this task yields very satisfactory results, in terms of precision and recall, even though the technique adopted does not produce analyses of sentences. The partial and transformational text processing adopted in this work felicitously marries efficiency and accuracy. It is a knowledge rich text mining technique that reports new linguistic phenomena, namely morphosyntactic variations, used by language for expressing the same concept under diverse linguistic forms.

8 Semantic Variation and Applications

In this chapter a final type of term variation is presented: *semantic variation*. As in the case of morphological variants, semantic variants are determined on the basis of elementary relationships among single words. Since semantic variation interact with morphological and syntactic variation, the new descriptive framework permits the combination of semantic links, morphological links, and structural transformations.

In addition some interesting applications of variant recognition to other related domains are presented: multilinguality, cross-lingual information retrieval, and cascaded information retrieval combining Web search and variant recognition.

8.1 Semantic Variation

FASTR is designed as a generic transformational parser that relies on syntactic transformations and morphological links between words in the base term and words in the variant. The same technological framework is now expanded in order to recognize semantic variants: in addition to morphological links, semantic links are expressed between source and target words. These variations represent the most generic family of terminological transformations; they are described in early studies on the application of natural language processing techniques to information management such as (Dunham, Pacak, and Pratt 1978). Recent studies propose large scale domain independent techniques for semantic variant recognition. Next section focuses on two of them and shows how the *FASTR* approach is related with these studies. First, a technique for *conceptual indexing* that amounts to the recognition of semantic variants is proposed for the English language by Woods (1997) and Ambroziak and Woods (1998). Second, a systematic description of semantic variants in the domain of industrial electricity is proposed for the French language by Hamon, Nazarenko, and Gros (1998). In the *IRENA* system (Arampatzis, Koster, and Tsoris 1997; Arampatzis et al. 1998), a notion of lexicosemantic similarity is also proposed. It is briefly described in section 2.3.6: the semantic similarity of two head/argument dependencies relies on the semantic relations of the heads and/or the arguments. However, more cannot be said on this proposition because of the lack of detail in the publication presenting the notion.

8.1.1 Related Work

The introductory chapter claims that an in-depth understanding of large textual databases is not a task at hand. Initial work on conceptual indexing, such as DeJong (1982) or Mauldin (1991), was focused on specific domains such as astronomy because the conceptual analysis of documents proposed in these studies required significant domain expertise. Such a situation is not realistic for processing large databases without involving a knowledge engineer in the loop.

A form of conceptual indexing is, however, possible on large data sets provided that no full analysis of the documents is required. For this purpose, an alternative solution to conceptual indexing is proposed in Woods (1997) and Ambroziak and Woods (1998). It relies on two basic processes: *subsumption* and *relaxation ranking* retrieval. Subsumption is used to take into consideration semantic variants and relaxation ranking to make correspondences between corpus occurrences and terminological forms in a query.

Through subsumption, complex terms are added into a conceptual taxonomy together with related concepts. For instance, *automobile steam cleaning* is related with *automobile cleaning*, *automobile upholstery cleaning*, *automobile washing*, and *car washing*. The assimilation of a new concept is performed by assigning a conceptual structure to the initial phrase and by determining what are the other related concepts and what relationships should be established between these concepts. The taxonomy is organized on the basis of generality (by subsumption). The structural subsumption between phrases depends on subsumption relationships among their constituents and a taxonomy of lexical atoms.

Relaxation ranking is a weighted approximate matching between a request and a document. The purpose of relaxation ranking is to find places in the indexed documents where the elements of a request are represented as nearly in the same configuration as in the initial request. Each relaxation from a requested concept to the actual occurrence is combined into a weighted penalty score.

The basic semantic relation used in Woods (1997) and Ambroziak and Woods (1998) is subsumption which corresponds to the *kind-of* relationship in KL-One like systems (Brachman and Schmolze 1985). Synonymy is considered as a reciprocal subsumption in which neither of both synonyms is more generic than the other one. There are, however, other types of semantic relationships between single words, each of them can be used to deduce semantic relationships between multi-word terms.

The study of Hamon, Nazarenko, and Gros (1998) describes several types of semantic variations that depend on the type of the atomic semantic relationships and on the position of the related words in the phrases. Basically semantic variations are recognized in case of synonymous relations between single words. Unlike Woods (1997), Hamon, Nazarenko, and Gros (1998) do not use transitivity because they claim it produces erroneous relationships. The second difference between these two studies is that Hamon and his colleagues calculate variation links between candidate terms that are produced by an automatic term extractor instead of using terms from a thesaurus. Last, these authors are not concerned by automatic indexing and finding text occurrences of queries. In Hamon, Nazarenko, and Gros (1998) three configurations are distinguished for calculating semantic relations between multi-word terms: synonymous head words, synonymous arguments, and simultaneously synonymous heads and arguments. The last case is reported to be rare and inaccurate (around 10% precision).

In addition to synonymy, it is shown that meronymy relationships (part-whole) and antonymy relationships between multi-word terms are produced from synonymy links between single words. For instance, *safety report* is a meronym of *safety analysis*, though *report* and *analysis* are given as synonyms in the atomic taxonomy. Similarly an antonymous relationship between *mechanical control* and *automatic order* is inferred from the synonymy of *mechanical* and *automatic*.

In both preceding studies the focus is on semantics. In Woods (1997) a sophisticated semantic representation of phrases is built. Then each new concept is inserted in relation with its most specific subsumer(s) and most generic subsumee(s). In Hamon, Nazarenko, and Gros (1998) attention is paid to the nature of the semantic relationship between two complex phrases in correlation with the semantic relationship between the single words. In this chapter the focus is on the interaction between syntax and semantics. In the chapters 3 to 5 the efforts were devoted to the modeling of the variant structures, highlighting the complex interactions between elementary transformations. In introducing morphological variations in chapter 7, we insisted on the synergy of morphological and syntactic transformations. This approach to semantics is also strongly connected to structural modifications: it relies on the correlation of structural transformations, morphological modifications, and semantic relationships.

8.1.2   Semantic Variation in *FASTR*

The case of morphosyntactic term variations, studied in chapter 7, can be seen as a special case of semantic variation. The conflation of two terms, in which two single words are morphologically related, such as *Muscle contraction* and *muscle contracted*, is legitimate if and only if the words *contraction* and *contracted* are semantically related. This is the case in the current example, but the verb *to contract* can have other meanings even in a restricted domain such as medicine: for instance, a patient can *contract* a disease. This meaning of the word *to contract* would not be acceptable in a variation of *Muscle contraction*.

In order to recognize semantic variations, the formalism of *FASTR* has been expanded and accepts semantic relationships between a word in a term and a word in a variant structure. For instance, *benign mouse skin tumors* can be recognized a semantic variant of *benign neoplasms* provided that there is a semantic link between the words *tumors* and *neoplasms* and that the insertion of the modifier *mouse skin* is accepted. This variation can be seen as a generalization of a modification—the insertion of a modifier between the argument and the head word presented in section 5.1.2—in which a semantic relationship between the head words is accepted.

In Jacquemin (1999) experiments on large-scale extraction of semantic variations are described for the French and English languages. Metarules are described for the English language and evaluations are performed on French data-sets. The semantic links used for extracting semantic variants in English are synonymy links of WordNet 1.6 (Fellbaum 1998). In Morin and Jacquemin (1999) corpus-based hyponymy links are used instead of thesaurus-based semantic links for extracting semantic variants.

The complete set of metarules for the English language is given in appendix A.5. Examples of semantic variations from [Medic] are given in tables 8.1 and 8.2. In the first column the identifier of the variation given in appendix A.5 is reported. The second column indicates the type of morphosyntactic variation and the third column gives the location of the semantic link (whether Head or Argument). The semantically related words are underlined.

The different types of variations are grouped into four prototypes:

• Semantic variation on the argument word The occurrence *transmissible disease* is a semantic variant of *Genetic disease* in which the arguments *transmissible* and *genetic* are linked by a synonymy link provided by WordNet 1.6. It is extracted by the following metarule of *FASTR*:

Metarule $\text{SemArg1}(N_1 \rightarrow X_2\,N_3) \equiv N_1 \rightarrow X_4\,N_3$:

$\neg(\langle X_4\ agreement\ number \rangle \doteq \text{'}plural\text{'})$

$\langle X_2\ cat \rangle \doteq \langle X_4\ cat \rangle$

$\langle X_2\ syn \rangle \doteq \langle X_4\ syn \rangle.$

The last equation in the metarule expresses that the argument word in the source term (X_2) and the argument word in the variant (X_4) are semantically related by a synonymy link to at least one common word.

For the English language, each word is linked to all the words in the synsets of Word-Net 1.6 to which it belongs. Thus *genetic* is linked to *familial*, *hereditary*, *inherited*, *transmitted*, *transmissible*, *genic*, and *genetical*. Similarly *transmissible* is linked to *catching*, *communicable*, *contagious*, *contractable*, *transmittable*, *familial*, *genetic*, *hereditary*, and *inherited*. In addition each word is linked to itself by a synonymy link. The equation $\langle X_2\ syn \rangle \doteq \langle X_4\ syn \rangle$ is satisfied because *transmissible* and *genetic* share five common synonyms: *familial*, *hereditary*, *inherited*, *transmissible*, and *genetic*.

• Double semantic variation on the argument and head words The variant *observational work* is a double semantic variant of *Experimental study* exploiting two synonymy links from WordNet 1.6. It is extracted by the following metarule:

Metarule $\text{SemArgHead}(N_1 \rightarrow X_2\,N_3) \equiv N_1 \rightarrow X_4\,N_5$:

$\neg(\langle X_4\ agreement\ number \rangle \doteq \text{'}plural\text{'})$

$\langle X_2\ syn \rangle \doteq \langle X_4\ syn \rangle$

$\langle X_2\ cat \rangle \doteq \langle X_4\ cat \rangle$

$\langle N_3\ syn \rangle \doteq \langle N_5\ syn \rangle.$

Table 8.1
Semantic and morphosemantic variants from [Medic]: Part 1

Id	Variant type	Semantic link	Controlled term and variant
SemArg1	—	Argt	Term: *Reaction rate*
	Variant: *response rate*		
SemHead2	—	Head	Term: *Anterior segment*
	Variant: *anterior part*		
CoorSemArg3	Head Coor	Argt	Term: *Primary response*
	Variant: *basal secretory activity and response*		
CoorSemHead4	Head Coor	Head	Term: *Cell death*
	Variant: *cell infiltration and destruction*		
CoorSemArg5	Argt Coor	Argt	Term: *Primary school*
	Variant: *elementary and intermediate school*		
CoorSemHead6	Argt Coor	Head	Term: *Electrical stimulus*
	Variant: *electrical and magnetic stimulation*		
CoorSemArg7	Argt Coor	Argt	Term: *Morphological change*
	Variant: *morphologic, ultrastructural and immunologic changes*		
CoorSemHead8	Argt Coor	Head	Term: *Respiratory distress*
	Variant: *respiratory, circulatory and alimentary problems*		
CoorSemHead9	Argt Coor	Head	Term: *Hypothesis test*
	Variant: *hypothesis, comparability, randomized and nonrandomized trials*		
InsSemArg13	Ins	Argt	Term: *Steady flow*
	Variant: *constant gas flow*		
InsSemHead14	Ins	Head	Term: *Plastic surgery*
	Variant: *plastic reconstructive procedures*		
InsSemArg15	Ins	Argt	Term: *Supernumerary chromosome*
	Variant: *extra copies of chromosomes*		
InsSemHead16	Ins	Head	Term: *malignant tumor*
	Variant: *malignant transformation of cutaneous neoplasms*		
InsSemHead20	Ins	Head	Term: *Pressure decline*
	Variant: *pressure (IOP) reduction*		
InsSemArg21	Ins	Argt	Term: *Electrical stimulus*
	Variant: *electric, acoustic stimuli*		

• Syntacticosemantic variation The two preceding variants are "pure" semantic variants in the sense that they do not involve structural or morphological transformations. However, each syntactic variation presented in chapter 5 and each morphosyntactic variation presented in chapter 7 can be transformed into an hybrid semantic variation by adding semantic links in the metarules. For instance, each coordination variation can be converted into a syntacticosemantic variation by adding a semantic link between the head or the argument word. Thus the occurrence *response and delay times* is a variant of *Reaction time* that

Table 8.2
Semantic and morphosemantic variants from [Medic]: Part 2

Id	Variant type	Semantic link	Controlled term and variant
PermSemArg22	Perm	Argt	Term: *Static* pressure
	Variant: *pressure was stable*		
PermSemArg24	Perm	Head	Term: *Heterogeneous reaction*
	Variant: *response is heterogeneous*		
PermSemArg27	Perm	Argt	Term: *Return* rate
	Variant: *rate of recurrence*		
PermSemArg28	Perm	Head	Term: *Pressure decline*
	Variant: *decrease in the mean arterial blood pressure*		
NtoASemHead32	Head NtoA	Head/Argt	Term: *Reaction* specificity
	Variant: *specific response*		
AtoNSemHead35	Argt AtoN	Head	Term: *Constrictive band*
	Variant: *constriction rings*		
AtoNSemHead36	Argt AtoN	Head	Term: *respiratory distress*
	Variant: *difficulty with respiration*		
AtoAvSemHead37	Argt AtoAv	Head	Term: *Surgical wound*
	Variant: *surgically generated lesions*		
AtoASemHead38	Argt AtoA	Head	Term: *Optical system*
	Variant: *optic Nd-YAG laser unit*		
NtoNSemArg39	Head NtoN	Argt	Term: *Simultaneous* measurement
	Variant: *concurrent measures*		
NtoNSemArg40	Argt NtoN	Argt	Term: *Flow* limit
	Variant: *airflow limitation*		
NtoVSemArg43	Head NtoV	Argt	Term: *Language* development
	Variant: *developed good speech*		
NtoVSemArg44	Head NtoV	Arg	Term: *Hypothesis* test
	Variant: *possibility was tested*		

involves simultaneously an argument coordination and a semantic link (a synonymy link on the argument word). It is extracted by the following metarule:

Metarule CoorSemArg5($N_1 \rightarrow X_2\ N_3$) $\equiv$ $N_1 \rightarrow X_4\ C_4\ \langle\{A|N|Np|V\}^{1-3}\rangle\ N_3$:

$\neg(\langle X_4\ agreement\ number\rangle \doteq\ 'plural')$

$\langle X_2\ syn\rangle \doteq \langle X_4\ syn\rangle$

$\langle X_2\ cat\rangle \doteq \langle X_4\ cat\rangle.$

• Morphosyntactico-semantic variation Similarly morphosyntactic variations can combine with semantic relationships. In order to maintain a reasonable level of complexity, morphological and semantic links are not composed. Instead, semantic and morphological relationships are stated on different pairs of words. For instance, a noun to noun morphological relationship between argument words can be associated with a semantic link between head words and result in the occurrence *developed good speech*, a variant of *Language development*. The variation is modeled by the following metarule:

Metarule NtoVSemHead42($N_1 \rightarrow N_2\ N_3$)

$$\equiv N_1 \rightarrow V_3\ \langle\langle D\ \{N|Np\}^?\ P\rangle^?\ D^?\ \{A|N|Np|V\}^{0-3}\rangle\ N_5:$$

$$\langle V_3\ root \rangle \doteq \langle N_3\ root \rangle$$

$$\langle N_2\ syn \rangle \doteq \langle N_5\ syn \rangle.$$

As indicated by the preceding examples, semantic variations combine with syntactic and morphosyntactic variations resulting in a large number of possible variational schemata.

In Jacquemin (1999) an evaluation of semantic term extraction is reported for the French language. The corpus is a 1.2 million word corpus of scientific abstracts in the agricultural domain [AGRIC] from INIST/CNRS. Two types of semantic links are exploited: links from the specialized thesaurus AGROVOC (a multilingual thesaurus in the agricultural domain; AGROVOC 1995) and links from the thesaurus of the word processor Microsoft Word97.[49] The semantic variations extracted by the metagrammar for the French language with these two semantic databases have been manually inspected for evaluation purpose.

The semantic links from AGROVOC yield 122 correct semantic variations, while the semantic links from Word97 produce 747 semantic variations. The semantic variations from the specialized thesaurus represent 5% of the variants while the variations from the Word97 thesaurus represent 24% of the variants. Since AGROVOC links are more accurate semantic relationships, the precision of the variants extracted with the links from AGROVOC outperforms the precision of the variants relying on the relationships from the thesaurus of the word processor. Table 8.3 compares the precision obtained with these two semantic databases in semantic variant extraction ([AGRIC] corpus).

Most extraction errors are due to polysemy. For instance, *white subjects* (white people who are the subjects of an examination) is extracted as a variant of *White matter* (a part of the brain) because of the semantic relationship between *matter* and *subject*. The spurious variation is due to the polysemy of the two semantically related words: *matter* and *subject*. These words are synonymous when they both denote the theme of an intellectual work. However, in this example, *matter* means substance, while *subject* means a person in an experimental context.

Despite word polysemy, the precision values for pure semantic variants reported in table 8.3 are high (78% of the Microsoft Word97 thesaurus and 91% for the AGROVOC thesaurus). The good results are due to the context in which semantic links are exploited.

Table 8.3
Precision of semantic variant extraction ([AGRIC] corpus)

	Word97	AGROVOC
Semantic variant (Argument)	76.3%	88.9%
Semantic variant (Head)	82.7%	91.3%
Total (semantic variants)	**78.1%**	**91.0%**
Coor + semantic link	44.8%	62.6%
Modif + semantic link	55.6%	87.5%
A to N + semantic link	44.9%	0.0%
N to A + semantic link	21.3%	0.0%
N to N + semantic link	0.0%	60.0%
N to V + semantic link	24.2%	44.4%
Total (morphosyntactico-semantic variants)	**29.4%**	**55.0%**

All the semantic relationships used to extract semantic variant are formulated in the context of a multi-word term. In such a small context the remaining content words disambiguate the semantically related words and eliminate the spurious variants in which the words would have different meaning. However some incorrect variants remain, such as the preceding example in which the adjective *white* is not selective enough to avoid a spurious variant. Such cases are fortunately rare.

In conclusion, restricting the use of semantic links to small contexts, with stable words in the vicinity of semantically related words, yields a high-quality semantic variant. Semantic variant recognition is not facing the difficulties that have been observed for semantic expansion in the information retrieval framework of Voorhees (1998). The lower part of table 8.3 shows that the combination of semantic variation with syntactic and/or morphological variation yields poorer results. The combination of semantic relation with other transformations tend to diminish the quality of the resulting variation. A deeper linguistic analysis remains to be done on semantic disambiguation and on the interaction of semantic relationships with morphosyntactic transformations in order to improve the quality of hybrid variations.

The presentation of semantic variation concludes the description of the different levels of variations that are currently accepted by *FASTR*. The transformational paradigm introduced for syntactic variations in chapters 3 to 5 concerns only the structural level. It was enriched by a paradigmatic level in chapter 7, and in this chapter, in order to express morphological and semantic relationships between single words. The high quality of the variants observed at the different levels and the descriptive facility of metarules demonstrate that the transformational paradigm is well adapted to the recognition of term variation. Semantic variant recognition by *FASTR* combines descriptive economy (because no explicit semantic description is required) and computational efficiency (because transformations can be implemented on transducers).

However, there are some promising applications and extensions of term variant recognition; they are presented in the next section.

8.2   Applications

The linguistic observations and the companion computational techniques developed in this book can be directly embedded in applications for automatic indexing. Normalized occurrences of terms can serve as phrase indexes for subsequent information access. The purpose of this section is to show that the recognition—or the generation—of term variants can be implemented in several other applications and serve a wide range of purposes. This line of research contains the seed for many other promising developments.

8.2.1   Multilinguality

The automatic term recognition approach presented in this book was conceived to support variant description in different languages. For this reason the application is composed of two distinct entities: a generic parser including a unifier and a variant generator, and the linguistic data associated with each language. Correct term spotting depends on good synergy between three different types of linguistic data: a list of single words with morphological and semantic links, a list of term rules, and a list of metarules that describe term variations.

In this book *FASTR* is applied to the English language, but other studies report similar work using French (Jacquemin, Klavans, and Tzoukermann 1997; Klavans, Jacquemin, and Tzoukermann 1997; Tzoukermann, Klavans, and Jacquemin 1997; Jacquemin and Tzoukermann 1999). The different linguistic systems for French and English result in different kinds of variations. Permutation does not exist in French because as a Romance language it is without Germanic compounding. French terms have a left-headed noun phrase structure: a nominal head with postmodifiers. However, French terms with a N P N structure can undergo *synapsy variations* (see section 2.2.4): the addition of a determiner before the second noun or the change of central preposition. For instance, *récolte de fruits* (fruit crop) is a synapsy variant of *récolte en fruits* in which the preposition *de* is replaced by *en*. Thus the three main families of variations in French are modifications/substitutions, coordinations, and synapsies. More details about the metarules in French are provided in the aforementioned publications.

In order to validate the capacity of *FASTR* to be extended to other languages with different linguistic rules, linguistic data—and, particularly, metarules—are currently being designed for the three following languages:

• Spanish and Catalan (in cooperation with Jorge Vivaldi, University Pompeu Fabra, Barcelona),

• German (in cooperation with Antje Schmidt-Wigger, Institut zur Förderung der Angewandten Informationsforschung, Saarbrücken),

• Japanese (in cooperation with Kyo Kageura and Fuyuki Yoshikane, National Center for Science Information Systems, Tokyo; published in Yoshikane et al. 1998).

8.2.2 Application of Variant Generation to Cross-Lingual Information Retrieval

The possibility of querying the same source documents in different languages has become popular in recent years. This topic is known a Cross-Lingual Information Retrieval (CLIR) and workshops on this theme were organized in ETHZ, Zurich (March 1997) and SIGIR 1997 (August 1997), for example. The purpose of CLIR (Grefenstette 1998) is to study techniques for accessing multilingual documents through queries in a single language without calling for document translation.

Multi-word term translation is known to be a complex problem in machine translation (Bouillon, Boesefeldt, and Russel 1992). This issue is addressed in the study on term translation for CLIR in Fluhr et al. (1998). Fluhr and his colleagues propose a technique for example-based translation of complex terms that relies on the combination of structural transformation and literal translation based on bilingual relationships between single words. Such a method can be straightforwardly implemented with *FASTR*, in which a mechanism for term variant generation is embedded. Instead of a blind translation, queries are translated in CLIR through the generation of cross-lingual variants followed by corpus investigation:

• Generation of candidate translations from cross-lingual pattern associations and word correspondences extracted from bilingual dictionaries. Starting from the English term *road map*, using the structural association $N_1 N_2 \rightarrow N_2 P N_1$ and the correspondences $T(road) = \{route, chemin, rue, voie\}$ and $T(map) = \{carte, plan\}$, the following candidates are generated: $\{carte\ de\ route, carte\ de\ chemin, carte\ de\ rue, carte\ de\ voie, plan\ de\ route, plan\ de\ chemin, plan\ de\ rue, plan\ de\ voie\}$.

• Corpus-based selection of correct translation based on term and variant extraction from corpora. The preceding candidates are now considered as a list of controlled terms. *FASTR* is used for extracting occurrences or morphosyntactic variants of these candidates in order to retain the correct variants.

The correct translation is *carte routière* in which *routière* (lit. roady) is an adjective built from the noun *route* (road) through suffixing. This translation is likely to be spotted by *FASTR* from *carte de route* through a noun to adjective variation such as:

$$\text{Metarule NtoA}(N_1 \rightarrow N_2\, P_3\, N_4) \equiv N_1 \rightarrow N_2\, A_5: \tag{8.1}$$

$$\langle N_4\ root \rangle \doteq \langle A_5\ root \rangle.$$

The key ideas of this proposition stem from earlier work on compound translation of Rackow, Dagan, and Schwall (1992). In this study compounds are translated through a transfer-based machine translation system that generates several competing target translations and selects the one that appears the most frequently in a corpus.

This approach differs from this earlier work in that it accepts a wide range of variants and does not interweave variation and transfer procedure. Instead, it uses a very simplistic transfer procedure which is complemented by the recognition of variations during corpus matching. It results in a more traceable approach of the discrepancies between candidate translations and selected corpus occurrences.

8.2.3 Document Filtering in Web Search

The tolerance of *FASTR* to term variability is a key quality for using *FASTR* in a system for information access through the Internet. First, Web search engines are known for their lack of consideration for linguistic variability. For example, plurals and singulars are not merged unless wild cards are being used at the end of the words (which may ultimately result in excessively inaccurate queries). Second, Web documents are typically not normalized. They include texts of various qualities and various origins in which similar concepts may be expressed through different linguistic formulations. Third, Web searchers produce lists of thousands of documents and leave to the user the task of selecting the most relevant documents.

Some preliminary experiments with *FASTR* for information access from the Internet showed an ability to take into account linguistic variability and to improve the filtering of documents.[50] A cascaded approach to Internet search was used along the same line as (Woods 1997). It combined a low-precision/high-recall retrieval through a classical Web search engine with blind query expansion followed by high-precision retrieval through term variant indexing. The experiment was divided into two steps:

1. *Query expansion.* During the expansion phase an Internet query is decomposed into binary dependencies and enriched with additional words. Additional words are taken in the morphological and/or semantic families of the words in the query. For example, the query *offers debt consolidation loans* is decomposed into three subqueries: *loan offer*,

consolidation loan, and *debt consolidation*. Then each subquery is enriched with words from the CELEX base that have the same root as the words in the subquery. (A similar expansion can be done on a semantic basis by adding synonymous words.) For example, the subquery *loan offer* is transformed into ((*loan | loans | loaned | loaning*)~(*offer | offers | offered | offering | offertory | offertories*)) in which | stands for disjunction and in which ~ is an operator that connects two expressions that must co-occur in a small text window (here ten words). The expanded subqueries are then provided to a Web search-engine and the *n*-best ranked documents are downloaded for subsequent filtering and re-ranking.

2. *Document filtering.* During this step the documents from the query expansion stage are processed by *FASTR* in order to spot the correct occurrences of the initial subqueries or their morphosyntactic or semantic variants. The documents that contain correct occurrences or variants of the three initial subqueries are ranked first. For example, the expanded subquery *loan offer* yields correct filtered occurrences such as *offering a fast on line real estate loan* or *offers all types of loans*.

The concurrent exploitation of, first, query expansion through the addition of semantically and morphologically related words and, then, document filtering through NLP with *FASTR* is likely to increase recall—because Web search engines do not perform any morphological nor semantic normalization—and to increase precision—because Web search engines exploit no linguistic information about the occurrences encountered in documents. Preliminary experiments indicate that the re-ranking of documents through the combination of linguistically motivated expansion and filtering is informationally relevant.

8.3   Other Interesting Directions

This chapter has sketched some complementary applications of term and variant spotting. Other works accompany the developments of *FASTR* over the last few years and are reported in other publications:

Corpus-Based Morphology

In Jacquemin (1997a) a specific mode of term variant recognition is implemented in *FASTR*. It relies on word truncation and co-occurrence. Through this nonmorphological stemming technique, new morphological families are discovered such as the relationship between *dopamine* and *dopaminergic* which results from the variation link between *dopamine transmission* and *dopamin-ergic transmission*. Such morphological relations are not encountered in exhaustive studies on English morphology, as by Marchand (1969), because they correspond to rare and domain-specific structures. The morphological associations extracted by

FASTR are ultimately clustered into morphological families through a greedy clustering technique based on a morphologically plausible distance.

Another approach to corpus-based morphology is proposed in Xu and Croft (1998) in which correlations between morphologically related words are found on statistical bases. The morphological links extracted from corpora are used by these authors to modify a stemmer in order to take into consideration language use in specific corpora.

Pre-parsing

In Jacquemin (1998b) it is shown how *FASTR* can be used as a bracketer in order to facilitate subsequent parsing or indexing. The occurrences of terms and variants generally constitute well-formed phrases or substructures of phrases that contain a head word and some of its contiguous modifiers. They can be combined in order to build shallow structures by organizing them in a hierarchical fashion. The texts thus structured can be iteratively parsed by *FASTR* for extracting new occurrences of terms and variants that will enrich the structures produced at the preceding step. The process halts when no new structure is built.

The brackets in the following sentence denote occurrences of terms and variants that are extracted through this iterative process: *La variation mensuelle de la [respiration du sol] et ses rapports avec l'[humidité et la [température du sol]] ont été [analysées dans le [sol] superficiel d'une [forêt] tropicale.]* (The monthly variation of the [respiration of the soil] and its correlations with the [moisture and the [temperature of the soil]] have been [analyzed in the surface [soil of a [tropical forest]]].) Through the algorithm for combining term occurrences into shallow structures, the last three occurrences are reorganized as follows: . . . *ont été [analysées dans le [sol superficiel d'une [forêt tropicale.]]]*

Term Clustering

Section 2.2 described a wide range of tools that are available for term acquisition. These tools provide terminologists with lists of candidate terms that are ultimately inserted into a thesaurus or a term bank. A pre-structuring of the candidates is desirable because the numbers of candidate terms acquired by term extractors form around 10% of the size of the corpus and because controlling and inserting the terminology into a database is a very demanding task.

For this purpose, I developed a two-step algorithm for the clustering of term candidates produced by the term extractor *LEXTER* (Bourigault 1994; Bourigault 1995). The work is reported in Bourigault and Jacquemin (1999). In the first step, terms are self-indexed: the set of candidate terms produced by *LEXTER* is considered as a corpus in which each term constitutes an individual sentence. This corpus of candidates is indexed on the candidates themselves through *FASTR*. In the second step, a graph of terms is built in which two terms are connected if and only if one of them is a variant of the other one. Then connected subgraphs are automatically calculated. Most of them have a star-shape structure with a central binary term such as *nucléole proéminent* (prominent nucleolus) and peripheral ternary variants such as *nucléole souvent proéminent* (frequently prominent nucleolus), *nucléole central proéminent* (central prominent nucleolus), and *nucléole parfois proéminent* (occasionally prominent nucleolus). This pre-structured terminology is then presented to the expert who can rely on the clusters to include only the central term in the conceptual database and to consider the other terms as linguistic variants. Since these terms have been recognized as variant by the indexer, they do not need to be included in the database to be subsequently recognized in documents.

Paraphrasing

Identification of thematically similar pieces of documents has several applications such as multi-document summarization in order to avoid redundancy (Barzilay, McKeown, and Elhadad 1999), information retrieval in order to facilitate identification of thematically similar documents or passages, document clustering in order calculate document similarity, translation memory in order to group semantically related samples, and text generation in order to tune the output of a generator by selecting the most relevant paraphrase in a given context (Iordanskaja, Kittredge, and Polguère 1991; Robin 1994; Dras 1997).

Identification of thematically related document requires detecting paraphrastic clauses or sentences. In Amghar and Levrat (1995) paraphrases are detected through a *generate and test* rule-based approach. Each rule represents a semantic transformation with lexical and semantic restrictions. In Barzilay, McKeown, and Elhadad (1999) sentences are first analyzed through a dependency-based parser. Then paraphrasing rules are used to relate canonical dependency forms of sentences.

The detection of term variants is a special case of paraphrase identification. For terms one of the compared structures is a noun phrase (the source term). *FASTR* could be extended to the recognition of paraphrastic sentences trough the definition of variation patterns in which both the source and the target structures are any type of phrase.

Domain Survey and Terminological Dynamics

It is a well-known fact that noun phrases represent the aboutness of a document. In Wacholder (1998) *LinkIt* uses simplex noun phrase extraction and head clustering to identify significant topics in a document. Judges agree that such head-clustered terms represent better the content of a document than keyword lists or repeated word sequences. However, since such well-organized simplex NPs only offer a static picture of the significant topics in documents, other techniques must be developed in order to observe the evolution of human knowledge.

In Polanco, Grivel, and Royauté (1995) terminological variation is exploited as a clue for analyzing the evolutions of scientific domains. Semantic drifts, creations of new terms through the modification or the combination of existing terminologies, imports of terminologies created in other neighboring domains, all these changes in terminological data reflect evolutions of sciences and techniques. They can be traced by observing term variations. Domains with higher rates of term variants are likely to be domains in which new concepts are produced, and correlatively, domains with high scientific productivity.

Along the same line, term variations are used by Ibekwe-SanJuan (1998) for analyzing trends and thematic evolutions of scientific domains. These results must be confirmed by more systematic studies on the correlation of terminological dynamics and scientific evolution. However, these works pave the way for very promising domains of research on the exploitation of term variability as a means for observing scientific evolution.

9 Conclusion

The exploitation of NLP techniques presented this book differs from preceding approaches to term spotting. It has focused on important, and to date unexplored, linguistic phenomena concerning the syntactic, morphosyntactic and semantic variations of terms that are encountered in technical and scientific documents. It proposes an original NLP technology based on local transformations, shallow unification-based parsing, and lexicalization that offers the necessary accuracy and efficiency for the tasks at hand.

The most natural approach to term recognition is to consider that terms are frozen expressions without modifications. This is, however, an ideal view of terms and it is inappropriate. The experimental results provided by this book show that variation is not an exceptional phenomenon. For the purpose of recognizing these variants, *FASTR* offers tools for spotting terms and variants together with a methodology for tuning the associated linguistic data.

Variations should not be connoted only negatively as an obstacle to the recognition of terms. Variation reveals facets of terms that would otherwise remain hidden. Through variations, terms combine with other terms, and thus allow for the acquisition of new terms and associated conceptual links. Through variations, verbal and adjectival phrases can be recognized as conceptually equivalent to nominal terms, and thus extend the domain of terminological knowledge beyond the frontiers of noun phrases. Through variations, corpus-based translation of terms is made possible despite its well-known difficulties. Through variations, scientific creativity can be observed and traced. Through variations, terms are considered as genuine linguistic objects reflecting the complexity and the richness of human cognition and not just frozen labels of concepts!

Although this work has simultaneously presented tools for term recognition and applications of variant recognition to other domains, much still remains to be done. First, other accurate descriptions of linguistic data for term recognition must be provided. For instance, Fabre (1998) explores the description of verbal variants and provides linguistic features that enhance significantly the quality of term extraction. Similarly Daille (1999) studies adjectival variants and focuses on a more accurate description of relational adjectives. Second, recognition of terms and variants can be applied to various domains in which data are corrupted and thus hard to process. For example, spotting terms in written transcriptions of speech documents, emails, or chat corpora are interesting challenges. Third, term normalization can also be applied as a means for improving other fields in computational terminology such as term acquisition, term understanding, or term translation. Some of these domains are currently explored at the author's laboratory (LIMSI-CNRS).

A Metarule Files

A.1 Paradigmatic Syntactic Metarules

```
Metarule Coor( X1 -> X2 X3 ) = X1 -> X2 (X{1-3}) C4 X3:.
Metarule Coor( X1 -> X2 X3 ) = X1 -> X2 C4 (X{1-3}) X3:.

Metarule Modif( X1 -> X2 X3 ) = X1 -> X2 (X{1-3}) X3:.

Metarule Perm( X1 -> X2 X3 ) = X1 -> X3 P4 (X{0-3}) X2:.

Metarule ExtC( X1 -> X2 X3 ) = X1 -> X2 X5 (X{4}) C4 X3:.
Metarule ExtC( X1 -> X2 X3 ) = X1 -> X2 C4 (X{4}) X3:.
Metarule ExtM( X1 -> X2 X3 ) = X1 -> X2 (X{4}) X3:.
Metarule ExtP( X1 -> X2 X3 ) = X1 -> X3 P4 (X{4}) X2:.
```

A.2 Filtering Syntactic Metarules

```
Metarule Coor( X1 -> X2 X3 ) = X1 -> X2 X5 C4 X3:
     <X2 cat> ! P
     <X5 cat> ! Pu.
Metarule Coor( X1 -> X2 X3 ) = X1 -> X2 C4 Pp5 X3:
     "pronominal coordination"
     <X2 number> = <Pp5 number>.
Metarule Coor( X1 -> X2 X3 ) = X1 -> X2 C4 X5 X3:
     <X2 number> ! plural
     <X5 number> ! plural
     <X5 cat> ! Pp
     <X5 cat> ! D.
Metarule Coor( X1 -> X2 X3 ) = X1 -> X2 X5 X6 C4 X3:
     <X2 number> ! plural
     <X5 number> ! plural
     <X5 cat> ! D
     <X5 cat> ! P
     <X5 cat> ! Pu
     <X6 cat> ! Pu.
Metarule Coor( X1 -> X2 X3 ) = X1 -> X2 C4 X5 X6 X3:
     <X2 number> ! plural
     <X5 number> ! plural
     <X6 number> ! plural
     <X5 cat> ! D
     <X6 cat> ! P.
```

```
Metarule Coor( X1 -> X2 X3 ) = X1 -> X2 X5 X6 X7 C4 X3:
     <X2 number> ! plural
     <X5 number> ! plural
     <X6 number> ! plural
     <X5 cat> ! C
     <X5 cat> ! D
     <X5 cat> ! P
     <X5 cat> ! Pu
     <X6 cat> ! C
     <X6 cat> ! D
     <X6 cat> ! P
     <X6 cat> ! Pu
     <X7 cat> ! C
     <X7 cat> ! D
     <X7 cat> ! P
     <X7 cat> ! Pu.
Metarule Coor( X1 -> X2 X3 ) = X1 -> X2 C4 X5 X6 X7 X3:
     <X2 number> ! plural
     <X5 number> ! plural
     <X6 number> ! plural
     <X7 number> ! plural
     <X5 cat> ! C
     <X5 cat> ! D
     <X5 cat> ! P
     <X5 cat> ! Pu
     <X6 cat> ! C
     <X6 cat> ! D
     <X6 cat> ! P
     <X6 cat> ! Pu
     <X7 cat> ! C
     <X7 cat> ! D
     <X7 cat> ! P
     <X7 cat> ! Pu.


Metarule Modif( X1 -> X2 X3 ) = X1 -> X2 X5 X3:
     "genitive"
     <X5 lemma> = 's'.
Metarule Modif( X1 -> X2 X3 ) = X1 -> X2 X5 X3:
     <X2 number> ! plural
     <X2 cat> ! P
     <X5 number> ! plural
     <X5 cat> ! D
```

```
        <X5 cat> ! P
        <X5 cat> ! C
        <X5 cat> ! Pu.
Metarule Modif( X1 -> X2 X3 ) = X1 -> X2 X5 X6 X3:
        <X2 number> ! plural
        <X2 cat> ! P
        <X5 cat> ! D
        <X5 number> ! plural
        <X5 lemma> ! 'be'
        <X5 lemma> ! 'have'
        <X5 cat> ! P
        <X5 cat> ! Pu
        <X6 number> ! plural
        <X6 cat> ! D
        <X6 cat> ! P
        <X6 cat> ! Pu.
Metarule Modif( X1 -> X2 X3 ) = X1 -> X2 X5 X6 X7 X3:
        "insertion between parentheses"
        <X2 number> ! plural
        <X2 cat> ! P
        <X5 lemma> = '('
        <X7 lemma> = ')'.
Metarule Modif( X1 -> X2 X3 ) = X1 -> X2 X5 X6 X7 X3:
        <X2 number> ! plural
        <X2 cat> ! P
        <X5 number> ! plural
        <X5 cat> ! D
        <X5 lemma> ! 'be'
        <X5 lemma> ! 'have'
        <X5 cat> ! P
        <X5 cat> ! Pu
        <X5 cat> ! Av
        <X5 cat> ! C
        <X6 number> ! plural
        <X6 cat> ! C
        <X6 cat> ! D
        <X6 cat> ! P
        <X6 cat> ! Pu
        <X7 cat> ! D
        <X7 cat> ! P
        <X7 cat> ! Pu.
```

```
Metarule NPerm( X1 -> X2 X3 ) = X1 -> X3 V4 X2:
     <V4 lemma> ! 'be'.
Metarule NPerm( X1 -> X2 X3 ) = X1 -> X3 P4 X2:
     <X2 tense> ! gerund
     <X2 cat> ! N.
Metarule NPerm( X1 -> X2 X3 ) = X1 -> X3 D4 X2:
     <X2 tense> ! gerund
     <X2 cat> ! N.
Metarule NPerm( X1 -> X2 X3 ) = X1 -> X3 P4 X5 X2:
     <X2 tense> ! gerund
     <X2 cat> ! N.
Metarule NPerm( X1 -> X2 X3 ) = X1 -> X3 P4 X5 X6 X2:
     <X2 tense> ! gerund
     <X2 cat> ! N.
Metarule NPerm( X1 -> X2 X3 ) = X1 -> X3 P4 X5 X6 X7 X2:
     <X2 tense> ! gerund
     <X2 cat> ! N.


Metarule Perm( X1 -> X2 X3 ) = X1 -> X3 V4 X2:
     <X3 number> = <V4 number>.
Metarule Perm( X1 -> X2 X3 ) = X1 -> X3 D4 X2:.
Metarule Perm( X1 -> X2 X3 ) = X1 -> X3 P4 X2:.
Metarule Perm( X1 -> X2 X3 ) = X1 -> X3 P4 X5 X2:.
Metarule Perm( X1 -> X2 X3 ) = X1 -> X3 P4 X5 X6 X2:
     <X6 cat> ! P
     <X6 cat> ! Pu
     <X6 cat> ! C.
Metarule Perm( X1 -> X2 X3 ) = X1 -> X3 P4 X5 X6 X7 X2:
     <X6 cat> ! P
     <X6 cat> ! Pu
     <X6 cat> ! C
     <X7 cat> ! P
     <X7 cat> ! Pu
     <X7 cat> ! C.


Metarule ExtC( X1 -> X2 X3 ) = X1 -> X2 X5 X6 X7 X8 C4 X3:
     <X2 number> ! plural
     <X5 number> ! plural
     <X6 number> ! plural
     <X7 number> ! plural
     <X5 cat> ! C
```

```
            <X5 cat> ! D
            <X5 cat> ! P
            <X6 cat> ! C
            <X6 cat> ! D
            <X6 cat> ! P
            <X7 cat> ! C
            <X7 cat> ! D
            <X7 cat> ! P
            <X8 cat> ! C
            <X8 cat> ! D
            <X8 cat> ! P.
Metarule ExtC( X1 -> X2 X3 ) = X1 -> X2 C4 X5 X6 X7 X8 X3:
            <X2 number> ! plural
            <X5 number> ! plural
            <X6 number> ! plural
            <X7 number> ! plural
            <X8 number> ! plural
            <X5 cat> ! C
            <X5 cat> ! D
            <X5 cat> ! P
            <X6 cat> ! C
            <X6 cat> ! D
            <X6 cat> ! P
            <X7 cat> ! C
            <X7 cat> ! D
            <X7 cat> ! P
            <X8 cat> ! C
            <X8 cat> ! D
            <X8 cat> ! P.
Metarule ExtM( X1 -> X2 X3 ) = X1 -> X2 X5 X6 X7 X8 X3:
            <X2 number> ! plural
            <X2 cat> ! P
            <X5 lemma> = '('
            <X7 lemma> = ')'.
Metarule ExtM( X1 -> X2 X3 ) = X1 -> X2 X5 X6 X7 X8 X3:
            <X2 number> ! plural
            <X2 cat> ! P
            <X6 lemma> = '('
            <X8 lemma> = ')'.
Metarule ExtM( X1 -> X2 X3 ) = X1 -> X2 X5 X6 X7 X8 X3:
            <X2 cat> ! P
```

```
    <X5 cat> ! D
    <X5 cat> ! P
    <X5 cat> ! Pu
    <X6 cat> ! C
    <X6 cat> ! D
    <X6 cat> ! P
    <X6 cat> ! Pu
    <X7 cat> ! C
    <X7 cat> ! D
    <X7 cat> ! P
    <X7 cat> ! Pu
    <X8 cat> ! D
    <X8 cat> ! P
    <X8 cat> ! Pu.

Metarule NExtP( X1 -> X2 X3 ) = X1 -> X3 P4 X5 X6 X7 X8 X2:
    <X2 tense> ! gerund
    <X2 cat> ! N.
Metarule ExtP( X1 -> X2 X3 ) = X1 -> X3 P4 X5 X6 X7 X8 X2:
    <X6 cat> ! P
    <X6 cat> ! Pu
    <X6 cat> ! C
    <X7 cat> ! P
    <X7 cat> ! Pu
    <X7 cat> ! C
    <X8 cat> ! P
    <X8 cat> ! Pu
    <X8 cat> ! C.
```

A.3 Paradigmatic Morphosyntactic Metarules

```
Metarule SingDer( X1 -> X2 X3 ) = X1 -> X4 <X 0-9> X3:
    <X2 root> = <X4 root>
    <X1 metaLabel> = 'XX'.
Metarule SingDer( X1 -> X2 X3 ) = X1 -> X2 <X 0-9> X4:
    <X3 root> = <X4 root>
    <X1 metaLabel> = 'XX'.


Metarule SingDerP( X1 -> X2 X3 ) = X1 -> X4 <X 0-9> X2:
    <X3 root> = <X4 root>
```

```
        <X1 metaLabel> = 'XX'.
Metarule SingDerP( X1 -> X2 X3 ) = X1 -> X3 <X 0-9> X4:
        <X2 root> = <X4 root>
        <X1 metaLabel> = 'XX'.


Metarule DoubDer( X1 -> X2 X3 ) = X1 -> X4 <X 0-9> X5:
        <X2 root> = <X4 root>
        <X3 root> = <X5 root>
        <X1 metaLabel> = 'XX'.


Metarule DoubDerP( X1 -> X2 X3 ) = X1 -> X5 <X 0-9> X4:
        <X3 root> = <X5 root>
        <X2 root> = <X4 root>
        <X1 metaLabel> = 'XX'.
```

A.4 Filtering Morphosyntactic Metarules

```
Metarule Coor( X1 -> X2 N3 ) =
                X1 -> X2 < {A|N|Np|V} 0-3 > N5 < Pu/','? > C4 N3:
        <X2 num> ! plu.
Metarule Coor( X1 -> X2 N3 ) =
                X1 -> X2 C4 < {A|N|Np|V} 0-3 > N3:
        <X2 num> ! plu.
Metarule Coor( X1 -> X2 N3 ) =
                X1 -> X2 Pu4 < {A|N|Np|V} Pu? > C5 < {A|N|Np|V} > N3:
        <X2 num> ! plu.
Metarule Coor( X1 -> X2 N3 ) =
                X1 -> X2 Pu4 < {A|N|Np|V} > Pu5 < {A|N|Np|V} Pu? >
                    C6 < {A|N|Np|V} > N3:
        <X2 num> ! plu.
Metarule Coor( X1 -> X2 N3 ) =
                X1 -> X2 < {A|N|Np|V} 0-3 > N5 < Pu/',' > C4 N3:
        <X2 num> ! plu.


Metarule Modif( X1 -> X2 N3 ) =
                X1 -> X2 < {A|N|Np|V} 0-3 > N3:
        <X2 num> ! plu.
Metarule Modif( X1 -> X2 N3 ) =
                X1 -> X2 < N P D? A? > N3:
        <X2 num> ! plu.
```

```
Metarule Modif( X1 -> X2 N3 ) =
            X1 -> X2 < Pu/')' {A|N|Np|V}? > N3:
     <X2 num> ! plu.
Metarule Modif( X1 -> X2 N3 ) =
            X1 -> X2 <  Pu/'(' C? {A|N|Np|V} 1-2 Pu/')' > N3:
     <X2 num> ! plu.
Metarule Modif( X1 -> X2 N3 ) =
            X1 -> X2 <  Pu/',' {A|N|Np|V}  > N3:
     <X2 num> ! plu.


Metarule Perm( X1 -> X2 N3 ) = X1 -> N3 V4 X2:
     <V4 lem> = 'be'.
Metarule Perm( X1 -> X2 N3 ) = X1 -> N3 Pu4 X2:
     <Pu4 lem> = '('.


Metarule Perm( X1 -> N2 N3 ) =
     X1 -> N3 < V? > P4 < D? {A|N|Np|V} 0-3 <{N|Np} C D? >? > N2:.
Metarule Perm( X1 -> Np2 N3 ) =
     X1 -> N3 < V? > P4 < D? {A|N|Np|V} 0-3 <{N|Np} C D? >? > Np2:.


"category grammar -> categorial grammar"
Metarule NtoA( X1 -> N2 N3 ) =
            X1 -> A4 < {A|N|Np|V} 0-3 > N3:
     <N2 root> = <A4 root>.
"data sparseness -> sparse data"
Metarule NtoA( X1 -> N2 N3 ) =
            X1 -> A4 N2:
     <A4 root> = <N3 root>.
"error tolerance  -> error tolerant"
Metarule NtoA( X1 -> N2 N3 ) =
            X1 ->  N2 A4:
     <A4 root> = <N3 root>.


"categorial grammar -> category grammar"
Metarule AtoN( X1 -> A2 N3 ) =
            X1 -> N4 < {A|N|Np|V} 0-3 > N3:
     <A2 root> = <N4 root>.
"general grammar -> generalization of grammar"
Metarule AtoN( X1 -> A2 N3 ) =
            X1 -> N4 < <C D?>? P D? {A|N|Np|V} 0-3 > N3:
     <A2 root> = <N4 root>.
```

```
"frequent word -> word frequencies"
"experimental result -> results of two experiments"
Metarule AtoN( X1 -> A2 N3 ) =
            X1 -> N3 < <P D?>? {A|N|Np|V} 0-3 > N4:
    <A2 root> = <N4 root>.

"previous method -> previously proposed methods"
Metarule AtoAv( X1 -> A2 N3 ) =
            X1 -> Av3 < {A|N|Np|V} 0-3 > N3:
    <A2 root> = <Av3 root>.

"syntactic information ->  syntactical information"
Metarule AtoA( X1 -> A2 N3 ) =
            X1 -> A3 < {A|N|Np|V} 0-3 > N3:
    <A2 root> = <A3 root>.

"word category -> word categorization"
"technical document -> technical documentation"
Metarule NtoN( X1 -> X2 N3 ) =
            X1 -> X2 < {A|N|Np|V} 0-3 > N4:
    <N3 root> = <N4 root>.

"category grammar -> categorization grammar"
Metarule NtoN( X1 -> N2 N3 ) =
            X1 -> N4 < {A|N|Np|V} 0-3 > N3:
    <N4 root> = <N2 root>.

"word class  -> classifications of unknown words"
Metarule NtoN( X1 -> N2 N3 ) =
            X1 -> N4 < P {A|N|Np|V} 0-3 > N2:
    <N4 root> = <N3 root>.

"index grammar -> indexed grammar"
"loan consolidation -> consolidate those loans"
Metarule NtoV( X1 -> N2 N3 ) =
            X1 -> V3 < <D {N|Np}? P>? D? {A|N|Np|V} 0-3 > N3:
    <V3 root> = <N2 root>.

"word category -> categorize words"
Metarule NtoV( X1 -> N2 N3 ) =
            X1 -> V3 < Av? P? <D {N|Np}? P>? D?
```

```
                    {A|N|Np|V} 0-3 > N2:
    <V3 root> = <N3 root>.


"word category -> words categorized"
"dictionary coverage -> dictionary entries cover"
Metarule NtoV( X1 -> N2 N3 ) =
            X1 -> N2 < {N|Np}? V/'be' ? > V3:
    <V3 root> = <N3 root>.


"probabilistic model -> probabilistic modelling"
"probabilistic model -> probabilistic language modelling"
"automatic acquisition -> automatic method for acquiring"
Metarule NtoV( X1 -> A2 N3 ) =
            X1 -> A2 < {A|N|Np|V} 0-2 <{N|Np} P>? > V3:
    <V3 root> = <N3 root>.


"generation system -> system for generating"
"negotiation subdialogues -> subdialogues to negotiate"
Metarule NtoV( X1 -> N2 N3 ) =
            X1 -> N3   <P Av?> V2:
    <V2 root> = <N2 root>.


"generalization method -> method (will) generalizes"
Metarule NtoV( X1 -> N2 N3 ) =
            X1 -> N3 < V? > V2:
    <V2 root> = <N2 root>.


"indexed grammar -> index grammar"
Metarule VtoN( X1 -> V2 N3 ) =
            X1 -> N4 < {A|N|Np|V} 0-3 > N3:
    <V2 root> = <N4 root>.
```

A.5   Filtering Semantic and Morphosemantic Metarules

```
Metarule SemArg1( X1 -> X2 N3 ) = X1 -> X4 N3:
    <X4 num> ! plu
    <X2 syn> = <X4 syn>
    <X2 cat> = <X4 cat>.
Metarule SemHead2( X1 -> X2 N3 ) = X1 -> X2 N4:
    <X2 num> ! plu
    <N3 syn> = <N4 syn>.
```

```
MMetarule CoorSemArg3( X1 -> X2 N3 ) =
        X1 -> X4 < {A|N|Np|V} 1-3 Pu/',''? > C4 < {A|N|Np|V}? > N3:
    <X4 num> ! plu
    <X2 syn> = <X4 syn>
    <X2 cat> = <X4 cat>.
Metarule CoorSemHead4( X1 -> X2 N3 ) =
            X1 -> X2 < {A|N|Np|V} 1-3 Pu/',''? >
     C4 < {A|N|Np|V}? > N4:
    <X2 num> ! plu
    <N3 syn> = <N4 syn>.


Metarule CoorSemArg5( X1 -> X2 N3 ) =
            X1 -> X4 C4 < {A|N|Np|V} 0-3 > N3:
    <X4 num> ! plu
    <X2 syn> = <X4 syn>
    <X2 cat> = <X4 cat>.
Metarule CoorSemHead6( X1 -> X2 N3 ) =
            X1 -> X2 C4 < {A|N|Np|V} 0-3 > N4:
    <X2 num> ! plu
    <N3 syn> = <N4 syn>.


Metarule CoorSemArg7( X1 -> X2 N3 ) =
        X1 -> X4 Pu4 < {A|N|Np|V} Pu? > C5 < {A|N|Np|V} > N3:
    <X4 num> ! plu
    <X2 syn> = <X4 syn>
    <X2 cat> = <X4 cat>.
Metarule CoorSemHead8( X1 -> X2 N3 ) =
        X1 -> X2 Pu4 < {A|N|Np|V} Pu? > C5 < {A|N|Np|V} > N4:
    <X2 num> ! plu
    <N3 syn> = <N4 syn>.


Metarule CoorSemArg9( X1 -> X2 N3 ) =
            X1 -> X4 Pu4 < {A|N|Np|V} > Pu5 < {A|N|Np|V} Pu? >
                C6 < {A|N|Np|V} > N3:
    <X4 num> ! plu
    <X2 syn> = <X4 syn>
    <X2 cat> = <X4 cat>.
Metarule CoorSemHead10( X1 -> X2 N3 ) =
            X1 -> X2 Pu4 < {A|N|Np|V} > Pu5 < {A|N|Np|V} Pu? >
                C6 < {A|N|Np|V} > N4:
    <X2 num> ! plu
    <N3 syn> = <N4 syn>.
```

```
Metarule CoorSemArg11( X1 -> X2 N3 ) =
            X1 -> X4 < {A|N|Np|V} 0-3 {N|Np} Pu/',' > C4 N3:
     <X4 num> ! plu
     <X2 syn> = <X4 syn>
     <X2 cat> = <X4 cat>.
Metarule CoorSemHead12( X1 -> X2 N3 ) =
            X1 -> X2 < {A|N|Np|V} 0-3 {N|Np} Pu/',' > C4 N4:
     <X2 num> ! plu
     <N3 syn> = <N4 syn>.


Metarule InsSemArg13( X1 -> X2 N3 ) =
            X1 -> X4 < {A|N|Np|V} 0-3 > N3:
     <X4 num> ! plu
     <X2 syn> = <X4 syn>
     <X2 cat> = <X4 cat>.
Metarule InsSemHead14( X1 -> X2 N3 ) =
            X1 -> X2 < {A|N|Np|V} 0-3 > N4:
     <X2 num> ! plu
     <N3 syn> = <N4 syn>.


Metarule InsSemArg15( X1 -> X2 N3 ) =
            X1 -> X4 < N P D? A? > N3:
     <X4 num> ! plu
     <X2 syn> = <X4 syn>
     <X2 cat> = <X4 cat>.
Metarule InsSemHead16( X1 -> X2 N3 ) =
            X1 -> X2 < N P D? A? > N4:
     <X2 num> ! plu
     <N3 syn> = <N4 syn>.


Metarule InsSemArg17( X1 -> X2 N3 ) =
            X1 -> X4 < Pu/')' {A|N|Np|V}? > N3:
     <X4 num> ! plu
     <X2 syn> = <X4 syn>
     <X2 cat> = <X4 cat>.
Metarule InsSemHead18( X1 -> X2 N3 ) =
            X1 -> X2 < Pu/')' {A|N|Np|V}? > N4:
     <X2 num> ! plu
     <N3 syn> = <N4 syn>.


Metarule InsSemArg19( X1 -> X2 N3 ) =
```

```
                X1 -> X4 <  Pu/'(' C? {A|N|Np|V} 1-2 Pu/')' > N3:
      <X4 num> ! plu
      <X2 syn> = <X4 syn>
      <X2 cat> = <X4 cat>.
Metarule InsSemHead20( X1 -> X2 N3 ) =
                X1 -> X2 <  Pu/'(' C? {A|N|Np|V} 1-2 Pu/')' > N4:
      <X2 num> ! plu
      <N3 syn> = <N4 syn>.


Metarule InsSemArg21( X1 -> X2 N3 ) =
                X1 -> X4 <  Pu/',' {A|N|Np|V}  > N3:
      <X4 num> ! plu
      <X2 syn> = <X4 syn>
      <X2 cat> = <X4 cat>.
Metarule InsSemHead22( X1 -> X2 N3 ) =
                X1 -> X2 <  Pu/',' {A|N|Np|V}  > N4:
      <X2 num> ! plu
      <N3 syn> = <N4 syn>.


Metarule PermSemArg23( X1 -> X2 N3 ) = X1 -> N3 V4 X4:
      <V4 lem> = 'be'
      <X2 syn> = <X4 syn>
      <X2 cat> = <X4 cat>.
Metarule PermSemHead24( X1 -> X2 N3 ) = X1 -> N4 V4 X2:
      <V4 lem> = 'be'
      <N3 syn> = <N4 syn>.


Metarule PermSemArg25( X1 -> X2 N3 ) = X1 -> N3 Pu4 X4:
      <Pu4 lem> = '('
      <X2 syn> = <X4 syn>
      <X2 cat> = <X4 cat>.
Metarule PermSemHead26( X1 -> X2 N3 ) = X1 -> N4 Pu4 X2:
      <Pu4 lem> = '('
      <N3 syn> = <N4 syn>.


Metarule PermSemArg27( X1 -> N2 N3 ) =
    X1 -> N3 < V? > P4 < D? {A|N|Np|V} 0-3 <{N|Np} C D? >? > N4:
   <N2 syn> = <N4 syn>.
Metarule PermSemHead28( X1 -> N2 N3 ) =
    X1 -> N4 < V? > P4 < D? {A|N|Np|V} 0-3 <{N|Np} C D? >? > N2:
   <N3 syn> = <N4 syn>.
```

```
Metarule PermSemArg29( X1 -> Np2 N3 ) =
     X1 -> N3 < V? > P4 < D? {A|N|Np|V} 0-3 <{N|Np} C D? >? > Np4:
  <Np2 syn> = <Np4 syn>.
Metarule PermSemHead30( X1 -> Np2 N3 ) =
     X1 -> N4 < V? > P4 < D? {A|N|Np|V} 0-3 <{N|Np} C D? >? > Np2:
  <N3 syn> = <N4 syn>.

Metarule NtoASemHead31( X1 -> N2 N3 ) =
             X1 -> A4 < {A|N|Np|V} 0-3 > N4:
     <N2 root> = <A4 root>
     <N3 syn> = <N4 syn>.


Metarule NtoASemArg32( X1 -> N2 N3 ) =
               X1 -> A4 N4:
     <A4 root> = <N3 root>
     <N2 syn> = <N4 syn>.


Metarule NtoASemArg33( X1 -> N2 N3 ) =
             X1 ->  N4 A4:
     <A4 root> = <N3 root>
     <N2 syn> = <N4 syn>.


Metarule AtoNSemHead34( X1 -> A2 N3 ) =
             X1 -> N4 < {A|N|Np|V} 0-3 > N5:
     <A2 root> = <N4 root>
     <N3 syn> = <N5 syn>.


Metarule AtoNSemHead35( X1 -> A2 N3 ) =
             X1 -> N4 < <C D?>? P D? {A|N|Np|V} 0-3 > N5:
     <A2 root> = <N4 root>
     <N3 syn> = <N5 syn>.


Metarule AtoNSemHead36( X1 -> A2 N3 ) =
             X1 -> N5 < <P D?>? {A|N|Np|V} 0-3 > N4:
     <A2 root> = <N4 root>
     <N3 syn> = <N5 syn>.


Metarule AtoAvSemHead37( X1 -> A2 N3 ) =
             X1 -> Av3 < {A|N|Np|V} 0-3 > N5:
     <A2 root> = <Av3 root>
     <N3 syn> = <N5 syn>.
```

```
Metarule AtoASemHead38( X1 -> A2 N3 ) =
          X1 -> A3 < {A|N|Np|V} 0-3 > N5:
     <A2 root> = <A3 root>
     <N3 syn> = <N5 syn>.


Metarule NtoNSemArg39( X1 -> X2 N3 ) =
          X1 -> X4 < {A|N|Np|V} 0-3 > N4:
     <N3 root> = <N4 root>
     <X2 syn> = <X4 syn>
     <X2 cat> = <X4 cat>.


Metarule NtoNSemHead40( X1 -> N2 N3 ) =
          X1 -> N4 < {A|N|Np|V} 0-3 > N5:
     <N4 root> = <N2 root>
     <N3 syn> = <N5 syn>.


Metarule NtoNSemArg41( X1 -> N2 N3 ) =
          X1 -> N4 < P {A|N|Np|V} 0-3 > N5:
     <N4 root> = <N3 root>
     <N2 syn> = <N5 syn>.


Metarule NtoVSemHead42( X1 -> N2 N3 ) =
          X1 -> V3 < <D {N|Np}? P>? D? {A|N|Np|V} 0-3 > N5:
     <V3 root> = <N2 root>
     <N3 syn> = <N5 syn>.


Metarule NtoVSemArg43( X1 -> N2 N3 ) =
          X1 -> V3 < Av? P? <D {N|Np}? P>? D?
                    {A|N|Np|V} 0-3 > N5:
     <V3 root> = <N3 root>
     <N2 syn> = <N5 syn>.


Metarule NtoVSemArg44( X1 -> N2 N3 ) =
          X1 -> N5 < {N|Np}? V/'be' ? > V3:
     <V3 root> = <N3 root>
     <N2 syn> = <N5 syn>.


Metarule NtoVSemArg45( X1 -> A2 N3 ) =
          X1 -> A5 < {A|N|Np|V} 0-2 <{N|Np} P>? > V3:
     <V3 root> = <N3 root>
     <A2 syn> = <A5 syn>.
```

```
Metarule NtoVSemHead46( X1 -> N2 N3 ) =
            X1 -> N5   <P Av?> V2:
     <V2 root> = <N2 root>
     <N3 syn> = <N5 syn>.


Metarule NtoVSemHead47( X1 -> N2 N3 ) =
            X1 -> N5 < V? > V2:
     <V2 root> = <N2 root>
     <N3 syn> = <N5 syn>.


Metarule VtoNSemHead48( X1 -> V2 N3 ) =
            X1 -> N4 < {A|N|Np|V} 0-3 > N5:
     <V2 root> = <N4 root>
     <N3 syn> = <N5 syn>.
```

A.6 Pattern Extractors

```
Metarule Coor( X1 -> X2 X3 ) = X1 -> X2 X5 C4 X3.
     Extractor ExtrCoor( X1 -> X2 X5 C4 X3 ) = X1 -> X2 X5.
Metarule Coor( X1 -> X2 X3 ) = X1 -> X2 C4 Pp5 X3.
     "pronominal coordination"
     Extractor ExtrCoor( X1 -> X2 C4 Pp5 X3 ) = *.
Metarule Coor( X1 -> X2 X3 ) = X1 -> X2 C4 X5 X3.
     Extractor ExtrCoor( X1 -> X2 C4 X5 X3 ) = X1 -> X5 X3.
Metarule Coor( X1 -> X2 X3 ) = X1 -> X2 X5 X6 C4 X3.
     Extractor ExtrCoor( X1 -> X2 X5 X6 C4 X3 ) = X1 -> X2 X5 X6.
Metarule Coor( X1 -> X2 X3 ) = X1 -> X2 C4 X5 X6 X3.
     Extractor ExtrCoor( X1 -> X2 C4 X5 X6 X3 ) = X1 -> X5 X6 X3.
Metarule Coor( X1 -> X2 X3 ) = X1 -> X2 X5 X6 X7 C4 X3.
     Extractor ExtrCoor( X1 -> X2 X5 X6 X7 C4 X3 ) = X1 -> X2 X5 X6 X7.
Metarule Coor( X1 -> X2 X3 ) = X1 -> X2 C4 X5 X6 X7 X3.
     Extractor ExtrCoor( X1 -> X2 C4 X5 X6 X7 X3 ) = X1 -> X5 X6 X7 X3.


Metarule Modif( X1 -> X2 X3 ) = X1 -> X2 X5 X3.
     "genitive"
     Extractor ExtrModif( X1 -> X2 X5 X3 ) = *.
Metarule Modif( X1 -> X2 X3 ) = X1 -> X2 X5 X3.
     Extractor ExtrModif( X1 -> X2 X5 X3 ) = X1 -> X5 X3.
Metarule Modif( X1 -> X2 X3 ) = X1 -> X2 X5 X6 X3.
     Extractor ExtrModif( X1 -> X2 X5 X6 X3 ) = X1 -> X5 X6 X3.
```

```
Metarule Modif( X1 -> X2 X3 ) = X1 -> X2 X5 X6 X7 X3.
     "insertion between parentheses"
     Extractor ExtrModif( X1 -> X2 X5 X6 X7 X3 ) = *.
Metarule Modif( X1 -> X2 X3 ) = X1 -> X2 X5 X6 X7 X3.
     Extractor ExtrModif( X1 -> X2 X5 X6 X7 X3 ) = X1 -> X5 X6 X7 X3.


Metarule Perm( X1 -> X2 X3 ) = X1 -> X3 V4 X2.
     "elementary permutation"
     Extractor ExtrPerm( X1 -> X3 V4 X2 ) = *.
Metarule Perm( X1 -> X2 X3 ) = X1 -> X3 D4 X2:.
     "elementary permutation"
     Extractor ExtrPerm( X1 -> X3 D4 X2: ) = *.
Metarule Perm( X1 -> X2 X3 ) = X1 -> X3 P4 X2:.
     "elementary permutation"
     Extractor ExtrPerm( X1 -> X3 P4 X2: ) = *.
Metarule Perm( X1 -> X2 X3 ) = X1 -> X3 P4 X5 X2:.
     Extractor ExtrPerm( X1 -> X3 P4 X5 X2: ) = X1 -> X5 X2:.
Metarule Perm( X1 -> X2 X3 ) = X1 -> X3 P4 X5 X6 X2.
     Extractor ExtrPerm( X1 -> X3 P4 X5 X6 X2 ) = X1 -> X5 X6 X2.
Metarule Perm( X1 -> X2 X3 ) = X1 -> X3 P4 X5 X6 X7 X2.
     Extractor ExtrPerm( X1 -> X3 P4 X5 X6 X7 X2 ) = X1 -> X5 X6 X7 X2.
```

B Structured Acquisitions

This appendix gives an exhaustive description of the acquisition of terms through variations. Tables B.1 and B.2 provide translations of the acquisitions from coordination variants of table 6.8 for binary and ternary terms.

Similarly tables B.3 and B.4 provide translations of the acquisitions from substitution variants of table 6.11 for binary and ternary terms.

Finally tables B.5 and B.6 show the pattern extractors associated with the compositions of permutations and substitutions of binary and ternary terms. In order to restrict the size of the metagrammar, and because of their low productivity, variations are not reported if their head or their argument is split by the insertion of an external string. These variations are indicated by a star ($\star$) in tables B.5 and B.6. There are only 19 such variations in the corpus [Medic]. Where there is ambiguity, as in lines 7, 8, and 10 of table B.6, the correct pattern is the longest one according to the decision made for substitution variants.

Table B.1
String of a candidate $f(\beta)$ as a function of the binary term $f(\alpha) = w_1\ w_2$ and its coordination variant $f(\gamma)$

Variant	$f(\gamma)$	Cutting up c_1, c_2	$f(\alpha)$	$f(\beta)$	Constraints
$C_{H,R}$	$w_1\ C\ c_3\ w_2$	c_1 impossible	—	—	—
$C_{A,R}$	$w_1\ C\ c_3\ w_2$	$\begin{cases} c_1 = \varepsilon \cdot w_1 \\ c_2 = w_2 \cdot \varepsilon \end{cases}$	$\varepsilon \cdot w_1 \cdot w_2 \cdot \varepsilon$	$c_3 \cdot w_2$	—
$C_{A,L}$	$w_1\ c_3\ C\ w_2$	c_2 impossible	—	—	—
$C_{H,L}$	$w_1\ c_3\ C\ w_2$	$\begin{cases} c_1 = \varepsilon \cdot w_1 \\ c_2 = w_2 \cdot \varepsilon \end{cases}$	$\varepsilon \cdot w_1 \cdot w_2 \cdot \varepsilon$	$w_1 \cdot c_3$	—

Table B.2
String of a candidate $f(\beta)$ as a function of the ternary term $f(\alpha) = w_1\ w_2\ w_3$ and its coordination variant $f(\gamma)$

Variant	$f(\gamma)$	Cutting up c_1, c_2	$f(\alpha)$	$f(\beta)$	Constraints
$C_{H,R}$	$w_1\ w_2\ C\ c_3\ w_3$	$c_1 = \varepsilon \cdot w_1 \cdot w_2$	$\varepsilon \cdot w_1 \cdot w_2 \cdot w_3$	$w_1 \cdot c_3$	—
$C_{A,R}$	$w_1\ w_2\ C\ c_3\ w_3$	$\begin{cases} c_1 = \varepsilon \cdot w_1 w_2 \\ c_2 = w_2 \cdot \varepsilon \end{cases}$	$\varepsilon \cdot w_1 w_2 \cdot w_3 \cdot \varepsilon$	$c_3 \cdot w_3$	—
$C_{A,R}$	$w_1\ w_2\ C\ c_3\ w_3$	$\begin{cases} c_1 = w_1 \cdot w_2 \\ c_2 = w_2 \cdot \varepsilon \end{cases}$	$w_1 \cdot w_2 \cdot w_3 \cdot \varepsilon$	$c_3 \cdot w_3$	—
$C_{A,L}$	$w_1\ w_2\ c_3\ C\ w_3$	c_2 impossible	—	—	—
$C_{H,L}$	$w_1\ w_2\ c_3\ C\ w_3$	$\begin{cases} c_1 = w_1 \cdot w_2 \\ c_2 = w_3 \cdot \varepsilon \end{cases}$	$w_1 \cdot w_2 \cdot w_3 \cdot \varepsilon$	$w_2 \cdot c_3$	—
$C_{H,L}$	$w_1\ w_2\ c_3\ C\ w_3$	$\begin{cases} c_1 = \varepsilon \cdot w_1 w_2 \\ c_2 = w_3 \cdot \varepsilon \end{cases}$	$\varepsilon \cdot w_1 \cdot w_2 \cdot w_3 \cdot \varepsilon$	$w_1 w_2 \cdot c_3$	—
$C_{H,R}$	$w_1\ C\ c_3\ w_2\ w_3$	c_1 impossible	—	—	—
$C_{A,R}$	$w_1\ C\ c_3\ w_2\ w_3$	$\begin{cases} c_1 = \varepsilon \cdot w_1 \\ c_2 = w_2 w_3 \cdot \varepsilon \end{cases}$	$\varepsilon \cdot w_1 \cdot w_2 w_3 \cdot \varepsilon$	$c_3 \cdot w_2 w_3$	—
$C_{A,R}$	$w_1\ C\ c_3\ w_2\ w_3$	$\begin{cases} c_1 = \varepsilon \cdot w_1 \\ c_2 = w_2 \cdot w_3 \end{cases}$	$\varepsilon \cdot w_1 \cdot w_2 \cdot w_3$	$c_3 \cdot w_2$	—
$C_{A,L}$	$w_1\ c_3\ C\ w_2\ w_3$	$c_2 = w_2 \cdot w_3 \cdot \varepsilon$	$w_1 \cdot w_2 \cdot w_3 \cdot \varepsilon$	$c_3 \cdot w_3$	—
$C_{H,L}$	$w_1\ c_3\ C\ w_2\ w_3$	$\begin{cases} c_1 = \varepsilon \cdot w_1 \\ c_2 = w_2 w_3 \cdot \varepsilon \end{cases}$	$\varepsilon \cdot w_1 \cdot w_2 w_3 \cdot \varepsilon$	$w_1 \cdot c_3$	—
$C_{H,L}$	$w_1\ c_3\ C\ w_2\ w_3$	$\begin{cases} c_1 = \varepsilon \cdot w_1 \\ c_2 = w_2 \cdot w_3 \end{cases}$	$\varepsilon \cdot w_1 \cdot w_2 \cdot w_3$	$w_1 \cdot c_3$	—

Table B.3
String of a candidate $f(\beta)$ as a function of the binary term $f(\alpha) = w_1\ w_2$ and its substitution variant $f(\gamma)$

Variant	$f(\gamma)$	Cutting up c_2	$f(\alpha)$	$f(\beta)$	Constraints
S_R	$w_1\ c_3\ w_2$	$w_2 \cdot \varepsilon$	$w_1 \cdot w_2 \cdot \varepsilon$	$c_3 \cdot w_2$	—
S_L	$w_1\ c_3\ w_2$	impossible	—	—	—

Table B.4

String of a candidate $f(\beta)$ as a function of the ternary term $f(\alpha) = w_1\, w_2\, w_3$ and its substitution variant $f(\gamma)$

Variant	$f(\gamma)$	Cutting up c_2	$f(\alpha)$	$f(\beta)$	Constraints
S_R	$w_1\, w_2\, c_3\, w_3$	$w_3 \cdot \varepsilon$	$w_1 \cdot w_2 \cdot w_3 \cdot \varepsilon$	$c_3 \cdot w_3$	—
S_L	$w_1\, w_2\, c_3\, w_3$	impossible	—	—	—
S_R	$w_1\, c_3\, w_2\, w_3$	$w_2\, w_3 \cdot \varepsilon$	$w_1 \cdot w_2\, w_3 \cdot \varepsilon$	$c_3 \cdot w_2\, w_3$	—
S_R	$w_1\, c_3\, w_2\, w_3$	$w_2 \cdot w_3$	$w_1 \cdot w_2 \cdot w_3$	$c_3 \cdot w_2$	—
S_L	$w_1\, c_3\, w_2\, w_3$	$w_2 \cdot w_3 \cdot \varepsilon$	$w_1 \cdot w_2 \cdot w_3 \cdot \varepsilon$	$c_3 \cdot w_3$	—

Table B.5

String of a candidate $f(\beta)$ as a function of the binary term $w_1\, w_2$ and its variant $f(\gamma)$, composition of a permutation and a substitution

Variant	$f(\gamma)$	Cutting up c_2, c_4	$f(\alpha)$	$f(\beta)$	Constraints
$PS_{T,I}$	—	—	—	—	—
$PS_{H,R}$	—	—	—	—	—
$PS_{A,R}$	$w_2\, P\, c_3\, w_1$	$c_4 = w_1 \cdot \varepsilon$	$\varepsilon \cdot w_1 \cdot \varepsilon \cdot w_2$	$c_3 \cdot w_1$	—
$PS_{A,L}$	$w_2\, P\, c_3\, w_1$	c_4 impossible	—	—	—

Table B.6

String of a candidate $f(\beta)$ as a function of the ternary term $w_1\, w_2\, w_3$ and its variant $f(\gamma)$, composition of a permutation and a substitution

Variant		$f(\gamma)$	Cutting up c_2, c_4	$f(\alpha)$	$f(\beta)$	Constraints
$P_1S_{H,L}$	$\star$	$w_2\, c_3\, w_3\, P\, w_1$	$c_2 = w_3 \cdot \varepsilon$	$w_1 \cdot w_2 \cdot w_3 \cdot \varepsilon$	$c_3 \cdot w_3$	—
$P_1S_{H,R}$	$\star$	$w_2\, c_3\, w_3\, P\, w_1$	c_2 impossible	—	—	—
$P_1S_{A,R}$		$w_2\, w_3\, P\, c_3\, w_1$	$c_4 = w_1 \cdot \varepsilon$	$\varepsilon \cdot w_1 \cdot \varepsilon \cdot w_2\, w_3$	$c_3 \cdot w_1$	—
$P_1S_{A,L}$		$w_2\, w_3\, P\, c_3\, w_1$	c_4 impossible	—	—	—
$P_2S_{H,L}$		—	—	—	—	—
$P_2S_{H,R}$		—	—	—	—	—
$P_2S_{A,R}$		$w_3\, P\, c_3\, w_1\, w_2$	$c_4 = w_1\, w_2 \cdot \varepsilon$	$\varepsilon \cdot w_1\, w_2 \cdot \varepsilon \cdot w_3$	$c_3 \cdot w_1\, w_2$	—
$P_2S_{A,R}$		$w_3\, P\, c_3\, w_1\, w_2$	$c_4 = w_1 \cdot w_2$	$\varepsilon \cdot w_1 \cdot w_2 \cdot w_3$	$c_3 \cdot w_1$	—
$P_2S_{A,R}$	$\star$	$w_3\, P\, w_1\, c_3\, w_2$	$c_4 = w_2 \cdot \varepsilon$	$w_1 \cdot w_2 \cdot \varepsilon \cdot w_3$	$c_3 \cdot w_2$	—
$P_2S_{A,L}$		$w_3\, P\, c_3\, w_1\, w_2$	$c_4 = w_1 \cdot w_2 \cdot \varepsilon$	$\varepsilon \cdot w_1 \cdot w_2 \cdot w_3$	$c_3 \cdot w_2$	—
$P_2S_{A,L}$	$\star$	$w_3\, P\, w_1\, c_3\, w_2$	c_4 impossible	—	—	—

C Corpus and Term Lists

The tuning of the metagrammar and of the acquisition patterns has been performed on the training corpus [Medic]: a 1.6 million word corpus of medical abstracts, and the training term list [Pascal] composed of 71,623 terms (figure C.1 and table C.1). The corresponding test corpus is a 120.000-word corpus of scientific abstracts in the metallurgy domain [Metal], associated with a list of 6,621 terms in the same domain [Pascal-Metal] (figure C.2 and table C.2). The term lists are extracted from thesauri used for manual indexing at *INIST/CNRS* and the corpora are collected from a large bibliographical database available at *INIST/CNRS*.

INIST/CNRS (Institut de l'Information Scientifique et Technique du CNRS) is a documentation center for scientific and technical information. It produces two bibliographical databases, PASCAL and FRANCIS, indexed with a controlled thesaurus. The work reported in this book is done in cooperation with the Department *Programme de Recherche Infométrie* of *INIST/CNRS*, a department for research and development of tools in information management. We would like to thank the researchers of this laboratory for their help and their support all along this work. We are specifically grateful to Jean Royauté and Xavier Polanco for their fruitful cooperation. Through their collaboration and their scientific feedback, interesting experiments have been conducted that would have been otherwise impossible to complete.

Table C.1
Twenty terms from the training term list [Pascal]

Limousin	*Limpet*
Limulus	*Limulus lysate assay*
Limulus polyphemus	*Limy bile*
Linaceae	*Linamarin synthase*
Lincoff implant	*Lindblad resonance*
Line (geometry)	*Line (plant)*
Line Islands	*Line contact*
Line graph	*Line of sight propagation*
Line overlapping	*Line segment*
Line spectrum	*Line stress*

000001 Ventricular dilatation may have important prognostic implications for the survival of patients with left ventricular dysfunction. To determine the manner and extent to which the left ventricle of the rat remodels and dilates after myocardial infarction, we obtained the passive pressure-volume relationships, chamber stiffness constants, and mass during both the early and late phase.

000002 The sequence of a Pst I restriction fragment was determined that demonstrates instability in fragile X syndrome pedigrees. The region of instability was localized to a trinucleotide repeat p(CCG)n. The sequences flanking this repeat were identical in normal and affected individual.

000003 A case of CDC group IVc-2 peritonitis in a patient on continuous ambulatory peritoneal dialysis (CAPD) is described. To the authors' knowledge, this is the first case reported of CAPD peritonitis in which a member of this unusual group of bacteria was isolated as the sole microorganism. As this microorganism is usually resistant to most antibiotics commonly used to treat peritonitis in patients on CAPD, microbiological investigations with identification and antimicrobial susceptibility tests are mandator.

000004 The p53 gene is a tumor suppressor gene located on chromosome 17p. Deletions of this chromosome and point mutations of p53 have been implicated in the development of colonic neoplasms. We have analyzed the loss of heterozygosity of the human p53 tumor suppressor gene in 40 cases of colorectal carcinoma using two restriction fragment length polymorphisms detected by BglII and AccII restriction enzyme.

Figure C.1
The first 4 abstracts of the training corpus [Medic].

Table C.2
Twenty terms from the test term list [Pascal-Metal]

Nomograms	*Exposure chart*
Abrasives	*Abrasion*
Metal penetration	*Absenteeism*
Absorbent materials	*Absorption*
Infrared absorption	*Optical absorption*
Radiation absorption	*X-ray absorption*
Ultraviolet absorption	*Linear accelerator*
Particle accelerator	*Acceleration*
Acceptance	*Welding accessory*
Gas supply accessory	*Accident*

000001 Spherical wave correction is also included. The present method is applied to structural analysis of Si(111)-('rac'3x 'rac'3)Ag adsorbed system in the lowest approximation where Hartree-Fock potential and only m=0 spherical wave correction are used. The present calculation recommends HCT and QH models where the outermost layer is Ag layer.

000002 Multiple-scattering (MS) calculations are presented for polar intensity scans of MgK'Alpha' excited Al2s emission from linear atomic Al chains, and compared to corresponding scans of CuLVV Auger emission from linear Cu chains. Such model calculations permit an assessment of the importance of multiple-scattering effects in substrate emission along low-index directions. Intensity reductions in forward scattering due to MS defocusing effects are seen for both Al and Cu. However, for Al they are found to be significantly slower in turning on with distance along the chain

000003 We have tested a new algorithm to perform first-principles molecular dynamics simulations. This new scheme differs from the Car-Parrinello method and is based on the calculation of the self-consistent solutions of the Kohn-Sham equations at each molecular dynamics timestep, using a fast iterative diagonalization algorithm. We do not use a fictitious electron dynamics, and therefore the molecular dynamics timesteps can be considerably larger in our method than in the Car-Parrinello algorithm. Furthermore, the number of basis functions is variable, which makes this method particularly suited to deal with simulations involving a cell with variable shape and volume.

000004 We discuss the application of a recently proposed thermodynamically self-consistent integral equation, the variational modified hypernetted chain (VMHNC) approximation, to the study of the structural properties of liquid metals. We show a comparison between the structure of the liquid alkali metals, as obtained within the VMHNC, and molecular dynamics simulations carried out using the same potentials and parametrization. The results show that the VMHNC is an accurate approximation for the study of the structure of liquid metals

Figure C.2
The first 4 abstracts of the test corpus [Metal].

D Grammar Files

Single-word rules and term rules are automatically generated from the tagged term lists. This appendix shows the first 5 single-word rules and the first five term rules built from the [Pascal-Metal] term list (see appendix C). These rules correspond to the words *3d*, *a15*, *ability*, *abrasion*, and *abrasive*, and the terms *nomogram*, *exposure chart*, *abrasive*, *abrasion*, and *metal penetration*.

```
Word '3d':
    <cat> =  N
    <inflection> = 1.
Word 'a15':
    <cat> =  N
    <inflection> = 1.
Word 'abilit':
    <cat> =  N
    <inflection> = 3.
Word 'abrasion':
    <cat> =  N
    <inflection> = 1.
Word 'abrasive':
    <cat> =  A
    <inflection> = 1.


Rule N1 -> N2:
    <N1 lexicalization> = 'N2'
    <N1 label> = '100000'
    <N2 lemma> = 'nomogram'
    <N2 inflection> = 1.
Rule N1 -> N2 N3:
    <N1 lexicalization> = 'N3'
    <N1 label> = '100001'
    <N2 lemma> = 'exposure'
    <N2 inflection> = 1
    <N3 lemma> = 'chart'
    <N3 inflection> = 1.
Rule N1 -> N2:
    <N1 lexicalization> = 'N2'
    <N1 label> = '100002'
    <N2 lemma> = 'abrasive'
```

```
        <N2 inflection> = 1.
Rule N1 -> N2:
        <N1 lexicalization> = 'N2'
        <N1 label> = '100003'
        <N2 lemma> = 'abrasion'
        <N2 inflection> = 1.
Rule N1 -> N2 N3:
        <N1 lexicalization> = 'N3'
        <N1 label> = '100004'
        <N2 lemma> = 'metal'
        <N2 inflection> = 1
        <N3 lemma> = 'penetration'
        <N3 inflection> = 1.
```

Glossary

Acquisition graph An acquisition graph is built by connecting each *candidate term*[51] to all the terms from which it has been acquired. For instance, if the variant *frontal or sphenoid sinus* of *frontal sinus* yields the candidate *sphenoid sinus*, the acquisition graph has an arc from *frontal sinus* to *sphenoid sinus* labeled "coordination."

Automatic indexing Automatic indexing is the association of descriptors to documents for the purpose of information retrieval.

Binary decomposition A term with more than two content words can generally be decomposed into binary substructures (substructures with two content words). For instance, the binary decomposition of *left coronary artery* is [*left* [*coronary artery*]].

Candidate term A candidate term is a term produced by automatic acquisition that has not been manually validated.

Co-occurrence (insertion or permutation ~) A co-occurrence associated with a *controlled term t* is a *text window* that contains its content words w_1 and w_2. If the order of the words in the co-occurrence is the same as in the controlled term, the co-occurrence is an insertion co-occurrence; otherwise, the co-occurrence is a permutation co-occurrence. Variations are a special case of linguistically motivated co-occurrence.

Collocation A collocation denotes a recurring association of two words, and the linguistic links between these two words as well. Collocations are divided into lexical collocations such as *doctor* and *hospital* and grammatical collocations such as *make* and *decision*.

Complex (or multi-word) and single-word terms A complex or multi-word term is a term that contains at least two content words; a term which contains one content word is a single-word term. The term *artery* is a single-word term, while *coronary artery* is a complex term.

Composition of variations (homogeneous or heterogeneous) A composition of variations is the result of the repeated transformations of a *controlled term* by these variations. The composition is homogeneous if and only if all the variations belong to the same family (coordinations, modifications/substitutions, permutations, morphological variations, or semantic variations). The example given for the definition of a *transformational path* is an heterogeneous composition because it involves a modification/substitution and a coordination.

Context-free skeleton The syntactic structure of a rule or a metarule is its context-free skeleton.

Controlled term A controlled term is a term that has been manually validated and inserted into a term bank or a thesaurus. Any *automatic indexing* based on controlled terms is called *controlled indexing* and *free indexing* otherwise.

Coordination variation A coordination variation is the association of two terms with a common substructure which is factorized in the variant. For example, *blood and bone marrow cell* is a coordination variant of *Blood cell* resulting from its coordination with *Bone marrow cell*. If the common substructure contains the head words, the variation is called an argument coordination. Otherwise, the variation is a head coordination. The preceding example is an argument coordination.

Deconstruction of variation *Coordination* and *modification/substitution* variations involve two terms, but their detection only relies on one *controlled term*. The deconstruction of a variation of a term *t* which involves another term *t′* is the extraction of the "hidden" term *t′*. For instance, the coordination variant *abdominal and thoracic artery*, computed from the controlled term *Abdominal artery*, yields through deconstruction the *candidate term abdominal artery*.

Dependence In the *binary decomposition* of a term, dependences are the relationships between heads and arguments. For instance, in the term [*left* [*coronary artery*]], *coronary* depends from *artery* (in the substructure *coronary artery*) and *left* depends from *artery* (in the upper structure *left* [*coronary artery*]).

Elementary variations The four basic types of syntactic variations (*coordination, elision, modification/ substitution* and *permutation*) are called elementary variations. They can be composed into complex variations (see *composition of variations*).

Elision variation An elision variation is a deletion of one or more content words but not the head word. For instance, *sunflower oil* is an elision variant of *Sunflower seed oil* resulting from the deletion of *seed*.

Endocentricity or exocentricity A complex lexical entry is endocentric if the complex lexical entry and the head word share the same features (syntactic and semantic features). For instance, *bone marrow cell* is an endocentric structure (in particular, because a *bone marrow cell* is a kind-of *cell*). By contrast, a term such as *nose bleed* is exocentric.

Extended co-occurrence An extended *co-occurrence* associated with a *controlled term t* is a *text window* that contains its content words w_1 and w_2, or one of their morphologically related words, or one of their semantically related words.

Extended domain of locality Since tree grammars are not restricted to immediate dependency, complex lexical entries can be described through a *lexicalized grammar* in which each grammar rule describes the structure of a lexical entry.

False negative A false negative is a correct variant wrongly accepted by a *negative filtering metarule*.

False positive A false positive is an incorrect variant wrongly accepted by a *positive filtering metarule*.

False drop A false drop is an correct variant wrongly rejected by a *positive filtering metarule*.

Feature structure A feature structure is a directed graph in which arcs are labeled by features and in which nodes without outgoing arcs are possibly labeled by values.

Filtering Filtering is the selection of a subset of data based on statistical or symbolic criteria. For instance, the pattern A N is a symbolic filter that discards *blood cell* and accepts *mononuclear cell*.

Finite closure Given a set of transformations (metarules) and a domain (terms), the finite closure of this system is the set of all the images of all the elements in the domain by all the possible finite *compositions* of transformations.

Free or controlled indexing Controlled indexing is a procedure for *automatic indexing* in which the descriptors are *controlled terms*. Otherwise, it is called free indexing.

Frontier of a tree The frontier of a tree is the sequence of words or syntactic label obtained by a prefixed depth-first traversal of the tree.

Harrisian transformation In Harrisian linguistics, transformations are used to generate the variety of observed linguistic forms from a core set of minimal phrases. These phrases represent the informational content of the texts in which their transformations are encountered.

Heterocategorial variation Heterocategorial variations are *morphological variations* in which the categories of the morphologically related words differ. For instance, the variation that associates *Muscle contraction* with *contracted muscle* is heterocategorial.

Hybrid variation Hybrid variations are compositions of at least two variations in at least two of the three following categories: *morphological variations, semantic variation,* or *syntactic variations*. For instance, the variation that associates *Nervous tissue* with *neural and nonneural human tissues* is hybrid because it is the composition of a syntactic variation (a coordination) and a semantic variation involving the semantic link between *nervous* and *neural*.

Isocategorial variation Isocategorial variations are *morphological variations* in which the morphologically related words have the same category. For instance, the variation which associates *Death certificate* with *death certification* is isocategorial.

Lexical anchor   The lexical anchor of a *complex term* is any subset of the set of its content words.

Lexicalization   A tree grammar is lexicalized if and only if each rule is related with one and only one (single- or multi-word) lexical item.

Metarule (filtering or paradigmatic ~)   A metarule is composed of a *context-free skeleton* and constraints. The context-free skeleton is a double tree: one for the source and one for the target. The constraints are optional. Metarules without constraints are called paradigmatic metarules; metarules with constraints are called filtering metarules.

Metarule (source and target of a ~)   A metarule is composed of a pair of trees: a source and a target. The transformation of a rule by a metarule is composed of two steps: first the rule is paired with the source of the metarule; then the transformed rule is obtained by copying the target of the metarule. For instance, the source of the metarule $Coor(N_1 \rightarrow A_2\ N_3) \equiv N_1 \rightarrow A_2\ C_4\ A_5\ N_3$ can be paired with the term *Cerebral artery* and produces the variant rule *cerebral* C A *artery*.

Modification variation   A modification variation is the insertion of a modifier in the structure of a *controlled term*. For instance, *automatic image analysis* is a modification variant of *automatic analysis* resulting of the modification of *analysis* by *image*. In this case, *image analysis* is not a *controlled term*; otherwise, the variation would be a *substitution variation*.

Morphological family   Two noncompound lemmas belong to the same morphological family if they have a *morphological link* with the same root word. For instance, *illiteracy* and *literateness* are in the same morphological family because they share the same root lemma *literate*.

Morphological link   There is a morphological link from lemma l to lemma l' if l is (one of) the root lemma(s) of l'. For instance, there is a morphological link from *literate* to *illiteracy*.

Morphological variation   A morphological variation is the transformation of one of the content words into a word in the same *morphological family*. For example, *abused intravenous drugs* is a noun to verb variant of *Drug abuse*.

n-gram language model   In the statistical analysis of a document, the model of language is an n-gram model if the elementary events are n-uples of words. If n equals 2 or 3, the model is said bi- or tri-gram.

Paradigmatic or filtered variants   Paradigmatic variants are extracted through *paradigmatic metarules* and filtered variants through *filtering metarules* that contain additional constraints.

Pattern extractor   A *variant deconstruction* is performed by extracting a syntactic pattern from a variant. The pattern is closely related to the structure of the metarule that has produced the variant.

Permutation variation   A permutation variation is the transformation of a structure of Germanic compounding such as *Growth rate* into a noun phrase with a post-posed prepositional modifier such as *rate of growth*.

Postfiltering   The *candidate terms* produced through *variant deconstruction* are called pre-candidate terms. Postfiltering is the process through which pre-candidate terms are *filtered* in order to retain *candidate terms*.

Precision   The precision of *controlled indexing* is the proportion of correct indexes among the indexes of the documents.

Precision of fallout   The precision of fallout in *controlled indexing* is the proportion of correct indexes among the rejected occurrences.

Prefixed variation   Prefixed variations are *morphological variations* in which the morphological relation involves prefixing. For instance, the variation that associates *Chemical exchange* with *chemical change* is prefixed.

Ratio (adjacency or dependency ~)   *Structural disambiguation* relies on the computation of correct substructures through *statistical measures of co-occurrence*. Adjacency and dependency ratios are two measures used for this computation.

Recall   The recall in *controlled indexing* is the proportion of extracted indexes among the correct indexes.

Relative frequency   The relative frequency of a term in a document is the ratio of its number of occurrences to the size of the document.

Semantic class   Two lemmas belong to the same semantic class if they have a *semantic link* with the same lemma. For instance, *refinement* and *intricacy* are in the same semantic class because they both have a semantic link with *elaboration*.

Semantic link   For instance, there is a semantic link from *elaboration* to *refinement*.

Semantic variation   A semantic variation is the transformation of one of the content words into a word in the same *semantic family*. For example, *recurrence rate* is a semantic variant of *Return rate*.

Subterm   In a term structure, any substructure that is a *controlled term* is a subterm. For instance, if *Bone marrow* is a controlled term, it is a subterm of [[*bone marrow*] *cell*].

Statistical measure of co-occurrence   A statistical measure of co-occurrence is a statistical measure of the co-occurrences of two or more words in a fixed-length text window.

Structural ambiguity   A term is structurally ambiguous if it accepts several substructures with respect to a grammar of terms. For instance, given a grammar of noun phrases {NP → NP N, NP → N NP, NP → N, N → *bone*, N → *marrow*, N → *cell*}, *bone marrow cell* is ambiguous because it accepts *bone marrow* and *marrow cell* as substructures.

Structural disambiguation   If a term is *structurally ambiguous*, the structural disambiguation of a term is the selection of the substructures that are linguistically plausible.

Substitution variation   A substitution variation is the replacement of a substantive word w by a *controlled term* whose head word is w. For instance, *congenital heart disease* is a substitution variant of *Congenital disease* in which the head word *disease* is substituted by the term *heart disease*. If the substituted phrase is not a term, the variation is a *modification variant*.

Syntactic pattern   A syntactic pattern is a tree structure in which leaf nodes are lexemes or syntactic categories. By extension, a syntactic pattern is also the frontier of such a tree structure.

Term recycling   Terminological data are lexical databases that can be used to build electronic dictionaries for the purpose of natural language processing. Term recycling is the transformation and the exploitation of such a term base in natural language processing.

Terminography   Terminography refers to the study, the collection, the classification, the definition, and the conceptual classification of terms.

Text coverage   The text coverage of a linguistic phenomenon such as *term variation* is the proportion of a given text that is covered by this phenomenon.

Text window   A text window is a sequence of n consecutive words in a document. For instance, *in this sentence* is a 3-word window in this sentence.

Training or test corpus   The training corpus is used for tuning a set of metarules for a given language. The test corpus is used for the *evaluation* of a set of metarules for a given set of terms and a given language.

Transformational path   A transformational path of a nonelementary variation is a sequence of elementary variations whose *composition* is equal to this variation. For instance, a transformational path corresponding to the variant *Kupffer and mononuclear macrophagic cells* of *Kupffer cell* is the composition of a modification/ substitution that transforms *Mononuclear cell* into *mononuclear macrophagic cell* and an argument coordination.

Variant generation The generation of a term variant rule through a metarule is made in two steps: the rule of the base term is paired with the *source of the metarule* and the rule of the variant is obtained by copying the *target of the metarule*. For instance, the metarule $Coor(N_1 \rightarrow A_2 \ N_3) \equiv N_1 \rightarrow A_2 \ C_4 \ A_5 \ N_3$ transforms the term *Cerebral artery* into the variant *cerebral* C A *artery* which extracts the occurrence *cerebral and carotid artery*.

Syntactic variation A syntactic variation only involves a structural modification of terms and possible inflections of their components. In English, four main types of *elementary variations* are observed: *coordinations*, *elisions*, *modifications/substitutions*, and *permutations*.

Notes

1. Nowadays it might be useful to institute a written language, which could be understood by people from any country, and could be translated into their idioms without distortion through common use. This language would only be devoted to scientific matters. It would only express combinations of basic ideas shared by everyone. It would only be used for rigorous chains of reasoning, for accurate and calculated processes of comprehension.

Then, by a complete revolution, observance of this very form of writing could serve to put off ignorance, becoming, in a philosophical sense, a useful instrument in the propagation of enlightenment and in the improvement of the sciences.

2. *FASTR* can be downloaded from *http://www.limsi.fr/Individu/jacquemi/FASTR/*. The tool is available free for research uses at noncommercial and academic institutions (contact *jacquemin@limsi.fr*).

3. The most ambitious project for conceiving an encyclopedic knowledge basis is *CYC* (Guha and Lenat 1994), the most detailed part of which is medicine. Because of its fatal incompleteness, *CYC* is not appropriate for information retrieval; so far, *CYC* has only been applied to very restricted prototypes. The ultimate goal of *CYC*, multi-domain knowledge representation, is still far from having been achieved.

4. Confusion between indexing and term extraction may be misleading. A skillful job has to be done to transform a set of term occurrences into a set of indexes that requires expert inferring and complementary analysis of the text under study. However, here the term *indexing* will be frequently used to mean *term extraction* because I do not study the postcoordination phase that transforms term occurrences into final descriptors of documents.

5. Terminological variation, the main linguistic theme of this book, is not related to the studies on spoken or written genres (Biber 1988). Biber's work deals with a notion of variation with its traditional meaning in linguistics and sociolinguistics: the different modes of linguistic expression according to the dimensions of the documents such as formal/informal, interactive/non interactive, literary/colloquial, and restricted/elaborated. His work accounts for structural and distributional differences between these different genres without any specific or a priori concern for terminological units.

Some linguistic studies on *linguistic variation* have focused more precisely on specialized languages and on terminology. Texts with different levels of technicality have vocabularies with different features. More precisely, Tagliacozzo (1976) shows that the technicality of a vocabulary varies according to the technicality of the text and to the specialty to which it belongs. Articles in the field of psychology (a "soft" science) show more overlap of vocabulary between technical and nontechnical papers than the "harder" sciences like biology and physics. Although working on specialized languages and terminology, the notion of variation in Tagliacozzo's study is related to its traditional meaning in linguistics: the variability of language across different textual dimensions. It is not related to terminological variation studied here: the variability for expressing a concept in texts with similar dimensions (highly technical documents).

6. By convention, the first word of controlled terms is written with a capitalized letter.

7. The applications of term and term variant extraction are not limited to their identification within large corpora. Extracting terms is another form of knowledge extraction. Generally, term variants are hybrid structures that connect the domain of syntax with the domain of compounding. Because of these specific linguistic features, term variants include other terms and reveal semantic and conceptual constraints on the involved morphemes. The high linguistic content of term variation is attested to by its frequent use in linguistic studies on compounding (Gross 1988; Cadiot 1992). Variants provide linguists with syntactic, semantic and conceptual knowledge on terms and compounds.

8. Chapters 3, 4, 5, and 6 contain scientific results that are also presented in an unpublished thesis, *Mémoire d'Habilitation à Diriger des Recherches*, (Jacquemin 1997b). Due to the constraints of space, some of the developments in the thesis are not reported in this book, and the interested reader may consult this work for more details.

9. Structural disambiguation in natural language processing through corpus-based statistics is discussed in section 6.2.2.

10. Mutual Information is different from the measure originally used in information theory, which in fact corresponds to *Average Mutual Information*. Average Mutual Information is based on the notion of conditional entropy and represents information about w_1 contained in w_2.

11. The reverse is chosen in *Xtract* (Smadja 1993a; Smadja 1993b): the statistical selection is performed within a window and is eventually filtered according to linguistic criteria.

12. Negative approaches to the description of noun phrases is found in early work on phrase indexing, for which part-of-speech tagging was not available. In Baxendale (1958), phrase indexes are extracted from English documents by detecting word sequences beginning after a preposition and ending before a preposition or a punctuation mark.

13. All these rules apply whatever the frequency of the subconstituents.

14. The corresponding minimal and deterministic finite-state automaton is calculated in section 2.1.4.

15. The different types of word associations are described by Calzolari and Bindi (1990) through a statistical criterion that combines Mutual Information and a measure of dispersion. Associations are classified into three groups corresponding to different degrees of flexibility. Strong and frozen associations are compounds and proper nouns. Semiflexible associations are idioms and technical terms. Fully flexible associations are lexical associations such as support verbs and corresponding predicative nouns.

16. The termers developed for Chinese and Japanese in Fung (1997) are presented separately in section 2.2.10 in the discussion of termers for Asian languages.

17. Their approach of combining uninterrupted collocations is more coarse than the technique of Frantzi and Ananiadou presented in the preceding paragraph: if one collocation is completely nested in another, the nested collocation is ignored. The case of partially overlapping collocations does not entail any rearrangement of the collocations, since each is extracted separately.

18. A similar argument is put forth by Bourigault(1994) who rejects the statistical filtering of terms and instead opts for a morphosyntactic description of terminological noun phrases.

19. Nevertheless, there can be a discrepancy between the indexes extracted from a document and the descriptors that are assigned to this document. For example, in the *AIR/PHYS* Controlled Indexer (Biebricher et al. 1988), a clearcut separation is made between indexes and descriptors. The descriptors are calculated from the indexes through relations between terms and descriptors found in a thesaurus.

20. This structure is also carefully observed in my description of variations through metarules.

21. Indexing with parse trees is also advocated in the presentation of the *Constituent Object Parser* presented in section 2.3.2. However, the actual mechanisms exploiting parse trees in information retrieval are not detailed in the *Constituent Object Parser*. Tree matching is precisely and convincingly described by Sheridan and Smeaton, whose approach is presented here.

22. [*In the study of any contamination*]$_N$ it [*is suitable to consider*]$_V$ [*the relative importance of physico-chemical and biological mechanisms*]$_N$ [*which can simultaneously occur*]$_V$.

23. The evaluations in chapter 5 and chapter 7 will explore the power and limitations of a nonsemantic approach to term extraction.

24. For the sake of conciseness the value of the *cat* feature is indirectly given by the identifier of the corresponding constituent. The identifier A_2 in the context-free skeleton is equivalent to an identifier X_2 with the additional constraint $\langle X_2 \; cat \rangle \doteq \text{`}A\text{'}$.

25. Similarly the value of the *lemma* feature for single words is provided by the identifier given in the first line of the rule.

26. See Jacquemin and Tzoukermann (1999) for a more detailed presentation of concatenative morphology in French.

27. The difference between these two structures could be accounted for by adding systematically a feature *bar level* to the root and frontier nodes of the grammar. (See the description of *GPSG* in Gazdar et al. 1985 for details on using the BAR feature form X-bar theory of Chomsky 1970 within a unification-based framework.) The values of this feature are 0 (morphological level), 1 (lexical level), and 2 (phrase level). There are two arguments for placing the terms and compounds at the lexical level 1 instead of the phrase level 2. First, terms and compounds are not lexical atoms: they have a syntactic structure (Barbaud 1994), and this local structure can be modified by variations. Second, compounds may have specific phonological constraints: the stress of a compound is different from the stress of a phrase structure (Sproat 1992, p. 238). A formulation of a phrase grammar of terms that accounts for the bar level in the framework of *LTAGs* is given in Daille et al. (1996).

28. The inflectional paradigm of the adjectives is used for building the agglutinated comparatives whenever it is possible.

29. The term rule builder used in this experiment is due to Jean Royauté of *INIST/CNRS*. It was built using *DELAF*, the lexicon of English inflected forms from the *Laboratoire d'Automatique Documentaire et de Linguistique* (*LADL*) of University of Paris 7.

30. Transformations are ordered according to their linear order in the metarule file.

31. As mentioned in definition 1.1, syntactic variations involve neither morphological nor semantic relationships. The recognition of morphosyntactic variants is presented in chapter 7 and the recognition of semantic variants in chapter 8.

32. Collocational information is used by Rackow, Dagan, and Schwall (1992) for choosing the correct translation of a compound noun containing polysemous words. For instance, the literal translation of the German word *Reformprozeß* in English is either *Reform process*, *Reform case*, or *Reform trial*. Statistics of lexical co-occurrences correctly suggest the first translation as the correct one.

33. Section 6.2.2 describes a method whereby the structure of a ternary term is chosen by statistical means.

34. To describe all the possible structural combinations involved in coordinations, these two figures would be symmetrically extended to left-argument and right-head coordinations.

35. The training corpus is [Medic], a medical corpus, while the test corpus is [Metal], a metallurgy corpus. Therefore variations that are specific to the medical domain do not influence the results on the test corpus.

36. The correct permutations wrongly accepted by a negative permutation are classified into the correct paradigmatic variants $\mathcal{P}_C$. The incorrect variations correctly accepted by a negative permutation are classified into the incorrect paradigmatic variants $\mathcal{P}_I$.

37. The classification along predicative or implicit links is somewhat artificial, since some linguistic constructions are predicative, even though no explicit lexeme carries the predicate. For instance, the interpretation of the compounds *cardboard box* and *cardboard plant* involves two different predicates (*CONTAIN* and *PRODUCE*) that are not explicitly stated by the compounds (Fabre 1996).

38. This criterion disagrees with Lauer (1995) who obtains better results when using the dependency ratio.

39. Since 99.3% of the variants are variants of binary or ternary terms (see figure 5.9), the calculus of variants of n-ary terms with $n \geq 4$ would only marginally enhance the results.

40. The only clue indicating a composition is the size of the inserted string: when the inserted string contains two or more words, it is probably due to a composition of variations. Then more than one candidate could be proposed instead of a single one in the current state of the system. For instance, the variant *penetrating cardiocerebral missile injury* of *Penetrating injury* results from a composition of substitutions. In this case, in addition to the "normal" candidate *cardiocerebral missile injury*, the subterms *Cardiocerebral injury* and *Missile injury* may also be proposed as candidates. Similarly the variant *subcutaneous and visceral adipose tissue* of *Subcutaneous tissue*, which results from the composition of a coordination and a substitution, can be associated with the three candidates *visceral adipose tissue*, *visceral tissue*, and *adipose tissue*.

41. The number of variants are lower than in section 5.5 because identical variants are reduced to a single variant. The variants of 4-word terms are not taken into consideration because of their small proportion (only 0.6% of the variants of 2- and 3-word terms).

42. The initial experiments on the recognition of morphosyntactic variations were performed on French. The morphological analysis that produced the list of morphological families and the part-of-speech tagging of the corpora was performed at Lucent Technologies (Bell Labs). They are described into greater details in Jacquemin, Klavans, and Tzoukermann (1997, 1997, 1997, 1999). The part of the work covered by this chapter is patented under Patent 113437. The results reported here were obtained on English by using morphological families derived from the CELEX base (http://www.ldc.upenn.edu/readme_files/celex.readme.html) and by tagging the corpora with Eric Brill's tagger (Brill 1992). The author would like to thank Evelyne Tzoukermann, Bell Labs, Lucent Technologies, and Judith Klavans, Columbia University, for their scientific cooperation to this part of the work. He also acknowledges the cooperation of Béatrice Daille and Emmanuel Morin, IRIN, University of Nantes, for their

assistance for the tagging and the lemmatizing of the English corpora, and Hongyan Jing, Columbia University, for giving him some advice about the CELEX base.

43. Implicitly a word without information on its root lemma is its own root.

44. The CELEX base is available from the Linguistic Data Consortium at http://www.ldc.upenn.edu.

45. Recall that in section 2.1.4 each regular set was shown to be associated with a unique minimum finite-state automaton.

46. These variants are also used as a reference set in the computation of the recall ratios provided in section 7.3.1.

47. Additional metarules are also used for ternary terms, but they are not reported in appendix.

48. The metarules presented in appendix A.4 do not describe variations involving more than one morphological link.

49. The author is grateful to Olivier Ferret (LIMSI/CNRS) for the Microsoft Word97 macro-function used to extract the thesaurus.

50. These experiments were performed during a visit to Lucent Technologies in collaboration with Evelyne Tzoukermann and Judith Klavans in the summer 1998. The author is grateful to Judith and Evelyne for their constant support and for their useful suggestions.

51. Italicized terms in the definitions refer to other definitions.

References

Aarts, Jan, and W. Meijs, editors. 1991. *Corpus Linguistics, Recent developments in the use of computer corpora in English language research*. Rodopi, Amsterdam.

Abeillé, Anne. 1991. *Une grammaire lexicalisée d'arbres adjoints pour le français*. Thèse de Doctorat, Université de Paris 7, Paris.

Abeillé, Anne, and Yves Schabes. 1989. Parsing idioms in Lexicalized TAGs. In *Proceedings, 4th Conference of the European Chapter of the Association for Computational Linguistics (EACL'89)*, pages 1–9, Manchester.

Abney, Steven P. 1990. Rapid incremental parsing with repair. In *Proceedings Waterloo Conference on Electronic Text Research*.

Abney, Steven P. 1991. Parsing by chunks. In Robert C. Berwick, Steven P. Abney, and Carol Tenny, editors, *Principle-Based Parsing: Computation and Psycholinguistics*. Kluwer Academic Publisher, Boston, MA, pages 257–278.

Agarwal, Rajev. 1995. *Semantic Feature Extraction from Technical Texts with Limited Human Intervention*. PhD Thesis, Mississipi State University.

AGROVOC, 1995. *AGROVOC—Multilingual Agricultural Thesaurus*. Food and Agricultural Organization of the United Nations. *http://www.fao.org/catalog/Book/products/v9669-e.htm*.

Ahmad, Khurshid. 1993. Terminology and knowledge acquisition: A text-based approach. In *Proceedings, Terminology and Knowledge Engineering (TKE'93)*, pages 56–70. Indeks Verlag.

Aho, Alfred V., Ravi Sethi, and Jeffrey D. Ullman. 1986. *Compilers*. Addison-Wesley, Reading, MA.

Aho, Alfred V., and Jeffrey D. Ullman. 1972. *The Theory of Parsing, Translation and Compiling, Vol. 1 : Parsing*. Prentice-Hall, Inc., Englewood Cliffs, NJ.

Aho, Alfred V. and Jeffrey D. Ullman. 1992. *Foundations of Computer Science*. Freeman and Co, New York, NY.

Aizawa, Akiko N., and Kyo Kageura. 1998. An approach to the automatic generation of multilingual keyword clusters. In *Proceedings, 1st Workshop on Computational Terminology (COMPUTERM'98)*, pages 8–14, Montreal.

Alshawi, Hiyan, editor. 1992. *The Core Language Engine*. MIT Press, Cambridge, MA.

Ambroziak, Jacek, and William A. Woods. 1998. Natural language technology in precision content retrieval. In *Proceedings, Natural Language Processing and Industrial Applications (NLP+IA'98)*, Moncton, New Brunswick, CA.

Amghar, Tassadit, and Bernard Levrat. 1995. Deux stratégies d'indexation sur PARAPH, système de diagnostic de paraphrase. In Philippe Blache, editor, *Proceedings, Conference Traitement Automatique du Langage Naturel (TALN'95)*, pages 238–245, Marseille.

Amsler, Robert A. 1980. *The Structure of the Merriam-Webster Pocket Dictionary*. PhD Thesis in Computer Science, University of Texas, Austin. TR-164.

Amsler, Robert A. 1989. Research toward the development of lexical knowledge base for natural language processing. In *Proceedings, 12th Annual International ACM SIGIR Conference on Research and Development in Information Retrieval (SIGIR'89)*, pages 242–249.

Andreewsky, A., Fathi Debili, and Christian Fluhr. 1977. Computational learning of semantic lexical relations for the generation and automatic analysis of content. In *Proceedings, IFIP Congress*, pages 667–673, Toronto.

Anick, Peter, and Suzanne Artemieff. 1992. A high-level morphological language exploiting inflectional paradigms. In *Proceedings, 14th International Conference on Computational Linguistics (COLING'92)*, pages 67–73, Nantes.

Arampatzis, A. T., C. H. A. Koster, and T. Tsoris. 1997. IRENA: Information retrieval engine based on natural language analysis. In *Proceedings, Intelligent Multimedia Information Retrieval Systems and Management (RIAO'97)*, pages 159–175, Montreal.

Arampatzis, A. T., T. Tsoris, C. H. A. Koster, and Th. P. van der Weide. 1998. Phrase-based information retrieval. *Information Processing & Management*, 34(6):693–707.

Aronoff, Mark. 1976. *Word Formation in Generative Grammar*. MIT Press, Cambridge, MA.

Assadi, Houssem. 1997. Knowledge acquisition from texts: Using an automatic clustering method based on noun-modifier relationship. In *Proceedings, 35th Annual Meeting of the Association for Computational Linguistics and 8th Conference of the European Chapter of the Association for Computational Linguistics (ACL - EACL'97)*, pages 504–506, Madrid.

Assadi, Houssem, and Didier Bourigault. 1996. Acquisition et modélisation de connaissances à partir de textes : Outils informatiques et éléments méthodologiques. In *Proceedings, 10th Congrès Reconnaissance des Formes et Intelligence Artificielle (RFIA'96)*, pages 505–514, Rennes. A.F.C.E.T.

Bach, Emmon. 1974. *Syntactic Theory*. Holt, Rinehart and Winston, New York, NY.

Barbaud, Philippe. 1994. Conversion syntaxique. *Lingvisticæ Investigationes*, XVIII(1):1–26.

Barkema, Henk. 1994. Determining the syntactic flexibility of idioms. In Udo Fries, Gunnel Tottie, and Peter Schneider, editors, *Creating and Using English Language Corpora*. Rodopi, Amsterdam, pages 39–52.

Barzilay, Regina, Kathleen McKeown, and Michael Elhadad. 1999. Informational fusion in the context of multi-document summarization. In *Proceedings, 37th Annual Meeting of the Association for Computational Linguistics (ACL'99)*, pages 550–557, University of Maryland.

Basili, Roberto, Maria Teresa Pazienza, and Paola Velardi. 1994. Modeling syntactic uncertainty in lexical acquisition from texts. *Journal of Quantitative Linguistics*, 1(1):62–81.

Bauer, Laurie. 1983. *English Word-formation*. Cambridge University Press, Cambridge.

Baxendale, P. B. 1958. Machine-made index for technical literature: An experiment. *IBM Journal*, October:354–361.

Becker, Tilman. 1994a. *HyTAG : A New Type of Tree Adjoining Grammar for Hybrid Syntactic Representation of Free Word Order Languages*. PhD Thesis in Computer Science, Universität des Saarlandes, Saarbrücken.

Becker, Tilman. 1994b. Patterns in metarules. In *Proceedings, 3e Colloque International sur les Grammaires d'Arbres Adjoints (TAG+ 3), Technical Report TALANA-RT-94-01*, TALANA, Université Paris 7.

Benson, Morton, Evelyn Benson, and Robert Ilson. 1986. *The BBI Combinatory Dictionary of English*. John Benjamins, Amsterdam.

Benveniste, Emile. 1966. Formes nouvelles de la composition nominale. *Bulletin de la Société Linguistique de Paris*, LXI(1):82–95. Reprinted, *Problèmes de linguistique générale*, 2, Gallimard, Paris, (1974).

Biber, Douglas. 1988. *Variation across Speech and Writing*. Cambridge University Press, Cambridge.

Biebricher, Peter, Nobert Fuhr, Gerhard Lustig, Michael Schwanter, and Gerhard Knorz. 1988. The automatic indexing system AIR/PHYS —from research to application. In *Proceedings, 11th Annual International ACM SIGIR Conference on Research and Development in Information Retrieval (SIGIR'88)*, pages 333–341.

Black, E., R. Garside, G. Leech, E. Eyes, A. McEnery, J. Laferty, D. Magerman, and S. Roukos. 1993. *Statistically-driven Computer Grammars of English: The IBM/Lancaster Approach*. Rodopi, Amsterdam.

Boguraev, Bran K., and Karen Sparck Jones. 1984. A natural language front end to databases with evaluative feedback. In Bran K. Boguraev and Karen Sparck Jones, editors, *New applications of databases*. Academic Press, London.

Bouillon, Pierrette, Kathrin Boesefeldt, and Graham Russel. 1992. Compound nouns in a unification-based MT system. In *Proceedings, 3rd Conference on Applied Natural Language Processing (ANLP'92)*, pages 209–215, Trento.

Bourigault, Didier. 1993. An endogeneous corpus-based method for structural noun phrase disambiguation. In *Proceedings, 6th Conference of the European Chapter of the Association for Computational Linguistics (EACL'93)*, pages 81–86, Utrecht.

Bourigault, Didier. 1994. *LEXTER un Logiciel d'EXtraction de TERminologie. Application à l'extraction des connaissances à partir de textes*. Thèse en Mathématiques, Informatique Appliquée aux Sciences de l'Homme, Ecole des Hautes Etudes en Sciences Sociales, Paris.

Bourigault, Didier. 1995. LEXTER, a terminology extraction software for knowledge acquisition from texts. In *Proceedings, 9th Banff Knowedge Acquisition for Knowledge-Based Systems Workshop*, pages 1–17 (vol. 5), Banff.

Bourigault, Didier. 1996. LEXTER, a Natural Language tool for terminology extraction. In *Proceedings, 7th EURALEX International Congress*, pages 771–779, Göteborg.

Bourigault, Didier, and Christian Jacquemin. 1999. Term extraction + term clustering: An integrated platform for computer-aided terminology. In *Proceedings, 9th Conference of the European Chapter of the Association for Computational Linguistics (EACL'99)*, pages 15–22, Bergen.

Brachman, R. J., and J. Schmolze. 1985. An overview of the KL-One knowledge representation system. *Cognitive Science*, 9:171–216.

Brill, Eric. 1992. A simple rule-based part of speech tagger. In *Proceedings, 3rd Conference on Applied Natural Language Processing (ANLP'92)*, pages 152–155, Trento.

Brown, Peter L., Vincent J. Della Pietra, Peter V. deSouza, Jennifer C. Lai, and Robert L. Mercer. 1992. Class-based *n*-gram models of natural language. *Computational Linguistics*, 18(4):467–479.

Bunt, Harald, and Masaru Tomita, editors. 1996. *Recent Advances in Parsing Technology*. Kluwer Academic Publisher, Boston, MA.

Busemann, Stephan, and Christa Hauenschild. 1988. A constructive view of GPSG or How to make it work. In *Proceedings, 12th International Conference on Computational Linguistics (COLING'88)*, pages 77–82, Budapest.

Byrd, Roy J., Nicoletta Calzolari, Martin S. Chodorow, Judith L. Klavans, Mary S. Neff, and Omneya A. Rizk. 1988. Tools and methods for computationl lexicology. *Computational Linguistics*, 13(3-4):219–240.

Byrd, Roy J., Judith L. Klavans, Mark Aronoff, and Frank Anshen. 1986. Computer methods for morphological analysis. In *Proceedings, 24th Annual Meeting of the Association for Computational Linguistics (ACL'86)*, pages 120–127, New York, NY.

Byrd, Roy J., and Evelyne Tzoukermann. 1988. Adapting an English morphological analyzer for French. In *Proceedings, 26th Annual Meeting of the Association for Computational Linguistics (ACL'88)*, pages 1–6, Buffalo, NY.

Cabré Castellví, Maria Teresa, Rosa Estopà Bagot, and Jordi Vivaldi Palatresi. 2000 *forthcoming*. Automatic term detection: A review of current systems. In Didier Bourigault, Christian Jacquemin, and Marie-Claude L'Homme, editors, *Recent Advances in Computational Terminology*. John Benjamins, Amsterdam.

Cadiot, Pierre. 1992. À entre deux noms : Vers la composition nominale. *Lexique*, 11:193–240.

Calzolari, Nicoletta, and Remo Bindi. 1990. Acquisition of lexical information from a large textual Italian corpus. In *Proceedings, 13th International Conference on Computational Linguistics (COLING'90)*, pages 54–59, Helsinki.

Carpenter, Bob. 1992. *The Logic of Typed Feature Structures*. Cambridge Tracts in Theoretical Computer Science. Cambridge University Press, Cambridge.

Charniak, Eugene. 1993. *Statistical Language Learning*. MIT Press, Cambridge, MA.

Chen, Kuang-Hua, and Hsin-Hsi Chen. 1994. Extracting noun phrases from large-scale texts: A hybrid approach and its automatic evaluation. In *Proceedings, 32nd Annual Meeting of the Association for Computational Linguistics (ACL'94)*, pages 234–241, Las Cruces, NM.

Chodorow, M. S., R. J. Byrd, and G. E. Heidorn. 1985. Extracting semantic hierarchies from a large on-line dictionary. In *Proceedings, 23rd Annual Meeting of the Association for Computational Linguistics (ACL'85)*, pages 299–304, Chicago, IL.

Chomsky, Noam. 1956. Three models for the description of language. *IRE Transactions on Information Theory*, 2(3):113–124.

Chomsky, Noam. 1970. Remarks on nominalization. In Roderick A. Jacobs and Peter S. Rosenbaum, editors, *Readings in English Transformational Grammar*. Ginn and Company, Waltham, MA, pages 184–221.

Choueka, Yaacov. 1988. Looking for needles in a haystack or locating interesting collocational expressions in large textual databases. In *Proceedings, Intelligent Multimedia Information Retrieval Systems and Management (RIAO'88)*, pages 609–623, Cambridge, MA.

Church, Kenneth W. 1988. A stochastic parts program and noun phrase parser for unrestricted text. In *Proceedings, 2nd Conference on Applied Natural Language Processing (ANLP'88)*, pages 136–143, Austin, TE.

Church, Kenneth W., William Gale, Patrick Hanks, and Donald Hindle. 1991. Using statistics in lexical analysis. In Uri Zernik, editor, *Lexical Acquisition: Exploiting On-Line Resources to Build a Lexicon*. Lawrence Erlbaum Ass., Hillsdale, NJ, pages 115–164.

Church, Kenneth W., and Patrick Hanks. 1990. Word association norms, Mutual Information and lexicography. *Computational Linguistics*, 16(1):22–29.

Colmerauer, Alain. 1984. Equations and inequations on finite and infinite trees. In *Proceedings, International Conference on Fifth Generation Computer Systems*, pages 85–99, Tokyo.

Condamines, Anne, and Josette Rebeyrolles. 1998. CTKB: A corpus-based approach to a Terminological Knowledge Base. In *Proceedings, 1st Workshop on Computational Terminology (COMPUTERM'98)*, pages 29–35, Montreal.

Corbin, Danièle. 1992. Hypothèses sur les frontières de la composition nominale. *Cahiers de Grammaire*, 17:26–55.

Corbin, Danièle. 1997. Locutions, composés, unités polylexématiques: lexicalisation et mode de construction. In Michel Martins-Baltar, editor, *La locution entre langue et usages*. ENS Éditions, Fontenay Saint-Cloud, pages 53–101.

Crouch, Carolyn J. 1990. An approach to the automatic construction of global thesauri. *Information Processing & Management*, 26(5):629–640.

Crouch, Carolyn J., and Bokyung Yang. 1992. Experiments in automatic statistical thesaurus construction. In *Proceedings, 15th Annual International ACM SIGIR Conference on Research and Development in Information Retrieval (SIGIR'92)*, pages 77–88, Copenhagen.

Dagan, Ido, and Kenneth W. Church. 1994. *Termight:* Identifying and translating technical terminology. In *Proceedings, 4th Conference on Applied Natural Language Processing (ANLP'94)*, pages 34–40, Stuttgart.

Daille, Béatrice. 1994. *Approche mixte pour l'extraction de terminologie: statistique lexicale et filtres linguistiques*. Thèse en Informatique Fondamentale, Université de Paris 7, Paris.

Daille, Béatrice. 1996. Study and implementation of combined techniques for automatic extraction of terminology. In Judith L. Klavans and Philip Resnik, editors, *The Balancing Act: Combining Symbolic and Statistical Approaches to Language*. MIT Press, Cambridge, MA, pages 49–66.

Daille, Béatrice. 1999. Identification des adjectifs relationnels en corpus. In *Proceedings, Conférence de Traitement Automatique du Langage Naturel (TALN'99)*, Cargèse.

Daille, Béatrice, Benoît Habert, Christian Jacquemin, and Jean Royauté. 1996. Empirical observation of term variations and principles for their description. *Terminology*, 3(2):197–258.

Daille, Béatrice, and Christian Jacquemin. 1998. Lexical database and information access: A fruitful association. In *Proceedings, First International Conference on Language Resources and Evaluation (LREC'98)*, pages 669–673, Granada.

Dal, Georgette, Nabil Hathout, and Fiammetta Namer. 1999. Construire un lexique dérivationnel: théorie et réalisations. In *Proceedings, Conférence de Traitement Automatique du Langage Naturel (TALN'99)*, Cargèse.

Damerau, Fred J. 1964. A technique for computer detection and correction of spelling errors. *Communication of the ACM*, 7(3):171–176.

David, Sophie, and Pierre Plante. 1990a. De la nécessité d'une approche morpho-syntaxique dans l'analyse de textes. *Intelligence Artificielle et Sciences Cognitives au Québec*, 3(3):140–154.

David, Sophie, and Pierre Plante. 1990b. Le progiciel TERMINO: de la nécessité d'une analyse morphosyntaxique pour le dépouillement terminologique des textes. In *Colloque International sur les Industries de la Langue: Perspectives des Années 1990*, pages 71–88, Montréal.

Davidson, L., J. Kavanagh, K. Mackintosh, I. Meyer, and D. Skuce. 1998. Semi-automatic extraction of knowledge-rich contexts from corpora. In *Proceedings, 1st Workshop on Computational Terminology (COMPUTERM'98)*, pages 50–56, Montreal.

de la Briandais, R. 1959. File searching using variable length keys. *AFIPS Western JCC*, pages 295–298.

Debili, Fathi. 1982. *Analyse Syntaxico-Sémantique Fondée sur une Acquisition Automatique de Relations Lexicales-Sémantiques*. Thèse de Doctorat d'État en Sciences Informatiques, Université of Paris XI, Orsay.

Deese, J. E. 1964. The associative structure of some common English adjectives. *Journal of Verbal Learning and Verbal Behavior*, 3(5):347–357.

DeJong, G. F. 1982. An overview of the FRUMP system. In W. G. Lehnert and M. H. Ringle, editors, *Strategies for Natural Language Processing*. Lawrence Erlbaum Ass., Hillsdale, NJ, pages 149–176.

Dice, Lee R. 1945. Measures of the amount of ecologic association between species. *Journal of Ecology*, 26:297–302.

Diller, Antoni. 1994. *Z: An Introduction to Formal Methods*. John Wiley, Chichester, second edition.

Dillon, Martin, and Ann S. Gray. 1983. FASIT: A fully automatic syntactically based indexing system. *Journal of the American Society for Information Science*, 34(2):99–108.

Dras, Mark. 1997. Reluctant paraphrase: Textual restructuring under an optimization model. In *Proceedings, Pacific Association for Computational LINGuistics (PACLING'99)*, pages 98–104, Ohme, Japan.

Dunham, George S. 1986. The role of syntax in the sublanguage of medical diagnostic statement. In Ralph Grishman and Richard Kittredge, editors, *Analyzing Language in Restricted Domains. Sublanguage Description and Processing*. Lawrence Erlbaum Ass., Hillsdale, NJ, pages 175–194.

Dunham, George S., Milos G. Pacak, and Arnold W. Pratt. 1978. Automatic indexing of pathology data. *Journal of the American Society for Information Science*, 29(2):81–90.

Dunning, Ted. 1993. Accurate methods for the statistics of surprise and coincidence. *Computational Linguistics*, 19(1):61–74.

Enguehard, Chantal. 1992. *Acquisition naturelle automatique d'un réseau sémantique*. Thèse en Contrôle des Systèmes, Université de Technologie de Compiègne, Compiègne.

Enguehard, Chantal, and Laurent Pantera. 1995. Automatic natural acquisition of a terminology. *Journal of Quantitative Linguistics*, 2(1):27–32.

Evans, David A., Kimberly Ginther-Webster, Mary Hart, Robert G. Lefferts, and Ira A. Monarch. 1991. Automatic indexing using selective NLP and first-order thesauri. In *Proceedings, Intelligent Multimedia Information Retrieval Systems and Management (RIAO'91)*, pages 624–643, Barcelona.

Evans, David A., and Chengxiang Zhai. 1996. Noun-phrase analysis in unrestricted text for information retrieval. In *Proceedings, 34th Annual Meeting of the Association for Computational Linguistics (ACL'96)*, pages 17–24, Santa Cruz, CA.

Fabre, Cécile. 1996. Interpretation of nominal compounds: Combining domain-independent and domain-specific information. In *Proceedings, 16th International Conference on Computational Linguistics (COLING'96)*, pages 364–369, Copenhagen.

Fabre, Cécile. 1998. Une classification des variantes nomino-verbales. *Carnets de Grammaire*, 23.

Fabre, Cécile, and Christian Jacquemin. 2000. Boosting variant recognition with light semantics. In *Proceedings, 18th International Conference on Computational Linguistics (COLING'2000)*. Sarrebrücken. ACL.

Fagan, Joel L. 1987. *Experiments in Automatic Phrase Indexing for Document Retrieval: A Comparison of Syntactic and Non-syntactic Methods*. PhD Thesis in Philosophy, Cornell University.

Fano, Robert M. 1961. *Transmission of Information: A Statistical Theory of Communications*. MIT Press, Cambridge, MA.

Fellbaum, Christiane, editor. 1998. *WordNet: An Electronic Lexical Database*. MIT Press, Cambridge, MA.

Fisher, David, Stephen Soderland, Joseph McCarthy, Fangfang Feng, and Wendy Lehnert. 1995. Description of the UMass system as used for MUC-6. In *Proceedings of the Sixth Message Understanding Conference (MUC-6)*, pages 127–140, Columbia,MD.

Fitzpatrick, Eileen, Joan Bachenko, and Don Hindle. 1986. The status of telegraphic sublanguages. In Ralph Grishman and Richard Kittredge, editors, *Analyzing Language in Restricted Domains. Sublanguage Description and Processing*. Lawrence Erlbaum Ass., Hillsdale, NJ, pages 39–51.

Fluhr, Christian, Dominique Schmit, Philippe Ortet, Faza Elkateb, Karine Gurtner, and Khaled Radwan. 1998. Distributed Cross-lingual Information Retrieval. In Gregory Grefenstette, editor, *Cross-Language Information Retrieval*. Kluwer Academic Publisher, Boston, MA, pages 41–50.

Fox, Edward A., J. Terry Nutter, Thomas Ahlswede, Martha Evens, and Judith Markowitz. 1988. Building a large thesaurus for information retrieval. In *Proceedings, 2nd Conference on Applied Natural Language Processing (ANLP'88)*, pages 101–108, Austin, TE.

Frantzi, Katerina T., and Sophia Ananiadou. 1996a. A hybrid approach to term recognition. In *Proceedings, NLP & Industrial Applications (NLP+IA'96)*, pages 93–98, Moncton, Canada.

Frantzi, Katerina T., and Sophia Ananiadou. 1996b. Retrieving collocations by co-occurrences and word order constraints. In *Proceedings, 16th International Conference on Computational Linguistics (COLING'96)*, pages 41–46, Copenhagen.

Fraurud, Kari. 1990. Definiteness and the processing of noun phrases in natural discourse. *Journal of Semantics*, 7:395–433.

Fredkin, E. 1960. Trie memory. *Communications of the ACM*, 3:490–499.

Frenkel, Karen A. 1991. The human genome project and informatics. *Communications of the ACM*, 34(11):41–51.

Fung, Pascale. 1997. *Using Word Signature Features for Terminology Translation from Large Corpora*. PhD Dissertation, Graduate School of Arts and Science, Columbia University, New York.

Gaussier, Eric. 1998. Flow network models for word alignment and terminology extraction from bilingual corpora. In *Proceedings, 36th Annual Meeting of the Association for Computational Linguistics and 17th International Conference on Computational Linguistics (COLING-ACL'98)*, pages 444–450, Montreal.

Gazdar, Gerald, Ewan Klein, Geoffrey K. Pullum, and Ivan A. Sag. 1985. *Generalized Phrase Structure Grammar*. Harvard University Press, Cambridge, MA.

Giorgi, Alessandra, and Giuseppe Longobardi. 1991. *The Syntax of Noun Phrases*. Cambridge University Press, Cambridge.

Gonzalo, Julio, Anselmo Peñas, and Felisa Verdejo. 1999. Lexical ambiguity and information retrieval revisited. In *Proceedings, Joint SIGDAT Conference on Empirical Methods in Natural Language Processing and Very Large Corpora (EMNLP/VLC'99)*, pages 195–203, University of Maryland.

Gonzalo, Julio, Felisa Verdejo, Irina Chugur, and Juan Cigarrán. 1998. Using EuroWordNet in a concept-based approach to Cross-Language Text Retrieval. In *Proceedings, COLING/ACL Workshop on Usage of WordNet in Natural Language Processing Systems*, Montreal.

Grefenstette, Gregory. 1994a. Corpus derived first, second and third-order word affinities. In *Proceedings, EU-RALEX'94*.

Grefenstette, Gregory. 1994b. *Explorations in Automatic Thesaurus Discovery*. Kluwer Academic Publisher, Boston, MA.

Grefenstette, Gregory, editor. 1998. *Cross-Language Information Retrieval*. Kluwer Academic Publisher, Boston, MA.

Grevisse, Maurice. 1988. *Le bon usage. Grammaire française*. Duculot, Paris, 12th edition.

Grishman, Ralph, and Richard Kittredge, editors. 1986. *Analyzing Language in Restricted Domains. Sublanguage Description and Processing*. Lawrence Erlbaum Ass., Hillsdale, NJ.

Gross, Gaston. 1988. Degré de figement des noms composés. *Langages*, 90:57–72.

Gross, Maurice. 1975. *Méthodes en syntaxe: Régime des constructions complétives*. Hermann, Paris.

Gross, Maurice. 1986a. *Grammaire transformationnelle du français, 2 – Syntaxe du nom*. Systématique de la langue française. Cantilène, Paris.

Gross, Maurice. 1986b. Lexicon-grammar, the representation of compound words. In *Proceedings, 11th International Conference on Computational Linguistics (COLING'86)*, pages 1–6, Bonn.

Guha, R. V., and Douglas B. Lenat. 1994. Enabling agents to work together. *Communications of the ACM*, 37(7):127–142.

Guilbert, Louis. 1965. *La formation du vocabulaire de l'aviation*. Larousse, Paris.

Guilbert, Louis. 1973. La spécificité du terme scientifique et technique. *Langue Française*, 17:5–17.

Haas, Stephanie W. 1992. Covering the vocabulary of technical abstracts using standard and specialized dictionaries. *Journal of Information Science*, 18:363–373.

Habert, Benoît. 1991. *OLMES* : a versatile and extensible parser in CLOS. In *Proceedings, TOOLS'91*, pages 149–160.

Habert, Benoît, and Christian Jacquemin. 1993. Noms composés, termes, dénominations complexes : problématiques linguistiques et traitements automatiques. *Traitement automatique des langues*, 34(2):5–42.

Habert, Benoît, Elie Naulleau, and Adeline Nazarenko. 1996. Symbolic word clustering for medium-size corpora. In *Proceedings, 16th International Conference on Computational Linguistics (COLING'96)*, pages 490–495, Copenhagen.

Hall, Patrick A. and Geoff R. Dowling. 1980. Approximate string matching. *Computing Surveys*, 12(4):381–402.

Hamon, Thierry, Adeline Nazarenko, and Cécile Gros. 1998. A step towards the detection of semantic variants of terms in technical documents. In *Proceedings, 36th Annual Meeting of the Association for Computational Linguistics and 17th International Conference on Computational Linguistics (COLING-ACL'98)*, pages 498–504, Montreal.

Harris, Zellig S. 1968. *Mathematical Structure of Language*. John Wiley, Chichester.

Harris, Zellig S., Michael Gottfried, Thomas Ryckman, Paul Mattick Jr., Anne Daladier, T. N. Harris, and S. Harris. 1989. *The Form of Information in Science, Analysis of Immunology Sublanguage*, volume 104 of *Boston Studies in the Philosophy of Science*. Kluwer Academic Publisher, Boston, MA.

Hatzivassiloglou, Vasileios. 1997. Predicting the semantic orientation of adjectives. In *Proceedings, 35th Annual Meeting of the Association for Computational Linguistics and 8th Conference of the European Chapter of the Association for Computational Linguistics (ACL - EACL'97)*, pages 174–181, Madrid.

Hatzivassiloglou, Vasileios, and Kathy R. McKeown. 1993. Towards the automatic identification of adjectival scales: Clustering adjectives according to meaning. In *Proceedings, 31st Annual Meeting of the Association for Computational Linguistics (ACL'93)*, pages 172–182, Columbus, OH.

Hearst, Marti A. 1992. Automatic acquisition of hyponyms from large text corpora. In *Proceedings, 14th International Conference on Computational Linguistics (COLING'92)*, pages 539–545, Nantes.

Heidorn, G. E. 1975. Augmented phrase structure grammars. In R. Schank and B. L. Nash-Webber, editors, *Theoretical Issues in Natural Language Processing: An Interdisciplinary Workshop in Computational Linguistics, Psychology, Linguistics, and Artificial Intelligence*. Lawrence Erlbaum Ass., Hillsdale, NJ, pages 10–13.

Hindle, Donald. 1983. Deterministic parsing of syntactic non-fluencies. In *Proceedings, 21st Annual Meeting of the Association for Computational Linguistics (ACL'83)*, pages 123–128, Cambridge, MA.

Hindle, Donald. 1990. Noun classification from predicate argument structures. In *Proceedings, 28th Annual Meeting of the Association for Computational Linguistics (ACL'90)*, pages 268–275, Berkeley, CA.

Hirschman, Lynette. 1986. Discovering sublanguage structure. In Ralph Grishman and Richard Kittredge, editors, *Analyzing Language in Restricted Domains. Sublanguage Description and Processing*. Lawrence Erlbaum Ass., Hillsdale, NJ, pages 211–234.

Hirschman, Lynette, Ralph Grishman, and Naomi Sager. 1975. Grammatically-based automatic word class formation. *Information Processing & Management*, 11(1-2):39–57.

Hobbs, Jerry R., Douglas Appelt, John Bear, David Israel, Megumi Kameyama, Mark Stickel, and Mabry Tyson. 1997. FASTUS: A cascaded finite-state transducer for extracting information from natural-language text. In Emmanuel Roche and Yves Schabes, editors, *Finite-State Language Processing*. MIT Press, Cambridge, MA, pages 383–406.

Hopcroft, John E. 1971. An n log n algorithm for minimizing the states of in a finite automaton. In Z. Kohavi and A. Paz, editors, *The Theory of Machines and Computations*. Academic Press, New York, NY, pages 189–196.

Hopcroft, John E., and Jeffrey D. Ullman. 1979. *Introduction to Automata Theory, Languages, and Computation.* Addison-Wesley, Reading, MA.

Hull, David. 1998. A practical approach to terminology alignment. In *Proceedings, 1st Workshop on Computational Terminology (COMPUTERM'98)*, pages 1–7, Montreal.

Ibekwe-SanJuan, Fidelia. 1998. Terminological variation, a means of identifying research topics from texts. In *Proceedings, 36th Annual Meeting of the Association for Computational Linguistics and 17th International Conference on Computational Linguistics (COLING-ACL'98)*, pages 564–570, Montreal.

Ikehara, Satoru, Satoshi Shirai, and Hajime Uchino. 1996. A statistical method for extracting uninterrupted and interrupted collocations from very large corpora. In *Proceedings, 16th International Conference on Computational Linguistics (COLING'96)*, pages 574–579, Copenhagen.

Iordanskaja, Lidija, Richard Kittredge, and Alain Polguère. 1991. Lexical selection and paraphrase in a meaning-text generation model. In C. L. Paris, W. Swartout, and C. Mann, editors, *Natural Language Generation in Artificial Intelligence and Computational Linguistics*. Kluwer, Boston, MA, pages 293–311.

Jacquemin, Christian. 1991. *Transformations des noms composés.* Thèse en Informatique Fondamentale, Université de Paris 7.

Jacquemin, Christian. 1994a. Les Entrées Lexicales Complexes : À l'interface entre le lexique et la syntaxe. In *Proceedings, Journées du PRC Communication Homme/Machine (TALN'94)*, pages 99–108, Marseille. PRC Communication Homme/Machine.

Jacquemin, Christian. 1994b. Optimizing the computational lexicalization of large grammars. In *Proceedings, 32nd Annual Meeting of the Association for Computational Linguistics (ACL'94)*, pages 196–203, Las Cruces, NM.

Jacquemin, Christian. 1996a. A symbolic and surgical acquisition of terms through variation. In Stefan Wermter, Ellen Riloff, and Gabriele Scheler, editors, *Connectionist, Statistical and Symbolic Approaches to Learning for Natural Language Processing*. Springer, Heidelberg, pages 425–438.

Jacquemin, Christian. 1996b. What is the tree that we see through the window: A linguistic approach to windowing and term variation. *Information Processing & Management*, 32(4):445–458.

Jacquemin, Christian. 1997a. Guessing morphology from terms and corpora. In *Proceedings, 20th Annual International ACM SIGIR Conference on Research and Development in Information Retrieval (SIGIR'97)*, pages 156–167, Philadelphia, PA.

Jacquemin, Christian. 1997b. *Variation terminologique: Reconnaissance et acquisition automatiques de termes et de leurs variantes en corpus.* Mémoire d'habilitation à diriger des recherches en informatique fondamentale, University of Nantes.

Jacquemin, Christian. 1998a. Analyse et inférence de terminologie. *Revue d'Intelligence Artificielle*, 12(2):163–205.

Jacquemin, Christian. 1998b. Improving automatic indexing through concept combination and term enrichment. In *Proceedings, 36th Annual Meeting of the Association for Computational Linguistics and 17th International Conference on Computational Linguistics (COLING-ACL'98)*, pages 595–599, Montreal.

Jacquemin, Christian. 1999. Syntagmatic and paradigmatic representations of term variation. In *Proceedings, 37th Annual Meeting of the Association for Computational Linguistics (ACL'99)*, pages 341–348, University of Maryland.

Jacquemin, Christian, Judith L. Klavans, and Evelyne Tzoukermann. 1997. Expansion of multi-word terms for indexing and retrieval using morphology and syntax. In *Proceedings, 35th Annual Meeting of the Association for Computational Linguistics and 8th Conference of the European Chapter of the Association for Computational Linguistics (ACL - EACL'97)*, pages 24–31, Madrid.

Jacquemin, Christian, and Jean Royauté. 1994. Retrieving terms and their variants in a lexicalized unification-based framework. In *Proceedings, 17th Annual International ACM SIGIR Conference on Research and Development in Information Retrieval (SIGIR'94)*, pages 132–141, Dublin. Springer Verlag.

Jacquemin, Christian, and Evelyne Tzoukermann. 1999. NLP for term variant extraction: A synergy of morphology, lexicon, and syntax. In Tomek Strzalkowski, editor, *Natural Language Information Retrieval*. Kluwer, Boston, MA, pages 25–74.

Joshi, Aravind K. 1987. An introduction to Tree Adjoining Grammars. In Alexis Manaster-Ramer, editor, *Mathematics of Language*. John Benjamins, Amsterdam, pages 87–115.

Justeson, John S., and Slava M. Katz. 1991. Co-occurrences of antonymous adjectives and their contexts. *Computational Linguistics*, 17(1):1–19.

Justeson, John S., and Slava M. Katz. 1995. Technical terminology: some linguistic properties and an algorithm for identification in text. *Natural Language Engineering*, 1(1):9–27.

Kageura, Kyo. 1999. Bigram statistics revisited: A comparative evaluation of some statistical measures in morphological analysis of Japanese kanji sequences. *Journal of Quantitative Linguistics*.

Karlsson, Fred. 1990. Constraint Grammar as a framework for parsing running text. In *Proceedings, 13th International Conference on Computational Linguistics (COLING'90)*, pages 168–173, Helsinki.

Karlsson, Fred, Atro Voutilainen, Juha Heikkilä, and Arto Anttila, editors. 1995. *Constraint Grammar A Language-Independent System for Parsing Unrestricted Text*. Mouton de Gruyter, Berlin.

Kasper, Robert T. 1993. Typed feature constraint systems: Structures and descriptions. In Harald Trost, editor, *Feature Formalisms and Linguistic Ambiguity*. Ellis Horwood, Chichester, pages 1–17.

Kasper, Robert T., and William Rounds. 1986. A logical semantics for feature structures. In *Proceedings, 24th Annual Meeting of the Association for Computational Linguistics (ACL'86)*, pages 196–203, New York, NY.

Kay, Martin. 1983. When meta-rules are not meta-rules. In Karen Sparck Jones and Yorick Wilks, editors, *Automatic Natural Language Parsing*. Ellis Horwood/Wiley, Chichester, pages 94–116.

Keen, E. M. 1977. On the generation and searching of entries is printed subject indexes. *Journal of Documentation*, 33(1):15–45.

Kilbury, James. 1986. Category cooccurrence restrictions and the elimination of metarules. In *Proceedings, 11th International Conference on Computational Linguistics (COLING'86)*, pages 50–55.

Kiraz, George Anton. 1997. Compiling regular formalisms with rule features into finite-state automata. In *Proceedings, 35th Annual Meeting of the Association for Computational Linguistics and 8th Conference of the European Chapter of the Association for Computational Linguistics (ACL - EACL'97)*, pages 329–336, Madrid.

Kister, Laurence. 1993. *Groupes nominaux complexes et anaphores: possibilités de reprise pronominale dans un "N1 de (dét.) N2."* Thèse en Sciences du Langage, Université de Nancy 2, Nancy.

Kittredge, Richard, and John Lehrberger, editors. 1982. *Sublanguage: Studies of Language in Restricted Domains*. Walter de Gruyter, New York, NY.

Klavans, Judith L., Christian Jacquemin, and Evelyne Tzoukermann. 1997. A natural language approach to multiword term conflation. In *DELOS Workshop on Cross-Language Information retrieval*, ETHZ, Zurich, Switzerland. ERCIM: European Consortium for Informatics and Mathematics.

Klavans, Judith L., and Min-Yen Kan. 1998. Role of verbs in document analysis. In *Proceedings, 36th Annual Meeting of the Association for Computational Linguistics and 17th International Conference on Computational Linguistics (COLING-ACL'98)*, pages 680–686, Montreal.

Klavans, Judith L., and Philip Resnik, editors. 1996. *The Balancing Act: Combining Symbolic and Statistical Approaches to Language*. MIT Press, Cambridge, MA.

Kleiber, George. 1989. *Paul est bronzé* versus *la peau de paul est bronzée*. Contre une approche référentielle analytique. In Harro Stammerjohann, editor, *Proceedings, Ve colloque international de linguistique slavo-romane*, pages 109–134, Tübingen. Gunter Narr Verlag. Reprinted in *Nominales*, A. Colin, Paris, 1995.

Koskenniemi, Kimmo. 1983. *Two-Level Morphology: a General Computational Model for Word-Form Recognition and Production*. PhD dissertation, University of Helsinki, Helsinki.

Kroch, A. 1987. Subadjency in a Tree Adjoining Grammar. In Alexis Manaster-Ramer, editor, *Mathematics of Language*. John Benjamins, Amsterdam, pages 143–172.

Krovetz, Robert. 1993. Viewing morphology as an inference process. In *Proceedings, 16th Annual International ACM SIGIR Conference on Research and Development in Information Retrieval (SIGIR'93)*, pages 191–203, Pittsburg, PA.

Langacker, Ronald W. 1987. *Foundations of Cognitive Grammar*. Stanford University Press, Stanford, CA.

Lauer, Mark. 1994. Corpus statistics meet the noun compound: Some empirical results. In *Proceedings, 32nd Annual Meeting of the Association for Computational Linguistics (ACL'94)*, pages 337–339, Las Cruces, NM.

Lauer, Mark. 1995. Corpus statistics meet the noun compound: Some empirical results. In *Proceedings, 33rd Annual Meeting of the Association for Computational Linguistics (ACL'95)*, pages 47–54, Cambridge, MA.

Lauriston, Andy. 1994. Automatic recognition of complex terms: Problems and the TERMINO solution. *Terminology*, 1(1):147–170.

Lehrberger, John. 1986. Sublanguage analysis. In Ralph Grishman and Richard Kittredge, editors, *Analyzing Language in Restricted Domains. Sublanguage Description and Processing*. Lawrence Erlbaum Ass., Hillsdale, NJ, pages 19–38.

Levenshtein, V. I. 1966. Binary codes capable of correcting deletions, insertions, and reversals. *Sov. Phys. Dokl.*, 10:707–710.

Lewis, David D., and W. Bruce Croft. 1990. Term clustering of syntactic phrases. In *Proceedings, 13th Annual International ACM SIGIR Conference on Research and Development in Information Retrieval (SIGIR'90)*, pages 385–404, Brussels.

Lewis, David D., W. Bruce Croft, and Nehru Bhandaru. 1989. Language-oriented information retrieval. *International Journal of Intelligent Systems*, 4:285–318.

Liddy, Elisabeth, Susan Bonzi, Jeffrey Katzer, and Elizabeth Oddy. 1987. A study of discourse anaphora in scientific abstracts. *Journal of the American Society for Information Science*, 38(4):255–261.

Losee, Robert M. 1995. The development and migration of concepts from donor to borrower disciplines: Sublanguage term use in hard & soft sciences. In *Proceedings, 5th International Conference on Scientometrics and Informetrics*, pages 265–274, Chicago, IL.

Losee, Robert M., and Stephanie W. Haas. 1995. Sublanguage terms: Dictionaries, usage and automatic classification. *Journal of the American Society for Information Science*, 46(7):519–529.

Lovins, Judith Beth. 1968. Development of a stemming algorithm. *Translation and Computational Linguistics*, 11(1):22–31.

Marca, David A., and Clement L. McGowan. 1988. *SADT*. McGraw Hill, New York, NY.

Marchand, Hans. 1969. *The Categories and Types of Present-Day English Word Formation*. C. H. Beck, München.

Marcus, Mitchell P. 1980. *A Theory of Syntactic Recognition for Natural Language*. MIT Press, Cambridge, MA.

Martinet, André. 1985. *Syntaxe Générale*. Collection U. Armand Colin, Paris.

Mathieu-Colas, Michel. 1990. Orthographe et informatique : établissement d'un dictionnaire électronique des variantes graphiques. *Langue Française*, 87:104–111.

Mathieu-Colas, Michel. 1994. *Les mots à traits d'union : problèmes de lexicographie informatique*. Didier Érudition, Paris.

Matthews, P. H. 1974. *Morphology*. Cambridge University Press, Cambridge.

Mauldin, Michael L. 1991. *Conceptual Information Retrieval : A Case Study in Adaptive Partial Parsing*. Kluwer Academic Publisher, Boston, MA.

Maurel, Denis. 1991. Préanalyse des adverbes de date du français. *TA information*, 32(2):5–17.

McCord, Michael C. 1980. Slot grammars. *Computational Linguistics*, 6:31–43.

McCord, Michael C. 1990. Slot grammar: A system for simpler construction of practical natural language grammars. In R. Studer, editor, *Natural Language and Logic: International Scientific Symposium*, Lecture Notes in Computer Science. Springer Verlag, pages 118–145.

Mel'čuk, Igor. 1984. *Dictionnaire explicatif et combinatoire du français contemporain*. Presses de l'Université de Montréal, Montréal.

Metzler, Douglas P., and Stephanie W. Haas. 1989. The Constituent Object Parser: Syntactic structure matching for Information Retrieval. *ACM Transactions on Information Systems*, 7(3):292–316.

Metzler, Douglas P., Stephanie W. Haas, Cynthia L. Cosic, and Charlotte A. Weise. 1990. Conjunction ellipsis, and other discontinuous constituents in the Constituent Object Parser. *Information Processing and Management*, 26(1):53–71.

Metzler, Douglas P., Stephanie W. Haas, Cynthia L. Cosic, and Leslie H. Wheeler. 1989. Constituent Object Parsing for Information Retrieval and similar text processing problems. *Journal of the American Society for Information Science*, 40(6):398–423.

Miller, George A., R. Beckwith, C. Fellbaum, D. Gross, and K. J. Miller. 1990. Introduction to WordNet: An on-line lexical database. *Journal of Lexicography*, 3:235–244.

Mitra, Mandar, Chris Buckley, Amit Singhal, and Claire Cardie. 1997. An analysis of statistical and syntactic phrases. In *Proceedings, Intelligent Multimedia Information Retrieval Systems and Management (RIAO'97)*, pages 200–214, Montreal.

Mohri, Mehryar. 1994. Compact representations by finite-state transducers. In *Proceedings, 32nd Annual Meeting of the Association for Computational Linguistics (ACL'94)*, pages 204–208, Las Cruces, NM.

Mohri, Mehryar. 1997. On the use of sequential transducers in natural language processing. In Emmanuel Roche and Yves Schabes, editors, *Finite-State Language Processing*. MIT Press, Cambridge, MA, pages 355–382.

Morin, Emmanuel. 1997. Extraction de liens sémantiques entre termes dans les corpus et les textes techniques: Application à l'hyponymie. In *Proceedings, Colloque Traitement Automatique des Langues (TALN'97)*, pages 178–182, Grenoble.

Morin, Emmanuel. 1999. Des patrons lexico-syntaxiques pour aider au dépouillement terminologique. *t.a.l.*, 40(1):143–166.

Morin, Emmanuel, and Christian Jacquemin. 1999. Projecting corpus-based semantic links on a thesaurus. In *Proceedings, 37th Annual Meeting of the Association for Computational Linguistics (ACL'99)*, pages 389–396, University of Maryland.

MUC-6. 1995. *Proceedings of the Sixth Message Understanding Conference (MUC-6)*. Morgan Kauffmann, San Mateo, CA.

Nagao, Makoto, and Shinsuke Mori. 1994. A new method of *n*-gram statistics for large number of *n* and automatic extraction of words and phrases from large text data of Japanese. In *Proceedings, 15th International Conference on Computational Linguistics (COLING'94)*, pages 611–615, Kyoto.

Noailly, Michèle. 1990. *Le substantif épithète*. Linguistique Nouvelle. Presses Universitaires de France, Paris.

Nunberg, Geoffrey, Ivan A. Sag, and Thomas Wasow. 1994. Idioms. *Language*, 70(3):491–538.

Oostdijk, Nelleke. 1991. *Corpus Linguistics and the automatic analysis of English*. Rodopi, Amsterdam.

Otman, Gabriel. 1995. *Les repésentations sémantiques en terminologie*. Thèse de doctorat es lettres et sciences humaines, UFR Langue Française Université de Paris IV - Sorbonne.

Paice, C. D., and V. Aragon-Ramirez. 1985. The calculation of similarities between multi-word strings using a thesaurus. In *Proceedings, Intelligent Multimedia Information Retrieval Systems and Management (RIAO'85)*, pages 293–319, Grenoble.

Pohlmann, Renée, and Wessel Kraaij. 1997. The effect of syntactic phrase indexing on retrieval performances for Dutch texts. In *Proceedings, Intelligent Multimedia Information Retrieval Systems and Management (RIAO'97)*, pages 176–183, Montreal.

Polanco, Xavier, Luc Grivel, and Jean Royauté. 1995. How to do things with terms in infometrics: Terminological variation and stabilization as science watch indicators. In *Proceedings, 5th International Conference on Scientometrics and Informetrics*, pages 435–444, Chicago, IL.

Pollard, Carl, and Ivan A. Sag. 1987. *Information-Based Syntax and Semantics. Volume 1: Fundamentals.* CSLI Lecture Notes, 13. Chicago University Press, Stanford, CA.

Porter, M. F. 1980. An algorithm for suffix stripping. *Program*, 14:130–137.

Pugeault, Florence, Patrick Saint-Dizier, and Marie-Gaëlle Monteil. 1994. Knowledge extraction from texts: A method for extracting predicate-argument structures from texts. In *Proceedings, 15th International Conference on Computational Linguistics (COLING'94)*, pages 1039–1043, Kyoto.

Pustejovsky, James, Sabine Bergler, and Peter Anick. 1993. Lexical semantic techniques for corpus analysis. *Computational Linguistics*, 19(2):331–358. Special Issue on Using Large Corpora II.

Rackow, Ulrike, Ido Dagan, and Ulrike Schwall. 1992. Automatic translation of noun compounds. In *Proceedings, 14th International Conference on Computational Linguistics (COLING'92)*, pages 1249–1253, Nantes.

Resnik, Philip. 1993. *Selection and Information: A Class-Based Approach to Lexical Relationships.* PhD Thesis in Computer and Information Science, University of Pennsylvania, Institute for Research in Cognitive Science.

Resnik, Philip, and Marti Hearst. 1993. Structural ambiguity and conceptual relations. In *Proceedings, Workshop on Very Large Corpora: Academic and Industrial Perspectives*, pages 58–64, Ohio State University.

Rey, Alain. 1995. *Essays on Terminology.* John Benjamins, Amsterdam.

Riloff, Ellen. 1993. Automatically constructing a dictionay for information extraction tasks. In *Proceedings, 11th Natioanl Conference on Artificial Intelligence*, pages 811–816, Cambridge, MA. MIT Press.

Riloff, Ellen. 1995. Little words can make a big difference for text classification. In *Proceedings, 18th Annual International ACM SIGIR Conference on Research and Development in Information Retrieval (SIGIR'95)*, pages 130–136, Seattle.

Robin, Jacques. 1994. *Revision-based Generation of Natural Language Summaries Providing Historical Background: Corpus-based Analysis, Design, Implementation, and Evaluation.* PhD Thesis, Department of Computer Science, Columbia University, New York.

Robison, Harold R. 1970. Computer-detectable semantic structures. *Information Storage and Retrieval*, 6:273–288.

Roche, Emmanuel, and Yves Schabes. 1997a. Deterministic part-of-speech tagging with finite-state transducers. In Emmanuel Roche and Yves Schabes, editors, *Finite-State Language Processing.* MIT Press, Cambridge, MA, pages 205–240.

Roche, Emmanuel, and Yves Schabes, editors. 1997b. *Finite-State Language Processing.* MIT Press, Cambridge, MA.

Rounds, William C., and Robert T. Kasper. 1986. A complete logical calculus for record structures representing linguistic information. In *Proceedings, 15th Annual IEEE Symposium on Logic in Computer Science*, pages 39–43, Cambridge, MA. IEEE.

Royauté, Jean, and Christian Jacquemin. 1993. Indexation automatique et recherche de noms composés sous leurs différentes variations. In *Proceedings, Colloque Informatique et Langue Naturelle (ILN'93)*, pages 5–23, Nantes.

Ruge, Gerda. 1991. Experiments on linguistically based term associations. In *Proceedings, Intelligent Multimedia Information Retrieval Systems and Management (RIAO'91)*, pages 528–545, Barcelona.

Rupp, C. J., M. A. Rosner, and R. L. Johnson, editors. 1994. *Constraints, Language and Computation.* Academic Press, New York, NY.

Ruwet, Nicolas. 1991. *Syntax and Human Experience.* Studies in Contemporary Linguistics. The University of Chicago Press, Chicago, IL.

Sager, Juan C. 1990. *A Practical Course in Terminology Processing.* John Benjamins, Amsterdam.

Sager, Naomi. 1981. *Natural Language Information Processing: A Computer Grammar of English and its Applications.* Addison-Wesley, Reading, MA.

Sager, Naomi. 1986. Sublanguage: Linguistic phenomenon, computational tool. In Ralph Grishman and Richard Kittredge, editors, *Analyzing Language in Restricted Domains. Sublanguage Description and Processing.* Lawrence Erlbaum Ass., Hillsdale, NJ, pages 1–18.

Salton, Gerard. 1971. Experiments in automatic thesaurus construction for information retrieval. In *Proceedings, Information Processing '71*, pages 115–123, Amsterdam. North Holland.

Salton, Gerard. 1989. *Automatic Text Processing: The Transformation, Analysis and Retrieval of Information by Computer*. Addison-Wesley, Reading, MA.

Salton, Gerard, and Michael E. Lesk. 1968. Computer evaluation of indexing and text processing. *Journal of the Association for Computational Machinery*, 15(1):8–36.

Salton, Gerard, and Michael E. Lesk. 1971. Information analysis and dictionary construction. In Gerard Salton, editor, *The Smart Retrieval System: Experiments in Automatic Document Processing*. Prentice Hall Inc., Engelwood Cliffs, NJ, pages 115–142.

Salton, Gerard, and Michael J. McGill. 1983. *Introduction to Modern Information Retrieval*. McGraw Hill, New York, NY.

Salton, Gerard, C. S. Yang, and C. T. Yu. 1975. A theory of term importance in automatic text analysis. *Journal of the American Society for Information Science*, 26(1):33–44.

Sampson, Geoffrey. 1995. *English for the Computer: The SUSANNE Corpus and Analytic Scheme*. Clarendon Press (Oxford University Press), Oxford, UK.

Savoy, Jacques. 1993. Stemming of French words based on grammatical categories. *Journal of the American Society for Information Science*, 44(1):1–9.

Schabes, Yves. 1990. *Mathematical and Computational Aspects of Lexicalized Grammars*. PhD Thesis in Computer and Information Science, University of Pennsylvania, Department of Information and Computer Science.

Schabes, Yves, Anne Abeillé, and Aravind Joshi. 1988. Parsing strategies with 'lexicalized' grammars. In *Proceedings, 12th International Conference on Computational Linguistics (COLING'88)*, pages 578–583, Budapest.

Schabes, Yves, and Aravind K. Joshi. 1990. Parsing with Lexicalized Tree Adjoining Grammar. In Masaru Tomita, editor, *Current Issues in Parsing Technologies*. Kluwer Academic Publisher, Boston, MA.

Schütze, Hinrich. 1993. Word space. In Stephen J. Hanson, Jack D. Cowan, and Lee Giles, editors, *Advances in Neural Information Processing Systems 5*. Morgan Kauffmann, San Mateo, CA.

Schwarz, Christoph. 1988. The TINA Project: Text content analysis at the Corporate Research Laboratories at Siemens. In *Proceedings, Intelligent Multimedia Information Retrieval Systems and Management (RIAO'88)*, pages 361–368, Cambridge, MA.

Schwarz, Christoph. 1989. Content-based text handling. *Information Processing and Management*, 26(2):219–226.

Schwarz, Christoph. 1990. Automatic syntactic analysis of free text. *Journal of the American Society for Information Science*, 41(6):408–417.

Selkirk, Elisabeth O. 1982. *The Syntax of Words*. Linguistic Inquiry Monographs. MIT Press, Cambridge, MA.

Senellart, Jean. 1998. Tools for locating noun phrases with finite state transducers. In *Proceedings, 36th Annual Meeting of the Association for Computational Linguistics and 17th International Conference on Computational Linguistics (COLING-ACL'98)*, pages 80–84, Montreal.

Sheridan, Paraic, and Alan F Smeaton. 1992. The application of morpho-syntactic language processing to effective phrase matching. *Information Processing & Management*, 28(3):349–369.

Shieber, Stuart M., Susan U. Stucky, Hans Uszkoreit, and Jane J. Robinson. 1983. Formal constraints on metarules. In *Proceedings, 21st Annual Meeting of the Association for Computational Linguistics (ACL'83)*, pages 22–27, Cambridge, MA.

Shieber, Stuart N. 1986. *An Introduction to Unification-Based Approaches to Grammar*. CSLI Lecture Notes, 4. Chicago University Press, Stanford, CA.

Shieber, Stuart N. 1992. *Constraint-Based Formalisms*. A Bradford Book. MIT Press, Cambridge, MA.

Shimohata, Sayori, Toshiyuki Sugio, and Junji Nagata. 1997. Retrieving collocations by co-occurrences and word order constraints. In *Proceedings, 35th Annual Meeting of the Association for Computational Linguistics and 8th*

Conference of the European Chapter of the Association for Computational Linguistics (ACL - EACL'97), pages 476–481, Madrid.

Silberztein, Max. 1990. Le dictionnaire électronique des mots composés. *Langue Française*, 87:71–83.

Silberztein, Max. 1993. *Dictionnaires électroniques et analyse automatique de textes: Le système INTEX*. Masson, Paris.

Smadja, Franck, Kathy R. McKeown, and Vasileios Hatzivassiloglou. 1996. Translating collocations for bilingual lexicons: A statistical approach. *Computational Linguistics*, 22(1):1–38.

Smadja, Frank. 1993a. Retrieving collocations from text: Xtract. *Computational Linguistics*, 19(1):143–177.

Smadja, Frank. 1993b. Xtract: An overview. *Computer and the Humanities*, 26:399–413.

Smeaton, Alan F., and Paraic Sheridan. 1991. Using morpho-syntactic language analysis in phrase matching. In *Proceedings, Intelligent Multimedia Information Retrieval Systems and Management (RIAO'91)*, pages 415–429, Barcelona.

Sparck Jones, Karen. 1971. *Automatic Keyword Classification for Information Retrieval*. Butterworth, London.

Sparck Jones, Karen, and John I. Tait. 1984a. Automatic search term variant generation. *Journal of Documentation*, 40(1):50–66.

Sparck Jones, Karen, and John I. Tait. 1984b. Linguistically motivated descriptive term selection. In *Proceedings, 10th International Conference on Computational Linguistics (COLING'84)*, pages 287–290, Stanford, CA.

Spivey, J. M. 1994. *La Notation Z*. Masson/Prentice Hall, Paris.

Sproat, Richard. 1992. *Morphology and Computation*. ACL-MIT Press Series in NLP. MIT Press, Cambridge, MA.

Srinivas, B., D. Egedi, C. Doran, and Tilman Becker. 1994. Lexicalization and grammar development. In *Proceedings, KONVENS'94*, pages 310–319, Vienna.

Srinivasan, Padmini. 1992. Thesaurus construction. In William B. Frakes and Ricardo Baeza-Yates, editors, *Information Retrieval: Data Structure and Algorithms*. Prentice Hall, London, pages 161–218.

Stiles, H. Edmund. 1961. The association factor in information retrieval. *Journal of the Association for Computational Machinery*, 8(2):271–279.

Strzalkowski, Tomek. 1994. Robust text processing in automatic information retrieval. In *Proceedings, 4th Conference on Applied Natural Language Processing (ANLP'94)*, pages 168–173, Stuttgart.

Strzalkowski, Tomek. 1995. Natural language information retrieval. *Information Processing & Management*, 31(3):397–417.

Strzalkowski, Tomek, and Peter G. N. Scheyen. 1996. Evaluation of the Tagged Text Parser. In Harald Bunt and Masaru Tomita, editors, *Recent Advances in Parsing Technology*. Kluwer Academic Publisher, Boston, MA, pages 201–220.

Strzalkowski, Tomek, and Barbara Vauthey. 1992. Information retrieval using robust natural language processing. In *Proceedings, 20th Annual Meeting of the Association for Computational Linguistics (ACL'92)*, pages 104–111, Newark, DE.

Su, Keh-Yih, Ming-Wen Wu, and Chang Jing-Shin. 1994. A corpus-based approach to automatic compound extraction. In *Proceedings, 32nd Annual Meeting of the Association for Computational Linguistics (ACL'94)*, pages 242–247, Las Cruces, NM.

Tagliacozzo, Renata. 1976. Levels of technicality in scientific communication. *Information Processing & Management*, 12(2):95–110.

Tanimoto, T. T. 1958. An elementary mathematical theory of classification. Technical report, IBM.

Tapanainen, Pasi, and Timo Järvinen. 1994. Syntactic analysis of natural language using linguistic rules and corpus-based patterns. In *Proceedings, 15th International Conference on Computational Linguistics (COLING'94)*, pages 629–634, Kyoto.

Tesnière, Lucien. 1959. *Éléments de syntaxe structurale*. Klincksieck, Paris. Fifth edition, 1988.

Thompson, Henry. 1983. Handling metarules in a parser for GPSG. In *Proceedings, 21st Annual Meeting of the Association for Computational Linguistics (ACL'83)*, pages 26–37.

Tzoukermann, Evelyne, and Christian Jacquemin. 1997. Analyse automatique de la morphologie dérivationnelle et filtrage de mots possibles. In *Actes, Forum de morphologie 1ères rencontres: Mots Possibles et Mots Existants*, Lille. SILEX, Université de Lille 3.

Tzoukermann, Evelyne, Judith L. Klavans, and Christian Jacquemin. 1997. Effective use of natural language processing techniques for automatic conflation of multi-word terms: The role of derivational morphology, part of speech tagging, and shallow parsing. In *Actes, 20th Annual International ACM SIGIR Conference on Research and Development in Information Retrieval (SIGIR'97)*, pages 148–155, Philadelphia, PA.

Tzoukermann, Evelyne, and Mark Liberman. 1990. A finite-state processor for Spanish. In *Proceedings, 13th International Conference on Computational Linguistics (COLING'90)*, Helsinki.

Tzoukermann, Evelyne, and Dragomir R. Radev. 1997. Use of weighted finite state transducers in part of speech tagging. In Andras Kornai, editor, *Extended Finite State Models of Language*. Cambridge University Press.

UMLS, 1995. *Unified Medical Language System, UMLS Knowledge Source*. National Library of Medicine, 6th experimental edition. *http://www.nlm.nih.gov/research/umls/UMLSDOC.HTML*.

Van der Eijk, Pim. 1993. Automating the acquisition of bilingual terminology. In *Proceedings, 6th Conference of the European Chapter of the Association for Computational Linguistics (EACL'93)*, pages 113–119, Utrecht.

Van Rijsbergen, C. J. 1975. *Information Retrieval*. Butterworth, London.

Velardi, Paola, Maria Teresa Pazienza, and Michela Fasolo. 1991. How to encode semantic knowledge: A method for meaning representation and computer-aided acquisition. *Computational Linguistics*, 17(2):153–170.

Véronis, Jean. 1992. Disjunctive feature structures as hypergraphs. In *Proceedings, 14th International Conference on Computational Linguistics (COLING'92)*, pages 498–504, Nantes.

Véronis, Jean, and Nancy Ide. 1991. An assesment of semantic information automatically extracted from machine readable dictionaries. In *Proceedings, 5th Conference of the European Chapter of the Association for Computational Linguistics (EACL'89)*, pages 227–233, Berlin.

Vijay-Shanker, K. 1992. Using descriptions of trees in a Tree Adjoining Grammar. *Computational Linguistics*, 18(4):481–518.

Voorhees, Ellen M. 1998. Using WordNet for text retrieval. In Christiane Fellbaum, editor, *WordNet: An Electronic Lexical Database*. MIT Press, Cambridge, MA, pages 285–303.

Voutilainen, Atro. 1993. *NPtool*, A detector of English noun phrases. In *Proceedings, Workshop on Very Large Corpora : Academic and Industrial Perspectives*, pages 48–57, Columbus, Ohio.

Voutilainen, Atro. 1997. Designing a (finite-state) parsing grammar. In Emmanuel Roche and Yves Schabes, editors, *Finite-State Language Processing*. MIT Press, Cambridge, MA, pages 283–310.

Wacholder, Nina. 1998. Simplex NPs clustered by head: A method for identifying significant topics within a document. In *Proceedings, COLING/ACL Workshoop on the Computational Treatment of Nominals*, pages 70–79, Montreal.

Wagner, Robert A., and Michael J. Fisher. 1974. The string-to-string correction problem. *Journal of the Association for Computational Machinery*, 21(1):168–173.

Wasow, Thomas, Ivan A. Sag, and Geoffrey Nunberg. 1984. Idioms : An interim report. In Shiro Hatori and Kasuko Inoue, editors, *Proceedings, 13th International Congress of Linguists*, pages 102–115, Tokyo.

Weischedel, Ralph M. 1983. Meta-rules as a basis for processing ill-formed input. *American Journal of Computational Linguistics*, 9(3–4):161–177.

Weisweber, Wilhelm, and Susanne Preuß. 1992. Direct parsing with metarules. In *Proceedings, 14th International Conference on Computational Linguistics (COLING'92)*, pages 1111–1115, Nantes.

Wermter, Stefan. 1995. *Hybrid Connectionist Natural Language Processing*. Chapman & Hall, London.

Woods, William A. 1997. Conceptual indexing: A better way to organize knowledge. Technical Report SMLI TR-97-61, Sun Microsystems Laboratories, Mountain View, CA.

Xu, Jing, and W. Bruce Croft. 1998. Corpus-based stemming using co-occurrence of word variants. *ACM Transaction on Information Systems*, 16(1):61–81.

Yoshikane, Fuyuki, Keita Tsuji, Kyo Kageura, and Christian Jacquemin. 1998. Detecting Japanese term variation in textual corpus. In *Proceedings, 4th International Workshop on Information Retrieval with Asian Languages (IRAL'99)*, pages 97–108, Academia Sinica, Taipei, Taiwan.

Zhai, Chengxiang. 1997. Fast statistical parsing of noun phrases for document indexing. In *Proceedings, 5th Conference on Applied Natural Language Processing (ANLP'97)*, pages 312–319, Washington.

Author Index

A page followed by an *"n"* indicates an endnote.

Aarts J., 23
Abeillé A., 130, 131
Abney S.P., 14, 59, 62, 107
Agarwal R., 227
Ahmad K., 37
Aho A.V., 26, 27, 32, 139
Aizawa A.N., 222
Alshawi H., 124, 135
Ambroziak J., 297, 298
Amghar T., 310
Amsler R.A., 129, 227
Ananiadou S., 59, 65, 66
Andreewsky A., 103
Anick P., 124
Aragon-Ramirez V., 43
Arampatzis A.T., 90, 92, 297
Aronoff M., 20
Artemieff S., 124
Assadi H., 44, 48, 266

Bach E., 188
Barbaud P., 122, 350
Barkema H., 22, 23, 25
Barzilay R., 310
Basili R., 226
Baxendale P.B., 350*n*
Becker T., 151
Benveniste É., 52
Biber D., 349
Biebricher P., 350
Bindi R., 350
Black E., 279
Boguraev B.K., 100
Bouillon P., 306
Bourigault D., 44, 48, 52, 107, 196, 234, 235, 309, 350*n*
Brachman R.J., 298
Brill E., 14, 89, 286, 351
Brown P.F., 34
Bunt H., 26
Busemann S., 157
Byrd R.J., 20, 228

Cabré Castellví T., 37
Cadiot P., 166, 349*n*
Calzolari N., 350
Carpenter B., 119, 123
Charniak E., 26, 32, 224
Chen H.-H., 65
Chen K.-H., 65
Chodorow M.S., 227, 268
Chomsky N., 30
Choueka Y., 40, 216

Church K.W., 32, 34, 59, 64, 89, 216, 223
Colmerauer A., 123, 124
Condamines A., 225
Croft W.B., 223, 277, 309
Crouch C.J., 43, 222, 223

Dagan I., 64, 307, 351
Daille B., 17, 35, 37, 59, 152, 164, 189, 216, 249, 313, 350
Dal G., 17
Damerau F., 187
David S., 49, 50
Davidson L., 225
Debili F., 91, 103, 105, 111, 118
Deese J.E., 224
DeJong G.F., 297
de la Briandais R., 138
Dice L.R., 34
Diller A., 119
Dillon M., 87
Dowling G.R., 42, 43, 187
Dras M., 310
Dunham G.S., 161, 297

Enguegard C., 41
Enguehard C., 40
Evans D.A., 71, 72, 74, 75

Fabre C., 227, 313, 351*n*
Fagan J.L., 93, 161, 206
Fano R., 33
Fellbaum C., 266, 300
Fisher M.J., 42, 43
Fitzpatrick E., 146
Fluhr C., 306
Fox E.A., 226
Frantzi K., 59, 65, 66
Fraurud K., 168, 169, 170
Fredkin E., 138
Frenkel K.A., 3
Fung P., 68, 69, 350

Gaussier É., 64
Gazdar G., 114, 122, 148, 149, 188
Giorgi A., 250
Gonzalo J., 93
Gray A.S., 87
Grefenstette G., 111, 223, 224, 306
Grevisse M., 21
Grishman R., 145, 223
Gross G., 23, 25, 147, 349*n*
Gross M., 24, 146, 169
Guha R., 349*n*
Guilbert L., 3, 217

Subject Index

Terms are defined on pages listed in **bold**. A page followed by an *"f"* indicates a figure; a *"g"* indicates a glossary entry, an *"n"* indicates an endnote, and a *"t"* indicates a table.